Medieval Britain, *c.* 1000–1500

Though England was the emerging super-state in the medieval British Isles, its story is not the only one Britain can offer; there is a wider context of Britain in Europe, and the story of this period is one of how European Latin and French culture and ideals colonised the minds of all the British peoples. This engaging and accessible introduction offers a truly integrated perspective of medieval British history, emphasising elements of medieval life over political narrative, and offering an up-to-date presentation and summary of medieval historiography. Featuring figures, maps, a glossary of key terms, a chronology of rulers, timelines and annotated suggestions for further reading and key texts, this textbook is an essential resource for undergraduate courses on medieval Britain. Supplementary online resources include additional further reading suggestions, useful links and primary sources.

David Crouch is Professor of Medieval History at the University of Hull. He is the author of many books, including *The Reign of King Stephen* (2002), *The Birth of Nobility: Constructing Aristocracy in England and France, 1000–1300* (2005), *The Normans* (2005), *The English Aristocracy, 1070–1272: A Social Transformation* (2011), *Lost Letters of Medieval Life: English Society, 1200–1250* (with Martha Carlin, 2013), *The Acts and Letters of the Marshal Family 1156–1248* (2015) and *William Marshal* (3rd edn, 2016).

CAMBRIDGE HISTORY OF BRITAIN

The Cambridge History of Britain is an innovative new textbook
series covering the whole of British history from the breakdown of
Roman power to the present day. The series is aimed at first-year
undergraduates and above, and volumes in the series will serve both as
indispensable works of synthesis and as original interpretations of
Britain's past. Each volume will offer an accessible survey of political,
social, cultural and economic history, charting the changing shape of
Britain as a result of the gradual integration of the four kingdoms and
Britain's increasing interaction and exchange with Europe and the
wider world. Each volume will also feature boxes, illustrations, maps,
timelines and guides to further reading as well as a companion
website with further primary source and illustrative materials.

VOLUMES IN THE SERIES

CAMBRIDGE HISTORY OF BRITAIN

Medieval Britain, *c.* 1000–1500

David Crouch

CAMBRIDGE
UNIVERSITY PRESS

CAMBRIDGE
UNIVERSITY PRESS

University Printing House, Cambridge CB2 8BS, United Kingdom

One Liberty Plaza, 20th Floor, New York, NY 10006, USA

477 Williamstown Road, Port Melbourne, VIC 3207, Australia

4843/24, 2nd Floor, Ansari Road, Daryaganj, Delhi – 110002, India

79 Anson Road, #06–04/06, Singapore 079906

Cambridge University Press is part of the University of Cambridge.

It furthers the University's mission by disseminating knowledge in the pursuit of education, learning, and research at the highest international levels of excellence.

www.cambridge.org
Information on this title: www.cambridge.org/9780521190718
DOI 10.1017/9780511844379

First published 2017

Printed in the United Kingdom by TJ International Ltd. Padstow Cornwall

A catalogue record for this publication is available from the British Library.

Library of Congress Cataloging in Publication Data
Names: Crouch, David, author.
Title: Medieval Britain, *c.* 1000–1500 / David Crouch.
Description: New York : Cambridge University Press, 2017. | Series: Cambridge history of Britain ; 2 | Includes bibliographical references.
Identifiers: LCCN 2016041197 | ISBN 9780521190718 (hardback)
Subjects: LCSH: Great Britain – History – Medieval period, 1066–1485. | BISAC: HISTORY / Europe / Great Britain.
Classification: LCC DA175 .C76 2017 | DDC 941.02/1–dc23
LC record available at https://lccn.loc.gov/2016041197

ISBN 978-0-521-19071-8 Hardback
ISBN 978-0-521-14967-9 Paperback

Additional resources for this publication at www.cambridge.org/crouch

Contents

Figures

Maps

Preface

This book is intended as an introduction to half a millennium of British history for degree-level students, though its breadth of coverage would make it useful also as a senior school text. It is not intended as a reference book so much as a guide to broad social, political and cultural change in a very long period of history. Because of the complexity of the intertwining story of the three nations of Great Britain (the English, Scots and Welsh), the emphasis of the book is on themes rather than events. It is not a reign-by-reign account of the kingdoms of Britain. A thematic approach does make more clear what political histories often fail to, that the history and lives of those three peoples did have a powerful 'British' rather than national dimension. Indeed, looked at in this way the period can be seen to have experienced a major shift in the idea of what Britain was. As a result, the book is organised in two narrative sections: before and after what is called here 'the great divorce', the collapse of the ancient understanding of the British peoples as being united under the informal presidency of the English king. After 1306 Britain was partitioned between two mutually hostile, warring states: England and Scotland. There was no healing of the rift within the rest of the period of this book. The thematic sections, however, make plain that the unrelenting hostility was an overlay on societies and states which were otherwise responding to the same developments in culture, agriculture, economy, disease and social change, and that all three peoples were interacting with forces beyond the British Isles. Ireland (which is part of the British Isles, but not Great Britain) is not specifically addressed in this study, as that would have made the book unmanageable and indeed incoherent. Nonetheless, reference is made to developments concerning Ireland which have a British context.

Within this book there are some major changes which have a significance for vocabulary. One is the change in understanding of the Gaelic kingdom of the north, which under David I (1124–1153) moved into the mainstream of European monarchies. So, before his reign, it is called by its ancient name of Alba, and after by the name it was increasingly given within and outside its borders, Scotland (*Scotia*). Likewise for England, the ruling dynasty which acquired the throne in 1154 and carried on until the very end of the period is called the 'Angevins' while it still maintained a claim to its ancient homeland in northern France (Anjou) and 'Plantagenets' thereafter (with no reference to its Lancastrian and Yorkist branches which became important after 1399). At the end of each section are reading lists, with those called 'Key Texts': landmark studies which offer the most authoritative as well as broadest coverage. 'Further Reading' includes important studies which have informed the writing of the chapter and which can form the basis for student research. The online companion site for this book offers further opportunities for research, including primary source material.

Introduction

People in Britain in the middle ages did not know they were medieval. Educated men in the twelfth century were in fact proud to be called 'modern' (Lat. *moderni*: 'the people of here and now'), a word that the century invented. Intellectuals of the day were very proud of their attainments in Latin literature, and the romance writer of the 1170s, Chrétien de Troyes, believed that in his own time French-speaking society had attained heights of civility and military culture unknown since Rome. For Chrétien, his society was rising to greatness, and it was not in a trough between waves of human attainment. 'Medieval' people of a reflective turn of mind believed their day and age were expansive and developing along the same lines as the great minds of the ancient world whom they studied and imitated with avid intelligence. The idea that they occupied a dark age of ignorance was not one they could have accepted, though it was a given for most of them that it was sinful. An idea that a decline had followed the days of the Roman Empire and continued until their own time was one that Italian grammaticists of the mid fourteenth century first smugly suggested, but when they did they were referring only to their standard of Latinity, which they claimed to have renewed to the standard Cicero had attained. It was not until the seventeenth century that people began to look back at the fifteenth century and those that preceded it as a 'middle age' between their own modern times and that of the Romans, and when they did it was to their superior, humanistic learning they were referring. It was the likes of the French philosopher Voltaire (1694–1778) who latched on to priest-ridden ignorance as the characteristic of the 'middle age', a view consolidated by nineteenth-century positivist humanists into an orthodoxy that if something was 'medieval' it was dark and blighted and suppressed the human spirit. It is a usage that is still common currency amongst politicians and journalists, which they apply to any practice they think socially retrograde, in a blithe demonstration of their own ignorance.

Reading these chapters will take you back among the 'medieval' people of Great Britain, and, if you've not met them before, I think you'll find they were not at all what you might expect from the use of that adjective. They certainly had a high idea of the Christian religion and its promises. Their fascination with its theology and their own limited world view are not now our own in general, for the modern world has found other sources of promise in the philosophies of social economics and natural science. But medieval people also had a high idea of the rights of the political community of their various realms and an ability to articulate it from which we still benefit. They despised and resisted political corruption; sought true justice; hoped the best for their own lives and for their children, whom they loved; met the horrors of pandemic and disease with a fortitude that humbles us, their descendants; and pursued their own prosperity with enterprise, doggedness and originality. They had an aesthetic sensibility in music, colour, form and stone that still delights and, in its symbolic science of heraldry, is still widely employed. The lions of England and Scotland in red or gold were already figuring on their kings' banners and shields by 1200. The medieval sense of humour left a lot to be desired, it's true, but medieval people could deploy vast reserves of irony against a sometimes harsh world, which is a triumph of the human spirit. They liked to laugh, eat and drink, and, when all is said and done, they lived not that far away from us. If eighty years is a frequently attainable life, then six such lives, laid end to end, take us back amongst medieval people. They knew that you should let sleeping dogs lie and not expect old dogs to pick up new tricks; that still waters run deep; that you should cover your mouth when you cough; and that you should be suspicious of the French (and all foreigners, in fact). They discussed the finer points of horses, dogs, beer and wine, and were very much into organised sport as both spectators and players. For all our differences, medieval people were our ancestors in thought, aspirations and manners, as much as in our genes.

This book covers half a millennium of the history of Great Britain, the principal island of a major archipelago on the eastern Atlantic continental shelf. As is the way of things in the world of medieval historians, it had to be written either by an 'early' medievalist or by a 'late' one, which in basic terms means someone who studies the period on either side of the year 1300. My period of specialist study falls into the earlier period. This has advantages and disadvantages. The resulting book is not going to be written to prove how it was that the world of 1500 came into being, by just writing the prehistory of the things that are perceived to be the key features of fifteenth-century history. History written backwards can be trapped into teleology, and, if (for instance) a historian thinks that its political constitution was what defined medieval England, then he will (as late medievalists tend to do) begin his history in 1215, the year of Magna Carta. Anything that came before would be irrelevant and perhaps also less sophisticated and interesting, as earlier societies inevitably seem to historians of later days. But an earlier medievalist knows that Magna Carta was part of a much older process, thrown up as one temporary solution to the basic inherent flaw of medieval monarchies, that they only worked when the personality of the king matched the expectations of the community of the magnates of his land, with whom the king had to negotiate to get anything done.

The problem of earlier medievalists writing later medieval history is the mirror image. We are prone to seize on later developments and claim our own period as having produced them. We also forget that occasionally entirely new developments arise which have little precedent in the earlier period. So for one like me the temptation is to claim Magna Carta as a central if not culminating event, the 'origin' of a British concern for social justice, the rule of law and democracy. It would give my period cachet and would make me feel good about it. Since I am aware of that temptation, the verdict you will find here is that Magna Carta was an emergency measure produced by the breakdown of what had been until the accession of King John an effective, long-term solution to the problem of kingship: government by council and consensus in which the frequently absent king took a back seat. It only accidentally became the banner for an aristocracy which saw itself as the guardian of the community against the abuses of an executive monarchy. Just like a later medievalist looking backward, my history looking forward is inevitably going to be handicapped by presuppositions.

Another problem in writing this book is that the island of Great Britain during its period was home to three peoples, the English, Scots and Welsh (which I have taken care here to put in alphabetical order, not in order of importance). Since the nineteenth century, each of these British peoples has developed its own historical tradition as the consciousness of its national identity was tested and contested by their modern world, where history's principal purpose was to tell the national story, almost always in relation to current political concerns. It is only since the 1980s that medievalists, principally under the impulse of Sir Rees Davies, have deliberately moved to looking at how the (four) peoples of the British Isles interacted. Talents like Rees Davies's are rare ones, but it helps to be Welsh. The view of medieval England of one brought up west of Offa's Dyke in a different culture will differ from a native of, say, Warwickshire (a county that has produced a remarkable number of distinguished living late medievalists, as it happens) to whom England tends to be central. As a Welshman myself and a writer on Welsh as much as English history, I can at least claim a close acquaintance with two out of three of the peoples studied here.

There is more to the difficulty of writing a coherent British history than the juggling of national stories. At the very beginning of the period of this book, the kingdoms of England and Alba were actors in a wider northern world, dominated by the seagoing Scandinavian powers, who had periodically colonised the British Isles, and indeed in 1000 ruled large parts of them. The influence of the Atlantic and North Sea world did not finally collapse so far as England is concerned until the 1080s, and it remained a larger factor in Scottish history until the very end of this period, when Scotland under

James IV sent a military expedition to the Baltic and deployed his navy to deny the North Sea to the English. But in the meantime the events of 1066 had abruptly drawn England into the Francophone cultural and political world to the south, a fact which would dominate its history for the rest of the period of this book. It was the Francophone world that principally shaped the religion, culture, social structure and literature first of the English, then the Scots and eventually even the Welsh. It was not so much that England had been 'colonised' in the twelfth century by the French; England was a vital French-speaking part of a wide cultural and political zone that it only began edging away from at the end of the thirteenth century. The traffic was also not by any means one way, for Anglo-French culture and literature were of interest to the continental French, and Capetian kings and princes visited English courts and shrines throughout the twelfth century. In 1216 the heir to France thought it perfectly within his rights to claim the throne of England. To write the history of Britain and ignore the European context is to admire the gem without seeing the artistry of the setting.

The treatment of politics within this book is deliberately selective, focusing on those developments which span the centuries and have a broader significance for medieval life. For instance, the reader may be surprised to find the Peasants' Revolt of 1381 absent from the political (though not the economic) treatment of the fourteenth century, but in my judgement its socio-political significance was minimal, other than for Marxist historiography. Reigns which lack major social and political changes, such as those of Richard I (1189–1199) or Henry IV (1399–1413), will tend to get a cursory treatment: not that things did not happen within them that were unimportant in their own day. The turbulent reigns of John (1199–1216) and Richard II (1377–1399) get by contrast a large amount of attention in several contexts, simply because their events were so significant in the long term for all the realms of Britain. In the long view, John's reign, like that of Robert I of Scotland (1306–1329), is very much a political and cultural nexus which transformed not just their own kingdoms, but also the island of Great Britain.

Part I
The Empire of Britain

TIMELINE: 1000–1217

	England	Alba/Scotland	Wales
979	Æthelred II, king		
1002	Æthelred marries Emma of Normandy		
1005		Máel Coluim II mac Coinneach, king of Alba	
1008	English raid on Normandy		
1014	Swein of Denmark invades England		
1016	Battle of Assandun. Death of King Edmund. Cnut becomes king		
1031		Cnut's great northern expedition	
1035	Death of Cnut, succession of Harold I		
1039			Gruffudd ap Llywelyn defeats Mercian earls

	England	Alba/Scotland	Wales
1040		Death of Máel Coluim II. Donnchadh king of Alba	
1042	Edward the Confessor, king		
1050	Exile of Earl Godwine of Wessex		
1055			Gruffudd ap Llywelyn dominant in Wales
1058		English expedition to Alba. Máel Coluim III Ceann Mòr, king	
1063			Earl Harold overthrows Gruffudd ap Llywelyn
1064	Earl Harold in Normandy		
1066	Battle of Hastings (14 October)		
1068		Edgar atheling flees to Scotland	
1069	Battle of Stafford. Danish invasion of the North		Welsh kings invade Mercia
1071			Caradog ap Gruffudd, dominant king in Wales
1072		William I's expedition to Scotland	
1075			William Rufus raids South Wales
1081			Death of Caradog ap Gruffudd. William I's expedition to Deheubarth
1086	Domesday Survey		
1087	William II Rufus, king of England. Robert II, duke of Normandy		

	England	Alba/Scotland	Wales
1091		William II Rufus's expedition to Scotland. Annexation of Cumbria	
1093		Death of Máel Coluim III in Northumberland	Conquest of Deheubarth and Gwynedd by marcher earls
1095	Rebellion against William II Rufus		
1100	Henry I king of England		
1106	Battle of Tinchebray		
1109	First known meeting of the Exchequer of England		
1113		David of Scotland made earl of Huntingdon	
1124		David I, king of Scotland	
1128	Oath to support Matilda's succession		
1134			Death of Duke Robert at Cardiff
1135	Death of Henry I		
1136		David I declares support for Matilda and invades. Treaty of Durham	Rising of the Welsh and revival of kingdoms of Deheubarth and Glamorgan
1137	King Stephen in Normandy		Death of Gruffudd ap Cynan of Gwynedd
1138	Rebellion of Earl Robert of Gloucester	Scottish invasion. Battle of the Standard near Northallerton	
1139	Empress Matilda in England	King David cedes Northumberland	

	England	Alba/Scotland	Wales
1141	First Battle of Lincoln. Stephen captured		
1147	Death of Robert of Gloucester		
1148	Matilda resigns her claim to her son Henry of Anjou		
1153	Peace settlement between King Stephen and Henry	Death of King David I. Succeeded by his grandson, Máel Coluim IV	
1154	Death of King Stephen		
1155			Rhys ap Gruffudd, king of Deheubarth
1157			Defeat of Henry II by Welsh at Ewloe
1158		Henry II reclaims Northumberland and Cumbria from Scots	
1162	Thomas Becket archbishop of Canterbury		
1164	Council of Clarendon. Becket in exile		
1165		Death of Máel Coluim IV. William the Lion, king. David II of Scotland, earl of Huntingdon	Henry II defied by Owain ap Gruffudd of Gwynedd, in alliance with other princes
1169			Anglo-Welsh invasion of Leinster
1170	Assassination of Becket		
1172			Rhys of Deheubarth made justiciar of the Welsh March
1173	Rebellion against Henry II		

	England	Alba/Scotland	Wales
1174		Capture of King William the Lion at Alnwick by English army	
1175		King William swears homage to Henry II on his release	
1189	Death of Henry II		
1190	Richard I on crusade		
1193	Rebellion of John of Mortain, the king's brother		
1197			Llywelyn ab Iorwerth, dominant prince in Gwynedd
1199	Death of King Richard		
1200			
1203	King John driven out of Normandy		
1204	Fall of Rouen to King Philip II of France		Llywelyn marries Joan, daughter of King John
1208	Interdict laid on England		
1211			John invades Gwynedd and defeats Llywelyn
1214	Interdict ends. Battle of Bouvines	Death of King William	
1215	Magna Carta		
1216	Invasion by Louis of France. Death of King John. Reissue of Magna Carta		
1217	Regency of William Marshal for King Henry III. Second Battle of Lincoln		

1 A Century of Conquest, 1000–1100

OVERVIEW

Though the least well-documented period of this book, this century included some major events in British history. Not only was England conquered twice (by the Danes in 1016 and the Normans fifty years later), the conquerors moved to assert their domination over all of Great Britain: Cnut in 1030–1031 and William I in 1072 and 1081. A major shift followed on from the Norman Conquest. Britain had been fully engaged since the ninth century with the North Atlantic world created by the Scandinavian seagoing powers. After 1066, England and subsequently Scotland turned south, culturally and economically, to the French-speaking world. The shift had a major consequence for English politics as the Norman dynasty maintained its hold on its French lands, and so England was drawn into perpetual rivalry and warfare with its Norman conquerors' neighbours and their overlord, the Capetian king of France. France became a factor in British politics for the rest of this period.

In 1000 Britain was a much troubled place. The dominant kingdom of England was disturbed by internal dissensions and a dysfunctional court under a king who was failing to deal with aggressive Danish incursions into his realm. Æthelred II had become king while a boy in 979 following the murder of his elder half-brother and a period of civil unrest. Danish raids on the coasts of England began soon after his accession. In part this may have had to do with the kingdom's internal problems, but it was also related to the fact that Britain belonged more to the northern world, for which the North Sea was a highway. Commerce, people and information freely circulated across the shallow seas of the North Atlantic coastal shelf, so Æthelred's problems were well known in the Norse world. England's relations with France and Germany were by contrast culturally distant.

The part of France closest to the coasts of England would hardly challenge its cultural isolation. 'Normandy' was still perceived as a Norse colony, its leaders characterised by other Frenchmen as 'pirate dukes', even though it was by 1000 a land whose former Viking aristocracy was entirely French in customs and lifestyle. But since the rulers of Normandy maintained close political relations with the Danes there was some reason for the confusion. In the 960s Duke Richard I was happy to employ Norse mercenaries, and in the 980s he allowed Danish raiders to cross the Channel to his ports to unload their loot and slaves. Rouen was still then, as it had long been, a major entry point of northern trade into the **Frankish** realms. King Æthelred tried his best to protect this exposed flank of his realm, negotiating a treaty with Duke Richard I in 991 by which the Normans promised to close their ports to the Danish raiders. But the overwhelming assault on England by a Danish fleet in the last years of the tenth century was too destructive for the Normans to resist, and they once more allowed Danish ships to land in the duchy. This explains why in 1002, once he had got rid of the latest wave of **Vikings**, King Æthelred tried once more to close off his southern flank to the Danes by marrying Duke Richard II's sister, Emma: a fateful alliance, as it turned out.

The tragedy and drama of the declining years of King Æthelred's reign were therefore acted out in numerous lands and involved the fates of several peoples in a time of conquest and often vicious warfare. One of the results of this was going to be that two generations later the unity and importance of the North Sea littoral would be disrupted, and influences on Britain would blow instead from the warmer direction of continental Europe and the French-speaking world. The desperate manoeuvres of Æthelred to protect his embattled kingdom would have long-lasting consequences both for it and for his dynasty, rather more than anyone could have anticipated at the time he was king. Equally significant but unappreciated at the time may have been the events of 1008, when Æthelred had fallen out with his Norman brother-in-law and mounted a seaborne raid on the Cotentin peninsula, only for his English troops to find themselves outmanoeuvred and worsted by the Norman cavalry at the disposal of the local vicomte: two different modes of medieval warfare had come into contact for the first time. In 1013, as the endgame of the Danish conquest of England was becoming clear to everyone, Duke Richard II welcomed King Swein to Rouen and formally allied with the Danes. But Normans were nothing if not pragmatic, caught as they were between two cultural worlds. The very next year Richard was willing to give refuge to his sister and her two sons by King Æthelred as they fled England. So the two Anglo-Norman '**athelings**' were honourably brought up as adolescents and young men in Normandy at their uncle's court, and Edward, the younger of them, became markedly French in his cultural outlook.

The Danish Conquest of Britain

It is difficult to say precisely when the Danish incursions into England in Æthelred's reign ceased to be the enterprise of aristocratic pirates with their private fleets and shifted to become a war of conquest sponsored by the Danish king and backed up by the formidable military resources of his realm. But by 1012 the English kingdom was so debilitated that its leaders could do nothing to prevent the plundering of the country and the sacking of Canterbury, whose **archbishop** was subsequently murdered. Æthelred's only response was to hire the fleet that was devastating his realm under its commander, Thorkell the Tall, at an immense price in silver and seek to use it to protect his coasts from other predators (see Fig. 1.1). The predator-in-chief turned out the next year to be King Swein of Denmark himself, drawn into warfare perhaps by the apparent defection of his dependant, the *jarl* Thorkell, to a rival king. When Swein arrived in the summer of 1013, it was with sufficient force to intimidate the **ealdormen** of Northumbria and Wessex into surrendering to him. Æthelred fled the country, presumably with the aid of Thorkell's ships, having sent his Norman wife and their

Fig. 1.1 Silver Penny of Æthelred II. The most common image of kingship in circulation in medieval England was that stamped on the penny, the basic unit of currency. The obverse of the coin shows the bust of the king, here holding a sceptre, the chief sign of kingship. This coin is from a Scandinavian hoard, probably the wages of a Viking mercenary in Æthelred's pay.

children ahead of him. Swein's rule over England was brief, for he died at the beginning of February 1014, but his army immediately proceeded to elect his younger son Cnut to be their king, at least in England.

The death of Swein brought an ever hopeful Æthelred back to England, and he found sufficient support from the surviving ealdormen to challenge Cnut, though Æthelred's principal military backing was made up of Danish mercenaries. Cnut vacated England, looking for support from his elder brother Harald, who had secured the kingdom of Denmark on Swein's death. Æthelred maintained himself as king until his death in April 1016, but always under threat of a new Danish onslaught, which he had to deflect with mercenaries recruited from the same nation. Cnut did indeed return to England before Æthelred died, appearing on the English coasts in the autumn of 1015. Bitter campaigning between Cnut and Æthelred's son, Edmund 'Ironside', ended with an English defeat at *Assandun* (probably Ashdon) in Essex on 18 October 1016. It forced a compromise by which, for the last time, England was divided between claimants, Cnut taking the land north of the Thames and Edmund retaining Wessex and, it seems, the actual title of king. Edmund's death on 30 November allowed Cnut to claim the entirety of the kingdom, as had probably been the agreement between the two men. So ultimately, after two years of warfare, a Danish prince was able to succeed unchallenged to the kingdom of the English and all its claims in the British Isles, and to dispose of the conquered realm to his own satisfaction, fifty years and two generations before the Normans had a chance to do the same.

Cnut's claim on England had nothing to do with heredity. He was formally elected king on more than one occasion, the first time by his own army following his father's death, and later through treaty and acclamation of an assembly by the English themselves, but the reality was that his claim to be king was by conquest, for all the appearance of formal submission that election and coronation gave him. He reinforced his claim where he could, marrying Æthelred's widow, Emma of Normandy, in 1017 and finding her a very willing and capable auxiliary in his rule of England. As his wife, Queen Emma could not, of course, support her sons, the athelings, against Cnut, so in this way Cnut artfully limited their threat. His rule was accommodating to English traditions of kingship, and Cnut maintained and repaired the structure of rule he found in the kingdom: shire courts, **sheriffs** and royal **writs** continued to be the basis for his government. Even the shift from English 'ealdormen' to Scandinavian '**earls**' at the top of society was only a change of name, not of function. Cnut's earls were mostly Danish immigrants, appointed after he violently disposed of the unreliable ealdormen who had survived Æthelred's reign, but he was willing later to promote others from among the English, notably Godwine, son of Wulfnoth Cild, a member of a Sussex landowning family, whom the king made earl of several Wessex **shires** around 1018. Apart from the earls, Cnut did not choose to dispossess the existing English aristocracy in favour of Danes. The Danish earls he appointed would have in any case been accommodated with the reserved ealdormannic lands in the shires which went with their office. Nobody would have been dispossessed to make way for the new foreign rulers. There are few known instances of Danish aristocratic immigrants being accommodated with actual grants of estates in England.

Cnut made sure to maintain the traditional primacy of the king of England over his British neighbours, for he intended to be more than just overlord of the English. He brought some talent and resources to the task of empire. He seems to have fought a punitive campaign north of the Tweed to put Máel Coluim II mac Coinneach of Alba (1005–1034) in his place as early as 1020. In 1031 Cnut asserted himself in force north of the Forth and, according to the Anglo-Saxon Chronicle, intimidated three northern kings: Máel Coluim, Macbethad son of Findláech (of the rival Moray branch of Máel Coluim's family) and Echmarcach Ragnaldson, a Norse king then probably dominant in the Hebrides. Cnut seems first to have conducted a military campaign as far as central Scotland to add to the sincerity of their submission (Map 1.1).

A praise-poem to Cnut attributed to the poet Ottar the Black depicts the king as ruler of the Danes, Irish, English and 'Island-folk', which indicates he did more than just assert himself in England and the North. Warfare noted in Irish and Welsh **annals** as being conducted by the Norse of Dublin and the English in Wales in 1030–1031, in which a king of Deheubarth died, may have been Cnut's way of asserting his overlordship both of Sihtric, king of Dublin (died 1042), and of the Welsh kings of the day, the one by tributary alliance and the other in warfare. In some ways, Cnut may have gone further down the road to empire than his West Saxon predecessors had done. As a king who visited both the German imperial court and the city of Rome, Cnut appears to have made parallels between the situation of his son-in-law, the Emperor Henry III (died 1056), and his position in the great realm he had engineered for himself. He apparently assumed a crown modelled on that of the Western emperor, and his wife's biographer implies that his view of his Atlantic and Baltic condominium was that it was not merely a temporary union of several kingdoms but a new Empire of the North. This was how the next generation viewed his hegemony: 'When King Cnut obtained rule of the realm of the Danes, he was emperor of five kingdoms, having secured the lordship of Denmark, England, Wales, Scotland and Norway.'[1]

 ## The Norman Conquest

Cnut's great ambitions did not, in the end, result in political change in the British Isles. His early death in 1035 led to the partition of his several realms. The most significant of his acts for Britain ultimately proved to be his choice to marry Emma of Normandy, mother of the exiled atheling Edward. She had ensured the boy would be brought up safely in the duchy as a French aristocrat within her own Norman family and would be

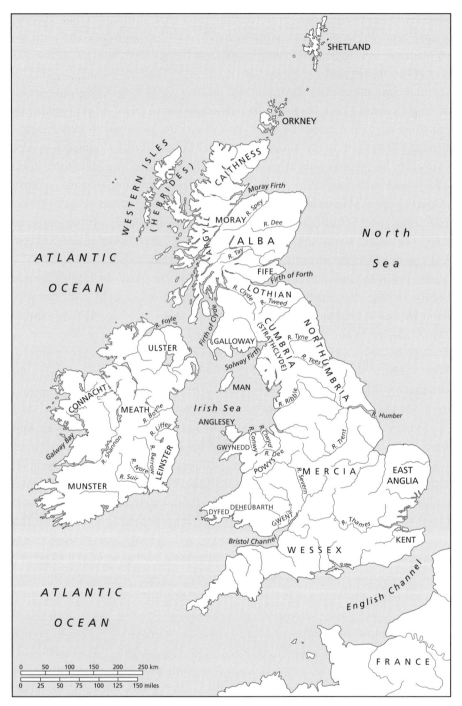

Map 1.1 Map of Britain, *c.* 1050

supported by them in his ambitions to reclaim England for his dynasty. She was also able to negotiate for Edward a place at the court of the son she had with Cnut, Edward's younger half-brother Harthacnut, king of Denmark from 1035 and of both it and England after 1040. Harthacnut recognised Edward as his heir once he had mastered England. Harthacnut's subsequent and unexpected death at the age of only twenty-four brought the Anglo-Norman atheling to the throne of England in 1042, chiefly due to the opportunistic but formidable support of Earl Godwine of Wessex and his sons.

England's new king had spent most of his life so far in France, and had been brought up from the age of thirteen at the Norman court, probably living on estates in the Seine valley given him by his uncle, Duke Richard II. He travelled on at least one occasion as far as Flanders seeking support for his claims, and it would be surprising had Edward not also visited the Capetian court, which was in close alliance with the Normans during the years he lived in the duchy. His sister Goda married the **count** of Amiens and the Vexin, a Norman ally, and Edward kept up links with her and her Anglo-French children. Edward thus paved the way for increasing French influence in England and, since he never produced any children of his own, opened the possibility of a Norman succession to his throne, in the person of his first cousin (once removed), Duke William II of Normandy.

Edward's favour towards the young duke of Normandy had as much to do with internal English politics as family affection and upbringing. The new king owed his throne to the support of Godwine of Wessex as much as to the favour of the late Harthacnut and the scheming of his mother. But Edward was astute enough to know that over-reliance on the support and counsel of Godwine would have been fatal to his effectiveness as king. He brought French followers to England, and favoured them as a way of balancing his court. It is quite possible that, as tension rose between the childless Edward and the powerful faction around Earl Godwine in the late 1040s, the king used the potential candidature of the Norman duke as his successor to keep the Godwine faction off balance. It is accepted nowadays that, in the political crisis of 1051–1052, when Godwine overreached himself and had to flee to Flanders, King Edward went so far as to assure Duke William that he favoured him as his heir for England and sent a son and grandson of Godwine to William's court as hostages for his good faith. The Normans naturally made a lot of this promise, probably more than Edward intended from what was principally a temporary factional strategy.

There were other relations Edward might have favoured, not least his Anglo-French nephews, the children of his sister Goda, countess of Amiens. Then there was Edward the Exile, his nephew, and Edward's half-Magyar children, though until 1057 they were far away in Hungary. It may be that Count Ralph of Mantes (died 1057), the king's Anglo-French nephew and son of Goda, had quite as much reason as William to see himself in the line of succession when he was enticed to England by Edward and in 1050 appointed as earl of several shires and commander of the fleet. But the possibility had been planted in William's head, and he continued to hold two minor members of the Godwine dynasty under his control at his court as a perpetual reminder. When Harold Godwineson arrived in Normandy in 1064 to reclaim his relations, he was allowed to take his nephew Haakon back to England, but not before he had been invested by Duke William with a banner and arms, as if Earl Harold had been one of his dependent counts. William was still calculating the odds on his succession to England in those years, when Edward had more or less resigned the rule of England to the Godwinesons.

King Edward was not as ineffective as his apparent reliance on Earl Godwin and his sons hints. The Godwinesons were balanced within England by the great Midland and Northern earls, on whom Edward counted to exert his wider influence in Britain, for it was Siward of Northumbria who intervened in the internecine strife between the two major branches of the royal house of Alba, by backing Máel Coluim III against Macbethad of Moray in 1058. The ascendancy of Earl Harold at King Edward's court was, however, all but complete in the 1060s, when the king married his sister Edith. Even had Edward produced children by the marriage, the Godwinesons' ascendancy would have survived the king's death. Harold can be glimpsed in those years ensuring that the realm of England maintained its traditional shape and claims, since in a sense they would represent his own future claims. This can be seen in the way he moved to deal with the threat posed to the imperial claims of the English over the Welsh. From his power base in Gwynedd, a young warrior, Gruffudd ap Llywelyn, had established his ascendancy over Wales and his military reputation by his catastrophic defeat of a Mercian army in the Marches in 1039. By 1055 his ascendancy was such that he ruled as high king over the entire extent of Wales, and the Anglo-Saxon Chronicle recognised Gruffudd as exactly that: 'king over the whole of Wales', a unique description that more than anything else recognises the danger Gruffudd posed to the established order of things within Britain. He was a direct challenge to English primacy within Britain, and the challenge became military when Gruffudd invaded and laid waste to Herefordshire in 1055, the year he established his dominance over all the other Welsh rulers. For the next two years, he had free rein in the **March**, terrorising the Severn and Dee valleys, sacking Hereford and raiding within sight of Gloucester. In the end he eliminated the Mercian settlements which had been made west of Offa's Dyke and forced the English to recognise his gains.

It was Harold Godwineson who undertook the task of re-establishing English primacy in what was an ongoing crisis which was to mark deeply the psyche of the Welsh borderlands for many generations. For decades to come, the English would fear a Welsh ability to duplicate Gruffudd's achievement or go even further and make good their claim to the lands they had lost to the Saxons in past centuries. In a combined naval and military operation in 1063, Harold devastated Gruffudd's lands from north to south with a huge army and eventually harried the Welsh to the extent that Gruffudd's fellow Welsh turned on him, and sent his head to Harold as a token of peace. Harold's campaign was significant in other ways. He did not just raid the Welsh borderlands; he showed every sign in 1063 of wishing to annex large coastal areas in the south-east, establishing a new **burh** as a military base at Portskewett on the Severn. It was on the basis of this campaign that his Norman successors would define their extensive claims on the March a few years later.

The Norman Invasion

The death of King Edward on 5 January 1066 found England long prepared for the succession of King Harold II Godwineson. The option of the king's teenage great-nephew, the atheling Edgar, was not even considered at this point. Harold had long been the chief mover in British politics, and even those earls not of his family chose not to oppose his succession, though he had no royal blood whatsoever in his veins. The English political community had chosen to forget King Edward's French relatives, and particularly William of Normandy, his nearest male blood relative, who had asserted his continuing interest in the succession only recently when he had been host to Harold at his court. William had a valid claim which was in due course to be accepted by the English, though they clearly preferred Harold and, when finally given a choice after Harold's death, young Edgar. But by then, with the English levies defeated and Harold and most of his brothers dead on the field of Hastings, there was no argument but that William of Normandy was the rightful king of England. The fact that the major-ity of English landowners were to support him militarily as king throughout the later 1060s and 1070s indicates that many admitted the validity of his claim, by blood and by nomination of his predecessor. It was the peculiar Anglocentricity of romantics and Victorians that was to label William as an invading usurper, a description that best fits the activities and non-existent claims of Harold Hardrada, king of Norway, whom Harold Godwineson defeated and killed at Stamford Bridge near York in the run-up to his own defeat at Hastings on 14 October 1066.

The invasion of England by Duke William was a remarkable enterprise, and Hastings was, as historians have commented, an unusual medieval battle. Edward's death had come at a convenient point in the duke's career. He had managed to establish an ascend-ancy in northern France and survived the aggression of his formidable enemies, King Henry of France and Count Geoffrey Martel of Anjou. He was allied with the counts of Brittany and Flanders, his neighbours. William's duchy was increasingly wealthy and his aristocracy was fully under his control: impressed by his long record of military success and formidable personal qualities, not least his austere piety. Duke William prepared well and took his time about it: collecting intelligence from England and assembling a huge fleet at the port of St-Valéry in the allied county of Ponthieu beyond the northern border of his duchy, which offered a shorter journey across the Channel. He recruited widely across northern and central France, contracting companies of **knights** for pay as a supplement to the retinues of knights and infantry promised by his own counts and **barons**. His logistical expertise in assembling the large force that gathered in Ponthieu was so effective that he was able to maintain it in the field, while by contrast across the sea King Harold had to dismiss his fleet and southern levies due to lack of provisions. The French fleet sailed with the tide on Thursday, 28 September 1066, and crossed the Channel by night, following the beacon blazing on the duke's flagship. Most made it to the designated landing site of Pevensey Bay and rendezvoused there with the duke's English agents. Harold in the meantime was returning from his defeat of the Norwegians near York. He settled at London to await reports on the Norman forces, while William established his headquarters in Hastings.

A week after his arrival in London, King Harold marched south into Sussex across the Weald. He hoped to catch the Franco-Norman army off guard, but his approach was detected and the duke was able to move his army north to confront the English. The engagement began well for Harold. In the cold dawn of Saturday, 14 October, his forces encountered the French on their northward march in a potentially strong defensive position: a wooded east–west ridge at the end of a spur of the Weald with a steep southward slope blocking the French advance. The duke's army was momentarily disorganised as the English lines appeared on the ridge above them, and in a bad position to deploy William's bowmen and infantry to the best advantage to weaken the English lines. The duke had to send parties of cavalry to search out the ends of the English lines; they were worsted in the process, and attempts to breach the main front by cavalry charges were frustrated by the nature of the ground. In places a retreat began amid rumours the duke himself had fallen.

It was at this point that the English made their fatal error. Some of their leaders concluded that a charge at this point would turn Norman disarray into rout but it seems that the consequent move off the hill misjudged the deadliness of the crossbow fire from below and the capacity of William's elite cavalry to recover and countercharge. At this point Harold's brothers Gyrth and Leofwine may have fallen leading the faltering advance. The unusual thing about Hastings was that the battle then continued throughout the day, whereas medieval battles in general were over in an hour once the advantage was clear. Both armies here, however, regrouped, with William sending his archers and crossbowmen to further deplete the shaken English line, and he spent hours carefully weakening and testing it until eventually, as the afternoon wore on, the English were no longer able to counter the armoured punch of William's cavalry squadrons. In the massacre that followed, most of the higher aristocracy of Wessex and Kent fell alongside their king.

Hastings was a decisive battle, but not just for military reasons. The leading earls of the Godwine family and their retinues did not survive the battle, and the shallowness of Harold's claim to the throne was revealed by his death: only his personal charisma (and, perhaps, his Englishness) had sustained it, and none of his family could inherit his political position. William's moral and hereditary claim on England was stronger than anyone else's, apart from Edgar atheling, the late King Edward's great-nephew, who was a teenager and whose candidature commanded little support. William spent weeks in Sussex after the battle, simply because he knew he was the only credible candidate for the throne, and it was only a matter of time before his new realm submitted without further resistance. The main danger to him at this point was a serious attack of illness, perhaps winter flu, which struck him and his army in Kent at the end of November, as he moved to put pressure on London. A **chevauchée** through the shires around the capital eventually produced the desired result, and the surviving English aristocracy and London submitted to William in mid December. He was crowned at the Confessor's shining white Romanesque abbey of Westminster on Monday, 25 December 1066, an auspicious day for a coronation.

Conquest of England and Domination of Britain

As the new king of England, William of Normandy had no particular enthusiasm for novelty. For several years after his coronation he would attempt to rule as his predecessors on the throne had done. He maintained the Midland and Northern earls who had not marched to Harold's support at Hastings and even put up with the objectionable Archbishop Stigand, Harold's close political friend, though he was wary enough to take them all back to Normandy with him in 1067, keeping his potential enemies close to him, as his court historian observed. For a while William even attempted to govern through the medium of English. He appears to have hoped that (like Cnut) he could manage England through viceroys and the occasional protracted stay, while he got on with his principal task of defending Normandy from the aggression of his French neighbours. But this was wishful thinking. The rapacity of the viceroys William had left behind in England inspired resentment, and the piecemeal redistribution of forfeited estates to incoming French that was under way by 1068 destabilised England. Harold's sons had fled to Dublin (as their exiled father had done in his day in 1052). Like him they recruited Norse mercenaries and ships and descended on the English coasts, seizing Bristol. Edgar atheling and his fearful family escaped to Scotland at the earliest opportunity, where they found shelter with King Máel Coluim III. King William would have learned for the first time from these events the complications, instabilities and cross-connections which were a part of political life in the British Isles, and the importance for a king of England of exerting and maintaining his wider claims to primacy over the archipelago.

So in 1068 William assembled his army and moved north, overawing the Mercian and Northumbrian earls and settling at York to receive ambassadors from Scotland, as a first step towards asserting the traditional place of the king of England within Britain. But his ostentatious progress north failed to have the desired effect, and on his return to Normandy a major revolt broke out in Northumbria, which commenced with a massacre of the Norman earl and garrison established at Durham in January 1069. The situation became rapidly more complicated as King Swein Estrithson of Denmark, the great Cnut's nephew, asserted his own claim to England. In this crisis it was only his enemies' mistakes that preserved William's new crown. York fell to the rebels, and King Swein's brother with his army landed on the Humber estuary to join up with the insurgents in September 1069. Exeter and Shrewsbury were besieged, and a Welsh army was operating with Mercian rebels deep into the Midlands. The king was able to destroy in person his enemies at Stafford, an obscure battle which may perhaps have been the most significant victory of his reign, for it allowed him to deploy north while his lieutenants dealt with lesser threats in the south. In a tour de force of military diplomacy he paid a heavy bribe for the Danish army to withdraw into a winter camp on the coast, and having divided his enemies he took the opportunity to inflict such a vicious wasting of Yorkshire that his English enemies were unable to stay in the field, and many had no choice but to submit to him.

From Easter 1070, England experienced a different William: ruthless, and indifferent now to past expedients in its kingship. Englishmen were purged from the highest ranks of the aristocracy and Church as too evidently uncommitted to his rule. Only Earl Waltheof of the East Midlands, the king's son-in-law, remained in a position of power until a false step in 1075 led to his execution. After that there were few English-born **magnates** left of any substance, and the few that remained were William's own creatures, raised by him with grants of lands from the dispossessed. By 1071, King Swein of Denmark had lost interest in England and the last pockets of resistance to William's rule had been mopped up. Thereafter threats to William's dominance came from outside England, and like his predecessors he was obliged to expend wealth and men to assert the British overlordship which he had inherited from the West Saxon dynasty, with the additional complication that William had simultaneously to maintain himself within the very different **polity** that was the kingdom of France. As for England, it became a place to be exploited for funds to finance the king's wider schemes. The great monument of the reign, the Domesday Survey of 1086, is a remarkable testimony to the organising ability of the Anglo-Norman state, but also to the way the wider world influenced it. The survey was commissioned as a response to the threat to its security by the aggressive posturing of a king of Denmark in 1085. The king wished to establish once and for all who owed what when the realm was taxed. It had to be taxed so that armies could be put in the field and navies floated to finance the king of England's wider ambitions and obligations.

The Anglo-Norman Empire

One of the most long-lasting effects of the Norman conquest of England was the way it reoriented England, and in due course the rest of Britain, away from the Scandinavian north-east and towards the south, to the **romance** cultures of Western Europe. The link between England and Normandy would last until 1204, occasionally broken (as it was between 1087 and 1096, 1100 and 1106, 1144 and 1154) but always repaired. In 1069 Norman power still included the much-contested county of Maine to the south, and it is some measure of the stress that the English rebellion of that year placed William's resources under that its seizure by the **Angevins** that year was never revenged or cancelled. The conquest of England came at a cost to the Normans, and has been characterised as 'imperial overstretch'. In the 1120s English commentators were already pointing out how much of an inescapable drag on England's resources the defence of Normandy had become. William had new French problems to deal with after 1066. One was the emerging talent of the young King Philip I of France (1059–1109), who took up his father's feud with the Normans with determination when he came of age in the 1070s. He inflicted two humiliating military defeats on William, at Dol (1076) and Gerberoy (1079), when the French benefited from the assistance of the king's own rebellious son, Robert. Philip was also able to weaken the Norman overlordship of neighbouring Brittany. If the balance of time that William spent between France and England after 1070 is any indication of his views, the king considered that Normandy was a much more pressing cause for concern than his realm across the Channel.

In part William's frequent absence may be because he had chosen to do no more than the least ambitious of his predecessors in relation to his kingdom, which was to maintain the status quo and the traditional imperial claim to British dominance he had inherited. After the conquest of England he continued the political ascendancy Harold Godwineson had enjoyed over the shires of Wessex by raising his close friend, William fitz Osbern (died 1071), as earl there. One of Earl William's main tasks was to reduplicate Harold's 1063 campaign, take possession of the areas on the fringes of Gwent and Brycheiniog which the English had colonised and reinforce the submission local kings had sworn to King Edward after Harold's defeat of Gruffudd ap Llywelyn. Welsh leaders and their warbands had taken advantage of the instability of the time, joining forces with English Mercian dissidents in 1067, and marching as far as Stafford with the rebels of 1069, to be crushed by the king personally.

An earl was set up in Chester in 1071 to continue that shire's position as a bastion of defence against the power of Gwynedd, and another was established at Shrewsbury to challenge any threat from the other major kingdom of Powys. The former English fortified outpost at Rhuddlan was reoccupied and became a castle and forward command post. Thereafter William's regime chose to ignore Wales, relying on the alliance with compliant kings, such as Caradog ap Gruffudd of Glamorgan, who was supported with French mercenaries when he extended his power across the entirety of South Wales. It was Caradog's death in 1081 in pursuit of his ambitions in Deheubarth that brought William's only venture across Offa's Dyke, when he marched unopposed along the coast from Gloucester through Glamorgan to St Davids, to intimidate any Welsh kings who might have taken advantage of Caradog's fall and thus exerting the king of England's traditional supremacy. The Welsh victors of 1081 over Caradog, Rhys ap Tewdwr of Deheubarth and Gruffudd ap Cynan of Gwynedd, saw the consequent advantage of becoming in their turn obliging clients of the Normans.

It was almost as if William was following a script for asserting British dominance he had borrowed from his predecessor, Cnut. The rebellion of 1069–1070 brought instability to his relationship with Máel Coluim III Ceann Mór of Scotland (died 1093), who by now had married Margaret, sister of the English atheling, Edgar, who had fled north to Lothian in 1068. Máel Coluim was himself half-English and had spent years at King Edward's court, so his awareness of the Anglo-French world of his day was greater than any previous king of Alba, which he reconquered between 1054 and 1057 and to which he added the breakaway kingdom of Moray. Máel Coluim's adroit handling of his multilingual collection of realms did more than anything else to define in contemporary consciousness the kingdom of Scotland out of Alba, Lothian, Galloway and Moray. Máel Coluim's sudden move against William after the rebellion of 1069–1070 is odd in view of his previous caution, and perhaps has most to do with sympathy and support for his new brother-in-law, Edgar the atheling. Máel Coluim's raids south across the river Tweed into troubled Northumbria and his close association with English rebels motivated King William's return to England in 1072 and a re-run of Cnut's great northern campaign of forty years earlier. An English naval and land force penetrated north as far as the river Tay, and forced Máel Coluim to meet William and acknowledge his overlordship at Abernethy on the northern border of Fife. The local knowledge William had of northern political and military conditions tells us that it can have been undertaken only in consultation with the established English leaders in Northumbria, and it connects William of Normandy directly to the policies and claims of his English and Danish predecessors.

William Rufus and the Struggle for Normandy

The death of William the Conqueror in 1087 temporarily separated England from Normandy, a separation which, had it continued, would have resolved many of the problems posed by such a dispersed and diverse realm which the events of 1066 had brought into being. But the new king William Rufus (1087–1100) was reluctant to let his elder brother Duke Robert II (1087–1106) enjoy Normandy in peace. In part this was politics. The fact that the greatest of the Norman magnates simultaneously enjoyed great estates in England introduced a new source of instability into Anglo-Norman politics. In 1088 a dangerous rebellion in favour of Duke Robert led by his uncles, Count Robert of Mortain and Bishop Odo of Bayeux, came near to unseating Rufus from his new throne. The rebels included many magnates who openly professed that they wanted to see England and Normandy reunited, but on their own terms. In 1088 the principal concern was the succession to both realms of the easy-going and incompetent Duke Robert.

Recognising this problem of allegiance, Rufus spent the following years investing great sums of English money and political capital so as to convince the greatest of the Norman nobles that it was in their interest that they should select him as their ruler. He did not take the option of warfare to assert his claims; instead he simply moved across the Channel in 1091 and set up an alternative court at Eu, in the northern corner of the duchy, the allegiance of whose count he had bought. His brother was obliged to accept Rufus as joint ruler of Normandy and resign himself to political impotence. Duke Robert occasionally attempted to evade the constraints of his enforced tutelage, but in the end his only escape from his brother's trap was to take a huge cash subsidy from Rufus in 1096 to finance his participation in the great **crusade** being proclaimed by Pope Urban. His departure for Constantinople left the mortgaged duchy in the hands of a king of England once again.

In the immediate run-up to Rufus's acquisition of Normandy, the king had been following up his father's work in subduing Britain with a good deal of enthusiasm and a new degree of ambition. In 1091 he had attempted to repeat his father's campaign against Máel Coluim III, though the elements proved to be unkinder to him. His fleet had been wrecked on the Northumbrian coast before it could assault Lothian and Fife. Nonetheless, the devastation of his army across the Scottish Lowlands had been enough to persuade Máel Coluim to make a formal act of submission to the king of England, in the negotiation of which Edgar atheling, a personal friend of Rufus, had been instrumental. It was at this point that Rufus revealed a closer engagement in British affairs than his distracted father had ever displayed. In 1092 he annexed Cumbria and fortified Carlisle, settling English colonists in the protection of the castle and fostering the erection of a line of **castellanries** along the Scottish border. The next year he began to give the Welsh March a similar degree of attention. The client kings Rhys ap Tewdwr of Deheubarth and Cadwgan ap Bleddyn of Powys had been growing in power at the expense of the divided and failing kingdoms of the south-east and Gwynedd. Rufus plainly saw the opportunity to duplicate his Cumbrian strategy in the Welsh border shires. In March 1093 he was assembling a great army in the Severn valley when he fell dangerously ill. His illness ruled him out of leadership in the subsequent incursions across **Offa's Dyke**, but he was still responsible for what became a major break with the insular strategies of his royal predecessors.

The inspiration for Rufus's Welsh campaigns may go back to 1075, when as a sixteen-year-old newly dubbed knight he was entrusted by his father with his first independent military command, which was to pursue followers of the Norman rebel earl, Roger de Breteuil of Hereford, across the frontier into Gwent and subdue Welsh resistance. There is an account of his success in forcing the Welsh king, Caradog ap Gruffudd, into submission and consolidating the English enclave originally set up eight years before by Earl Harold of Wessex along the coastal levels of Gwent as far as the river Usk. His youthful success appears to have stuck in Rufus's mind and become in due course the basis of a plan for broader incursions. In 1093 in furtherance of this he despatched his friend Robert fitz Hamo (died 1106), whom he had made lord of Gloucester, to extend this coastal lordship, and it seems that Robert was able to seize the entire coastal region of Gwent and Glamorgan unopposed, establishing a new lordship from the river Usk as far west as the river Tawe and in effect annexing the ancient kingdom of Gwlad Morgan.

This annexation was an entirely unprecedented development in Anglo-Welsh relations. What made the year 1093 even more dramatic in Wales was that the marcher earls of Chester and Shrewsbury were making simultaneous pushes westward from their own advance posts. In the course of these incursions, the dominant king of the day, Rhys ap Tewdwr, was killed in Brycheiniog, which effectively decapitated any organised native resistance. Perhaps to their own surprise, Earls Hugh of Chester and Roger de Montgomery of Shrewsbury found themselves masters of coastal Gwynedd and Deheubarth. They established new castles and lordships deep within Wales, at Deganwy, Pembroke, Brecon and Cardigan, which were to define in future the scope of conflicts between English marcher and Welsh native lords. Only the dynasty of Powys survived the catastrophe; the surviving members of the royal families of Deheubarth, Glamorgan and Gwynedd were for decades to be dispossessed refugees or prisoners. After this year, marvelled the chronicler of Worcester (a little prematurely, as it happened), there were no more kings in Wales. But that indeed appears to have been William Rufus's plan in 1093, and in embracing that ambition he made the first step to redefining the king of England's *imperium* over Britain into a legal, rather than tributary, lordship.

The Tyranny of William Rufus

William Rufus is one of the more enigmatic kings of England. All three of the Conqueror's sons who survived to adulthood were in their way formidable men. Even Robert Curthose was a brave and talented soldier, for all his political wilfulness and ineptitude. His long-term popular reputation in the middle ages was as the indomitable and modest hero of the First Crusade, the duke who turned down the offer of the kingdom of Jerusalem and coronation on the Temple Mount. William Rufus was the sort of king whose military virtues aligned closely with the aspirations of his own aristocracy, which enlisted their sympathies for him. Yet no one could deny the darker side of his personality. He was suspicious and greedy for treasure, and not too particular how his officers secured it for him. His chief minister, Ranulf Flambard, had influence with his master because he was so unscrupulous in extracting money from his aristocracy, Church and realm. Flambard was already hard at work on filling the king's treasury in 1090, and it was his efforts which provided the wherewithal for the destabilisation of Normandy and the purchase of the duchy. Whenever a church appointment fell vacant, Flambard would install managers and siphon off the income for the treasury, a measure that particularly offended the bishops, especially when Canterbury itself was transformed into a cash cow on the death of Archbishop Lanfranc in 1088. Lanfranc was not replaced until 1093 and then only because the king suspected he was on his deathbed and wished to negotiate the problem with God by appointing to Canterbury the Church's own candidate for the post, Abbot Anselm of Bec.

The king's own character is enough to explain the conspiracy against him in 1095. The plot that was uncovered amongst some of the leading members of his aristocracy was to murder Rufus and replace him with his first cousin, the count of Aumale, who was not in on the plot (though his father was). The major motivation was not to replace Rufus with his brother Robert, therefore. It was simply to get rid of a king who was far too domineering for the taste of the plotters, such as one of the more powerful of the leaders, Robert de Mowbray, earl of Northumbria, whose own authority in the north the king was happy to undermine. The king reacted decisively and ruthlessly, seizing Earl Robert's castles and dragging him out of his refuge in Tynemouth priory where he was cornered. Terrified plotters willingly implicated others, and a vengeful witch-hunt followed. The kinship of Count William of Eu with the king was not enough to prevent his blinding and castration when he failed to win a judicial duel into which he was hounded by the king. Flambard made the most of the situation by levying huge fines to clear their guilt on anyone stigmatised as a conspirator.

Modern historians have tended to approve of Rufus because of the detachment and irony he displayed in his dealings with his contemporaries (detachment and irony being the characteristic vices of historians themselves). He appears unusually secular for one of his family, as if he were a modern man out of time. But in fact he was very much a man of his own day: he was merely reacting as others did to the stifling piety of his father's court. Rufus was devoted to another contemporary cult: the hard-living and excessive knightly culture of the military camp and tournament, to which the Church was deeply opposed. His inappropriate humour and carelessness of consequences were very much of his day and his class. The Church's condemnation of his wild and unconstrained language was not because he was an unbeliever, but because he represented a king without self-control, and his greed and paranoia were a real threat

Fig. 1.2 Westminster Hall. From 1099 the main stage of English kingship, and the original meeting place of the Exchequer Court. From John's reign it was where the central court of Common Pleas met, and later housed the King's Bench and Chancery courts. The outer walls are still those built for William II Rufus's original hall in the 1090s. The hammerbeam roof dates from a rebuilding in 1395–1397.

to his own realm, as the rebellion against him in 1095 indicated. Like many egotistical rulers he developed grandiose building projects, such as the great hall he had built in Westminster Palace, designed to be the biggest in Europe (see Fig. 1.2). He was in fact a king who was well on his way to being stigmatised a tyrant when on 2 August 1100 a chance error in a hunting party in the New Forest sent a crossbow bolt into his chest rather than a passing buck. The general relief evident in the aftermath of his death, the prompt arrest of Flambard and the solemn undertaking of his successor to the political community to renounce the abuses of Rufus's reign tell us quite how far down the road to tyranny he had gone before his unexpected death. The fact that he had no chance to confess on a proper deathbed was enough proof anyone needed that God had struck him down for his sins.

 POSTSCRIPT

The shift by William Rufus in the degree of his ambition in Britain in 1092 was to have long-term consequences, as the *next chapter* will explore. England was now more deeply engaged in the weak Welsh polity than it ever had been and the new Welsh March drew in English lords and colonists who fundamentally challenged the older form of Welsh society. The kings of Alba after Máel Coluim III found themselves obliged either to resist or to imitate the new model of kingship in the south. Meanwhile, in England, Rufus's tyrannical rule inspired a long-term reaction in the political community, forcing his successor to negotiate with his magnates as partners in his rule, and to devise new and ultimately revolutionary ways of governing his realm.

KEY TEXTS

ENGLAND

The Anglo-Saxons, ed. J. Campbell (Penguin, 1991), offers fascinating essays on the Anglo-Saxon background and the period up to 1066. • Chibnall, M. *Anglo-Norman England, 1066–1166* (Blackwell, 1986), deals adroitly with the post-Conquest period.

SCOTLAND

Duncan, A. A. M. *The Kingship of the Scots, 842–1292: Succession and Independence* (Edinburgh University Press, 2002), persuasive and magisterial telling of the history of Scotland. • Woolf, A. *From Pictland to Alba, 789–1070* (Edinburgh University Press, 2007), offers an up-to-date and imaginative new ethnic model of the emergence of the Scots.

WALES

Davies, R. R. *The Age of Conquest: Wales 1063–1415* (Oxford University Press, 1991), a comprehensive and unsurpassed reconstruction of the emergence of Wales into the new Europe.

FURTHER READING

Barlow, F. *Edward the Confessor* (Eyre Methuen, 1970). • Barlow, F. *William Rufus* (Eyre Methuen, 1983). • Bates, D. *The Normans and Empire* (Oxford University Press, 2013). • Bates, D. *William the Conqueror* (Yale University Press, 2016). • Crouch, D. *The Normans: The History of a Dynasty* (Hambledon, 2002). • Lawson, M. K. *Cnut: The Danes in England in the Early Eleventh Century* (Longman, 1993). • Williams, A. *Æthelred the Unready: The Ill-Counselled King* (Hambledon, 2003). • Williams, A. 'The King's Nephew: The Family and Career of Ralph, Earl of Hereford', in *Studies in Medieval History Presented to R. Allen Brown*, ed. C. Harper-Bill et al. (Boydell, 1989), 327–43.

NOTE

1. *Encomium Emmae Reginae*, ed. A. Campbell (Camden Society, 3rd ser., 72, 1949), 34 (c. 1041).

2

Francophone Britain, 1100–1217

OVERVIEW

A new factor in the history of the British Isles in the long twelfth century is that what gave it a semblance of cultural unity was no longer its past history as some sort of tributary empire of the West Saxon kings, but the twelfth-century fact that it was part of a much bigger French cultural sphere, which embraced Scotland and Ireland as much as England. Until the expulsion of Louis of France from England in 1217, Frenchmen of all sorts moved easily across England, into Wales and Scotland and eventually Ireland, without leaving their own Francophone aristocratic world. This was not entirely due to the fact that the king of England was also a French prince throughout the twelfth century. French culture was predominant outside the French frontier, and was attractive as much to Germans as it was to Scots.

Between 1066 and 1217 there were only ten years when the king of England did not also directly rule over parts of France: those were between 1087 and 1091 when William Rufus was in England attempting to secure a lordship of his own in Normandy and between 1100 and 1106 when King Henry was gathering himself to emulate his brother's achievements. Even when King Stephen was ousted from Normandy in 1144, he still ruled over the county of Boulogne until his death. Before 1141 the English king tended to spend considerably more time in northern France than in England. After 1154, the centre of gravity of the Angevin royal house shifted the king's usual haunts even further south, to a heartland between the Loire valley and Rouen. The young king of Scots himself went on tour in France in 1166, to some acclaim. After the 1130s the Scots royal family consistently married female aristocrats from northern France or scions of the Angevin royal house. We can see the cultural and linguistic meshing that followed on from this in some striking cross-fertilisation between peoples and cultures quite early on. A fine example is that of Osbert of Arden, an aristocrat impeccably English in lineage and a retained knight of King David of Scotland. He expected to make regular tours of northern French tourneying grounds in the 1120s.

If the royal houses of Britain operated within a European framework as well as British and national ones, the same was as true for their upper aristocracy. It is possible to offer several striking illustrations of this. The earl of Leicester Henry I created in 1107 was the lord of much of the right bank of the city of Paris, and Versailles came within his French lordship. The marshal of Richard Strongbow's invading army which landed in Ireland in 1169 was recruited from the leading Capetian vassal dynasty of Montmorency. Through his Franco-Norman mother, Máel Coluim IV of Scotland had a rather more direct descent from Charlemagne than did his contemporary, Louis VII of France. When William Marshal, regent of Henry III, took the field at Lincoln in 1217, the invading French were commanded by his young first cousin, Count Thomas of Perche. He was consequently rather upset by the count's death during the course of the battle, for all that it marked the effective end of the Capetian attempt to conquer England.

The fact that the greatest of England's magnates were also Normandy's greatest magnates had consequences. It dictated the course of Anglo-Norman politics between 1087 and 1144. In 1088, 1095, 1100–1101, 1106 and 1136, numbers of magnates chose – or attempted to impose – the candidate for the English throne whose candidacy was most to the advantage of their cross-Channel interests. Down to the knightly level, there were people in the twelfth century who were landowners on both sides of the Channel whether in England, Wales or Scotland, which brought French influence directly to bear on English county courts, the Scottish Lowland lordships and the Welsh marcher liberties. It was for this reason that Latin became the language of record in the developing government of the English and Scottish states, as it was theoretically accessible to all: Breton, Norman, Cornish, Welsh, English and Gael. So in 1070 the Conqueror's

Chancery stopped communicating in English, and in the early thirteenth century the English government did not join the drift towards the French vernacular in legal business that was occurring across northern France.

The Revolutionary Reign of Henry I of England (1100–1135)

Henry was a king who more than any of his predecessors effortlessly bestrode the several spheres in which history and dynasty placed him. Whether as king of England, lord of an Anglo-Norman condominium or as a dominant ruler within the British Isles and northern France, he seemed equally at home, which is a tribute to his intellectual capacity. His ability to comprehend and manipulate the warring Welsh kingdoms and the complex power-politics of Picardy and Flanders, while simultaneously pacifying the fractious lords of Normandy and exploiting the resources of England, has been recognised by historians and generally admired. Some contemporaries, particularly the Norman historian Orderic Vitalis, were equally impressed. A large part of Henry's success was built on his ability to delegate to effective subordinates while he prioritised and concentrated on the key issue, which he diagnosed as the management of Normandy and relations with his Capetian adversary, Louis VI (1109–1137), a man of not dissimilar talents.

Louis VI was a kingdom-builder, using his effective control of the Seine basin in the 1120s to extend his influence northwards into Picardy and Flanders and constructing an alliance with the powerful count of Blois to the south-west. Louis had an unerring instinct for exploiting Henry I's weaknesses: the dynastic problem of Henry's young and dispossessed rival, his nephew William Clito (died 1128); the unstable march of Normandy, whose magnates looked as much to Paris as to Rouen; and the troubled relationship of the Normans with the rival military power of Anjou to the south. If Henry I of England's achievements in orchestrating his complex transnational interests and domains were impressive, the achievements of Louis VI of France in making life uncomfortable for him while patiently assembling the components of a Capetian state are even more so. It is worth reflecting on how Henry's dazzling successes proved in the end to be of the moment, while Louis's proved to be the foundation of a glittering political and cultural empire which by 1216 could presume to add England to its provinces.

But in his day Henry I of England was formidable, artfully unseating his elder brother from his rightful rule over Normandy in 1106 and persuading the world he had done both Robert and the duchy a favour. A clue to understanding his reign was in the way he came to power in England, an episode itself of some broad significance in British history. By 1100 Henry had spent well over a decade exploiting and being exploited by his elder brothers, learning his political skills the hard way. By 1100 he had for four years assumed the role of obedient henchman and courtier to his brother

William Rufus, which had at least gained him recognition of his precarious claim to a county in western Normandy. His career at court had also given a keen appreciation of the personalities and issues amongst his fellow magnates.

When his brother fell dead in a shooting accident on a hunt in the New Forest on 2 August 1100, Count Henry found himself standing over the corpse with a few companions, while the unfortunate Frenchman who had shot the bolt that killed the king rode for his life. After what must have been a rapid strategy conference, the small party of nobles rode for Winchester to seize the treasury and have the dead king buried decently, if hastily. Within two days, Henry was in London and had talked the bishop of London into consecrating him at Westminster on 5 August, which was done without much grandeur but at least with appropriate formality. At this, the very beginning of his reign, Henry was forced to a strategy which would shape relations between king and kingdom for the rest of the middle ages. On the same day he was crowned he drafted a declaration to be read out in every shire court and, to make sure everyone understood its implications, a parallel English text was issued alongside the Latin one.

The 1100 coronation charter was at one level a fraud. It declared confidently that Henry I had been crowned 'by common counsel of the barons of my realm of England' when the only participants in the liturgy of consecration had been his hunting party, other barons then in London, the monks of Westminster and two harassed bishops. But it was a manifesto designed to appeal to a kingdom ground down by 'unjust exactions'. Henry had to address directly the concerns of the political elite of his time if he were to gain their support. Since he too had been a baron and member of his brother's court until Rufus was cut down by a crossbow bolt meant for a deer, Henry knew very well what his fellow barons found irksome in his brother's rule of England, and indeed in their father's, which was one reason he harked back to the good laws of Edward the Confessor, rather than the good laws of the Conqueror.

The charter repeated his coronation oath to protect the Church and promised not to hang on to the estates of vacant bishoprics and abbeys, taking their profits for himself. As far as his barons were concerned, the king distanced himself from his brother's ruthless tendency to charge what he could get away with for the relief payments which were due to him on succession to their lands. Henry would ask a 'lawful and just' figure, but he did not actually go so far as to specify what that might be. The English aristocracy was seething about the treatment of its women, and had been even before the Norman Conquest. It was an issue with a long history. Norman kings had claimed the right to marry off females who came into their wardship, and they even tried to control the marriage of women who were in the care of their families. Henry promised consultation. Henry also surrendered the right his predecessors had claimed to marry off widows to whomever he wanted without their consent. More generally, the Conqueror and Rufus had imposed fines for offences and recognised no upper limit. Henry again promised to be reasonable in what he asked. The new king was in a desperate situation and would promise a lot to gain support, and it is likely that he had little intention at the time of sticking to his promises. What he may not have realised in the circumstances of 1100 was that he had constructed a reform agenda for the magnates of England and, in putting his seal to copies of it, had begun a dialogue his successors would be less than happy to be engaged in, and which would bring several of them low. Formal negotiations between the Crown and people of England over their just rights had begun, and the executive officer of the English state had recognised that his power had limits, even if it was only that he should be reasonable in what he asked.

Henry I survived the crisis of 1100–1101, and negotiated even the acquiescence of his elder brother, Duke Robert of Normandy, in his seizure of the throne of England. In the crisis Henry exerted himself to charm Anselm, the estranged archbishop of Canterbury, back from exile in Burgundy to England. Anselm even dutifully raised troops to defend the king from his brother's invading army. Henry then promptly went back on his settlement: victimising his brother's supporters in England, reneging on their deal and driving Anselm back into exile. Everything was organised, in fact, so that the new king would have the cash to raise the paid troops that would be the backbone of an army to invade and take Normandy, and so that the majority of the Anglo-Norman aristocracy would take his part and continue to support him. Henry was not intending to insinuate his lordship into Normandy as his brother had; he would take it. With an eye to future legitimacy, he married the king of Scotland's sister, a lady directly descended from Alfred the Great, so as to give their children an ancestry with which his English subjects could identify.

In 1106, at the battle of Tinchebray Henry achieved his aim; his isolated and unhappy brother was defeated and captured, and sent into supervised custody in a series of castles until he died at Cardiff in 1134. But once again, in pursuing a short-term objective, Henry ignored the possible long-term implications. He had inherited from his father and brother a huge reserve of royal estates readily available to grant out to win support. He added to it by the confiscation of his brother's supporters' lands in England, and the many opportunities for patronage that his rights as lord of England gave him. To extend his base of support he indulged in an orgy of patronage to construct an aristocracy deeply obliged to his generosity and tied to his fortunes. In so doing he began the process by which the balance of resources in England shifted away from the king and towards his aristocracy which would become increasingly embarrassing to the English monarchy in the thirteenth century. Despite the impressive nature of the monarchy Henry I of England constructed, with its ability to generate and monitor cash through a strict monetary policy and a finance office, it had already overreached itself by his death, and his successors were left with his debts.

But in his day Henry was nonetheless formidable. His selection of subordinates and willingness to give them free rein itself had consequences. Perhaps the most significant of these subordinates was Bishop Roger of Salisbury, a clerical friend of his from his difficult years in the political wilderness. Roger and his nephews gained a grip on the administration of England which they developed in new ways, not least in the improvement and systematising of the biannual financial audit called by 1109 the 'Exchequer', which was generating by at least 1118 annual summaries of royal income and expenditure. It gave the king and his officers both an ability to plan and a way to call regional officers and magnates alike to account. Characteristically, it also gave King Henry another resource for patronage. The 'pipe rolls' of the Exchequer are full of pardons from debt and taxation that the king granted to favoured individuals. The reform – one of the key steps in making the English state tangible and definitive – arose from a small trusted circle around the king: Bishop Roger; the king's soul mate and key supporter, Count Robert of Meulan; and possibly also his young queen, Matilda of Scotland. It seems they were well aware of the significance of what they were doing: the count had instituted a private exchequer on his own extensive English estates before his death in 1118. They may also have been aware that their fiscal vision of England helped define the nation: England could now be said to be that territory which answered to the Exchequer's demands for information and cash.

In retrospect, Henry I's reign in England was a remarkable episode of civil peace and state-building, which deeply impressed contemporaries on the continent, as Pope Innocent II himself tells us in the aftermath of Henry's death. He had so much success in England because he was willing enough to buy it at a high price, as his principal aims lay outside Britain. In 1100 he was perfectly ready to forswear the more objectionable methods of his tyrannical brother so as to win the sympathy of his brother's oppressed aristocracy. He recruited his leading magnates into his schemes and employed his earls and barons in the government of his realm, and for this he rewarded them lavishly. Tax exemptions were offered for those who supported his government. Royal estates were granted out on a huge scale to favoured magnates, and apparently with little expecta-tion of any return other than their loyalty. William earl of Warenne (died 1137), who had fought for Curthose in 1100, was a leader of the royalists by 1106. He was bought over by easy pardons and then fattened by lavish grants of former royal estates. He was a key Anglo-Norman magnate, whose support tipped the balance in Henry I's favour in both England and Normandy. He fought loyally for his royal master and acted as his agent and justice in both England and the duchy, being indeed elected lieutenant of Normandy by his fellows on the king's death in December 1135, until the succession question was decided. The problem for Henry's successors was that magnates loyal to him would not necessarily be loyal to them, and all the bribes he had offered could not keep the magnates constant to the oath he forced them to swear to support his daughter's candidacy for the throne. To this extent, Henry's actions laid the ground for the civil upset that followed his death, though one could hardly say he was responsible for it.

Civil War and Reconstruction in England

King Stephen of England (1135–1154) started well but he began his reign with unavoidable disadvantages which eventually brought him down. The first was the existence of a major rival with a good claim against him. Matilda, daughter of Henry I of England and former empress of Germany, had returned to England in 1125 after her husband's death to occupy the position of heir apparent to her father, a position reinforced by public oaths of the magnates to support her succession on his death. Stephen had ignored that inconvenient fact in December 1135 when he staked his claim to the crown, and was followed in it by the archbishop of Canterbury and the majority of the Anglo-Norman bishops and magnates. Pope Innocent II chose to accept Stephen's *fait accompli* when the new king's claim to England and Normandy was sent to him to arbitrate at Rome in February 1136. Louis VI of France himself wrote in Stephen's support, for the simple reason that Stephen was a member of the allied dynasty of Blois, on which the French king counted for support against Anjou, to whose ruling count Matilda had been unhappily married since 1128.

Initially, Matilda the empress received little support in either England or Normandy. Her pragmatic half-brother, the powerful earl of Gloucester, offered his own support to the house of Blois and attended Stephen's first great court at Oxford at Easter 1136. Her most formidable remaining supporter was her uncle, King David of Scotland, who had occupied Cumberland and Northumberland when news reached him of Henry I's death, and who had proclaimed Matilda queen. But in February 1136, faced with an impressive mercenary army led into the North by Stephen, and with little support from elsewhere, David too backed down and accepted the status quo. It was at this point that other parts of King Henry's legacy caught up with Stephen. In the great Easter court of April 1136 Stephen proved parsimonious with his favours, causing at least one major baron to storm off to the provinces swearing rebellion. Fortunately for Stephen the baron in question, Richard de Clare, walked straight into a Welsh ambush near Talgarth and was murdered. A consequence which was less fortunate, however, was that the Welsh then rose against the lords of the March and within a couple of months had wiped out all the territorial gains the English had made in Wales since the 1090s (Map 2.1).

Stephen's advisers knew that their king had to appear to be the kind of king Henry had been reputed to have been, but could not afford the largesse that Henry had thrown around. Perhaps for that same reason Stephen issued nothing more than a generalised coronation charter which in fact promised his realm nothing other than what was in his consecration oath. The late king's decisive and interventionist way with the Welsh kings had also now come home to roost, and Stephen's dithering as to how to respond to the March in flames demonstrated his serious limits as a king. While Wales was in

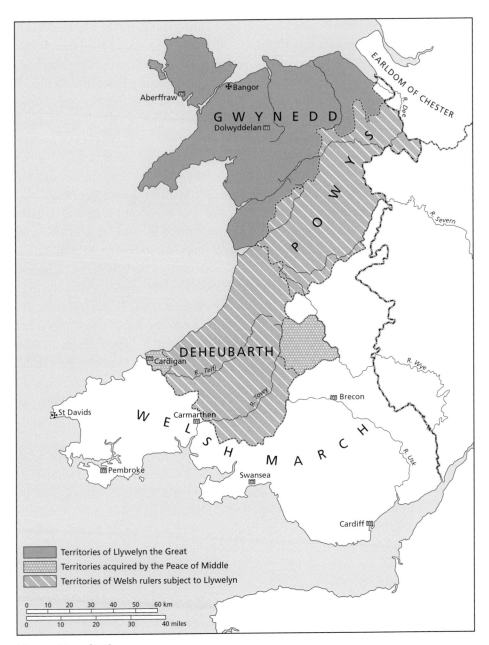

Map 2.1 Map of Wales, *c.* 1200

tumult, Stephen sat in front of Exeter in a show siege trying to demonstrate that he was as remorseless as his late uncle in dealing with rebel barons. Instead, he lost the respect of the embattled marcher community and sacrificed English military dominance in Wales for several generations.

The qualities of Stephen as king have fascinated historians since the nineteenth century, as have the reasons for the outbreak of civil war in 1139. As we have seen, he had a negative legacy from his predecessor to deal with. Stephen's limits as king also had a lot to do with it, not least his unfortunate inability to maintain a balance of factions at his court. From trusting his brother, the bishop of Winchester, and Henry I's former confidant, the bishop of Salisbury, Stephen veered at the end of 1137 to over-reliance on a noble cabal headed by the ambitious and mercurial Count Waleran of Meulan, appointed his lieutenant of Normandy in 1136. His reliance on either faction can only have alienated Earl Robert of Gloucester, the late king's eldest (if illegitimate) son, one of those marcher barons who already had cause for complaint against Stephen.

Earl Robert had tired of Stephen by 1138, and sent the king his formal defiance from Normandy. He had the option of appearing moral in doing this by declaring for his half-sister, the empress, and her Angevin husband. Robert's rebellion did not initially prosper, as he was hounded across Normandy by Count Waleran. A premature rising of his allies in England in April 1138 was brutally suppressed by the king, and David of Scotland's attempted military intervention was humiliatingly crushed by Stephen's loyalists near Northallerton in Yorkshire. Yet by the end of 1139 civil war had nonetheless set light to England. Earl Robert's daring coup in September in crossing the Channel with the empress herself was the key event. With the Empress Matilda now in England, and a core of rebellion still active in the southern March, she had a credibility she had until then lacked. New supporters emerged, and the empress was able to secure a rebel heartland in the Severn valley, maintaining herself there against the king.

Stephen failed to eliminate the rebel 'Angevin' party during the rest of his reign, though he strove to do so with admirable energy and fortitude. He too had a heartland in the south-east, based on the loyalty and wealth of London, while retaining also the allegiance of towns, castles and loyalists in the Midlands and Yorkshire. A military stalemate gradually emerged. Both sides had low points, not least the king's capture at the battle of Lincoln, 2 February 1141, and subsequent nine-month imprisonment. But it was retrieved by the empress's humiliation at the hands of the Londoners when she rode to Westminster for her coronation, and her own subsequent military catastrophe at Winchester, which led to the capture and imprisonment of Robert of Gloucester. A prisoner exchange at Winchester on 1 November 1141 cancelled all the empress's advantage. But Stephen too was weakened by his loss of Normandy to an Angevin invasion and the defection of his Norman agent, the count of Meulan. Stalemate continued for six years after Lincoln. The one major change in circumstances was the death of Robert of Gloucester in 1147, which led to the empress's tired withdrawal to Normandy from her capital at Devizes early in 1148, and the resignation of her claims to her teenage eldest son, Henry. But the civil war nonetheless sputtered on insolubly until its unexpected resolution in 1153.

What was most remarkable about England's twelfth-century civil war was the manner of its ending, which had little to do with the rivals for the throne themselves. Exhaustion at the ongoing tragedy played its part, as is the general case with such wars. But the key factor that emerged in the end was an English political community that took charge of events over the heads of the principals of the warring factions. There were already signs of this in the aftermath of the death of Earl Robert of Gloucester in November 1147. The earl's personal animus against the king had provided the energy to keep the fight going for years, though he had told Stephen to his face at the handover of prisoners in 1141 that it was nothing personal but a matter of principle that kept him in the field. The civil war of the mid twelfth century was in fact rationalised by both parties as a matter of principle, not dynastic conflict. The core of this was one close to aristocratic hearts, the principle of loyalty and good faith. When both sides came to exchanging words about why they were fighting, as in the debate between the bishop of Winchester and Brian fitz Count, rebel lord of Wallingford, it was their oaths to Henry I and the empress that were the basis for finger-pointing.

Once Robert of Gloucester was dead and the empress had left England, the earl's son and heir began negotiating local peace pacts with his neighbours, whatever party they nominally belonged to. Ignoring the king and his new rival, Henry Plantagenet, the great magnates attempted to limit the damage done England, and began discussing possible solutions to the civil war. Warfare consequently died down to limited annual campaigns by Stephen to force a passage into the rebel heartland in the Severn valley. Stephen was generally admitted to be part of the problem, and there was a reluctance to concede his family any future on the throne. As early as 1150 his plan to have his eldest son and heir, Eustace, crowned associate king was being thwarted by the archbishop of Canterbury in conjunction with a now hostile papacy. The summer of 1153 saw an attempt to reopen the war by Henry Plantagenet, already a young warrior of repute and duke of Normandy in succession to his father, who had died in 1151.

Henry's arrival in England led to significant defections from the king, but also brought the peace movement to a head. Both king and duke were personally determined on a final confrontation and a battle to the death, but when they manoeuvred to achieve it at Wallingford in August 1153 they found themselves outmanoeuvred by their own supporters, who refused to fight and demanded a peace conference. Not only that, but the bishops and earls of England were ready with the heads of the proposals for peace. Fate eliminated the obstacle of Eustace, who fell victim to **dysentery**, and the bereaved king his father accepted the inevitable, which was to adopt Henry Plantagenet as his heir despite having still one other teenage son. A formal peace settlement was agreed in November 1153, and in March 1154 Duke Henry left for Normandy and his pressing military problems in France, still on speaking terms with the 57-year-old king. Not a happy man, perhaps, Stephen nonetheless soldiered on and reasserted himself as undisputed king of England, until his death at Dover in October put the succession question entirely beyond question and ushered in the dynasty that would rule England for the rest of the middle ages.

Henry II became king with some assurance. He did not hurry to cross back to England to claim his crown at Westminster. This was neither a parade of bravado nor because of the distraction caused by French commitments. England was for Henry a problem, which though not fully solved could be left to itself for a while. For most of his reign his major preoccupation was going to be the enormous complex of domains he had inherited and acquired by marriage in France, as it would be also for his successors well into the next century. Henry arrived in England for his coronation the best part of two months after his old rival's death to find it peaceful under the rule of the archbishop of Canterbury and the great earls, one of whom he appointed his **justiciar**, or chief agent, the earl of Leicester. He co-opted the late King Stephen's principal officer, Richard de Lucy, to assist Leicester.

The earls and bishops had settled England's wars in 1153, and it became apparent during the course of 1155 that the new king was going to leave them to get on with it. Conciliar rule had come to England. Henry II was not going to challenge the dominance of his earls. The one serious attempt he made to strike down an earl as being over-mighty in the spring of 1155 was against Roger of Hereford, a veteran leader of his own party in the civil war. But when Roger deployed Welsh mercenaries and put his castles into defence, the king backed away from confrontation and sought compromise. Compromise encouraged the former earl of York, William of Aumale, to give up his notorious and obnoxious gains in the North from the previous reign. When Henry moved against any magnate, he made sure they were isolated first. So he confiscated Pembroke from its young and friendless earl, though he let him keep the status of the title. Worcester was taken from Waleran of Meulan, but he was already disgraced and marginalised in Normandy and his twin brother, Earl Robert of Leicester, had bought into a future with the new dynasty.

Henry was back in France at the beginning of 1156, where he was, in the end, to spend nearly two-thirds of his reign. He had two strategies to deal with this forced separation: the development of an administrative and judicial alter-ego in the person of a justiciar, who presided on the **bench** of the Exchequer, which gave him financial and legal predominance in the kingdom. The other was the tacit concession of control of the realm to the aristocracy, at least in the first years of his reign. Staged set-pieces of the king sitting in state in council issuing assizes and judgements declared to posterity that all was done by the counsel and consent of bishops and magnates. So Henry II continued the alliance that had brought the civil war to a close. It paid off as a strategy, though it had consequences, not least this view (preached in French at his own court by his own chaplain): 'The king cannot please himself, he is there for everyone; if he did what he wanted to do, he would not be worthy. He has to heed the common will, if its wishes are for the good of all.'[1] The advantage was that none were more vocal in their support of the king against his enemy Thomas Becket at Clarendon in 1164 than Henry's magnates, and it was four of his curial barons who were so offended by the archbishop's disrespect to their lord that they eventually murdered him. The magnates included among their numbers those with the skills to reconstruct and indeed improve on the machinery of the state that survived Stephen's reign. For all that Richard fitz Nigel (son of the bishop of Ely, nephew of Roger of Salisbury) claimed it was his father who had restored the wrecked Exchequer, it was an earl who presided there throughout this period, supported by the late King Stephen's constable and friend, Richard de Lucy.

Historians are willing to believe that Henry I's financial innovations actually survived the reign of his successor. The Exchequer was there to be revived rather than reinvented. The trick was to restore its authority, institute effective local officers and reclaim what royal estates could be recovered. A lot of progress had been made towards this by 1159, particularly in increasing judicial revenues in the face of an inevitable decline in the ancient national land tax (the geld) and in revenue from royal manors and boroughs, many of which never returned to royal hands after Stephen's reign. The king's agents busily innovated in the face of necessity and found new sources of revenue in exploiting as a form of tax the military exaction known as **scutage**, which assisted the king in funding mercenary forces in the field from fines from unperformed knight service. It was to be this innovation, which in its collection approached rapacity at times, which made so much possible of what Henry and his sons achieved, but success relied on the complaisance of a political community that Stephen's reign had brought into being and which identified itself as much with the fortunes of the kingdom as those of the man who wore its crown.

State-Building in Scotland and Wales

The kingdom of England had already had a long-term effect on its neighbours to its north and west before 1066. The kingdom of the Scots in the eleventh century had in Lothian and Cumbria regions where **Anglian** culture, language and ecclesiastical structures were long established. Máel Coluim III (1058–1093) was married to the celebrated Margaret, granddaughter of King Edmund Ironside; their four eldest sons were given West Saxon royal names. One of them, King Edgar (1097–1107), took a seal which had as its inspiration that of the Confessor, and entered into a close relationship with William Rufus. It was his younger brother, King David (1124–1153), who has the justified reputation of being the conscious reformer of Scotland on an English template. David served an apprenticeship at the court of Henry I of England where his sister Edith (called Matilda in England) was queen and where he arrived around 1113 to be honoured with a marriage which brought him the English earldom of Huntingdon. Even before he became king, David was active in his Lowland fief establishing burghs at Roxburgh and Berwick and importing French monks to Selkirk. As king he brought Anglo-French aristocrats bodily into his realm and offered them estates to be held in the customary manner with which they were familiar from elsewhere in the Francophone world. David established sheriffs as royal officers across the Lowlands and Fife and as far north as Perth. His new towns had mints which issued silver pennies in his name on the English model. So far as his circumstances allowed he duplicated what he could of the English state in his own realm. He manufactured a Scotland recognisable as another of the realms of the Francophone area of north-western Europe. It is no surprise to find his grandson King William (1165–1214), who used his mother's Norman surname 'de Warenne', tourneying as a young king across northern France, a pursuit that David himself has been credited with embracing in the 1120s.

The frontier between England and Scotland was permeable to clerics and aristocrats alike in the twelfth and thirteenth centuries, and many of the aristocrats of Scotland and England had possessions in both kingdoms, which produced the same sort of complications as aristocrats with lands in both England and France experienced. It also brought the Scottish royal family bodily into English politics. Members of it played a part in all the major upheavals of the reigns of the early Angevin kings, and cadets of the family held English earldoms of Huntingdon and Chester. Another factor was that the Scots kings had long harboured claims to an extensive earldom of Northumbria. King David and Máel Coluim IV had briefly managed to make it good between 1139 and 1158, and it was a claim William the Lion continued to pursue in his turn. This did not mean the Scots had any ambition to subtract Cumbria and Northumberland from England and add them to Scotland. The phantom earldom was still being pursued by King Alexander II against King John in the thirteenth century. But embracing the mainstream of European politics and culture only went so far in Scotland. Most of the developments I have described concerned only eastern, central and Lowland Scotland. Norse-Gaelic and Galwegian Scotland had a far less European relationship with the royal house of Alba. That said, the native **mormaers** of the north were adopting the aristocratic mores of the Anglo-French by the thirteenth century, with household knights, castles and the title of 'earl' masking the solidly Gaelic origins of the mormaers of Menteith, Strathearn, Fife and their like.

Wales is a more complex example of the influence of the Anglo-French model of rulership. Between 1080 and 1121 the south and east of Wales was subject to remorseless and occasionally ruthless colonisation licensed by the English king, and sometimes participated in by him. No Welsh ruler attempted the sort of cultural assimilation the Scottish kings embraced, though they seem at least to have aspired to and mastered contemporary European military technology, building and besieging castles with some finesse. It was the collapse of the March of Wales in the 1130s which changed this state of affairs. The generation of Owain ap Gruffudd of Gwynedd (1137–1170) and Rhys ap Gruffudd (the Lord Rhys) of Deheubarth (1155–1197) accommodated itself to the fact and power of the English state, but did so from a position of strength. Owain of

Gwynedd inflicted two defeats on Henry II of England in the field and corresponded with Louis VII of France as an independent princely power. Rhys of Deheubarth for his part used the weakness of King Henry II in Wales to negotiate in 1172 a position of his justiciar there outside Gwynedd, giving him theoretical control over Welsh and English alike. In return Welsh mercenaries filled the ranks of Angevin armies and became feared across the battlefields of northern and central France.

The cultural accommodation between Welsh rulers and the Francophone mainstream proceeded subtly. By the 1170s Welsh rulers dropped their aspiration to kingship and selected a more European title of 'prince' to claim a sovereign but non-royal status, recognisably the same as that exercised by the dukes of France, Italy and Germany: greater than counts but subordinate to kings. It was in John of England's reign that all these developments came together in the remarkable person of Llywelyn ab Iorwerth, prince of Gwynedd (1197–1240) and grandson of Owain. While pursuing a thoroughly traditional Welsh hegemony over the other native rulers, Llywelyn created a court more oriented to the contemporary Francophone world, where his princess, King John's eldest daughter Joan, 'the Lady of Wales', was arbiter of its culture. He offered generous patronage to **Cistercians** and **Franciscans**, employed jurists who constructed a somewhat unhistorical view of the prince of Gwynedd as supreme source of a national Welsh law, built boroughs and stone castles (see Fig. 2.1), employed seneschals and flaunted a

Fig. 2.1 Dolwyddelan Castle. State-building in Wales by the princes of Gwynedd included strategic castle-building, such as this impressive fortress built by Llywelyn ab Iorwerth (died 1240) to defend a mountain pass giving access to the Vale of Conwy. Captured through treachery in 1283, it was formidable enough to be absorbed into the English network of garrisoned castles in Wales.

heraldry alluding to the royal house of Anjou into which he and his uncle Dafydd had married. It was in his day and in his court that the flickering image of a Welsh state emerged which his son and grandson attempted to solidify.

King John and the Collapse of the Angevin Regime

The conciliar rule of England that King Henry II sanctioned in the 1150s persisted, though the initial good relations between the king and his magnates, let alone the Church, did not survive the 1160s. The king was formidable as an intellectual and as a politician, and the realm he inherited and acquired – for all it was ramshackle – made him the most obviously powerful ruler in Europe other than the Hohenstaufen emperor. In England and Normandy aristocratic support got him through the crisis represented by Thomas Becket, but that crisis itself illustrated the difficulty of the king's aggressive personality, subject to wilful and remorseless dislikes. He excluded and marginalised magnates he simply could not abide, such as his cousin and one-time chief support, Earl William of Gloucester, and his younger contemporary Earl Richard Strongbow. He was not beyond extra-judicial arrest and deprivation in his dealings with his magnates, which generated discontent and unease. By 1173 this was sufficient to create a formidable party among his Anglo-French aristocracy which was happy to support the internal rebellion led by Henry's eldest son and associate king, the Young Henry (1170–1183) which, when allied to the resurgent Capetian monarchy and a Scots invasion, came within an ace of toppling him. The capture of the king of Scots and the defeat of the earls of Leicester and Norfolk by loyalist barons in 1174, as well as the political ineptitude of his own son, preserved Henry's throne in England.

It may be that the increasing absorption of the king in the challenging problem of his French domains and the threat posed by Philip II of France was what principally accounted for the relative quiet in England for the rest of his reign, left to its loyal bureaucracy to rule. His reign ended ingloriously, for he was never able to resolve the problem caused by his inability to let go of control of his realm. He apparently found even nominating an heir hard to do, as in his head it would set the seal on his departure. It was that weakness that allowed Philip II of France to manipulate the only credible heir, his elder surviving legitimate son, Count Richard of Poitou, into rebelling in 1189 against his mortally ill father, and it was in the throes of the humiliating military defeat that followed that Henry II died.

The absence from England of the king and the delegation of power to aristocratic bureaucrats continued into the reign of King Richard (1189–1199), who famously spent no more than six months of his reign in England. One of the most striking features of his reign was that, nonetheless, England was ruled effectively and provided him with the resources to pursue his endless campaigns in the Mediterranean and France. This was principally due to his decision to continue the rule of England through his father's aristocracy and established bureaucracy, not perhaps that he had much choice in the matter. He was also able to take many of his most active and capable aristocracy on campaign, being one of those kings of England who was able to identify thoroughly with his aristocracy through their shared military aspirations. One aristocrat he did not take with him to Sicily, Cyprus and Palestine was his brother John, count of Mortain and earl of Gloucester. So when Richard departed on crusade in 1190 John was able skilfully to use the tensions caused by his brother's poor choice of justiciar, William de Longchamp, over the heads of the established royal officers, to lever himself into power in England. He was supreme there between 1191 and 1193, though he too ended up dependent on the support of a committee of Angevin bureaucrats. These were the same men who were to combine to bring John to the throne in the aftermath of the unexpected and childless death of his brother in 1199.

And so began the reign of John (1199–1216), one of the most transformative in English medieval history. It might be added that it was transformative too in terms of British history, for John was a king, like Henry I, who had a formidable vision of himself as a ruler dominant over all the isles of Britain. In part that aspiration was due to an early immersion in the rule of Ireland, of which he was formally made 'lord' in 1185, though he lost the status temporarily after his disgrace in 1194. The responsibility for the collapse of Angevin rule in France north of the Loire between 1203 and 1205 may not be entirely attributable to John, for he inherited an exhausted Normandy and an alienated Norman aristocracy. But his mercurial and difficult personality was already taking a toll on his relations with his English magnates by 1203. His retreat from Normandy to England at the end of that year proved irreversible and created a new balance of power in northern France in favour of the Capetians. In English terms there were consequences for the separation of England and Normandy in the fact that after 1203, for the first time in several decades, the kingdom had a king in long-term residence. The conciliar rule of the realm ended as the king himself assumed an executive role in policy and the machinery of finance and judiciary, and it so happened that John was a king obsessed with finance and the seat of judgement.

These changes might have in fact assisted his ambitions had it not been for John's personality. His grandson Edward I was a man equally as directive and aggressive in British terms, but Edward at least was able to count on his aristocracy for much of his reign. But trust was not part of John's nature, nor was he a man the military aristocracy could identify with, for all that he was in his way a talented soldier and had demonstrated personal bravery in the field on more than one occasion. He would take up a new intimate for a while and then cast him down. It was only those very few friends he made as a child and an adolescent prince that he ever remained loyal to. It cannot be said of him that he was a bloody tyrant: he was simply bloody-minded. Though he has been blamed by history for the deaths of his nephew Arthur in 1203 and members of the Briouze family in 1210, failed gaol breaks and gaol fever are equally credible explanations of these deaths. Like his father, John had an appetite for nubile teenage girls which contemporaries found quite as distasteful as the present day does, for all that kings could get away with much in his time. But the overstated and sometimes ludicrous propaganda of the emerging opposition baronial party in 1210, which was adopted by his Capetian enemies in Paris, is the basis of the case against him adopted in turn by Victorian historians. The main charge on which he can be convicted is that, unlike his predecessors since Stephen, he did not work with his magnates in the rule of his realm, but actively defied and despised them. Two generations after his death this was what defined his historical reputation even on the continent: a Franciscan moralist writing in France said of John's nemesis King Philip that he knew how to value a good man, whereas John of England was disinherited because he could not.[2] John was thus in contemporary terms a tyrant, a rogue king.

John managed to stabilise his control over Aquitaine in France in 1206 and established a favourable truce with the Capetians. He made efforts to compensate English magnates who had lost lands in France in part by redistributing lands of those who had gone over to the Capetians. He built up a treasury and naval control over the Channel. Until as late as 1210 John appeared to be a king who was holding his own in struggles with his arch-rival, King Philip Augustus of France (1180–1223), and a hostile papacy. But there were ominous developments. He saw Ireland as his own playground, and wished to reduce the power of the great Irish provincial lordships: Leinster, Meath, Ulster and Limerick. But he experienced a setback in 1207–1208 when he moved against William de Briouze, a former close and intimate friend who had been one of the prime movers of his succession. Though Briouze was dispossessed of his Welsh lands and Limerick, he was defiantly harboured by his Irish fellow magnates. Never willing to let an issue go, John in due course assembled a huge army and fleet and descended in force on Ireland in the summer of 1210, rounding up the Briouze family, humiliating the lords of Meath and Leinster and driving into exile Hugh de Lacy, the earl of Ulster he had himself created.

For all that this remarkable campaign of 1210 demonstrated John's military skill and political will, it also convinced his magnates that not even the greatest amongst them was safe from the king's wilfulness. The situation was compounded by the subsequent death of William de Briouze's much admired wife, Matilda, and his eldest son in captivity at Windsor, about which wild rumours were soon circulating amongst the political community. Although John followed up his Irish triumph with an equally stunning campaign against his son-in-law Llywelyn of Gwynedd in Wales in 1211, the alienation of his magnates was by then all but complete. Issues had emerged to feed their insecurity: John recognised no limits when he had them at his financial mercy; he clearly put more trust in his Norman and Angevin captains and officials than he did in his English barons, and the partnership by which England had long been governed was dead. The point had been reached when the magnates wished to re-establish it, and John had sufficient enemies and difficulties now for the magnates to be able to impose on him.

While preparing at Nottingham for a second campaign against Llywelyn in August 1212, John was informed that an attempt would be made to topple or even kill him on the campaign. Some believed the warning had come from his daughter Joan, the princess of Gwynedd. It was not unprecedented for assassinations to be attempted against English kings (Henry I, Stephen and Henry II had all been targeted at one time or other), and there was no doubt John was shaken by the news of a plot. A chronicler based in the East Midlands reports that behind it were letters (presumably from the pope or someone claiming to be the pope) absolving the barons of their allegiance and encouraging rebellion. Some believed that the crusading hero and John's personal enemy since 1209, Simon de Montfort, had been secretly elected as John's replacement. The king had just set up an intrusive national enquiry into the service owed him by the barons, who may well have feared that this was the preliminary to major new impositions on them as the king geared up for a decisive French campaign. Other complications occurred at this time. The king got into a personal confrontation with Robert fitz Walter over a homicide committed by Robert's son-in-law, Geoffrey de Mandeville. Robert apparently came armed with his military household to Nottingham for an interview with the king. Following this, fitz Walter, Eustace de Vesci and their families fled England for the Capetian court, which developed into a major problem for John. The two exiled barons damaged John considerably. It was Vesci and fitz Walter who provided the Capetians with the characterisation of John as a rapist, murderer and enemy of mankind. It was at this time that the prophet Peter of Pontefract (or Wakefield) began publicly preaching that John would not be king after the next feast of the Ascension (23 May 1213). Quite a few chose to believe him.

John made notable efforts as a result of the plot to conciliate the kingdom, threatened as he was by the tightening papal **interdict**. He took back into favour the venerable and popular earl, William Marshal, lord of Leinster; he moderated his demands for money and returned some hostages. Most importantly he began to negotiate peace with the pope in February 1213, and allowed the return of the exiled bishops and barons as part of the deal with Pandulf, the papal negotiator. Apart from a hard core of opposition among the Northern barons, the rest of the magnates submitted to John's more conciliatory and reasonable stance concerning their individual claims and grievances, hoping perhaps that the good old days were at last returning. Apart from the North, the major barons supported John's climactic 1214 French campaign, a grand alliance with the emperor and the count of Flanders which was to restore him to power in his lost lands. The failure of John in France revived the dispute, however. John lost his gamble, and the stakes were now called in.

The barons could resort in this crisis to the broad agenda of subjects against their king which had long ago been set out in Henry I's coronation charter, which had, as we have seen, allowed that his subjects could reasonably claim some rights as their own. Copies of this charter were to be found in a number of local archives available to the barons. Some may even have had their own copies in their family papers. In the second week of January 1215, the first planning meeting of the baronial party convened. The adherence to the barons of Saher de Quincy, earl of Winchester, was a serious development for John. He had been a prominent Angevin loyalist, judge and captain since the time of Henry II and had done very well out of John, to whom he owed a wife, an earldom and great wealth. His defection to the dissidents indicates that the pillars of the Angevin monarchy had shattered under the weight of the king's greed and wilfulness. The middle managers of its power structures were now out against the king, and Saher was the sort of man who would have known all about the 1100 charter and its significance.

Magna Carta and the Decline of Francophone England

For all that John stalled and the pope was recruited to offer his mediation, on 5 May near Brackley (Saher de Quincy's castle) the barons defied the king by letter and marched with banners unfurled (that is, in a state of war) to besiege nearby Northampton, a royal castle. The rebellion was already wider than England: the king of Scots and the prince of Gwynedd sent messages of support to the barons. The king's prospects abruptly collapsed when baronial troops seized London on 17 May. All over the country, royal parks and manors were attacked and sacked. The king retreated to Winchester, unable to engage usefully with the rebels. John knew his position was untenable, and so he negotiated with the barons. As early as February 1215 the king's spokesman was Earl William Marshal, while the mouthpiece of the baronial party was Archbishop Stephen Langton, who had himself defied the king in March 1215 by refusing to excommunicate the dissidents. The king actually discussed the barons' terms in a surviving letter to Pope Innocent sent at the end of May, after the baronial defiance, so we know he had already broadly agreed to abolish the supposed 'evil customs' tactfully ascribed to his brother and father, and proposed a commission to decide what needed reforming. Negotiations were non-stop and largely focused on the 'meadow of Staines', a place called Runnymede on the bank of the Thames where the borders of Middlesex, Surrey and Berkshire met, an ancient meeting place for the men of the region. By 10 June a basic settlement had been ironed out between the parties. On 15 June the two parties met and sealed the final draft of the settlement: the 'Great Charter'.

The Magna Carta of 1215 has sixty-three clauses, within which there is the makings of a social revolution, as contemporaries (notably Pope Innocent) easily recognised and, in the pope's case, resented. John himself must have been aware of it, and historians have generally assumed that he sealed it because he had no intention of keeping to the terms, but of ignoring the settlement as soon as it felt safe to do so. Historians have disputed as to what precisely the barons thought they were doing at Runnymede. Some deny that they had the intellectual resources to articulate their concerns, and many have adopted the unreliable chronicler Wendover's belief that it was really the work of the brilliant academic Archbishop Langton and his fellow bishops. Others have been more generous to the intellectual capacities of the magnates and see Magna Carta as a natural consequence of the way Angevin kingship was implemented in England before John's reign, with the barons being conceded a stake in a conciliar style of government which John had abandoned. It was their way of reasserting their stake in affairs.

The sources are such that we know how all these developments were received by contemporaries. A Flemish political commentator who visited England at this time (a man called by historians 'the Anonymous of Béthune') singles out three particular issues about Magna Carta he picked up on his travels and conversations in England: disparagement, forest offences and limits on the size of fines. The king's arranging of unsuitable marriages for their women had been a major complaint of the barons in 1100, and features heavily in the charter, a complaint which goes along with the king's unfair exploitation of wardships. The rapacity of the king's foresters was another issue. In 1100 Henry I had clearly been challenged on the same subject, but had made minimal concessions. Restraining the king's ability to fine and tax his subjects at will was a major concern in 1100, and John had made it more pressing still. Power without restraint was tyranny, and this was no longer to be allowed John, by setting actual ceilings for his demands and institutionalising consent. It was only slightly moderated by imposing similar restrictions on the barons themselves. The Anonymous did not, however, take notice of the clauses which immortalise Magna Carta: that no free man may be brought to law without the 'lawful judgement of his peers' and 'to no one will we sell, to no one will we deny or delay right or justice' (cc. 39, 40). These clauses decisively limited royal power ever afterwards in England. The Anonymous did notice – and make much of – the clauses which appointed Twenty-Five Barons to monitor the implementation of Magna Carta and keep the king in check. This too had a long-term impact. The repeated baronial coups over the next two centuries were likewise to appoint committees to limit the king's power to act and tie him to their agenda.

Pope Innocent's condemnation of Magna Carta was decisive: the king had accepted it 'by force and fear'; it was 'demeaning and shameful, but also illegal and unjust'. The barons must 'voluntarily renounce this settlement, making amends to the king and his people for the losses and wrongs inflicted on them'.[3] He may have recognised that John was the problem and the barons had a case of sorts, but all he could do was offer his mediation. The barons would hardly accept what the pope offered, and so full-scale civil war broke out. The rebels, as in Stephen's day, sought legitimacy by embracing an opposing candidate for the throne, in this case Louis of France, King Philip's son, whose own claim was shakily underpinned by his marriage to a granddaughter of King

Henry II, Blanche of Castile. Louis's landing on Thanet on 22 May 1216 was a shattering blow to John. A poem on the occasion is significant of the general mood:

Everything had been in the dark, but light returned with morning;
A joyful day without cloud or mist.
The shadows fly as the one who caused the dark times himself flees
And new light dawns with the rising sun.
The tyranny of madness ends, days of freedom are now ours,
The necks of the English are liberated from their yoke.[4]

Barons defected, even the king's until-then loyal half-brother, Earl William Longespée, who joined Louis in London. The French army pursued John, retreating on Winchester; the Scots crossed the frontier once more, and the Welsh renewed pressure on the royalist marcher barons. What followed was very much a British war. With London and Winchester gone, John retreated to his last heartland of loyalism, the West Midlands and March of Wales, where several earls still remained Angevin supporters. The pregnant queen and the king's heir Henry were removed from threatened Corfe to the safer fortress of Bristol, from which escape by ship to Ireland was possible. Ireland at least stayed firmly Angevin.

Things might have been worse for John had not differences begun to emerge between the French and the English barons. Louis was pressured by his principal French supporters to reward them out of confiscated loyalist lands: so the count of Nevers was given much of Hampshire, and the count of Dreux was given Marlborough. Louis also was having limited success with two particularly stubborn loyalist fortresses: Dover and Lincoln (the latter held by a female constable, Nicola de la Haie). The xenophobia of the English was allowed to develop unchecked: a guerrilla war broke out against French forces in Kent, and ships from the Cinque Ports of Kent and Sussex began to attack Louis's supply ships. John was still capable of offensive action, making raids through Berkshire to support his men besieged in Windsor. He mounted a chevauchée in September 1216, riding a column of troops up through the east of England with the intention of driving off the rebels beseiging Lincoln. He may have planned to head further north and support the royalist garrisons resisting the Northerners and the Scots in Durham and Barnard Castle. But at Lynn in October 1216 he contracted dysentery, which rapidly worsened until he reached Newark, where it became evident that he was going to die.

John's death, leaving a nine-year-old boy heir, delivered England back to the magnates, in whose hands it was to remain for over a decade. The man of the moment was the venerable earl, William Marshal of Pembroke, one of the great courtiers of his age. He had been for two decades one of the leading curial magnates, always loyal to the Angevin dynasty, yet on good terms with John's opponents: the Capetian king, the **papal legate** and the baronial opposition. He was also decisive. He staged a prompt political coup, taking control of the late king's funeral and custody of the boy Henry III. He railroaded the claims of the other great earl, Ranulf of Chester, and reached a rapid accommodation with the legate and John's officers and captains. With such a man advertising himself as regent and with the degree of animosity directed at the French, most of the rebels had little cause to fight on. Marshal, though now in his seventies, seized the chance to destroy the divided French army at Lincoln on 20 May 1217. Following that defeat, Louis's position in England became untenable, and the interception and sinking of a reinforcement fleet sailing down the Channel on 24 August brought him to terms. He resigned his claim to the English throne and left for France with no more obligation than to persuade his father to think about restoring Normandy to the Angevins. The Welsh and Scots too got easy terms, and peace of a sort returned to the British Isles.

In retrospect, 1217 takes on great significance. This is not so much because it was the last serious foreign invasion of England, for it was not. In some ways the French invasion of 1216–1217 was similar to the events of 1688, with the political community seeking to replace an impossible king with a viable foreign candidate who had a wife with a good degree of royal blood. What 1217 did do was to increase the separation of England from the Francophone world of which it had previously been such a major part. Henry III was to make ineffectual bids to reassert his rights in northern France, but apart from the earl of Pembroke (until 1234) and the countess of Eu (until 1249) English magnates now operated only in the British Isles. Opportunities for Frenchmen in England declined rapidly once the generation of King John's hated Norman and Angevin mercenary captains was ousted from the country. Indeed, by the 1230s the sort of opportunity a young Frenchman might be looking for in England was more likely to be as an au pair to inculcate French manners and 'the French of Pontoise' in a noble household, for England's aristocracy was thought by then to lack a certain *je ne sais quoi*, not to mention *savoir vivre*. France was still the source of high culture and higher education, but England had been cast adrift from its firm anchorage in the French world. English xenophobia was already rising in John's reign, and the reign's problems taught the English that the French were arrogant usurpers seeking the overthrow of their realm. English concerns now became insular.

POSTSCRIPT

John's reign was the watershed of medieval British as much as English history. Some developments I have identified continued unchanged through it: notably the growth in the ambition of government and the dominance of Francophone culture, which impinged now even on Wales. In other ways it was a sharp break. Since most of the former Angevin lands on the continent were lost to the king, British concerns came to the fore in his policy, which would affect the political development of Wales and Scotland (not to mention Ireland). Since the king was now mostly in England, he came into conflict with the older idea of conciliar government when he tried to exert executive and judicial control. The old office of justiciar did not long survive in the next reign as a result. But Magna Carta provided his aristocracy with a moral rallying point in any future conflict, and Henry I's decisions to unload much of the royal estates left the king weak against the combined power of his bishops and magnates in any crisis. These are developments which will come to the fore in the next narrative section (see Part III).

KEY TEXTS

Carpenter, D. *Magna Carta* (Penguin, 2015), by far the most comprehensive and current text on this key development in English history. • Carpenter, D. *The Struggle for Mastery: Britain, 1066–1284* (Penguin, 2004), a detailed narrative of British history during this period. • Clanchy, M. T. *England and Its Rulers 1066–1272* (2nd edn, Blackwell, 1998), a fluent and insightful overview of the period. • Crouch, D. *The Reign of King Stephen, 1135–1154* (Longman, 2000), a study which identifies the conciliar transition in politics. • Davies, R. R. *The First English Empire: Power and Identities in the British Isles 1093–1343* (Oxford University Press, 2002), in many ways a revisionist history of the British middle ages. • Huscroft, R. *Ruling England, 1042–1217* (Longman, 2005), as fluent as Clanchy but more up to date in terms of historiography.

FURTHER READING

NORMAN PERIOD AND CIVIL WAR

Bradbury, J. *Stephen and Mathilda: The Civil War of 1139–1153* (Sutton, 1996). • Chibnall, M. *Anglo-Norman England, 1066–1166* (Blackwell, 1987). • Chibnall, M. *The Empress Matilda: Queen Consort, Queen Mother and Lady of the English* (Blackwell, 1991). • Crouch, D. *The Normans: The History of a Dynasty* (Hambledon, 2002). • Davis, R. H. C. *King Stephen* (3rd edn, Longman, 1990). • Green, J. A. *Henry I* (Cambridge University Press, 2006). • Hollister, C. W. *Henry I*, ed. A. C. Frost (Yale University Press, 2003). • Huneycutt, L. L. *Matilda of Scotland: A Study in Medieval Queenship* (Boydell, 2003). • King, E. *King Stephen* (Yale University Press, 2011).

RECONSTRUCTION

Amt, E. *The Accession of Henry II in England: Royal Government Restored 1149–1159* (Boydell, 1993). • White, G. *Restoration and Reform 1153–1165: Recovery from Civil War in England* (Cambridge University Press, 2001).

SCOTLAND

Barrow, G. W. S. *The Anglo-Norman Era in Scottish History* (Clarendon, 1980). • Barrow, G. W. S. *Kingship and Unity: Scotland 1000–1306* (repr. Edinburgh University Press, 2003). • Taylor, A. *The Shape of the State in Medieval Scotland, 1124–1290* (Oxford University Press, 2016).

ANGEVIN BRITAIN

Crouch, D. *William Marshal* (3rd edn, Taylor Francis, 2016). • Gillingham, J. *The Angevin Empire* (2nd edn, Hodder Arnold, 2001). • Gillingham, J. *Richard I* (Yale University Press, 1999). • *Henry II: New Interpretations*, ed. C. Harper-Bill and N. Vincent (Boydell, 2007). • Holt, J. C. *Magna Carta* (2nd edn, Cambridge University Press, 1992). • Mortimer, R. *Angevin England 1154–1258* (Blackwell, 1996). • Turner, R. V. *King John* (Longman, 1994). • Turner, R. V. *King John: England's Evil King?* (Tempus, 2005). • Turner, R. V. and R. R. Heiser, *The Reign of Richard Lionheart* (Longman, 2000). • Warren, W. L. *Henry II* (Methuen, 1973, repr. Yale University Press, 2000). • Warren, W. L. *King John* (repr. Yale University Press, 1997).

NOTES

1. Stephen de Fougères, *Le Livre des Manières*, ed. R. A. Lodge (Droz, 1979), 68.
2. *Le Miroir des Bonnes Femmes*, University of Pennsylvania Special Collections, ms 659, fo. 80v.
3. *Selected Letters of Pope Innocent III Concerning England, 1198–1216*, ed. C. R. Cheney and W. H. Semple (Nelson, 1953), no. 83.
4. R. Bartlett, *Gerald of Wales* (Oxford University Press, 1982), Appendix II, 222.

Part II
Living in Medieval Britain

3 Peoples and Languages

OVERVIEW

Britain was one of the more culturally and ethnically diverse
parts of medieval Europe with three of the recognised nations
of Europe calling it home, as for a while also did a people
who had no nation, the Jews. It is not surprising that medieval
Britain throws up dramatic evidence of ethnic oppression and
xenophobia as minorities struggled to deal with the dominant
English, who came as colonisers to parts of the island outside
England. The English themselves had to deal for a while with
subordination to an external international cultural power, that of
the French. Ethnic and national identity is one of the major and
most uncomfortable themes of medieval British history.

⚭ Ethnic Diversity

Britain in 1000 was an island of several distinct peoples, who were principally defined by language, not by any political unit. Language was regarded as the chief feature of ethnicity in the middle ages, when what we call a 'people' was often called a 'tongue'. England was, of course, as it had been for a long time, the land of the English, but within the kingdom of Æthelred II were other ethnic identities: 'Britons' (that is, Welsh speakers) occupied corners of his realm in the north-west and Cornwall, and indeed still hung on at the western fringe of Herefordshire. More recent migrants also retained an identity. The Norse and Danes who had arrived in the ninth century maintained a distinct cultural and legal identity in the north and east of England, though they had by now integrated linguistically. But Scandinavian identity was in 1000 in the process of being massively reinforced by the reappearance of Danish armies and mercenaries in England in some numbers.

The same diversity applied to the kingdom of Alba. Here the Scots, the Gaelic speakers of the west and centre, had political dominance under their king Coinneach II mac Máel Coluim. English speakers were broadly predominant in Lothian and Fife, and a form of Gaelic was spoken in Galloway. Alba too had its Scandinavian element, which was concentrated in Caithness in the far north. Wales was at least mostly Welsh, for all its political fragmentation, though there was some penetration of English personnel into the ranks of the Church in the southern kingdoms and even into the royal families: a character called Edwin ab Einion was dominant in Deheubarth in the years before 1000 allied with English ealdormen. Likewise, Irish Gaelic speakers were to be found active in Gwynedd and Ceredigion, usually in a mercenary capacity, but there is some place-name evidence of Gaelic settlement in the west.

This diversity of language and cultures did not much change throughout the middle ages. So around 1140 a Yorkshire cleric could write, 'At present there are five peoples dwelling in Britain: namely the Britons in Wales, Picts in the far north, the Gaels in Alba but principally English and Normans dwelling throughout the island amongst the others.'[1] There had been even by then some shifts and new penetrations. Cumbrian Welsh was to fade away as a linguistic group in the north-west under the pressure of a deliberate policy of English colonisation in the late eleventh century, as did the border Welsh in the marches. The Galwegians were long regarded as a separate ethnic division in the kingdom of Scotland, but it is difficult to find any linguistic trace of their distinctiveness after the twelfth century; English gained ground in the southern dales of Galloway and the new burghs of Clydesdale and the eastern coastlands, while the Gaelic language remained dominant in the centre and west of Scotland, even if it lost out to French and English as the language of the court, since the political focus of the realm moved to the Lowlands after 1200. In the far north, the extension of

Scottish lordship into the Hebrides and Orkneys reduced the Norwegian influence in the population. Large-scale colonisation by English and Flemings in the early twelfth century irrevocably changed the linguistic makeup of Wales, and by the thirteenth century marcher lordships like Glamorgan and Pembroke distinguished between upland 'Welshries' and lowland 'Englishries', where law and language were different. In the Englishries, field and even stream names were largely Anglicised and many new villages with English names appeared. Urban life began in Wales in the 1090s and the new towns were Anglophone from the beginning even where their names referred to earlier Welsh settlements or districts. In Edward I's reign, Welshmen were routinely excluded from trading and even residence in the new and self-consciously English boroughs of the conquered principality.

There were newcomers to the British ethnic mix, not least (though not strictly speaking situated in the British archipelago) the French speakers of the Channel Islands, which were after 1204 the last fragment of the duchy of Normandy to remain under the lordship of the king of England. Rather more of an impact was experienced from the migration of a large Jewish community from Rouen and the Rhineland to establish itself in London in the 1070s. It occupied a large quarter of the City north of Cheapside and spread to a score of other English towns, though it was to London that all medieval Jews were taken for burial. Jews never seem to have penetrated into the lightly urbanised economies of Wales and Scotland in any numbers, or even perhaps at all in the middle ages. During their stay in England, members of the Jewish community maintained their ethnic and religious separation, appointed their rabbis (whom the English called 'Jewish bishops'), met in their synagogues (which neighbouring Christians regarded as 'schools' from the low-key and bookish nature of the worship and study that went on there) and maintained their rites: ritual baths which were used by the communities have been found both in London and Bristol (see Fig. 3.1). At least one major **Talmudic** scholar made his home in London in the twelfth century.

The Jewish experience in England was not in general a happy one before the group's final expulsion from England in 1290. Denied the possibility of activity as craftsmen or landowners, the English Jews took to moneylending, commodity trading, rental agency and pawnbroking. While some accumulated a precarious wealth, it was always at the mercy of the king's intermittent desperation for ready cash. As the king's **peasants**, the Jews were heavily protected but could be taxed at will without consent, and their inheritance of property and goods always depended on the king's consent. The religious and ethnic apartness of the Jews extended to dress and language. Because of their continental origins, Jews dealt with their neighbours by preference in French, which probably did not endear them to monoglot Englishmen. In times of high religious excitement, notably at the time of the Second (1145–1148) and the Third Crusade (1187–1190), Jews became ready targets. It was medieval Britain's disgrace that the notorious 'blood libel' – which alleged that Jews mocked Christ's redemptive crucifixion by ritually murdering

Fig. 3.1 Mikvah from the London Jewry. Jewish ritual practices demanded purification baths, and examples of mikva'ot have been found by excavation on the sites of the twelfth-century Jewries of London and Bristol.

a Christian boy at Pesach (Passover) – first surfaced on these islands in the writings of a cleric by the name of Thomas of Monmouth, in a rather murky attempt to pin a child murder on the Jewish community in Norwich in the 1140s. Child murders – real or supposed – became the excuse for rousing antagonism against Jewish communities on several occasions thereafter, made perhaps the more seedy by the fact that these children were being promoted as saints to bolster the finances and status of local churches. Conniving gentry, who were creditors of local Jewish moneylenders, took the opportunity in 1190 to remove their burden by orchestrated riots and violence in York, a strategy which was repeated in several other English towns. It was that same social group which used Parliament to pressure Edward I to finally expel the Jews from his realm in 1290, a move being urged on the king by some churchmen and aristocrats since the 1240s.

English Ethnicity

Consciousness of ethnic difference was unsurprisingly high in such a diverse and politically divided island, and as a result xenophobia was rife in insular societies, as immigrant Jews learned to their cost. The conquest of England placed the native English in a socially disadvantaged position. The Conqueror's court was French-speaking, and by 1075 only a very few magnates were native Englishmen. There remained many thousands of English-born free landowners by the time of Domesday Book (1086) but only a minority of them controlled multiple manors, and those few that did have access to the king and substantial estates were men the Conqueror had himself selected for promotion. The Norman court was not necessarily hostile to the English past, because it had its uses. Lanfranc, the Lombard archbishop of Canterbury (died 1088), was willing to admit that English saints were as good as those of any other nation, and even referred to himself as 'an Englishman, though somewhat green'. Queen Matilda (II), the wife of Henry I and descendant of King Alfred, once proudly claimed the Anglo-Saxon saint Aldhelm as her kinsman in conversation with the monks of Malmesbury. Henry II, her grandson, was in his day happy to be regarded as the descendant of the West Saxon royal house, and was greeted as its renewer by his English subjects in 1154.

The English freeholder adapted within a generation to new circumstances, as he must. By 1100 most English landholders of any substance and social ambition had adopted French customs and language, and the knight of English descent was as common a sight as the French one. Some of the interaction was promoted by marriages between English and French families, but that was probably only a small part of the process. Much of it was fuelled by the need to fit into a new society more geared to interaction with Francophone Europe, and it happened that some English landholding families prospered in the new environment. English male names disappeared rapidly from the stock of landed families after 1100; Godwines, Siwards and Æthelwulfs gave way to Richards, Henrys and Williams, though Alfred still survived as an option, probably because it was a name the Normans had given their own children before 1066. English names survived in numbers for a generation more in urban society, and female names for longer yet. It was at the level of the peasant that monoglot English language and naming practice survived longest. Conservative rural society was insulated from that of the elite French-speaking world of the court, and it is significant that the customary Latin name for the English bonded peasant was *nativus*, or *naif* in French ('someone born here'). It reveals the opinion of the peasants' betters that it was one of the sources of the modern word 'knave'. It was still possible to find numerous Old English personal names in the peasant society of the time of King John, but by the end of his son's reign they were long gone.

In Henry III's time, certain Old English names, Edward and Edmund, resurfaced in the royal family, for they were names of venerated English royal saints. So, to that extent, Englishness was being rediscovered in the thirteenth century, as the consequences of war and politics distanced England once again from the continent. This was an unexceptionable form of Anglicisation as it was a matter of choice, but the reverse of the cultural coin was that the French-speaking aristocracy of England found itself being increasingly stigmatised for its Englishness by the French of France. The process was well under way in the days of the early Angevin kings, and there is evidence the English did not like it much. The Capetian propagandist Peter Riga in 1160 taunted the French subjects of Henry II as all being 'English' even if they lived in Normandy or Anjou, and mockingly suggested that they might therefore be accused of having tails. This particular insult directed at the English appears in the twelfth century, supposedly as the result of a curse by St Augustine of Canterbury on the Kentishmen who crudely taunted him and his missionary monks when they landed in England in AD 597. It was a long-lasting way of goading the English, as when in 1407 the retinue of a Scottish earl travelling north came to Navenby in Lincolnshire and took over the village, mocking the intimidated locals as 'tailed English dogs' when they tried to resist his impositions.

Peter Riga also satirised the ancient Latin wordplay which equated the word 'angels' (*angeli*) with 'English' (*Angli*), suggesting 'con artists' (*anguli*) might be more appropriate. Already by the 1180s Parisian satirists were deploying their skills to undermine the legend of King Arthur, by then as popular in France as in England. The Angevin kings had adopted Arthur as their secular patron of kingship, and indeed hijacked him as a king of the English, not the Britons. French writers throughout the middle ages depicted the English as loud-mouthed, moody drunkards and ineffectual knights who did not share in the high aristocratic culture found in the twelfth century at its international apogee in the great **tournament** meetings held in Hainaut and Picardy. Tournaments had in fact been banned in England by Henry II because of their disruptive effect on society, and were to be proscribed from most of the reign of Henry III too. These bans put the English aristocracy at a permanent chivalric disadvantage. One of the most cutting attacks on the unpopular King Philip III of France (1270–1285) was that he never took the tourney field and had resigned leadership of international chivalric society to Edward of England.

Xenophobia

The English for their part were just as guilty of ethnic stigmatisation. Living on the same island with a variety of linguistic and ethnic groups gave them every opportunity to practise the worst elements of what we call racism, including that conjured up by the sinister euphemism, 'ethnic cleansing'. Racial rhetoric was rife in Anglo-Norman society from the beginning. Archbishop Lanfranc might have been willing to admit the past sanctity of the English Church, but in 1075 he described the Breton subjects of his king as 'so much shit'. The Normans came to England already prone to despise their Breton neighbours as wayward, semi-barbaric nomads, without cities or culture. A pithy Norman view of its ethnic neighbours is preserved in a poem of the 1140s exalting a duchy which had subdued so many peoples, including the 'boastful' English, the 'cold-blooded' Scot and the 'savage' Welshman. How then were the Normans in England going to regard the Welsh, Scots and Irish?

The half-Norman writer William of Malmesbury might have been expected to have a balanced view of the English, and indeed when commenting on his parents' generation remarked quirkily that 'the English are scornful of any superior and the Normans cannot endure an equal'.[2] But he was not by any means prone to tolerance of other ethnic groups. He deployed his considerable literary talents in the 1120s in portraying the Welsh in particular as treacherous, barbaric, savage subhumans, not properly to be regarded as one of the Christian peoples and therefore to be eliminated with as much conscience as would be displayed to pagans. He even extended his contempt to the as-yet-untouched Irish, characterised as dirty and bucolic, the very opposite of the English and French with their commerce, civilisation and cities. It was in Malmesbury's time that Welsh populations were being displaced from the more productive lowlands of their country and replaced by English colonists, something Malmesbury's twisted racial rhetoric justified.

Some Welsh early on adapted to this imposed foreign image, so as to live within the new order and gain some benefit from it. The ethnically Welsh bishop of Glamorgan in 1119 referred to the 'treachery' and 'viciousness' of his fellow Welshmen when soliciting help from Rome and Canterbury to reform and restore his **cathedral**. The Welsh never escaped this characterisation of their casual savagery and deceit: 'talking Welsh' was in later medieval England a way of saying someone was lying. A model letter of the mid thirteenth century depicts the king urging a marcher lord to join him to defeat the 'traitorous' Welsh and drive them back into their forests and 'bestial lairs'. Indeed the Angevin and later Plantagenet kings deliberately recruited companies of Welsh mercenaries for their French wars to exploit the fear their reputation inspired in their opponents, as graphically demonstrated in 1233 when English troops ambushed by rebels in Wiltshire panicked and ran, concluding they were being assailed by Welsh infantry led by Prince Llywelyn in person. It was only in the fourteenth century that the rhetoric directed at the Welsh moderated, though the ethnic condescension continued. English writers were already congratulating themselves in the 1290s that the newly conquered Welsh were abandoning their nomadic pastoralism and settling down to the 'English' idea of peaceful commerce and property-holding. The historian Ranulf Higden reflected that in his day the Welsh dressed, worked and lived as any Englishman might, even to the wearing of shoes, and 'they might be now judged English rather than Welsh'. This reflected in part the fact that by the 1350s Welshmen were to be found as much in English markets, Inns of Court and universities as in English armies.

The Scots came in for their share of racial abuse from the English, and in much the same terms as the Welsh, especially during times of border warfare. Fourteenth-century English government records are not shy of complaining of the untrustworthiness and savagery of the Scot. There was a persistent conviction among medieval English writers brought up on **Bede**'s *History* that the savage tribes of the Picts still survived in the far north even in the thirteenth century, a belief indeed cherished as late as 1995 in a portrayal of the Edwardian conquest produced in Hollywood. So in 1138 the invading multiracial army of David I of Scotland in Yorkshire was described by a Hexham writer (who should have known better) as being made up of Cumbrian Britons, Norman knights and English from Lothian, but also barbarian Picts and Scots, who were principally responsible for the savage wasting of Northumbria and the murder and rape of women and children. He explained his anachronism by asserting that the Picts had lingered on into the modern world as inhabitants of Galloway. However, the emergence of a powerful Scottish state under King David, which extended its sway south to the river Tees in the 1140s, tended to moderate the rhetoric, for to writers south of the border King David had been the great bearer of modern civilised values to the wild north. A French-language account of the Anglo-Scottish war of 1173–1174, though composed in England, could not but portray King William the Lion as a French-speaking and fully royal *cusin* of the king of England, the ruler of a prosperous realm which boasted *cuntes* (earls), *barun* (barons) and *chevaliers* (knights), though it does insinuate that he was fonder of the French than he was of his own people. It was supposedly the bad advice of the native Scots aristocrats which induced him to attack England and brought him into captivity.[3]

Scotland came to be accepted as one of the great club of European kingdoms. A Scottish 'nation' was, for instance, a division of the student body in the university of Orleans, an institution favoured by Scots students after Oxford and Cambridge became unwelcoming in the fourteenth century. Scotland's royal family was thought fit to marry into other princely houses, though Louis IX of France (1228–1270) is on record as stating that the (unlikely) succession of a Scot to his throne would be one of the worst things that could happen to France. There was even an occasional Scottish presence on the northern French international tournament circuit, where the Scots were accepted as a tourneying nation, unlike the Welsh, who proved to be very interested in French military technology but unimpressed by its military and chivalric culture. However, this did not necessarily mean there was much affection in England for the Scots, especially in the North which suffered periodic devastations from Scots armies and raiders, particularly severe in the fourteenth century. To the Northern English, the Scots were 'rivelings', from the crude rawhide boots their raiders supposedly wore. The English historian Robert Mannynge railed against the 'scabby' Scots of the 1330s, who dared to resist the power of his king and laid waste the border region, so that he felt threatened even in his home in Lincolnshire. Memories of this were long. A fifteenth-century Yorkshire will left a handsome sum of money to be distributed after the testator's funeral to poor vagrants at the church door, 'except they be Scots'.

Particularism

To complicate the picture further, it should be added that there was not necessarily any solidarity within ethnic groups in medieval Britain. Scottish national identity was particularly vexed. Within Scotland the word *Scotia* described not the extent of the kingdom, but the historical kingdom of Alba, the mainland area north of the Forth, which some writers subdivided between 'Lesser Scotia' (south of Moray) and 'Greater Scotia'. Within that area the Gaels were dominant and regarded themselves as the true Scots (*Albanaig*, the 'people of Alba') and saw themselves as more closely linked to the Irish Gaels (*Goidel*) whose Gaelic culture they shared than to their ethnic neighbours. Until the thirteenth century, a 'Scot' within Scotland would have been the inhabitant of only a quarter of the landmass of the kingdom. The rise of a Scottish monarchical state eventually provided some overlay of identity to the mix, and before 1290 inhabitants of Galloway and Lothian, being subjects of the king of Scotland, would accept the designation of Scot. Moreover, the pressure of the Edwardian invasion obliged the Scottish political class to find a historical '**origin myth**' on which to erect a common ethnic identity to fit the new and expanded concept of the Scot.

But such is human nature that, as early as the twelfth century, those regions distant from the more prosperous and Anglicised Scottish Lowlands where the king resided, such as Galloway, began to be characterised as being rude, barbaric and the lair of bestial savages. The Gaelic-dominated Highlands, once the power base of the kingdom of Alba, was described by the later fourteenth-century Scots chronicler John Fordun in the same terms William of Malmesbury described the Welsh, as 'a savage and untamed nation, rude and independent … and exceedingly cruel', whereas the English speakers of the coast and Lowlands of Scotland were 'domestic and civilised'. Yet both linguistic groups were Scots, even if, as the cleric Andrew Wyntoun (died *c.* 1422) said, they were 'wild, wicked Helande men'. Welsh, Scottish and English identity was by no means monolithic; ethnicity and nation were fractured by particularism all across Britain.

The Welsh consciousness of their own ethnicity and antiquity as a people within Britain and possession of a vernacular culture of huge energy was not matched by any feeling of shared nationhood, an idea which was imposed upon them from outside. A Welsh clerk writing in Glamorgan around 1030 depicted his land as hemmed in by hostile English and the rival Welsh of Gwent to the east, with the Welsh of Brycheiniog and Deheubarth to north and west as being hardly less alien than the hated Saxons. He considered that fraternal amity between his province and the surrounding Welsh was something only divine intervention could secure.[4] Looking to the kingdom of England to find a high idea of ethnic coherence and solidarity would also disappoint. In England, provinces and regions might have a higher regard for themselves than they had for the English of other shires. A late twelfth-century essay on Chester and Cheshire would barely admit that the Cheshire folk were English, describing them instead as a sort of Anglo-Welsh hybrid people enjoying the superior characteristics of both the Welsh and the rest of the English. A contemporary writer was equally voluble on the vile customs and depravity of the people of Norfolk, so much so that a Norfolk writer composed a reply in its defence. That he wrote in Latin and his name was John de St-Omer tells us a lot about the continuing complications of local identity around 1200. Such local feelings could as readily spawn violence as vicious character assassination, such as the student riots in Cambridge in 1261 between Southern and Northern English youths, who were organised as separate 'nations' within Oxford and Cambridge.

To conclude this section, however, it is worth bearing in mind that, prejudice notwithstanding, people can surprise, even kings. King John entertained a long-lasting friendship with an Irish Cistercian monk, Ailbe Ua Máel Muaid (died 1223), whom he promoted to the **see** of Ferns and loyally supported against his English enemies. Ailbe occasionally visited the king in England and appears to have been one of his principal advisers on Irish affairs, which earned him the enmity of the English magnates in Ireland. The same king also showed considerable favour to his father's former lover, the Welsh noblewoman Nest of Caerleon, and to her child, his Anglo-Welsh half-brother, Morgan. In the mid thirteenth century a resident of the town of Warwick was indicted for burning down an outhouse which was the subject of a lawsuit, and, to evade the consquences of his act, he blamed the arson on his neighbour, a Jewish lady. Curiously, a jury of his neighbours chose not to fall for his blatant attempt to rouse them against the small Jewish community in his town, but instead convicted him unanimously of deceit and arson. Sometimes medieval people chose not to obey their worst impulses in the matter of their alien neighbour.

Speaking and Writing

The English language by 1000 had developed a dominant dialect in use in the West Saxon royal court and the higher echelons of society. It had been modified by exposure to Scandinavian settlement, which had to an extent streamlined it, stripping it of all but one of the various cases of nouns English had once shared with continental German. The surviving **genitive** case is nearly all that remains of the ancient form of the English language's nouns nowadays. This was the English in which the national historical register, the Anglo-Saxon Chronicle, was kept. Eleventh-century English was a literary and administrative language used widely both in official documents such as property conveyances and wills, and also for religious poetry, sermons, hagiography and theology. But this great inheritance of vernacular literacy was abandoned in the aftermath of conquest, though the Anglo-Saxon Chronicle was kept up at Peterborough Abbey as a local product until Stephen's reign. By 1250 English-speaking monks at Worcester Cathedral library were barely able to decipher the Old English books their library still possessed in some numbers, the vernacular had changed so radically since the Conquest two centuries before.

French colonisation of Britain following the Norman conquest had a far more powerful cultural impact than that of the Danes in 1016. The dominant role of the English language was immediately compromised. The thousands of French who settled in England, and indeed Scotland, were to have a major linguistic impact, aided by the fact that from 1066 French was the language of the court and aristocracy in England, and from 1124 increasingly so in Scotland as well. But although it was customary until as late as the reign of Richard I to commence charters in England by addressing them 'to all men and friends, French and English' and in Wales to 'French, English and Welsh' (sorted into a revealing hierarchy of cultural priority), the French speakers of England were in their own heads 'Englishmen' because they lived in England, even if their origins might have been in Normandy, Flanders, Brittany or Poitou.

Multilingualism became the norm in England for several centuries after 1070. It was an advantage for a man of affairs in England in the twelfth century to have several languages, so the Anglo-Welsh courtier, Walter Map, had a high opinion of Bishop Gilbert Foliot of London (died 1187) 'who was very accomplished in three languages – Latin, French and English – and could explain himself fluently in each'.[5] Knowing only English was a social disadvantage, especially in the Church. The urbane Anglo-Norman historian William of Malmesbury in the 1120s had nothing but contempt for the older generation of monks of his house, who he claimed could communicate only in English, not Latin. Immigrant bishops in the twelfth and thirteenth centuries, such as the Norman William Longchamps of Ely, the Burgundian Hugh of Avalon of Lincoln and the Poitevin Peter des Roches of Winchester, never bothered to acquire English at all. Latin was of course a language widely spoken, not just read, in all areas of Britain, and very useful as an administrative language as a result, since it was the cultural and religious heritage of all the British peoples. It was spoken as much at court as in the Church in the Angevin period, when we find that Bishop Hugh of Lincoln was able to share a joke in Latin with the king's foresters guarding the entry flap of the royal pavilion.

From their idiom, it appears that King John actually dictated certain of his letters and writings to his clerks directly in Latin, one of them being the lengthy list of grudges he had against his subject, William de Briouze, in 1210. It may well be he could speak English too, as he was born and spent his infancy with foster parents at the royal residence of Gillingham in Dorset. His elder brother Richard was similarly fostered in England at St Albans. However, John was soon shifted to where he could pick up the elegant and cultivated French of his family's ancestral lands in the Loire valley, being moved overseas to the French environment of the nunnery of Fontevrault in Anjou at the age of three or four. It is probable enough that every English king after John could at need speak the indigenous language, and by the time of Henry IV (1399–1413) kings ordinarily spoke and wrote in English by preference. Interestingly, the Scottish magnate, George Dunbar earl of March, knew this and wrote in 1400 to Henry IV in English rather than French, because, as the earl said, although he knew French well enough, 'the Englishe tongue is maire cleare to myne understanding'.[6] By the turn of the fifteenth century, the political elites throughout Britain were finding the cultural pre-eminence of French tiresome and were reverting to English as their common tongue.

When writing, the post-Conquest generations long turned to Latin and sometimes French to express themselves. The consequence of this is that the earliest version of the *Song of Roland*, the French national **epic**, was apparently written down in England even if it was not composed there. The earliest moral treatise (Philip de Thaon's *Le Comput*) and the earliest historical writing in the French language (Geoffrey Gaimar's *L'Estoire des Engleis*) were committed to parchment before 1140 on the north side of the English Channel. The French of England (what we call 'Anglo-Norman' French) was a distinct dialect by the 1160s, increasingly dissimilar from its Norman parent, which to some extent demonstrates its dynamism. Since the Plantagenet court-French of that period was the French of the Loire valley, and the educated clerk trained in Paris spoke the French of the Île-de-France ('françois' or 'francilien'), those who acquired their French in England were increasingly apologetic about its *faute de chic*. When King Henry II commissioned a suitable dynastic history in the 1160s, he abandoned the Norman author he first went to and went instead to Benoît de St-Maure, a native of the Touraine; so also did the great English aristocrat William Marshal the younger (died 1231) when he wanted a professional poet to write his father's biography.

The impact of French vocabulary on the English language was enormous, displacing in several generations much of the Germanic vocabulary of pre-Conquest Old English, and adding some 10,000 new nouns, verbs and adjectives, with the pace of borrowing increasing rapidly in the later thirteenth century. There is more than arrogance in the chauvinistic comment of the French statesman Georges Clemenceau that the English language is French pronounced badly. 'Le', 'les' and 'the' were interchangeable as the definite article in England throughout the period of this volume, and it still survives in some quaint place-names, such as Newton-le-Willows (Lancashire). However, even in its centuries of obscurity and social eclipse, English remained the language of common currency in at least the countryside, and failure to acquire it put people at a disadvantage. In the middle of the twelfth century, the monoglot French canons of Shobdon priory in Herefordshire had to be replaced by the abbot of their Parisian mother house by others who were born and bred in England, priests 'who knew how to speak and understand the language of England and were versed in English manners'.[7] But it is clear enough that until well after 1300 it was regarded as a mark of social inferiority to be an English monoglot. This was why there were handbooks that taught French to the socially ambitious. So we find the comment in a popular mid-thirteenth-century (French) poem *Urban li Cortois*, which urged its English readers to 'make sure you can speak French well, for it is a prestigious language much appreciated by gentle folk'.[8] Petitions addressed to the king of England or his lord chancellor were customarily (and often quaintly) expressed in French, the language of the court and courtliness, until the very end of the middle ages, and still cram many files in the National Archives.

English remained the language acquired from wet-nurses and foster families in infancy in England, even by royal children, as we have seen. So it is no surprise that the highly aristocratic clerk, Waltheof of Melrose (died 1159), born in England in the 1090s to the Picard nobleman Earl Simon de Senlis and Matilda, niece of William the Conqueror (queen of Scotland after 1124), spoke both English and French 'eloquently and fluently'. But the English of the twelfth century had no English-speaking court to impose a socially dominant form. Middle English (as it is called) was as a result a deeply fractured language, markedly different in vocabulary and syntax even from shire to shire. It was notorious already in the twelfth century within East Anglia that the English spoken in Norfolk was very different from that spoken in Suffolk, the county to its south. Surviving surnames such as Kentish, Cheshire, Cornish, Sotheron, Norris and Devenish still recall a time when a person's dialect easily identified his origin to strangers. William of Malmesbury complained that the English spoken north of the Trent was more or less incomprehensible to Southerners. Much the same was said in the fourteenth century from the other direction, when a Yorkshire writer redrafted an English-language universal history in his own 'language' because the dialect of Southerners 'no other Englishman can read'.

The English language in the eleventh century had of course spread rather further than England, and was present in those areas of Scotland where Northumbrian kings had once ruled but where the Gaelic kings of Alba were now dominant. As opposed to its cultural dominance in pre-Conquest England, the English language in Alba was just one of the multi-ethnic kingdom's many languages, and probably not used in the royal household until King Máel Coluim II (1005–1034) married the daughter of Earl Siward of Northumbria. The English of Scotland was likewise to develop as a distinct dialect, though retaining much in vocabulary and syntax that was common to Northern English south of the border, as indeed it still does. But, just as in England, French for a long while retained social prominence in Scotland amongst the aristocracy and the clergy. The dialogue between the Scots Guardians and council and Edward I in 1292 over the sovereignty of Scotland was carried out in French, as the language common to all cultured aristocrats of whatever nation.

The Resurgence of the Vernacular

English began to regain traction as a literary and civil language in the fourteenth century. A key point came in 1362 when it was no longer required to plead cases in the king's courts in the French dialect of England, but in English, though lesser courts, such as those of English boroughs and manors, had shifted to the vernacular as their business language a long time before that, even if the written records they generated were in Latin or French. Literary English emerges strongly in the fourteenth century in Scotland as much as England. Not surprisingly, perhaps, its first manifestations are in the writing of national histories. Although they allude back to the legendary Brutus, invented in the 1130s by Geoffrey of Monmouth as the eponymous founder of 'Britain', the historical works of Robert of Gloucester (writing in the 1290s) and the **Gilbertine** canon Robert Mannyng (died c. 1338) proudly proclaim 'the story of *Inglande*', because to them Englishness had considerably more appeal than being reckoned as Britons, which, according to Mannyng, was a practice he believed to be out of fashion.

Mannyng was writing in the aftermath of Edward I's attempt to refashion Britain as a greater England. The failure of the king's project can only have reinforced the retreat of national identity on a littler England and made the national language more acceptable in the mouths of the educated and patriotic. These writers make a point of characterising William the Norman and his eclectic French nobility as alien foreign conquerors, and identifying themselves with the English-speaking conquered. Curiously, the failure of the Edwardian conquest was also ultimately responsible for the appearance around 1375 in Scotland of a major English-language historical poem on Robert Bruce by John Barbour (died 1395), one of the northern kingdom's earliest literary monuments. Barbour's several patriotic historical works (all but one now lost and all dedicated to his Stewart patrons) were in English and set the pattern for fifteenth-century Scottish literature in the English language, in which the Edwardian war was a major theme up until the time when Barbour's *Bruce* was eclipsed in popular affections by Blind Harry's heroic characterisation of William Wallace in the 1470s.

When English became once again the language of the court in England it began to respond to the same force of standardisation it had experienced in the days of the West Saxon monarchy several centuries earlier. When English began to predominate as the language of king and aristocracy is not easy to say. Richard II certainly had a taste for English literature, and it is in his reign in the 1380s that the works of Geoffrey Chaucer, Thomas Usk and John Clanvow were received with favour at court. The Scotland of Robert II (1371–1390) and Robert III (1390–1406) carried out its foreign correspondence in French, but when it needed to discuss in Parliament the truce of Leulinghem between England and France (1389) the government had to pay for its translation into Scots English, as French-speaking was something only the Scottish higher aristocracy cultivated. Richard II's Lancastrian successors favoured the vernacular for their correspondence as much as their daily conversation.

The English dialect of the king was that shared and used by the Signet Office and Chancery which issued his vernacular letters and orders. The king's English was in fact drawn from the East Midlands dialect, as spoken by the Londoner, author and courtier Geoffrey Chaucer (died 1400) as well as by the graduates of Oxford and Cambridge universities, who were recruited into the government and Church hierarchy. The Inns of Chancery in London were the schools which first employed and taught a standard form of English spelling and syntax acceptable in business and the courts, and when William Caxton (died 1492) set up his presses in Westminster in 1476 this was the form of the vernacular in which he printed his books, so as to give them general appeal. Caxton himself in 1490, in a meditative preface to one of his last books published, reflected as to how in his own lifetime the variance of English from shire to shire still continued, but that the upper classes had formed an idea of correct English speech, the one in which he published.

The fate of Welsh is a marked and instructive contrast to that of English, for though Wales was a politically fractured nation, its language did not fragment in the middle ages to the extent that Middle English did. Unlike English, Welsh was not displaced in the courts of native princes by a foreign tongue; Welsh literature and poetry retained aristocratic patrons throughout the period of this book. In the twelfth century, Wales supported a class of admired elite poets (*gogynfeirdd*) who found praise and patronage at the courts of princes, some of whom were themselves accomplished poets such as Hywel (died 1216), son of Owain ap Gruffudd, king of Gwynedd. Welsh variation in dialect was by no means as wide as it was in English in the middle ages. Pride in its purity of language was one of the few cohesive characteristics of medieval Wales. Even after the fall of the native principalities in the thirteenth century, a national culture of poetry continued in a new generation of less exalted poets (*cywyddwyr*), who were able to attract the patronage of the Welsh, and sometimes Anglo-Welsh, gentry households of the fourteenth and fifteenth centuries. Notable among these was Dafydd ap Gwilym (viv. 1350), the quality of whose output ranks him amongst the foremost vernacular poets of his day anywhere in Europe.

Welsh literature was not entirely insulated from European influences, however. The ancient cycle of tales of the Mabinogi was added to early in the thirteenth century by a 'fourth branch': three romances inspired by the Arthurian world of Chrétien de Troyes. Around the same time the *Song of Roland* was translated for the benefit of a Welsh noble household. For all that, the Welsh language, unlike English, borrowed few words from French, or even from English for that matter. Welsh culture was consequently sealed from its neighbours in an unusual way, and was transmitted intact into the early modern period. Gaelic in Scotland did not quite share the social decline of English after the Conquest, but neither did it maintain its place in aristocratic favour as Welsh did in Wales. Nonetheless the Spanish ambassador in Scotland reported of James IV in the 1490s that, as well as being highly accomplished in Latin, he had an extraordinary acquaintance with the main European vernaculars: French, German, Flemish, Italian and Spanish; not only that but he also spoke his 'own Scottish language' (meaning Lowlands English) and 'the language of the savages who live in some parts of Scotland and on the Islands'.

The vernacular historical tradition in England and Scotland developed strongly in the fourteenth century, as we have seen, energised in the case of Scotland by the memory of the traumatic national struggle of the early fourteenth century. The Welsh tradition here again is an instructive variant. A national chronicle was kept up in Latin in Wales perhaps under the influence of the Anglo-Saxon Chronicle. It seems to have first been compiled in Deheubarth but in the early twelfth century migrated to central Wales, to the collegiate church of Llanbadarn and then to the Cistercian abbey of Strata Florida. It was largely independent of the state-building dynasty of Gwynedd, though it became less parochial as the twelfth century progressed. It continued to be maintained long after the fall of the house of Gwynedd, and after 1300 was translated into Welsh in several versions for the benefit of the gentry in whose collections it survived, although the original Latin version is now largely lost. Even more popular as a way of constructing a Welsh past was the way that Geoffrey of Monmouth's *History of the Kings of Britain* was translated into Welsh in versions of which a dozen copies survive from before 1300. Geoffrey's work was published around 1136 as a tongue-in-cheek rival version of British history to set against Bede and the Anglo-Saxon Chronicle, borrowing freely from Welsh materials. Geoffrey's book had huge success across Europe and internationalised the Welsh vernacular hero, Arthur of the Britons. The Welsh after 1200 were happy to reclaim him for their own vernacular, and in so doing signalled their own realisation of the great contribution their own national culture had made to that of Europe.

POSTSCRIPT

Language and culture played a major part in the drive to define the nature of the medieval nations of Britain in relation to England. Their power can be seen in particular with the Welsh, who despite political fragmentation and conquest retained a distinct identity and sense of themselves as a people into the early modern period. The same might be said of the English, whose culture and identity underwent serious challenge and mutation from the dominant Francophone culture of the continent before 1300, but in the end English identity reformed itself as a new and flourishing vernacular. Regrettably, its other means of survival relied on xenophobia and the belittling of its neighbours as part of the process of conquest and colonisation. This was not just an English response to a situation of threat, as the Scots used the same mechanisms to escape the challenge of England's domination. These were the social developments which underlay and reinforced the long-term trends in monarchy and government that we will go on to discuss in the next chapters.

KEY TEXTS

Bartlett, R. *England Under the Norman and Angevin Kings, 1075–1225* (Oxford University Press, 2000), not a political history, as you might expect from the title, but a wide-ranging and original cultural one. • Brown, M. *Disunited Kingdoms: Peoples and Politics in the British Isles, 1280–1460* (Pearson, 2013), a thorough and distinctly British history which foregrounds cultures other than the English. • Davies, R. R. *The First English Empire: Power and Identities in the British Isles, 1093–1343* (Oxford University Press, 2000), a revisionist history of the British middle ages. • *Image and Identity: The Making and Remaking of Scotland Through the Ages*, ed. D. Broun et al. (John Arnold, 1998), a series of original historical essays on what it was and is to be Scots.

FURTHER READING

Baugh, A. C. and T. Cable. *A History of the English Language* (5th edn, Routledge, 2002). • Bennett, M. J. 'The Court of Richard II and the Promotion of Literature', in *Chaucer's England: Literature in Historical Context*, ed. B. Hanawalt (University of Minnesota Press, 1992), 3–20. • Gillingham, J. A. *The English in the Twelfth Century: Imperialism, National Identity and Political Values* (Boydell, 2000). • Goldstein, R. J. *The Matter of Scotland: Historical Narrative in Medieval Scotland* (University of Nebraska Press, 1993). • *A History of the English Language*, ed. R. Hogg and D. Denison (Cambridge University Press, 2006). • Nicholson, R. *Scotland: The Later Middle Ages* (Oliver & Boyd, 1974). • *Normandy and Its Neighbours, c. 900–1250: Essays for David Bates*, ed. D. Crouch and K. Thompson (Brepols, 2010). • Rose, E. M. *The Murder of William of Norwich: The Origins of the Blood*

Libel in Medieval Europe (Oxford University Press, 2015). • Ruddick, A. 'Ethnic Identity and Political Language in the King of England's Dominions: A Fourteenth-Century Perspective', in *The Fifteenth Century*, VI, ed. L. Clark (Boydell, 2006), 15–31. • Sharpe, R. 'Addressing Different Language Groups', in *Multilingualism in Medieval Britain (c. 1066–1520)*, ed. J. A. Jefferson et al. (Brepols, 2013), 1–40. • Thomas, H. M. *The English and the Normans: Ethnic Hostility, Assimilation and Identity, 1066–c. 1220* (Oxford University Press, 2003). • Turville-Petre, T. *England the Nation: Language, Literature and National Identity, 1290–1340* (Oxford University Press, 1996). • Williams, A. *The English and the Norman Conquest* (Woodbridge, 1995).

NOTES

1. Alfred of Beverley, *Annales*, ed. T. Hearne (Clarendon, 1716), 10 (c. 1140).
2. *Gesta regum Anglorum*, ed. R. A. B. Mynors, R. M. Thomson and M. Winterbottom (2 vols., Clarendon, 1998–9), I: 356.
3. Richard of Hexham, *De Gestis Regis Stephani*, in *Chronicles of the Reigns of Stephen, Henry II and Richard I*, ed. Richard Howlett, III (Rolls Series, 1886), 150–64; *Jordan Fantosme's Chronicle*, ed. and trans. R. C. Johnston (Oxford University Press, 1981).
4. *Liber de Llan Dâv*, ed. J. G. Evans (Oxford University Press, 1893), 256.
5. *De Nugis Curialium* (Oxford University Press, 1980), 36.
6. R. Nicholson, *Scotland: The Later Middle Ages* (Edinburgh University Press, 1974), 274.
7. *Monasticon Anglicanum*, ed. J. Caley et al. (8 vols., Record Commission, 1817–30), VI: 345.
8. R. Parsons, 'Anglo-Norman Books of Courtesy and Nurture', *Proceedings of the Modern Language Association of America*, 44:2 (1929), lines 18–20.

4 Monarchy

OVERVIEW

The central political fact of medieval life was kingship, and Britain gives us much material to see how the idea developed and functioned over a half-millennium, in more than one realm. Kingship in England and Scotland was, however, defined on a wider stage, and much of its ideology was borrowed from the early medieval kingdom of the Franks. Kings were not above looking outside their own kingdoms for attractive models of power, so the Anglo-Saxon and Danish kings looked to Germany for inspiration while time and again Plantagenet kings looked to Capetian and Valois France for the way kingship should be done properly. The Scottish kings looked south to England for ideas to exalt themselves as monarchs, much to the annoyance of the English. The king enthroned at Westminster did not look kindly on an imitator within Britain.

In 1000 Britain was an island of many kings. There was no part of it where a man described by the Latin title *rex* did not rule. The most considerable of them was of course Æthelred II (979–1016), *rex Anglorum*, 'king of the English'. He was without a rival in Britain in terms of land, wealth and military power, though by 1000 a lot of the sparkle had gone from his crown. In the north of Britain the kingdom of Alba under Coinneach II mac Máel Coluim exercised a hegemony over diverse peoples, Gaels (*Scotti*), Britons and Norse, from Caithness south to the Forth. English ealdormen still ruled as far north as Edinburgh, and the incorporation of Lowland, English-speaking Lothian under the Scottish king (*rí Alban*) was as yet in the future, but even so Coinneach's kingdom had a certain strength, relying on effective provincial governors (mormaers) to control the people and repel invasions. Around the fringes of northern Britain were other royal jurisdictions. The Western Isles and the Orkneys were under the remote suzerainty of the king of Norway, through Sigurðr the 'great earl' of Orkney. The Isle of Man was under the overlordship of the Norse king of Dublin. In Wales, kings were many and kingdoms were fluid. In 1000 rival royal dynasties based in Deheubarth (west Wales) and Gwynedd (north-east Wales) were fighting it out – as they had long been doing – for dominance. But there were many other men called 'kings' (*rhi, brenhinedd*) in Wales. Even so small an area as lower Gwent had its own dynasty and ambitions, though its extent was not much more than that of two modern county boroughs.

Royalty

All these men were described in Latin by contemporary writers as *rex*, and they and their families treasured their royal status, which everywhere was believed to be hereditary within dynasties. But their understanding of what kingship was, and how it could be expressed, was not necessarily the same. All would have agreed, even the Norse kings, that kingship belonged in certain families and that the longer they had held it, the more royal they were. As a matter of course, the kings of the Scots possessed lists of predecessors going back far beyond Coinneach mac Ailpein (died 858), creator of the kingdom of Alba, to his Dál Riatan Gaelic predecessors who had come to the Western Isles from their Ulster homeland in the sixth century. Such lists were their title deeds to royalty and were going to continue to be copied and updated in monasteries under the Scots king's patronage right up to the late medieval period. At the king's inauguration at Scone as late as the thirteenth century, it was the duty of the court poet (*ollamh*) to stand up and recite in Gaelic the new king's genealogy as proof of his title to rule. But of course, royal descent might justify more than one man claiming kingship, with internecine warfare sure to follow. So in Alba between 1040 and 1058 two rival branches of the dynasty of mac Ailpein disputed the kingdom. King Macbethad mac Findláech (Shakespeare's Macbeth) used a northern power base in Moray to oust the southern branch led by Máel Coluim III Cenn Mór, who had to fight his way back to his kingship with English military support.

Royal descent was promiscuously spread through Welsh society, and the consequence was political fragmentation in Wales. Several Welsh dynasties proudly and probably authentically traced their lineage back to one Llywarch Hen ('the Old'), a refugee from the north of Britain who supposedly settled in Wales and established his dynasty in the sixth century. On that basis, scores of men in every generation claimed royal status. Their court poets, just like the Scots, made a lot of their ancient, heroic predecessors and grafted in all sorts of historical sources of dignity into the stock, such as the Emperors Constantine and Magnus Maximus and the exiled Trojan, Aeneas, who founded Rome. Some Welsh genealogies even claimed cousinship with the family of the Virgin Mary. According to Gerald of Wales in the 1180s, Welsh poets had books and directories to assist their genealogical outpourings; and, academic as he was, he was doubtful about their accuracy. But Llywarch's rather less critical twelfth-century Welsh descendants deeply cherished the antiquity of their lineage. So in Gwynedd in the 1150s a clerk celebrated his king's ancestry and took it back further from Llywarch the Old to Brutus, founder of the kingdom of the Britons, then past Brutus through Aeneas and Priam of Troy to the god Saturn and thence through Noah to Seth 'son of Adam son of God'.

English kings were just as determined to prove the deep roots of their own dynasty, and under the same impulse to assert their credibility. Most of the greater English royal dynasties were claiming prestige from their long pedigrees already in the seventh century. The dynasty of the West Saxons, which united all the English under its sway in the tenth century, boasted a pedigree that took it back beyond King Ine of Wessex (688–726) to some distinctly unusual forebears, appropriating a genealogy of a British lineage whose early members, Caradoc (Cerdic) and Cynwrig (Cynric), would have ruled the Thames basin in the sixth century, if, that is, they had ever existed.

The Norman conquest made little difference to this need for royalty to demonstrate antiquity. About six months before Duke Henry Plantagenet came to the throne of England in 1154, his supporter, Abbot Aelred of Rievaulx, himself a man of a long English descent, celebrated the royal Saxon lineage Henry had through his grandmother Matilda, the queen of Henry I. Aelred did not stop at Cynric, but traced the West Saxon line through many fanciful names to Woden and thence in his turn to end up at Seth 'who was son of Adam, the father of all'. Aelred addressed his genealogy to Duke Henry, 'as it is the most pressing impulse towards acquiring the best conduct to know that one has achieved nobility of blood from the very best of people'.[1] The Norman dukes before the Conquest of England were just as well aware of this need and were all too conscious of the embarrassment of their short Viking lineage. So around 1026 the obscure Viking leader Hrólfr (fl. 911 × 25), who founded the Norman dynasty, was portrayed by Duke Richard II's propagandist, Dudo of St-Quentin, appropriately if vaguely as a refugee Danish nobleman of royal lineage. Dudo was unable to take back his duke's descent more than a century, regrettably. This primitive justification for royal claims by descent was transmitted on into the later middle ages almost unconsciously in England.

One King to Rule Them All

All the kings of Britain shared a view of their royalty: that it came from the past and was transmitted by blood. But the justification and exaltation of that kingship was better articulated in England than elsewhere in Britain. The title 'king of the English' (*rex Anglorum*, *Engla cining*) was relatively new in 1000. It had been adopted by King Æthelstan (925–940) to signal his unification of all the speakers of English, from Lothian to Kent, under his rule. But Æthelstan was himself the heir of centuries of elaboration of the ideology of Christian kingship, begun as far back as sixth-century Gaul where it was devised by the bishops for the moral education of their Frankish lords. It had been brought to its fullest development at the courts of the eighth-century **Carolingians**, rulers of most of Western Europe. The West Saxons in England, as much as the **Capetians** who succeeded the Carolingians in France and the **Ottonians** who followed them in Germany, were its beneficiaries. King Æthelstan used this royal ideology to the utmost. He was crowned sole king of the English in 925 at the royal estate of Kingston upon Thames, symbolically on the border of the two ancient kingdoms of Wessex and Mercia which he united in his person. He was emphasising that England had but one crown and the crown had one possessor. His nephew Eadwig (955–959) came under criticism for breaking up the 'unity' that was by then believed to be England's natural state, whereas his other nephew Edgar (959–975) was praised for restoring it.

By the mid twelfth century the idea that there might be two people simultaneously anointed as sovereign ruler of the English was inconceivable. In the period between February and June 1141, when the crowned king was in captivity and England was preparing to anoint a ruling queen, the anomaly of what to do with Stephen, the dethroned but indelibly consecrated monarch, could be resolved only by suggesting he go off to Jerusalem to spend the rest of his natural life as a pilgrim. Æthelstan's inauguration at Kingston in 925 followed a rite devised to align the somewhat antiquated English rite with the one then current in West Francia. It used the full symbolic range of regalia: the ring, sword and rod as well as the crown. The ceremony proclaimed the king as defender of justice and the Church, the one who brought peace and unity. He was anointed and so was Christ (Gk. *Christos*: 'the anointed one'). He was the mediator between God and mankind. The rite used in 925 at Kingston was the template for that used for the consecration of every subsequent medieval king of England: West Saxon, Danish, Norman and Plantagenet.

The physical image of the king projected by the English monarchy in the eleventh century was consciously European, gilded by the imperial legacy of **Charlemagne**. It was to be found everywhere and not even the humblest of his subjects could avoid seeing it, even if he never saw the king in person. Every writ coming into the shire and hundred courts of Edward the Confessor was authenticated by his seal, imprinting the wax disk with his image enthroned with rod, crown and sword, as he would have been on his coronation day: a design ultimately adapted from the seals of the German emperors. The millions of silver pennies in circulation in his realm were stamped with a bust depicting the king bearded, crowned with a diadem and robed like a latter-day Augustus. His royal diplomas might go so far as to hail him 'king and ruler of the whole land of Britain, by the superabundant grace of God'. The hand of a protective God adorned the back of the coins of King Æthelred II, just to bring home the message of his sanctity to the whole realm. It was not unusual for the imperial styles of 'basileus' and 'imperator' to be appropriated by the clerks of Edward and his predecessors. This language of imperial, divinely sanctioned power was vital to the establishment of the prestige of the English monarchy, and it had been deployed that way since the time of Æthelstan. It had an inevitable impact on the surrounding British kings, who could compete neither in wealth nor in royal ideology with the English. A London clerk pronounced confidently and imperiously around the time of King John (1199–1216): 'There is only one monarch and one kingdom, and it is called the kingdom of Britain, though nowadays people call it England.'

Demoting Kingship Outside England

In 1109, the court poet of the king then ruling the Welsh of Morgannwg and Dyfed (a ruler only by grace of the English, who had imposed him on the region) called his lord 'greatest of the kings of the west, up as far as London'. Even for this unrealistic flatterer there was no denying the grandeur of the king who ruled from Westminster. Welsh kings had been brought to acknowledge their inferiority in dignity now for centuries. The Welsh and Cumbrian kings who attended Æthelstan's court in the 930s would be routinely described by his clerks as *subreguli* ('kinglets' or 'under-kings'), the same word deployed in other contexts for the king of England's ealdormen. The degree of kingship they were conceded depended on their context. They were more royal at home. Even in the twelfth century there were Welsh kings who were valiantly asserting their true roy-alty, despite the Worcester chronicler's statement that, after William Rufus's conquests of 1093, 'no more kings ruled in Wales'. So a king like Gruffudd ap Cynan of Gwynedd (died 1137) might have officers round his court who took the same titles as officials to be found at the English royal court. He may not have worn a crown, but he rejoiced in a royal treasure, he wore royal robes and his wife would be called queen. But when English barons and earls were ruling large swathes of Wales, Welsh claims to kingship could only have looked slightly comical, and no aristocrat wishes to look ridiculous. So when King Cadell ap Gruffudd of Deheubarth (retired 1151) had a seal fashioned for him in the 1140s, he took as the model the seal of the earl of Pembroke, with his image charging on a horse, armed as a knight. He was not shown enthroned and crowned as a European king. No Welsh king ever did what several Scottish and the occasional English king did, and go to the external authority of the pope for an affirmation of his royalty. Welsh kings knew they lacked credibility within wider Christendom.

The weakness of Welsh kingship was in part because the ideal of a single royal authority never made any headway in Welsh society. Without that, there was little foundation for the compelling royal ideology of justice and authority that underpinned English and eventually Scottish kingship. There were occasional Welsh kings who came near recognition of over-kingship of all Wales. A king like Gruffudd ap Rhydderch (died 1056) could impose himself from his heartland of Deheubarth on South Wales in the 1040s, and defy the rising power of Gwynedd. A clerk such as his might certainly talk the talk of unitary kingship, and issue a diploma in his name for a distant beneficiary describing his lord as 'Gruffudd king of Britain, and as I will assert, of all Wales from one side to the other'. But Gruffudd was still eventually cornered and killed by his dynastic rivals for power. Thirteenth-century Welsh jurists liked to imagine that Welsh kings in the past had issued law codes as Alfred the Great and Cnut had done, and when they assembled a compendium of Welsh law they attached to it the name of Æthelstan's contemporary Hywel ap Cadell (Hywel Dda), king of Deheubarth and Gwynedd. The Laws depict Hywel holding court at Whitland and assembling legal authorities from all over Wales. Presiding as a latter-day **Justinian**, Hywel is said to have codified and amended the good laws in council, and to have given the collection the stamp of his royal authority. But this wistful and unconvincing picture of a golden age of Welsh kingship and unity belongs to a time when Welsh law was coming under pressure from the model of English Common Law, which was imposed from the King's Bench at Westminster. The tragic truth about Welsh kingship in its heyday was that it was too often about murderous competition between dynastic rivals in the royal kin-group (*aelodau'r brenin*) and the rape of communities by naked military force. From Gildas onwards the Church in Wales bemoaned its kings; it did not trumpet any royal ideology in their support.

The kings of England spared little expense in the way they belittled any kingship other than their own in Britain. The erection of the great hall of Westminster palace by King William Rufus was conceived as a suitable theatre for the performance of English kingship and its dominance. The recollection of his first great court held there in 1099 depicts it in just such a way, with the inaugural procession used as a way of demonstrating the subordination of the Welsh kings present. They were to carry the ceremonial swords in front of the king, and so accept a role as underlings, which was still too prominent a role for the liking of the English earls present. It was no wonder, therefore, that in the decade of the 1160s Welsh rulers began to abandon kingship of their own volition. The title they chose as an alternative also had a European significance. The rulers of Gwynedd, Powys and Deheubarth took up the title of 'prince' (Lat. *princeps*, Welsh *tywysog*). It was a style of high dignity, for the princes of southern Italy and the

Holy Land were sovereign rulers of a higher status than mere counts, who were their subordinates. For the Welsh to adopt the title showed that they were accepting a view of royalty and authority much wider than that of the British Isles and their own Iron Age past, and were seeking an accommodation within it. The climactic moment came in May 1240 at Gloucester Abbey, when King Henry III invested as prince his young nephew, Dafydd ap Llywelyn of Gwynedd, in a ceremony during which he placed a coronet on Dafydd's head. The coronet was called the *garlanda*, a lesser crown, the same as used in the investiture of a duke of Normandy. The English and Welsh had come to a compromise which accepted that the rulers of Wales were ducal figures, more than counts but decidedly a step down from kings.

A quite different path was followed in relations between the kings of England and Scotland, though the demand by the English that the Scots accept a subordinate royalty was just as real. In 1031, King Cnut of England (1016–1042) journeyed north to meet the kings of Alba and the king of Dublin. His intention was to extort an acknowledgement of his suzerainty from King Máel Coluim II mac Coinneach, made doubly effective because it was extorted without the need for a military campaign. He found Máel Coluim and his northern rival, Macbethad of Moray, very willing to submit to him and acknowledge their dependence, despite the fact that Scottish territorial power was by then moving south into English-speaking Lothian and into direct conflict with English claims. The dependency expressed in 1031 was the sort of undefined over-kingship of Britain characteristic of the early medieval period. What happened in 1031 was but the first of many such acts of formal submission by the king of the Scots to the king of the English over the next two centuries, enacted in many different ways and in different circumstances, but expressing the dependence of the Scottish king on the English.

 Regal Ambition

But the power of the English model of kingship might have quite the opposite effect on surrounding rulers than it had in Wales: it might provide a model for aspiration. King Edgar of Alba (1097–1107) was using a seal which copied that of the pre-Conquest English kings, depicting him complete with throne, crown, sword and sceptre. It even gave him the title 'basileus' as favoured by the Confessor. The fact of dependency on England sat oddly with the Scottish king's assertion to be as much a king as any other in Christendom, and sitting oddly makes for discomfort. The English king's view of Scottish kingship was not sympathetic. In 1250 Henry III wrote to the pope requesting that he not permit the child king of Scots a crown and the rite of consecration unless with Henry's consent, since, he said, the Scottish king was his dependant and did homage to Henry. It had come to Henry's attention that the Scots had asked for this recognition and, though the pope apparently made no decision on the matter, he did not admit King Henry's right to ask what he had. As an adult, King Alexander III showed a flash of the same spirit in 1278, asserting to Edward I's face that, though he might be the English king's man for his lands in England, he held Scotland of nobody but God himself. The danger became obvious when a king such as Edward I of England decided to institutionalise and assert his status as Scotland's 'superior lord', as he put it. To Edward after 1296 Scotland was a 'land' under his rule, not a 'kingdom', since he had decided he had the power to absorb it into his own greater kingship, where Britain became England writ large. In 1328 the end result of his failed wars was an admission from the Mortimer regime that Scotland was a realm 'divided in all things from the realm of England, entire free and quit and without any subjection, servitude, claim or demand'.[2] Under David I (1124–1153), a constant inhabitant of the English court for a decade before assuming the rule of Scotland, we find plenty of evidence that Scottish royalty was being asserted by its holder to be part of the European mainstream. That the king of Scotland was *rex* and his wife *regina* was not disputed by anyone in the twelfth and thirteenth centuries. Although dynastic rivals still appeared and contested the kingship, particularly in Moray, there was nonetheless only one king of the Scots, who demanded the homage of his magnates, did justice in his realm and took its profits. From 1173, William the Lion (1165–1214) added to documents issued in his name that he was king 'by the grace of God', as any other king might, and indeed, when writing to his brother of England, the king of Scots would assert that he was king 'by the same grace'. Pope Lucius III in 1182 obligingly honoured William as one amongst the body of Christian rulers by sending him a gift of a rose figured out of gold, already then established as a sort of international prize for princely virtue. When heraldic rolls of arms appear across Europe in the thirteenth century, the arms of Scotland are depicted and listed alongside those of the other Christian kings of the West, while kings of Scotland not infrequently appear as characters in French romance literature of the thirteenth and fourteenth centuries. The boy-king Alexander III's council nonetheless had to solicit a later pope in 1250 for the right to use the regalia other Christian kings had long employed to signal their greatness amongst men, and they were unsuccessful.

It was at the point of inauguration that Scottish kingship was most handicapped. In Scotland, magnates and bishops assembled at the abbey of Scone for the king-making ceremony held in the churchyard. There was some sort of benediction ritual over the enthroned king, who took an inaugural oath which might have included the same sort of statement on royal ideology heard in England.[3] But the anointing and coronation which the kings of England, France and Germany experienced were not offered to the king of Scots even in Alexander III's reign. Several symbols of royalty were adopted. The king of Scotland was using the sceptre, the chief ensign of royalty, in the twelfth century. Seal images show thirteenth-century Scottish kings associating themselves with other insignia: sword of state, rod and orb, presented to them perhaps after enthronement. These items were looted from Scotland by Edward I and presented to Westminster Abbey in 1297 (see Fig. 4.1). The seals of Alexander III (1249–1286) and John Balliol

Fig. 4.1 Stone of Scone. The 'Stone of Destiny' was part of the ancient regalia of the kings of Alba shipped south by King Edward I to Westminster in 1296. It was kept until 1996 in a slot beneath the coronation chair. In the fourteenth century it was believed that the kings of Alba and Scotland sat on it during their investiture, which is why this replica at Scone Abbey is exhibited like a seat. Recent archaeological examination indicates the stone was in fact used as a portable altar table for the celebration of mass during the inauguration.

(1292–1296) actually show the king sporting a coronet. But sacral anointing and the use of the royal crown were not formally recognised to be a right of the king of Scots by the pope until 1329. It took the civil tumult of the early fourteenth century and the severing of links between the kingdoms of England and Scotland before the king of Scots fought his way to a parity of status with the king of England within Britain, and shed the inconvenient heritage of the Iron Age.

The Problem of Succession

The early middle ages justified claims to kingship by blood and descent. This idea was transmitted on into the age of universities and parliaments. Its chaotic implications effectively destroyed kingship in Wales by 1170. But it remained a justification for claiming rulership in Wales even after the native royal dynasty had been destroyed: Owain ap Gruffudd of Glyndyfrdwy (Owain Glyndŵr) asserted his title to be prince of Wales in 1400 on the basis of his lines of descent from the three great Welsh royal houses. Wales was one extreme in terms of succession; the other was France. Here the potential for internecine warfare was tamed for much of the middle ages by a stricter regulation of the succession and often by the coronation of the heir in his father's lifetime. France experienced no internal family competition for the crown from the tenth to the fourteenth centuries. Commentators in the early thirteenth century shook their heads at the customary violence of the English succession contrasted with the ordered succession of the French. Gerald of Wales (died 1226) used the contrast to account for the rise of the Capetian monarchy and the collapse of Plantagenet power on the continent.

England would never attain the French level of dynastic serenity in the middle ages, and succession could be a matter of individual opportunism by ambitious members of the royal kin-group. The case of Harold II Godwineson proves that succession custom was so unstable in England that even a powerful man without royal descent might dare to seize the crown by force. Once an English king was on the throne, it was more than likely that he would have to deal with relatives who did not accept the fact. So Henry I had to face the rivalry of his elder brother, Robert, and then his nephew, William Clito; Stephen had to deal with his cousins Matilda and Henry Plantagenet; John had to combat the claims of his nephew, Arthur of Brittany; and Henry III's guardians had to defeat in battle Louis of France, husband of Henry's cousin, Blanche. Even Richard I succeeded irregularly. He was at war with his father when the old king died in 1189. In January 1194, as Richard was preparing to return to England from his German imprisonment, his brother John agreed with the king of France that John should be recognised as ruler of the family lands in France in defiance of Richard's kingship. This act of dynastic treachery was no more than Richard had himself done to his father, which was perhaps why Richard forgave John so readily several months later. It was not until

Edward I succeeded Henry III in 1272 that England experienced a royal succession in any way uncontested and routine, on the French model. The Plantagenet dynasty eventually fell back into its old ways as a result of the political chaos of the reign of Richard II. Scotland was not immune to such instability, for all that the mac Ailpein dynasty provided a generally regular succession of monarchs from 1058 to 1286. Other mac Ailpein branches, notably the Moray family of mac William, led challenges to the king even as late as the reign of Alexander III.

Dynastic insecurity in England had major consequences for the realm. It made possession and manipulation of ancient, royal descent a serious matter for its kings from the eleventh to the fifteenth centuries. The Anglo-Saxon roots of English kingship became ever more important to the later medieval kings, as the sanctity of England's holy king Edward the Confessor became a touchstone of legitimacy. His shrine-church at Westminster became the traditional site of coronation, and by the end of the twelfth century it was staking a claim to have been the repository of the regalia of England since before the Conquest. Illuminated genealogical rolls demonstrating lawful royal succession burgeoned in the fourteenth and fifteenth centuries, and never more so than in the reign of Edward IV (1461–1483), whose title to the throne on which he sat was so very debatable. Edward was forced to make great play of his genealogy, even to the extent of soliciting support among the Welsh on the basis of his perfectly genuine line of descent from Llywelyn ab Iorwerth, prince of Gwynedd (c. 1197–1240). Edward's dispossession of Henry VI in February 1461 had to be justified in any way possible: by sermon at St Paul's Cross in London; by the staged acclamation of his succession of thousands of people outside the City; by political pamphlets and published manifestoes. His party even went so far as to retrospectively hail his mother, never more than a duchess, as 'rightful queen', since her dead husband should have been king, by their account of things. Yet, in the end, Edward of York could only appeal to force and reason. As his restoration proclamation of 1471 put it, 'in such divisions and controversies arising between princes about the high sovereign power of kings, there can be had no more obvious proof or declaration of truth, right and God's will than reason, right and victory in battle'.[4]

As a result of this lack of stability in succession customs, the period following the death of a king was a routinely fraught one in England. In eleventh- and twelfth-century England there was no idea that kingship was an abstract state that passed to the next heir as soon as the old king exhaled his last breath. The dying king might very well express a preference as to who should succeed him, as Harthacnut, William the Conqueror, Henry I and Richard I are all said to have done, but their nominee's succession was never assured. Until the king-to-be asserted dominance and secured consecration, there was in effect no law in twelfth-century England since in the interregnum there was no king whose majesty could be offended by crime. Thus the murderers of William Maltravers in December 1135 escaped punishment because he had been done to death at Pontefract before Stephen secured coronation at Westminster. The same defence was put forward in 1199 by a party of Warwickshire knightly house-breakers; when challenged by their victim on their violent offence against the king's peace, one of them shouted out that the king 'had gone somewhere where he would never see him and that he was dead!'⁵ This defence may not have been accepted, but it shows why it was that prudent aristocrats immediately fortified and garrisoned their castles when news of the king's death reached them, as Roger of Howden says indeed happened on Richard I's death. An interregnum was a time to settle scores and stake claims. English kings were well aware the interregnum was a problem, whether through family concerns or a less selfish commitment to public peace. In 1150, King Stephen began an unsuccessful campaign to get his elder son Eustace crowned in his own lifetime in the Capetian manner, so as to pre-empt the claims of Henry of Anjou. Stephen failed to secure papal approval for the innovation, but Henry II in his turn attempted the same, for less selfish dynastic reasons. In 1170 his then eldest son, the Young Henry, was crowned king of England, and remained associate king until his death in June 1183. The experiment was not repeated for the next eldest son, Richard.

The Crown

The idea that England had a single royal crown which travelled from the head of one monarch to the next took a while to evolve. The Conqueror divided his principal regalia in his deathbed testament between the abbeys of St Stephen of Caen and Battle in Sussex, his crown, sword and sceptre going to his burial church of Caen, his royal mantle to Battle.⁶ A king's successor, if he wanted his predecessor's crown back, had to redeem the gift by a counter-gift of his own, as was done to Caen by both William Rufus and Henry I. Henry II was crowned with a diadem brought from Germany by his mother in 1125, which she left to the abbey of Bec in Normandy when she was buried there in 1164. We know John had to have his own coronation crown made for him in London in 1199, as his brother was buried at Fontevrault in his. He subsequently reclaimed his grandmother's imperial diadem from the abbey of Bec, and took it to England. He used her regalia in his ceremonial courts of 1207 and 1215.

It was not until 1272 that we can be certain that the old king's principal diadem was passed on to the king his heir, when the late Henry III's 'great royal crown with most precious rubies and other valuable stones' was handed over to his son's treasurer. This was the crown that had been made for Henry III's second coronation in 1220, already then being called 'St Edward's crown', and it was in turn used for Edward I's in 1274. It was the crown itself which in the end provided the resolution to the problem of the interregnum. By the 1130s the dignity of the king and his **prerogative** was being called 'the Crown': for instance, the king's rights to do justice in criminal cases were 'pleas of the Crown' and the shire officer charged to record and investigate them was the 'coroner' (from the Latin word for crown: *corona*). Although the sceptre was believed by theologians to be the true sign of royalty, the crown gradually took over the role, so much so that 'coronation' eventually became the name for the ceremony of consecrating the king or queen. There may not always have been a living king, but the 'Crown' was an undying body of royal rights.

Circumstances took a hand in helping define the nature of English kingship on the succession of Edward I. He was beginning his return from crusade on something of a grand European tour when his father died on 16 November 1272, and he did not reappear in England until August 1274. But Edward was regarded as king from the ceremony at Westminster, four days after his father's death just after the funeral while the old king's grave was still open, when the magnates and prelates of England assembled to swear faith to him in his absence. Edward had already had cause to reflect on this point. He had been in Tunis just after Louis IX had died there on 25 August 1270. Philip III had immediately taken up the powers of king of France, including being Edward's overlord for Aquitaine, despite Philip's not yet being crowned. Kingship was becoming a disembodied quality independent of consecration and coronation. Accession was now to be reckoned from the death and burial of the old king. On Edward's own death in 1307, and for almost every succession thereafter until 1461, the date of accession was reckoned as the day after the old king's death (or deposition). On Edward IV's seizure of the crown in 1461, even that one day's grace between reigns was abolished. The king of England could no longer die, because his kingship was perpetual. The issue was where the butterfly of immortal royalty would alight once the old king was dead or otherwise disposed of. Orderly and predictable succession in England was never to be a problem the middle ages settled.

In Scotland, the succession was more regular. A surprisingly large proportion of Scottish kings produced the requisite sons in a Scottish succession almost as ordered as that of the Capetians. Even when the childless David II (1329–1371) manoeuvred deliberately to deny the succession to his nearest male heir, his nephew, the detested Robert the Steward, he failed, and the Steward was duly crowned as King Robert II (1371–1390). Stewart successions likewise were curiously lacking in contentiousness within the realm of Scotland, for all the English attempts at external intervention. This was remarkable, considering the minorities and premature successions that were characteristic of the Scottish monarchy throughout the fifteenth and sixteenth centuries. So the eight-year-old James III smoothly followed his father in 1460 with no discord within the family about the succession, despite a multiplicity of ambitious uncles and cousins. The important question in 1460 was who would be his guardian. The comparison with the brief reign of Edward V of England in 1483 is telling. Even though the Stewart family descended into internecine conflict in the 1480s – and indeed James III's son, the teenage duke of Rothesay, was ultimately responsible for the deposition and death of his own father in 1488 – one reason James IV got away with his patricidal politics was because as the king's eldest son he was the heir on whom the political community had fixed its hopes.

Queenship

The nature of kingship affected the king's wife. All the languages used in medieval Britain had an ancient female equivalent for 'king' (Lat. *rex*; Eng. *cyning*; Fr. *rei*; Wel. *brenin*; Sc. Gael. *rìgh*), which was 'queen' (*regina*; *cynincges wif, cwen*; *reine*; *brenhines*; *ban-rìgh*). It will be immediately apparent from this linguistic exercise that the word was created by the feminisation of the male title, which sums up the essential truth of medieval British queenship: the queen was the moon to the king's sun, itself already an ancient gendered metaphor in Western society in 1000. The theology and status of queenship were complex. Could a queen rule? The anarchic succession customs of Britain meant that theoretically a woman might ascend the throne and take up the sceptre, if the circumstances were favourable. It so happens that no woman did this between 1000 and 1500 in England or Scotland. But that it might happen was not the issue. When Henry I despaired of male issue in 1127 he proclaimed that he wished his only surviving legitimate child, the Empress Matilda (1102–1167), to succeed him. He induced his magnates in England and Normandy to swear homage to her in a great court at January 1128, and when he died in 1135 a significant party of magnates, including King David I of Scotland, was actually prepared to fight for her right to be crowned ruling queen. Only her political miscalculation as to the mood of the Londoners prevented her coronation at Westminster Abbey in June 1141, when she was already being hailed as 'Lady of England'. In the end her limited victory was the acceptance by the political community of the rights of her eldest son to succeed as king in 1154. Likewise in 1290 Margaret, granddaughter and sole direct heir of Alexander III, was on the brink of inauguration as child-queen of Scotland, with no dissent from the realm and in fulfilment of the marriage contract between her mother and father which stipulated that Scotland would devolve on their child, when she died. This was the background to the accession of the first ruling queen of Scotland in 1542 and of England in 1553. It could not be argued against Mary Stewart, Mary Tudor or Matilda that their gender excluded them from the throne, as it might have done elsewhere in Europe.

It is difficult to talk of an ideology of queenship, when the quality of medieval royalty was so closely identified with the male. Even the regalia employed for both was the same, with the significant exception of sword and spurs at the coronation. A duty to judge, correct and coerce was not symbolically awarded to women. What was expected of her, according to an English tract (the *Exeter Book*) written just before 1000, was a domestic eminence. The queen was often called *hlæfdige* (lady) in English, a word which meant in essence a 'hostess', the food-maker. A queen, it was said, must preside in the king's hall and be a friendly host to his guests; she must dispense gifts liberally and maintain cheerfulness and good nature in his court. However, it recognised some political role. The queen was expected openly to give counsel to her husband and engage in diplomacy at a high level. A queen was always more than a noblewoman wearing a crown. From the time of Ælfthryth in 973, the English queen was anointed and consecrated. As early as 1017 her coronation service hailed the queen as 'sharer in authority' with her husband, though she was not asked to swear the oath that was her husband's contract with his kingdom. The omission of the oath from the queen's coronation was also the case in Scotland in the fourteenth century, as it was elsewhere in Europe. Queens were the only medieval British females to be offered a degree of sacrality, but they did not share the responsibilities that defined their husband's status under God.

When Eleanor of Provence was crowned in 1236 it was done at Westminster Abbey by the archbishop of Canterbury. On that occasion we hear for the first time of the pageant of state accompanying a queen's consecration. She was escorted by bishops and preceded by chanting clergy; swords were carried before her by the earls, the earl of Chester taking precedence as in the ceremony for the king. One natural difference was that the crowned king preceded her from the hall to the abbey under his own canopy. The great court officers served at the banquet which followed and took the same fees as if it were a king's. The Scottish queen's coronation ritual developed late, but it seems to have also imitated that of the king, and indeed could not occur until after he was crowned, even if the two had married before his accession. It too usually took place at Scone. During and after the coronation, men had to behave to the queen with the same deference as they would to a king. Her large estates – including in England at various times the cities of Winchester and Exeter, the towns of Cambridge, Gloucester and Arundel, and the counties of Shropshire and Rutland – were generally hers to control. Such resources made a queen an independent source of patronage. Though her children were often raised by foster parents, they might very well cherish close relations with their mother, and – like Matilda I and Eleanor of Aquitaine – the queen's relationship with her sons might become a dominant factor in court politics.

There was a reluctance in society to visualise women in the sacral role they did in fact occupy in England. A queen of Scotland was not indeed sacrally inaugurated until Joan of England was crowned at Scone with her boy-husband, David II, in 1331, nearly three and a half centuries after the first crowning of an English queen. This reluctance is betrayed by the way that queens' seal effigies in Western Europe did not generally show them enthroned, even in the later middle ages, but as standing in the same pose as in any image of a contemporary noblewoman, though they do at least appear crowned from the later twelfth century and some hold sceptres, the chief sign of royalty in Europe. The only exception – and a natural one – is that of the Empress Matilda (1102–1167), whose image sits enthroned as Queen of the Romans, featuring both diadem and sceptre.

This symbolic reticence is all the more surprising in view of the widespread contemporary depictions as early as 1000 in both sculpture and image of the Coronation of the Virgin Mary as a possible model. A queen's political role might not be so hesitant. Kings tended to rely on their wives for disinterested counsel and support. The queen's intercession was always a good cover for a king who had second thoughts about a decision. To take her advice did not look like weakness, but graciousness.

Queens were the logical choice for regents, and a succession of queens of England from Matilda II (who presided at the Exchequer in 1109) to Philippa of Hainaut took the chief place of state in their husbands' protracted continental absences. This happened in Scotland too, where Anabella (died 1401), queen of Robert III (1390–1406), was often to be found in the 1390s conducting state business in her ineffectual husband's absences in his kingdom's remoter fastnesses. The queen's writ as much as the king's could initiate legal action in both kingdoms. The extreme was of course when the queen seized power from her ineffectual husband. This happened only once in Britain between 1000 and 1500, when Isabel of France conspired in her husband's overthrow and subsequent murder, ruling England between 1327 and 1330 in her underage son's name, with the aid of her lover. Society's verdict on this interlude was very harsh on Queen Isabel, called *lupa* (the whore) by her contemporaries. More common was the lavish praise given the likes of Matilda III (died 1152), the queen of Stephen, who took charge of his army after his capture at Lincoln on 2 February 1141, and over the course of a year successfully campaigned for his rival's defeat, triumphantly securing her husband's freedom. She was otherwise active during his reign in leading diplomatic missions to France and Rome in her husband's support. This sort of political energy and military action was thought admirable in a queen, because it did not transgress the expectations of her gender; it assisted her husband.

We have less direct information about Scottish queens, though that is compensated for in the survival of a biography of the remarkable Queen Margaret (died 1093), the wife of King Máel Coluim III Cenn Mór. She brought the English view of queenship with her to Scotland, for she was the granddaughter of King Edmund Ironside (died 1016). She was the sort of queen who secured an ascendancy over her sons and was trusted by her husband with an active political role, as much as the management of the royal household, where we are told she introduced English court customs, display and dress. Her biographer flattered her by fulsome comparison with righteous queens: the biblical Esther and the Empress Helena, mother of Constantine. Her confessional and charitable piety was as exemplary as that of any great queen ought to be. Thereafter she provided a pattern for saintly queenship in her adopted kingdom and even further abroad. Her daughter, Queen Matilda II of England (died 1118), consciously used her mother as the pattern for her own conduct. Her son David I venerated her memory and pursued her pious causes. Her great-grandson, King William the Lion, attempted to use her sanctity in his interest by keeping vigil at her tomb at Edinburgh before his projected invasion of England in 1199. St Margaret (canonised in 1248) is an example of the sort of moral influence a queen might attain, and it was not inconsiderable in the affairs of her realm.

 ## Embodying the Kingdom

The bodies of medieval kings were negotiable. As well as hosting the transitory quality of kingship itself, they came to symbolise their kingdom. At the same time the kings themselves adopted other bodies: those of holy kings on whom they patterned themselves and their image. The idea of summing up the kingdom by the person of the king is an ancient one. When Peter Riga, canon of Reims, chose to satirise the English in 1161 he concentrated all their vices in the person of their king. They were deliberately melted one into the other. Henry II personified the treachery, luxury and unmanly conduct typical of his nation, according to Peter. Henry was actually called 'England' by Peter, as his rival Louis VII was 'France'.[7] It was this identification of king and nation that produced the late medieval ritual of investing kingship in a lifelike image of the dead king during an interregnum, placing it on top of the royal coffin in procession, or on the royal bed of state during the mourning period. This is first known to have happened in England for Edward II in 1327. Since his death long preceded his funeral, it was not possible to display his corpse to the people on a bier, robed in state, as had been the general custom for centuries across Europe. Instead the body was represented by a lifelike wooden effigy in the robes and regalia of the dead king. Similar effigies were rapidly fashioned to represent Edward III (see Fig. 4.2) and Henry V after their deaths, and the custom was exported to France when Charles VI died in 1422 under English control. It was also extended to the queen, and the effigy of Queen Anne of Bohemia, the face based on her death mask, survives from 1394. Before the end of the fifteenth century, the effigy became more than simply an aspect of funeral ceremonial, but was regarded as a repository of immortal kingship in the absence of a living royal body.

This idea of embodiment produced the long-running medieval street theatre of the coronation procession, when an attempt was made to enact the entire nation rather on the lines of St Paul's image of Christ as the head of the kingdom and the believers as its limbs. John of Salisbury (died 1180) in his *Policraticus* used this very image in reference to the king and his people. It surfaces again in the rhetoric surrounding the deposition of Edward II in 1327, where the 'sickness of the head' was taken as an image for what was wrong with the realm. We have very early evidence as to how the embodiment was staged at coronations. The order for the procession made at the re-coronation of King Stephen in Canterbury at Christmas 1141 was preserved for us when the Norman order for the occasion was taken as the model for the re-coronation of Richard I in Winchester on Low Sunday (24 April) 1194, after his release from his German captivity.

Fig. 4.2 **Funeral Effigy of Edward III**. From 1307 lifesize effigies of the kings and queens of England were displayed in royal robes on beds of state during the mourning period after their deaths. It was a practice last used for Charles James Stewart (the Young Pretender) as late as 1788. After the burial, the effigies became the property of Westminster Abbey, which still has the relics of the one constructed for Edward III in 1377.

So we know that a Norman king processed from his palace to the crown-wearing at mid morning in his royal vestments, already wearing his great crown and carrying rod and sceptre, led by his bishops. The bishops in copes led, processing behind **acolytes** and **thurifers** in order of their date of consecration, except for the archbishop of York and bishop of London, who walked to the right and left of the archbishop of Canterbury. Behind them came the abbots and the attendant monks and clerks. The king came behind the chanting clergy, flanked to left and right by bishops. Four barons carried lit candles in front of him, and four more shaded his head with a silk pavilion carried on four poles. Three ceremonial swords were borne upright in their gilded sheaths by senior earls. The earl of Chester was said by another source to claim the right to be premier earl and carry the king's sceptre, but that would apply only to his first coronation, not the subsequent crown-wearings. At the church, the king knelt before the altar for the opening invocation of the **mass** and then took his throne, set up in the choir, led there by the archbishop of Canterbury and the bishop of London. After the collect (the dedicatory prayer of the mass) the king heard the *laudes regiae* (royal anthem of praise) sung by his clerks. We are told that at King Stephen's re-inauguration in 1141 the singing of the *laudes* was a shambles, as the monks of Canterbury and the royal clerks had not settled who was to do it, and the two sets of clergy competed for the honour (and the fees which went with it).[8]

What was parading through Canterbury in December 1141 and Winchester in April 1194 was the kingdom in motion. The Church led the way as its first estate, intercession, sung anthems and incense symbolising its duty of prayer for the realm. The focus of the show was the king in splendour, supported and sheltered by his magnates, whose duty was to protect and fight for the realm. The confiding of the swords which represented justice and command to the earls was deliberate, as they too took swords as their own particular symbol of authority. Magnates and prelates alike were marshalled in strict precedence, affirming a hierarchy of status which gave sense to the realm. For that reason, the queen when she was crowned had all the insignia which expressed royalty, other than the sword of corrective power. Even the common people had a function, which was to acclaim their king and so affirm his power. Such symbols counted for a lot and were meant to be understood. For the people's sake, the king took his coronation oath in the language of daily life, not in Latin. The dissonance of the duelling choirs at Canterbury in 1141 before King Stephen was taken as a metaphor for the disharmony of his war-torn realm. Henry of Huntingdon, the historian, greeted the designate king Henry Plantagenet in 1153 as one who would adorn the sceptre and rods which symbolised his peace-giving and just kingship. Unlike Stephen, Henry II would play his part in the political theatre with conviction. Henry as king would have no shortage of courtier clerks who would press home his kingship and what it symbolised. One, Peter of Blois, made great play with the theocratic power wielded by a king who was by coronation 'Christ the Lord'. He reflected heavily on the king's miraculous power to cure by his touch those afflicted with scrofula: tubercular sores afflicting the ganglions of sufferers' necks.

There is comparatively little information about the manner of the celebration of the kingship of Scotland, other than that we know the pope sanctioned the use of a crown and oil in 1329 for King Robert I (though he was already dead when the decision was made). What retrospective indications there are, however, point to the Scots in the later middle ages using a ritual comparable to that of England and for the same reasons. It included a procession involving prelates, **peers** and officers of state, the use of holy oil by a bishop to anoint the king and the display of relics associated with the ancient realm of Alba, as well as the usual Western Catholic regalia of crown, sword and sceptre. Some elements of these actually survive from the middle ages for Scotland, whereas the remaining medieval regalia of England were destroyed under the Commonwealth (apart from the ampulla and spoon for the oil of anointing). But the sceptre of Scotland is still largely the elegant one presented to King James IV by Pope Alexander VI in 1494 (along with another golden rose). The present crown of Scotland is, however, no older than 1540, even if it re-uses jewels from earlier diadems. The coronation oath for Scotland was that which had featured in Western orders for centuries, and the king's crown was touched by the assembled peers when they swore **fealty**, just as in later English coronations. The fraught consecration and coronation of James IV were held at Scone in 1488. The ceremony occurred on the inaugural mound used by the mac Ailpein dynasty, the first time it had been used for the purpose since the coronation of James I in 1424. In view of the circumstances, James and his council had to appeal to tradition, for the new king had mounted the throne over the body of his father. The symbolism had to be used to mitigate the damage James's own regicide had done to the Scottish monarchy. The parallel with the English re-coronations of 1141, 1194 and indeed 1471 is obvious. It is likely enough that the Scots were willing to borrow English rites and rituals since they provided so prestigious a model of sacral kingship. Homage to England went at least that far after Robert the Bruce.

The theatre of kingship continued to mutate during the middle ages, adapting to new circumstances and new audiences. A feature of the usurping inaugurations of Henry IV, Edward IV and Richard III was the intensification of the symbolism of crown and anointing, and a new emphasis on the pre-coronation rituals, strengthening the idea of acclamation by the political community as a way of making the elevation of the usurper all the more real. So before coronation Edward was hailed as rightful king by seating him in robes and the cap of state (a furred red cap on which a crown was set) on the chancellor's marble seat in Westminster Hall, the symbolic heart of the Common Law of England. There, with a sceptre in his hand, Edward made the same promises as he would later make before God in the abbey during his coronation. Since he made them *after* the acclamation as king and before he left the palace, he was enacting the fact that his kingship was real and rightful, not relying on anything other than his blood and claims. Political circumstance made this new rite of acclamation more urgent than the traditional procession to the abbey and the consecration which followed. Just to further make the point, after his coronation Edward gave an additional lecture to the abbey congregation about the truth of his claims to the throne he was sitting on.

 ## Contractual Kingship and Deposition

The quality of anointed kingship, which the king embodied, was enacted by symbol and theatre. But it also had an ideology, which was more problematical for the king, as it was expressed in words and promises, which could be taken as having the force of contract by troublesome subjects if they thought they were being broken. It was summed up in his coronation oath, the most binding and discussed document on kingship. As we have seen, it drew on a theology that had its roots in the Scriptures and their application in the early Frankish kingdom. It was on this basis that successive kings of

England, Henry I, Stephen and Henry II, issued coronation charters guaranteeing first and foremost the liberty of the Church they had just sworn to uphold. Stephen's failure to honour his bishops was made into a justification for rebelling against him. So when a London clerk wrote about what made a good king during the troubled reign of John (1199–1216) the first duty of the king was, he said, to honour and protect the Church and to expel the wicked from its midst. But he went on, 'if he does not do this and does not maintain his kingship in these matters then indeed he is no king'.[9] There was a penalty for a king in failing to honour the contract with his subjects. Likewise, the king ruled justly only when he maintained good laws and took the advice of the magnates, his natural counsellors. The justification for deposing a king was in fact implicit in royal ideology.

Edward II (1307–1327) was a king who suffered much because of the coronation oath. The one he swore in February 1308 was in fact amended so that he had to promise specifically to uphold the laws his subjects might 'rightfully and reasonably choose'. This was most likely a consequence of his father's failure to live up to his promises to his people; the new king's noble councillors were ensuring that a loophole in his contract with his realm was closed as a return for their support. And within months, after the first crisis inspired by Peter Gaveston, Edward II's magnates stated as a fact that a king who fell short in royal dignity and trespassed against his oath had made himself liable to their correction. Their oaths of fealty at his coronation were cited as a justification to defy him, because it was to the ideals represented by the crown, not the living king himself, that they were loyal. In due course, Edward became the first king to be deposed within the period of this book. Criticism of his failures was widespread even before his arrest and deposition. In 1317, his native Irish subjects wrote to the pope explaining that they had repudiated his kingship because of his failure to offer them the even-handed justice he was bound to do. When in 1327 the arguments were drawn up by which he was to be deprived of his kingship, the list of his defects presented to Parliament included breaking his oath to respect the Church and listen to his magnates, as well as his all-round incompetence. By this date his sacral status was no longer enough to keep him royal, as it had been for the captive Stephen in 1141. From the point when Edward II was defied by his people and his son proclaimed king in his stead, he was merely 'the lord Edward, the king's father'. Yet legalism only went so far, for Edward was, nonetheless, buried and entombed as a king.

As a result kings knew very well the dangers implicit in their oath. A report of a conversation Richard II had in 1398 as his unhappy reign drew to a close says that Richard poured scorn on his rival, Henry of Bolingbroke, then duke of Hereford, because 'if ever he be king he would be as wild a tyrant to Holy Church as ever was any!'[10] King Richard also took some satisfaction in having 'trampled the necks of the proud underfoot', in the words of his letter to the Byzantine emperor; overthrowing and thwarting the wicked were what kings had long been supposed to do. He said as much in person to the Commons when he addressed the English Parliament in 1386. Unfortunately for Richard, too few of his subjects agreed with his self-evaluation as king, and thus felt justified in rebelling against him. Richard's fixation on the grandeur of his kingship was in part his undoing. Like Henry III, Richard found his inspiration for his high view of his dignity in his royal brother, the king of France, whose court treated its lord with a formality that opened up a great gulf of dignity between the king and even the great princes of his realm. Charles V of France (1364–1380) had in particular offered a model of a royal court as centre of elaborate ceremony, learning and high cultural patronage. Richard attempted to rival and even exceed the sumptuous state of the French royal court, as seen especially in 1396, when he and Charles VI met at Ardres on the border between English-ruled Calais and France, and Richard attempted to outdo the French in the opulence of his gifts and dress. But Richard wanted more than just the gilded image of power; he embraced an academic and high theological view of the king as the only legitimate source of power in his realm and any other power existed in it only at his will. Such a view could only antagonise a political community which had a long history of disputing its king's authority on the basis of customary rights which were not negotiable.

❧ Excusing Kingship

The degree to which kings celebrated their sacral status generally depended on the king. Henry III (1216–1272) and Richard II (1377–1399) were kings who founded their view of their own kingship in high theocratic terms. Both kings celebrated the royal cult of their predecessor Edward the Confessor (renowned as the fount of England's good laws), and both patronised artistic representations of themselves as set far apart from other lay people in a special relationship with the divine. Henry III's corpse was placed in the vacant tomb of the sainted Confessor at Westminster while his own was being prepared. Richard II's celebrated taste for portraiture depicted him in robes of the celestial blue which the Virgin Mary customarily wore, with angels bearing his livery badges, while his royal arms after 1390 featured those attributed to the Confessor. It has to be said that both men were notoriously insecure and compromised monarchs, and their exaltation of their kingship by symbolic means readily provoked counter-attack. Henry III deliberately dropped the sword from his great seal in 1259 for a dove-headed rod. It was intended to assert his imperial status under God, but it was criticised by contemporaries as an admission of his own military incompetence as king. The same king's enthusiastic and lavish attempt to associate his kingship with a relic of Christ's blood at Westminster in 1247 was humiliatingly snubbed by the indifference of his people to the cult he so expensively promoted. Yet so martial a king as Henry V (1413–1422) demonstrated in his brief reign that a high theocratic view of his office was not just a characteristic of incompetents. His ambitious remodelling scheme for Sheen included three monasteries in the close vicinity of his riverside palace, Carthusian, Celestine and Bridgetine, symbolically placing austere confessional prayer at the heart of his monarchy.

The closer a king associated his kingship with God, the closer he approached to what early modern historians call 'absolutism'. In practice very few of the medieval kings of England or Scotland ever lost sight of the limits of their power. None of them was allowed to treat the kingdom as their own property and their own will as above dispute, for all that Roman law as it was developing in the schools of twelfth-century northern Italy theorised that 'the king's will was law'. When King John of England heedlessly attempted to implement such a view, he was eventually overthrown by an outraged political community. Medieval kingship had an elective element which it could not rid itself of. King Henry I, within a few days of his unexpected accession to his brother's throne in 1100, issued a manifesto for support in which he carefully notified his new subjects, with an inaccuracy as blithe as any spin doctor's, 'you should know that I have been crowned king of England by the mercy of God and the common counsel of the barons of the realm'. He had in fact been crowned with no more baronial support than that of the hunting party which witnessed his brother's death and not by an archbishop of Canterbury. As we have seen, the theatre of monarchy demanded peers and magnates as spear-carriers, and for good reason; but all too often they also wanted a speaking part. There were long periods in the history of both of the British kingdoms when the magnates were in fact dominant in government. In the reigns of the first two Angevin kings, a conciliar form of government tacitly allowed the magnates power over England. In the long minorities of Henry III and Henry VI of England, and of David II and James III of Scotland, an aristocratic leadership formally took the helm of the state and acquitted itself responsibly, if not entirely selflessly.

There were medieval British voices willing to articulate an aggressive view of kingship, though it is not easy to say how influential they were outside a narrow intellectual circle which did not always include the king. When kings themselves cite the source of their beliefs about their office they talk of their coronation oath, of the rights of their ancestors, of biblical, classical or saintly figures or, most often of all, of the mythical King Arthur of Britain. Arthur's cult was first cultivated at the courts of Henry II and his sons. He was given status as a historical monarch and rebranded as an ideal king of England to set against France's Charlemagne. Arthur certainly provided a justification for expansionist kings of England within Britain and France throughout the middle ages. He also provided an impulse towards the military kingship rejoiced in by Edward I and Edward III. Edward I believed he possessed Arthur's crown and sword, and his grandson set up his courtly order of the Garter as a restored Round Table. We occasionally know the message on kingship preached before kings at court, even in quite early days. Henry II's Breton chaplain, Master Stephen de Fougères, included his notes on kingship in his set of French sermons about the conditions of men. The court would have heard from him the traditional ideas that kings should be serious in promoting peace and justice, should honour the Church and correct the wicked. Stephen dwelt on the alleged sayings of the wisest of kings, Solomon of Israel, in the Books of Wisdom to provide a pattern of the wise and peace-giving prince. The sting was in the tail, for Stephen turned the image of the king as embodiment of his people back on the king: 'kings should be pure and chaste, for the people pursue all too readily those vices which their prince adopts'.[11] But such a message cannot have much offended the king, for he promoted Stephen to be a bishop in 1168.

Occasionally the king himself sponsored a more radical preaching of his kingship, which approached theocratic absolutism. John of England (1199–1216) was a genuinely tyrannical king, and there is evidence that he was seeking the support of friendly intellectuals to justify his defiance of the pope in 1207. One, Master Alexander Mason (an 'amateur theologian' according to jaundiced commentators), was encouraged by the king to preach the king's absolute right to chastise his people 'like a rod of iron' in the apocalyptic language of David's psalms and the Book of Revelation, 'which he proved by suchlike specious arguments'.[12] Yet, when he himself had to justify his tyrannical actions, as he did in 1210, King John still claimed he was acting within the law and custom of England. Tyranny in England might seek precedent as a mask, not radical theology or Roman law, because people believed good kingship was founded on custom.

When academics and lawyers worked in the king's interest, they might well follow their logic to extremes in their definition of their lord's authority and power. The ammunition to load into their intellectual artillery had been manufactured in the universities of northern Italy and Paris in the preceding centuries. It directly inspired the aggressive rhetoric by which Richard II pronounced himself above any constraints on his kingship, and the paranoia its use inspired amongst the political community fuelled the violence of the political community against him. A further example of this academic absolutism is in the coterie of university-educated lawyers and advisers surrounding James III of Scotland (1460–1488). The king was dealing with a realm where parliamentary consensus was at the heart of the political community and was seen as a check on royal power. So the king and his council from the 1460s began to stress the king's imperial authority within his realm, not so much to override papal claims of superiority (as was done in Philip VI's France and Henry VIII's England), but to exalt the king against the powerful parliament of estates he had to deal with. In 1469, James's first adult act declared, 'our sovereign lord has full jurisdiction and free empire within his realm'.[13] The ancient treasonous offence of lèse majesté (insulting the king) was sharpened in the 1470s to become any act perceived to be against the king's interests, not just his status, and was used to overthrow enemies. In due course a violent reaction to this programme led to regicide.

The intellectual counterblast to such ideas had also long been stockpiled. It is typified in England by Gerald of Wales (died *c.* 1223), who spent many of his latter years drafting his *On the Education of the Prince*, which became a hostile critique of the way aggressive Angevin kingship operated. To write such a work was dangerous. Gerald's alienated nephew and namesake threatened to use his uncle's incautious rhetoric to blackmail him by charging him with *lèse majesté*, a convenient catch-all offence which was always ready to be deployed against the king's enemies. Significantly, Gerald's attacks on the reputation of Henry II were based on the king's failure to live up to those very coronation promises on which Stephen de Fougères had preached to Henry's court. Gerald's work warns against kings who fall into sinfulness through pride, in this case his failure to honour the Church. In Gerald's eyes, the Capetian kings of France were the prime example of kings who took their coronation oath seriously, and he exhorted King Alexander II of Scotland to follow the French example, not the English. Louis (VIII) of France is the book's hero, not any Angevin king.

A more academic theory designed to domesticate medieval monarchy developed at the same time as aggressive imperial theories. Thomas Aquinas (died 1274) produced the work which became central to the theory of medieval monarchy. Aquinas approached the subject not through the significance of the coronation oath but through a rational consideration of the common good of a realm, which kings were obliged to maintain in peace, unity and justice. Kings were tyrants if they were motivated by self-interest rather than that of the community. This is a line we find adopted in the criticism of the kingship of Edward II (1307–1327). It became embedded ultimately in the theory of English kingship. The *Regement of Princes* (*Rule for Princes*) of Thomas Hoccleve (died 1426), a government clerk, which was dedicated to the youthful Henry of Monmouth, prince of Wales (later Henry V), also takes Aquinas's line. A king had to sum up the will of the commonwealth of his people and serve the common interest. The king who embraced virtue would have the moral eminence to speak for and direct his realm. Hoccleve's views were derived from earlier academic scholarship, notably the development by Giles of Rome (died 1326) of Aquinas's theory. But, being published in English as well as Latin, its ideas circulated more widely than its predecessors, and numerous manuscripts survive. It would be in Hoccleve's time that in England the academic interpretation of kingship as having a duty to the commonwealth surfaced in the nation's political minds. The traditional interpretation based on the king's promises to the Church and to his subjects as an individual human being before God faded, with all the long-term consequences for monarchy that such a rationalisation opened up.

POSTSCRIPT

The monarch was central not just to his kingdom and its political life, but to his realm's understanding of itself. For that reason the medieval idea of the 'Fisher King' was so powerful: if the king was ill and incapable then his realm too languished. For that same reason a king could very well call himself by the name of his kingdom: he was 'England'. The weight of ritual and symbolism that lay on a monarch's shoulders was immense and demanded some capacities from the man himself. If he failed to live up to expectations, the ideology that bolstered his power could also crush him. As a result it was not easy for a king to be a tyrant in the middle ages and get away with it. The bad news for his people was that, if his personality and competence were not up to the job of rulership, his centrality meant that the whole kingdom inevitably suffered, as we will see in the *next chapter*.

KEY TEXTS

Kantorowicz, E. H. *The King's Two Bodies: A Study in Mediaeval Political Theology* (Princeton University Press, 1957), the eternal classic on the nature and theology of kingship. • *Medieval Queenship*, ed. J. Carmi Parsons (Sutton, 1994), a series of essays which sums up current research on a neglected topic. • *The Welsh King and His Court*, ed. T. Charles-Edwards, M. E. Owen and P. Russell (University of Wales Press, 2000), a series of essays on the hybrid nature of Welsh kingship.

FURTHER READING

ENGLAND

Armstrong, C. A. J. 'Inauguration Ceremonies of the Yorkist Kings', *Transactions of the Royal Historical Society*, 4th ser., 30 (1948), 51–73. • Biddle, M. 'Seasonal Festivals and Residence: Winchester, Westminster and Gloucester in the Tenth to Twelfth Centuries', in *Anglo-Norman Studies*, VIII (Boydell, 1986), 51–63. • Binski, P. *Westminster Abbey and the Plantagenets: Kingship and the Representation of Power, 1200–1400* (Yale University Press, 1995). • Campbell, J. 'The United Kingdom of England: The Anglo-Saxon Achievement', in *Uniting the Kingdom: The Making of British History*, ed. A. Grant and K. J. Stringer (Routledge, 1995), 31–47. • Carpenter, D. A. 'The Burial of King Henry III, the Regalia and Royal Ideology', in *King Henry III* (Hambledon, 1996), 427–61. • Cowdrey, H. E. J. 'The Anglo-Norman Laudes Regiae', *Viator*, 12 (1981), 37–78. • Garnett, G. 'The Origins of the Crown', *Proceedings of the British Academy*, 89 (1996), 171–214. • Harvey, A. and R. Mortimer. *The Funeral Effigies of Westminster Abbey* (Woodbridge, 1994). • *Henry V: The Practice of Kingship*, ed. G. L. Harriss (Oxford University Press, 1985). • Huneycutt,

L. L. *Matilda of Scotland: A Study in Medieval Queenship* (Boydell, 2003). • Koziol, G. 'England, France and the Problem of Sacrality in Twelfth-Century Ritual', in *Cultures of Power: Lordship, Status and Process in Twelfth-Century Europe*, ed. T. N. Bisson (University of Pennsylvania Press, 1995), 124–48. • Molyneaux, G. 'Why Were Some Tenth-Century English Kings Presented as Rulers of Britain?' *Transactions of the Royal Historical Society*, 6th ser., 21 (2011), 59–92. • Nelson, Jinty. 'The First Use of the Second Anglo-Saxon Ordo', in *Myth, Rulership, Church and Charters*, ed. J. Barrow and A. Wareham (Ashgate, 2008), 117–26. • Perkins, N. *Hoccleve's Regiment of Princes: Counsel and Constraint* (Cambridge University Press, 2001). • Richardson, H. G. 'The Marriage and Coronation of Isabella of Angoulême', *English Historical Review*, 61 (1946), 289–314. • Richardson, H. G. and G. O. Sayles. 'The Undying King', in *The Governance of Medieval England* (Edinburgh University Press, 1963), 136–55. • Stafford, P. 'The King's Wife in Wessex, 800–1066', *Past & Present*, 91 (1981), 3–27. • Stafford, P. *Queen Emma and Queen Edith: Queenship and Women's Power in Eleventh-Century England* (Oxford University Press, 1997). • Turner, R. V. 'King John's Concept of Royal Authority', *History of Political Thought*, 17 (1996), 157–78. • Vincent, N. 'The Court of Henry II', in *Henry II: New Interpretations*, ed. C. Harper-Bill and N. Vincent (Boydell, 2007), 278–334. • Vincent, N. 'Twelfth- and Thirteenth-Century Kingship: An Essay in Anglo-French Misunderstanding', in *Les idées passent-elles la Manche? Savoirs, répresentations, pratiques (France–Angleterre, Xe–XXe siècles)*, ed. J.-P. Genet and J.-F. Ruggiu (Presses de l'Université de Paris-Sorbonne, 2007), 21–36. • Walker, S. 'Richard II's Views on Kingship', in *Rulers and Ruled in Late Medieval England*, ed. R. E. Archer and S. Walker (Hambledon, 1995), 49–63. • Watts, J. *Henry VI and the Politics of Kingship* (Cambridge University Press, 1996).

SCOTLAND

Anderson, M. O. *Kings and Kingship in Early Scotland* (Rowman & Littlefield, 1973). • Broun, D. *The Irish Identity of the Kingdom of the Scots* (Boydell, 1999). • Downie, Fiona. 'Queenship in Late Medieval Scotland', in *Scottish Kingship, 1306–1542: Essays in Honour of Norman McDougall* (Edinburgh University Press, 2008), 232–54. • Hudson, B. T. 'Cnut and the Scottish Kings', *English Historical Review*, 127 (1992), 350–60. • Lyall, R. J. 'The Medieval Scottish Coronation Service: Some Seventeenth-Century Evidence', *Innes Review*, 28 (1977), 3–21. • Nelson, Jessica. 'Scottish Queenship in the Thirteenth Century', in *Thirteenth-Century England*, XI, ed. B. K. U. Weiler, J. E. Burton and P. R. Schofield (Boydell, 2007), 61–81. • Reid, J. J. 'The Scottish Regalia', *Proceedings of the Society of Antiquaries of Scotland*, 24 (1889), 18–48. • Rodwell, W. *The Coronation Chair and Stone of Scone: History, Archaeology and Conservation* (Oxbow, 2013). • *Scottish Kingship, 1306–1542: Essays in Honour of Norman McDougall*, ed. M. Brown and R. J. Tanner (Edinburgh University Press, 2008).

WALES

Davies, W. *Patterns of Power in Early Wales* (Oxford University Press, 1990). • Pryce, H. 'Welsh Rulers and European Change, c. 1100–1282', in *Power and Identity in the Middle Ages*, ed. H. Pryce and J. Watts (Oxford University Press, 2007), 37–51.

NOTES

1. Aelred of Rievaulx, Genealogia Regum Anglorum, in *Patrologiae cursus completus: series Latina*, ed. J.-P. Migne (221 vols., Paris, 1847–67), CXCV: cols. 716–17.
2. *Anglo-Scottish Relations, 1174–1328*, ed. E. L. G. Stones (Oxford University Press, 1965), 324.
3. The retrospectively famous Stone of Scone long held in Westminster Abbey seems to have initially been the base of a portable altar used in the inauguration ceremony, rather than that of a seat: A. A. M. Duncan, *The Kingship of the Scots, 842–1292: Succession and Independence* (Edinburgh University Press, 2002), 140–44.
4. T. Rymer, *Foedera, Conventiones, Litterae et Acta Publica*, ed. A. Clarke and F. Holbrooke (7 vols., Record Commission, 1816–69), VII: 709–11 (modified into modern English).
5. *Rotuli Curiae Regis, 1194–1199* (Record Commission, 1835), 51–2.
6. The tract *de obitu Willelmi* purporting to describe the Conqueror's death says the unspecified *regalia* were given to William Rufus, but the tract was an adaptation of a much earlier essay on the death of Charlemagne and cannot be trusted on details.
7. B. Hauréau, 'Une poème inédit de Pierre Riga', *Bibliothèque de l'École de Chartes*, 44 (1883), 7–11.
8. *Gervasii monachi Cantuarensis Opera Historica*, ed. W. Stubbs (2 vols., Rolls Series, 1879–80), I: 524–7.
9. *Die Gesetze de Angelsachsen*, ed. F. Liebermann (3 vols., Halle, 1903–16), I: 635.
10. *Chronicles of London*, ed. C. L. Kingsford (Oxford University Press, 1905), 52, discussed in S. Walker 'Richard II's Views on Kingship', in *Rulers and Ruled in Late Medieval England*, ed. R. E. Archer and S. Walker (London, 1995), 50.
11. Stephen de Fougères, *Le Livre des Manières*, ed. R. A. Lodge (Droz, 1979), c. 37, p. 67 (my translation).
12. Roger of Wendover, *Flores Historiarum*, ed. H. G. Hewlett (3 vols., Rolls Series, 1886–9), II: 53.
13. *The Records of the Parliaments of Scotland to 1707*, ed. K. M. Brown et al. (University of St Andrews, 2008), 1469/70 (www.rps.ac.uk), English modernised.

5 The State

OVERVIEW

Government arises naturally out of the ambition in rulers to mobilise resources and people for all sorts of reasons, of which the most respectable is a concern for the security of the lands they have accumulated under their sway. It can happen on a basic level, and what are called 'states' can be primitive enough social entities. It was not until the seventeenth century that European thinkers began consciously to describe the 'state' as a political, territorial and social entity which demanded the allegiance of all its inhabitants and organised their lives. But even in 1000 kings had ambitions to exert control over the lives of their subjects, and in England were doing so. What we see over the following centuries is a steady increase in an ambition to monitor and exploit resources within the kingdoms of Britain, and an inventiveness in the way it could be done which had considerable consequences for daily life and ideas of community for, if the king saw himself as having a right to exploit his kingdom, his subjects would feel entitled to some return for what they contributed.

A medieval kingdom already possessed some of the elements of the state and occasionally a lot of them. England by 1000 was an infant Leviathan. It was a well-articulated kingdom with an energising and exploitative government at its heart which demanded the compliance and allegiance of its king's subjects. It had recognised borders, a single imperial ruler, a standardised vernacular language and its own idea of law. It even had a national administrative and financial structure which could generate the wealth by which navies could be launched and armies could be fielded. The same could be said to a lesser degree about the stable Gaelic kingdom of Alba to its north, which also had a military and judicial organisation to give it reality and expression. But if the volatile and shifting Welsh kingdoms in the west of Britain could be called 'states' then they were at a very basic level of development: their kings' sole aim was to extract a surplus from their tributary districts so as to finance the military household which guaranteed their local hegemony and defended them from their predatory kinsfolk. There was little in Wales of the mutual interest between ruler and ruled which you expect from the word 'state', and any social organisation was at the level of family and church. What you mostly hear from eleventh-century Wales is the infuriated complaints of clerics about the inadequacies of the aggressive, greedy and immoral local rulers who disrupted their lives and communities, rather than protecting them. From what Welsh clergymen read and understood of contemporary England and Carolingian France, we know that they were aware there was a better form of kingship to be found elsewhere.

Embodying England

The West Saxon monarchy had remarkable success during the tenth century in organising the unitary kingdom of England, to a degree unknown elsewhere in Western Europe. The English may have been taxed and conscripted from the top, but there was also a recognisable common interest among king, aristocracy and people which made the English state a reality. It was expressed in a governmental structure. By 1000 almost all the realm had two tiers of local government. The kingdom was subdivided into shires as far north as the rivers Tees and Mersey (see Map 5.1). These were units of government which the king supervised through his appointed sheriffs, who were responsible for royal estates within them and exercised a variety of executive functions. The king's ealdormen, who were also appointed officials, oversaw one or more shires on the level of public order and defence, and monitored and mobilised local aristocratic society. The king was able to communicate directly with his officials through his formal orders, writs (OE *gewritas*), sealed mandates written in English, some intended to be read out publicly in the shire moots, the tribunals where communal justice was done. Shires were subdivided into hundreds in most of the realm, though Scandinavian equivalent units and assemblies called 'wapentakes' had taken their place in most of

Yorkshire (apart from the East Riding) and the north Midland shires. Hundreds and wapentakes too had their reeves and communal assemblies. The law administered in these courts was local, though their assemblies paid attention in their verdicts to the past edicts issued nationally by English kings. The laws formulated by King Edgar were very much a live issue in the reign of Cnut, who embraced them publicly as a guarantee that he would be a king for all the people of England, Danes and English alike. The shires provided a tax base for the kingdom, which had been assessed at some time in the past in tax units called 'hides' over most of England (but 'carrucates' in the North Midlands and the North). A 'hide' was not a standard unit, though it was supposed to be the value of the amount of land which would support a well-off freeman. Taxes were collected through local assemblies by the sheriff. So it could be said that, wherever assemblies answered to the king's writs, heeded his law and paid him taxes, there was, in very real terms, England.

There were other ways to express the idea of England. Silver coinage had been deployed in England for centuries as a vehicle for advertising royal authority as much as to enable commerce and taxation. Pre-Conquest English government has been perceived as at its most formidable in the way it created, monitored and exploited its currency, which had long penetrated every economic level of English society, and even by 1000 had spread to the lands of its British neighbours, not to mention being exported in large quantities as both wages and tribute to Scandinavia. The governments of Æthelred II (978–1016) and Cnut (1016–1035) have been estimated to have kept £20,000 to £50,000 of silver coinage in circulation (that is, between 4.8 million and 12 million silver pennies) from its mints (see Fig. 1.1). Care was taken to issue centrally from London the dies by which pennies were struck, and to monitor silver content by periodically calling in the old coinage and reissuing it. Each coin was marked with its maker and the place of issue, and, most symbolically, stamped with the image of the king under whose authority it was issued.

The heart of the kingdom was the royal court. It was not central, in the sense that it was stationed permanently in any particular place, though already before the Conquest King Edward had made Westminster a favoured residence. It was just upriver of the greatest city in his realm, convenient both for provisioning and for access to news and emissaries from the North Sea world. Even in his days, the great earls had found it convenient to have their own halls in the vicinity of Westminster and London, as Earl Godwine had at Lambeth, across the Thames. But King Edward did not stay stationary: he toured his realm so as to exploit its resources, to visit and worship at its notable shrines and particularly to enjoy the hunting grounds he so loved. But, where the king was, was the centre of England, in the sense that it was the place from which executive orders were issued, and the place to which his magnates and prelates were regularly summoned – as they had been since at least the beginning of the tenth century – to give him their counsel, in a body known as the *witenagamot*. A dialogue between king

Map 5.1 Counties of England

and his most influential subjects was already going on in the eleventh century, and was informing the decisions his officials executed. All these factors allow us to say that England was already in the eleventh century operating as a fully realised and mobilised 'nation-state' capable of dominating the rest of Britain.

Each medieval century built on this Anglo-Saxon foundation of symbolism. Edward the Confessor's royal seal was imitated and improved on by his French successors. It became itself a symbol of the king's authority, impressed on expensive green wax hanging from his writs and charters of grant. The display of the seal by a royal messenger was a badge of his office. Royal officers in Henry II's day, dressed in his livery, shouted out in French as they went about their master's business 'Realx!' (King's men!) as a demand for deference to royal authority. The household knights who murdered Becket intimidated his servants by crying 'Realx!' as they forced their way into his lodgings, claiming to be on the king's business. It was in the same reign that the Angevin device of a gold lion (initially on blue) became more than just a dynastic symbol, and came to feature on banners and the uniform coats of his soldiers and servants as a stamp of English royal authority wherever they were displayed. In John's reign, the three lions on red took on their still familiar heraldic meaning, as a symbol for England as much as its monarch, displayed on linen and silk banners above the king's ships, castles and armies even when he was not present (up to the time of the Hundred Years War the king displayed a gold and red silk dragon banner, devised like a windsock, when he was personally in the field). The royal arms of England were so powerful a sign that their influence leaked symbolically across Britain early in the thirteenth century, with King John's relatives, the Scots king and the prince of Gwynedd, taking variants on the red and gold lion design to symbolise their own realms and authority. The lions of England were the focus and expression of national feeling. When King Edward III claimed the throne of France in 1337, and in 1340 adopted a new coat of arms which symbolised his claims by 'quartering' the English lions with the lilies of France, the design gave priority to the French arms, which caused some angst, as Edward himself recognised. He issued a pamphlet explaining that France was, after all, the more ancient kingdom. The French were not too impressed with the way he had pirated their national symbol, and deliberately redesigned it to differentiate *their* lilies from the ones the Plantagenets had hijacked.

The Rise of Bureaucracy

There was no basic difference between the degree of government England experienced under King Cnut (1016–1035) and under King William Rufus (1087–1100), in that both were foreign monarchs operating the same system and both were frequently absent from England in their other realms, entrusting their power while they were gone to viceregal proxies. The most obvious difference in the two kings' governments perhaps, as far as the general populace was concerned, was that Cnut and his officers – though foreigners – governed England through the medium of English, while Rufus did it through the medium of Latin, a reform his father had initiated in or around 1070 as a way of making his will understood in assemblies in which English and French speakers had to be addressed simultaneously. Latin was a neutral language which both ethnicities could be expected to know. By 1130, however, the complexion of English government had changed, and in changing it sparked further changes across Britain, as the possibilities of executive authority were expanded and came to be imitated by other British rulers, notably the kings of Scotland.

The principal catalyst of the change was the energy and insecurity of King Henry I (1100–1135), though in carrying out his changes it is clear that he formulated his ideas in consultation with a small group of talented advisers: principally his close friend, Count Robert of Meulan and Leicester (died 1118) and the cleric, Bishop Roger of Salisbury (died 1139). But it was the personality of the king himself which motivated the revolution. Henry in 1100 was ambitious to deprive his elder brother of his duchy of Normandy and then to hold it against the aggression of his Angevin and Capetian rivals, which required money, and lots of it. William Rufus, his predecessor on the throne, had achieved just that through outright extortion and chicanery, which left Henry to deal with a legacy of bitterness amongst the English aristocracy; Henry himself thought in the longer term. He had an inexhaustible appetite for information and indeed control. In the first decade of his reign he commissioned surveys of property-holding in various counties, quite as intrusive as Domesday Book, several of which have survived. He was believed to have kept a register of all his barons and the fees they were owed when they came to court, and detailed the allowances of his household officers down to the number of candle stubs (a list we know about because it was presented to his successor on the throne). Knowing his resources, he was better placed to use them, and his use of the patronage he had available to him left a long-lasting (but not necessarily helpful) legacy to his successors.

Out of King Henry's personal quirks came England's first impulse towards bureaucratic organisation, through the creation of a financial office. This was the Exchequer, which gets its name from the checker-board cloth (*scaccarium*) on which was calculated the amounts owed by the king's local officers, in a manner resembling that of an abacus. The Exchequer was a debt-collection agency, which we are told created appropriate terror in the way it intimidated sheriffs when they were called to present their accounts. It also became a specialised law court run by its 'barons', the king's appointed auditors and justices. They created the Exchequer's own customs, privileges and lore, which were to be written down in the 1160s in the days of Henry's grandson. Two things made the Exchequer revolutionary. It did not need the king to be present for it to meet; indeed in its first recorded meeting in 1109 the queen presided in the king's absence, and otherwise his alter-ego, the justiciar, filled the chair. The other significant fact about it was that it generated extensive accounts (called 'pipe rolls') which recorded annually, shire by shire, what was owed the king, what was actually paid and what still remained owing. As a result the king not only knew his income, but also could use the information to monitor costs and budget for future expenses. He could manipulate his subjects by deferring the collection of what they owed him, or ruin them by calling all the debt in if they took a wrong step. The earliest surviving pipe roll comes from 1130, but it carries on it unpaid debts that went back as far as 1118. There may well have been earlier forms of financial record keeping. The wooden **tallies** the Exchequer issued as receipts for payments made at the board were apparently something that had been employed before the creation of the Exchequer itself. But the pipe rolls were far more than this: they bureaucratised the state's ability to generate and deploy wealth; they imposed checks on local officers, and provided the impulse to enrol and archive government records systematically. All of a sudden England had a memory.

The significance of this twelfth-century moment should not be underestimated, for it solidified the concept of England as a land where the populace was subject to the executive authority of a king. Wherever the king's officers collected his revenues from estates, individuals and corporations, the English state was a reality, and the Exchequer board was the way the state made systematic and permanent links to the margins of its tributary territory. The writs issued to sheriffs, constables and **bailiffs** by king or justiciar from the board expressed the will of the centre, and demanded answers from the periphery. It is not difficult here to fall into the medieval imagery of a kingdom as a body with the king as directing intelligence, the precursor of Hobbes's image of the state as a corporate Leviathan. It would soon be reinforced by another powerful impulse, towards national law and the central dispensation of justice.

Lords and Order

Henry I evidently had a sincere wish to live up to his coronation oath so far as it concerned offering justice to his realm. It was this mixture of idealism and ambition to control on his part which provided a further push towards the bureaucratisation of England. English government had long expressed its will through the writ (see Fig. 5.1), in English before 1070 and in Latin afterwards. It has been calculated that in 1130 the king's four known working scribes issued between them around 4,500 letters and writs, which would mean they would each have written three a day: not impressive, perhaps, in terms of the paperwork generated by a more modern state, but a new thing in the middle ages. So the writ was already a useful and well-used administrative tool by Henry's day. But during Henry's reign the writ began to mutate as new uses were found for it.

Fig. 5.1 Writ of Henry I of England. This sealed strip of parchment is an example of one of the executive orders developed by the English royal Chancery as far back as the tenth century to convey instructions to royal officers. It was later developed into a legal instrument, of which the writ *Habeas corpus* remains the most famous example.

Determined to take responsibility for the conduct of justice where it offended the promises he had made in his coronation oath, King Henry took national responsibility for crimes against the peace of which he was guarantor under God. Being Henry, he did it in a systematic way. From the first decade of his reign justices were selected from amongst his household officers and barons who had a liking for that sort of work and who were sent out in teams of three or four on national circuits (the 'eyre' or 'travels') to sit in the communal courts and there advise the local assemblies about the justice they were doing in the king's name, and also to enquire into the king's rights, presented by a new local officer, the coroner (meaning 'crown agent'). As they made their circuit from shire court to shire court, the king's justices brought with them something new: a central idea of the way justice should be done and verdicts reached, which had authority because it came from the steps of the king's throne, supported as it was on lion's feet, as had been the seat of King Solomon of old. Law in England was being standardised; it was becoming 'common'. The justices also brought with them the forceful concerns of the king about his local rights, particularly the abuse of his prerogatives such as the forest, so it would not be quite true to say these men were entirely welcome in the shires, but their authority was inescapable.

Less easy for the king to monitor was an innovation that the Conquest had brought to England, though, oddly enough, in the end it was to reinforce royal authority over justice. Northern French lords were used to doing justice on their own tenants with little or no reference to a king whose authority was non-existent outside the region of Paris, and not much more to the duke who ruled from Rouen. They saw no reason why they should not carry on doing the same on their new estates in England, and the Conqueror did not disagree with them. Doing justice was a moral and financial prerogative for any effective lord in France, and the Conquest brought the idea to England, where justice had been done differently until then. Strangely, chaos did not follow on from this confusion over where the right to seek justice lay. In general, people went to the court where they thought they would get the best verdict. In difficult property cases, where the tenants of different lords were appealing to each other's court for a verdict, King Henry, however, insisted in 1108 that the two parties should go to a convenient neutral tribunal, such as the shire or hundred court.

These overlapping jurisdictions could be made sense of by looking up to the king as the supervisor of the whole process, as his coronation oath obliged him to be. This was the impetus that produced the specialised judicial writ issued by the king's Chancery to ensure justice was done in a particular case. Such a writ did not give a verdict; it simply ordered in the king's name that justice should be done to a particular plaintiff in a particular court, or there would be consequences. These writs had to be obtained from the royal Chancery by the payment of a fee, and thereafter the writ followed the case around like a parchment Post-it note, ensuring that it was dealt with. In the stroke of a pen, it placed the king in the centre of the judicial web of English courts, imposing his will on all of them and guaranteeing there would (at least in theory) be a process of judgement and settlement in every case, wherever it was heard. This is why the 'writ of right' is so important: more than a one-off document such as the law codes of Edgar and Cnut, it actually created a national legal 'system'. It grew out of Henry I's ideology of royal justice, but such writs first appear in the reign of his successor Stephen (1135–1154), a king usually otherwise blamed for disorder in England. However, it was in the reign of the jurist-king Henry II (1154–1189) that its full potential was realised, and the centralisation of justice on the king and his court taken to an entirely new level.

If the king was the guarantor of justice, it must soon have occurred to sensible people that the best verdict, and sometimes the cheapest, would be gained by taking their case directly to the king's presence. The king's court was a tribunal from which there was no appeal (other than to the pope in Rome, and that only for specialised cases). Though it cost a lot to get a case heard before the king or his commissioners and took much travel and expense to attend a hearing, in the end it may have been the cheaper option for a plaintiff. In twelfth-century England, when the king was across the Channel for years at a time, he might be inaccessible for all practical purposes. But the fact that he left a legal and administrative alter-ego behind him in the person of his chief justiciar meant that there was always one superior court functioning in England, and after the 1160s it focused more and more on Westminster, where the chief justiciar was to be found on the Exchequer bench with his colleagues at Easter and Michaelmas and the weeks following these high feasts, men who thus formed a 'bench' of justices.

So more or less accidentally, but perhaps inevitably, a central court of justice began to coalesce in England in the 1170s. Before the end of the decade the body of skills and traditions of these men had inspired one of them to write a handbook of legal procedures they implemented, England's first common law legal manual. It was called 'Glanvill' after Ranulf de Glanville, one of Henry II's most formidable justices and administrators, though he probably was not the author. Central record keeping soon followed, just as it had done already with England's finances, first at Winchester and later at Westminster. By the 1170s the justices at Westminster were issuing and retaining sealed copies of the verdicts they delivered on property cases (called 'final concords' or 'feet of fines'). The advantages of keeping a record of the actual deliberations of the court which led up to the verdict is obvious, and such records were kept by individual justices in Henry II's reign. One of them, Richard of Ilchester, is known to have kept his own set of rolls while on eyre in the 1160s, apparently on his own initiative. But during the 1190s rolls recording the pleas before the king's justices at Westminster and the justices in eyre in the provinces began to be not just demanded but centrally archived, and so England's legal memory began, the result of which can still be seen in the many thousands of hefty parchment rolls from before 1500, dark with centuries of the dust from London's coal fires, which occupy the shelving of the National Archives at Kew.

The Spread of Bureaucracy in Britain

The best evidence of the impact the English state was having on the mentality of its ruling class is the way its bureaucratic processes were copied and spread. Within a decade of the first appearance of the royal Exchequer an English earl had formed his own at Leicester, and reorganised his lands so his own officers presented accounts at its board for their areas of responsibility. Since the earl in question was Henry I's close friend, Robert of Meulan, it is possible to see how the diffusion of bureaucracy happened. By 1200 numerous other earls, barons and bishops had formed audit and accounting offices for their estates (called either exchequers or 'chambers'), and were generating their own financial records. More fateful were the lessons which a young Scottish earl, the king's brother-in-law, drew from what he witnessed at the English court. David of Huntingdon became king of Scotland in 1124, and before the end of his reign in 1153 he had implemented changes of organisation which were intended to replicate elements of the English state in Scotland. He imported the idea of a justiciar of Scotland as a legal alter-ego for himself, with delegated authority. The Gaelic areas of Scotland in fact already had provincial justices (*brithems*) with a comparable but limited responsibility. Once there was a national legal figurehead, the same move towards a Scottish 'common' law could begin. Royal writs (*brieves*) on the English pattern begin to be issued in Latin in David's reign, and in the 1160s we find in Scotland the same insistence on them we find in England, that justice should be done in private courts, and, if not, the king's sheriff or his justiciar would intervene to make sure it was.[1]

Royal supervision was the ambition, though in fact Scotland did not have the uniform structures of government that had been established across England before the Conquest which made possible a more intense bureaucratisation of society. Galloway and the Gaelic mormaerdoms of the north and centre of Scotland remained difficult for the king to influence directly unless they came into his wardship. It was in the Anglophone south, the province of Lothian which had once been Northumbrian, and in Fife and along the east coast that shires appeared, and sheriffs were appointed to supervise the king's interests and receive his writs. But the trend had nonetheless been set towards centralisation: a dozen Scottish sheriffdoms in 1160 had become a score by 1214. There was less obvious Scottish centralisation in finance than in England. When Exchequer rolls appear in Scotland in the thirteenth century (the earliest survivor is from 1264, though it is likely rolls had been compiled many decades before that date) they have less national coverage than those of England. The king's sheriffs account for the consumption of food, fish and firewood by the royal household as it travelled through their areas, just as an English magnate's bailiffs might for their lord. On the other hand, the Scottish Exchequer rolls link the king to the sheriffs, bailiffs, constables and foresters who administered his assets and monitored his rights, and the commission of auditors who inspected the accounts under the chamberlain were vigilant in their master's interests. They indicate a Scottish state that had a strong degree of bureaucratic control in the south and east of the realm.

Scottish sheriffs began to hold courts for their shires, however limited their authority. Already in the reign of William the Lion (1165–1214) there was the same insistence as in England that certain offences were the king's to investigate and punish: the criminal pleas of murder, rape, housebreaking and arson. Just as in England, the law of Scotland expanded to become common to the realm and in the same way. Just as King Henry II of England issued statements of law (assizes) in council which applied to all his kingdom, so did William the Lion of Scotland in the 1190s. Just as the legal handbook called Glanvill envisioned the law of England as common to the whole realm, a similar (but rather later) tract called *Regiam Majestatem* did the same for Scotland late in the reign of Alexander III, and indeed copied out chunks of Glanvill when it did so. Scotland never centralised royal justice on permanent courts as England did at Westminster. The nearest it came to this was to invest supreme judicial authority in Parliament, which never settled in one place in medieval Scotland, however. But in theory no part of the realm was beyond the reach of the king's justiciars, who in Alexander III's time divided up the realm into three circuits (Caithness acquired a fourth justiciar later).

The problems of attaining any sort of Welsh 'statehood' were too enormous for any Welsh ruler to succeed at it in the twelfth or thirteenth century. But the ambition to do so can at least be detected. Twelfth-century people understood there to be four 'realms' in Britain: those of the English, the Scots, the Irish and the Welsh (or Britons). A 'realm' (Lat. *regnum*) did not necessarily need a king (*rex*) but there was an expectation that it should have a single ruler (*rector*). Wales was a political dust cloud but an effective ruler might give it the centre of gravity it needed to coalesce as a state. Even before 1200, the princes of Gwynedd wanted that position, though for a while Rhys ap Gruffudd (died 1197), prince of Deheubarth, gave them a run for their money. Before the 1190s princes of Gwynedd had negotiated with the Capetians and married Angevin women, thus claiming a small space at the table of European princes. Even before Rhys's death, the remarkable talent of Llywelyn ab Iorwerth (died 1240) had brought him to predominance in Wales, a ruler eventually able to exert influence throughout all its ancient regions and demand the homage of all Welsh magnates, whom he regarded as no more than barons owing him homage. The rival princes of Powys had problems with that particular ambition of his until he beat them into submission.

One of the many challenges that occupied Llywelyn was the need to mobilise Gwynedd to provide the resources for him to deal with his English rivals and their king. By the time he died in 1240 Llywelyn had gone surprisingly far in achieving his ambition. He had created an administration which was not dissimilar (other than in the Welsh titles of its officers) to those of any contemporary prince: with bailiffs (*rhaglawiaid*) answering to his seneschal (*distain*), and a chancellor responsible for his written acts and archive. There was even something resembling a financial office though, in a society where horses were the most valued form of exchange between lords and men, its usefulness had its limits. Llywelyn built masonry castles over which his red and gold lion banner flaunted, garrisoned by soldiers in his green and white livery, and his mounted **sergeants** patrolled the provinces under his rule. Llywelyn's court gave some serious thought to its lord's primacy over Welsh customary law, and there were jurists associated with it who attempted to codify it under his authority, casting the semi-legendary king of Deheubarth and Gwynedd, Hywel Dda (*c.* 904–950), as a founding genius of Welsh customary law, which was in this way characterised as having been given from the hand of a prince. Llywelyn was to be hailed as Hywel's successor in a bid to seek a princely primacy over Welsh law. He needed to assert himself so he could use such an authority to change the rules of succession to his realm and so preserve it in the hands of one heir. In this of course he failed, but he and his successors clearly appreciated the need to couple authority over law to their princely coronet, the way the English crown was the symbolic focus of justice in the king's realm.

 The Departments of State

In a wry attempt to explain the twentieth-century British civil service, Cyril Northcote Parkinson (1909–1993) observed in *The Economist* in 1955 that 'administrators are more or less bound to multiply', since 'an official wants to multiply subordinates, not rivals'.[2] He was not a medievalist (though he was in fact the feudal lord of several Guernsey fiefs), but Parkinson might well have been explaining the dynamic behind the expanding Plantagenet bureaucracy of the thirteenth and fourteenth centuries. The English royal household in 1200 was not much different in overall size and its basic departmental structure from that of 1400, varying between 400 and 700 people receiving fees and maintenance. What did change were the numbers and specialisms of the departmental officials who did not follow the king's mobile court but took his salaries and worked from Westminster palace and its neighbourhood, which already by the 1180s was a permanent focus of government, where the Exchequer bench heard pleas under the pillared roof of the king's huge hall, and justices and clerks were generating records which were forming an increasingly large archive. Public activity thronged the palace hall, the nearby chapter house of the abbey and the growing suburb along King Street towards the Strand (where the financial centre of the London Temple formed another centre of public activity, at least until the reign of Edward II). The borough of Westminster and its northern suburb became in the later middle ages a burgeoning bureaucratic and legal enclave, its inns crowded with plaintiffs, messengers, clerks and, increasingly from the mid thirteenth century, professional lawyers and the law students who studied under masters and attended the lecture courses regularly offered by the justices of the bench. The celibate clerks employed by the government likewise settled in their own communal inns, with the western London ward of Farringdon being their particular enclave. By the end of the fourteenth century, the Inns of Chancery were being run as training schools for young bureaucrats by senior clerks, as parallel institutions to the Inns of Court.

Administrative careers in government became possible, and by 1300 there were a number of routes into the Plantagenet bureaucratic elite. Ambitious university-trained clerks, willing to put up with (or dodge) the requirement for celibacy, sought higher places in the administration, which could be richly rewarded by appointments to the church benefices, **canons'** stalls and ecclesiastical offices in the king's gift. Quite a few among them ended up as bishops, and after 1250 the majority of English bishops got their promotion after years of government service. Provincial **gentry** families were the principal recruiting ground for such men. Fathers were willing to invest in their sons' higher education in hopes of just such preferment. Such a path was followed by Anthony Bek (died 1311), a graduate of Oxford and a member of a Lincolnshire family of modest local importance but with a court connection to the earl of Lincoln. Anthony attracted the notice of the Lord Edward, the son of King Henry III, and obtained an appointment as a royal clerk. He spent nearly two decades as a diplomat, financial and parliamentary agent and military quartermaster, accumulating numerous church benefices along the way. Promotion to the bishopric of Durham in 1283 did not end his activities; he was at the centre of his master's diplomatic and military manoeuvres in Scotland and Gascony in the 1290s. In 1298, in his early fifties, he commanded a division of the English army in Scotland, led a siege and fought at the battle of Falkirk. Apparently, amongst his many other worldly enthusiasms he had a passion for horsebreeding. Oddly enough, despite this, Bek had a reputation for chastity and pastoral concern and was promoted to the titular Latin patriarchate of Jerusalem by the pope. Some at Durham Cathedral priory later regarded him as a candidate for sainthood.

The great majority of government clerks had to expect far less than Bek obtained. The autobiographical writings of Thomas Hoccleve (*c.* 1367–1426), a low-ranking clerk in the Privy Seal office from 1387, portray the experience of the majority. He eventually got promotion to senior clerk and a modest income from an annuity. He spent most of his life living in a communal inn with other clerks just off the Strand where they drank rather too much in its taverns as young males. Poverty was a theme of his complaints about his life: in 1410 he gave up hopes of a church appointment and married to escape the lonely grind of his life, which had led him to experience stress and disabling anxiety attacks. A further form of escape for him was a literary life that got him some wider attention, and earned him the notice of Geoffrey Chaucer as a young literary aspirant.

By 1300 the establishment of the Chancery had multiplied into three departments answering to the principal clerical officers: the chancellor, the Keeper of the Privy Seal and the officer who came to be known during the fourteenth century as the King's Secretary. Two of these departments were based at Westminster, the Keeper's department by 1360, though the Secretary's signet office continued to travel with the king to manage his personal correspondence. Each officer kept a distinct seal, the chancellor the great seal, the Keeper the lesser privy seal, and the Secretary the king's signet (or 'secret') seal, each of which had a history already going back over a century. By 1380 the chancellor's department consisted of a hierachy of more than 100 clerks of various ranks and responsibilities, and a support staff of various servants including the man whose job it was to warm the wax before it was pressed on to documents. The Keeper's department also grew over the century, from four to a dozen clerks by 1400. Though the signet office was a much smaller affair, and kept no files and rolls like the bigger state departments, its clerks tended to be university-trained, and closeness to the king brought them better prospects of promotion in the Church.

These three departments were issuing and keeping copies of as many as 40,000 letters between them in any year in the reign of Edward III (1327–1377), as opposed to the estimated 4,500 issued by Henry I's writing office two centuries before. On top of this they managed and archived the ten classes of Chancery record and justice rolls, and the king's huge incoming correspondence of letters and petitions. Unmarried clergy dominated personnel until the fifteenth century and continued to do so in the upper ranks; they had to stay celibate to have hopes of the highest ecclesiastical preferment. But by the middle of the century around a third of the more junior offices of the Chancery were occupied by married men. Similarly the clerks of the signet, too, after 1437 were no longer required to be in clerical orders, and made their way by appointments to profitable **sinecures** in the king's gift.

The financial offices swelled in their numbers of staff correspondingly. Here the leading officer remained the treasurer, presiding over a large and varied staff including judicial officers (or barons) and many clerks, whose departmental chief was the chancellor of the Exchequer. In Edward II's reign (1307–1327) the Exchequer was a department of more than 100 office-holders. But already in King John's reign there had been subdivision in the financial department. A supplementary financial office called the 'chamber' filled the need to administer that avaricious king's travelling treasury, as he preferred to keep his money close to him. It once amused John to pile up his cash in a great stack of barrels in a castle courtyard and gloat over it, much to his courtiers' distaste. Since the king's household comprised a permanent military contingent of **bannerets**, knights, sergeants and archers, the Chamber became the heart of military administration for much of the middle ages. It also managed the chests of plate, furs, jewels and luxury goods that accompanied the king on the road, though by John's reign royal castles such as Corfe and Devizes were already being used as safe deposits of royal treasure. Edward I expanded the Chamber into his chief financial department under the pressure of war finance and, though the harshness of its exactions made it unpopular, the flexibility of the Chamber was going to bring it into prominence in the reign of any military king, as it did in the time of Henry V (1413–1422). Just as the clerical offices became permanently based at Westminster, the Chamber in the fourteenth century set up permanent bases in the City of London: from 1361 the Great Wardrobe off Cheapside commissioned and purchased from the neighbouring City merchants and craftsmen the king's plate, robes and luxury goods and managed their warehousing; a Privy Wardrobe at the Tower of London specialised in military supplies. Like the clerical offices, these great departments too generated records, deploying and employing hundreds of officers, clerks and servants.

The Limits of Bureaucracy

In view of this steady expansion in the staff and scope of these government offices, the appearance of career hierarchies and professionalisation of their skills, it might be odd that this section talks of the 'limits' of bureaucracy. It is very easy for a historian to become mesmerised by the astonishing breadth and survival of the records of the medieval English state and the intricacies of its procedures, and assume that such an impressive organisation was itself a measure of state power, and many have been. But it would be a misleading assumption. Take, for instance, the lesson given by the Plantagenet lordship of Ireland. During the course of the thirteenth century, English government in Ireland reproduced a parallel hierarchy of exchequer, chancery and court of common pleas, with similar administrative, clerical and judicial offices and responsibilities drawing on a hinterland of shires, sheriffs, local **escheators**, justices and coroners. The city of Dublin was itself a setting designed to project the power and authority of the state: a city deliberately built by the Plantagenets to impress as a centre of dynastic power, a Westminster on the banks of the Liffey, with a massive fortress, a busy port, a mayor and corporation, two cathedrals, hospitals and great monasteries asserting the city to be the peer of London, Rouen, Bordeaux and Angers. Dublin too accumulated permanent state departments, while its castle's Bermingham Tower was stacked with a large archive of record rolls and files (tragically destined to be mostly burned in the civil unrest of 1922). But the scope of government and royal justice in Ireland was limited, often ineffectual and compromised both by the power of aristocratic liberties outside the **Pale** and by the persistence of native magnate power in the north and west of the island. The Irish Plantagenet state was a parchment tiger.

The same mismatch between bureaucratic ambition and real power might be observed in Scottish royal government, which, for all the disruption of Edward I's wars of conquest, developed along lines broadly similar to England's. But though there were state officers and offices in fourteenth-century Scotland, there was no equivalent to a centralising Plantagenet Westminster, or even Dublin. Yet despite the devastation of the Edwardian wars, we can glimpse evidence that thirteenth-century Scottish government had also generated records in some quantity. In 1292 King Edward shipped off to England 307 separate items which constituted the accumulated archive of government rolls, schedules and charters he found in Edinburgh Castle, the inventory of which still survives, though the originals do not. There were undoubtedly more records kept in other repositories, because there still survived in Scotland after 1306 Exchequer records and rolls going back to the time of Alexander II (1214–1249). As in England, the chancellor headed the clerical offices. A royal 'chapel' (that is, the office of royal clerks) at Edinburgh issued charters and legal brieves in return for fees. The keeper of the privy seal (called the secretary in Scotland) and his clerks travelled with the court, managing the king's correspondence and authorising the issue of charters under the great seal from the chapel clerks in Edinburgh. By the end of the reign of James I (1406–1437) Scotland, like England (and in deliberate imitation of it), had three clerical departments operating under chancellor, keeper and secretary and, although it was on a more modest scale than England's, the Scottish chancery was still able to generate a not unimpressive eighty-two record rolls before 1400, fifty-two in the troubled reign of David II (1329–1371). Unfortunately for posterity all but a few of these records went down in the North Sea with the ship that was transporting them south in 1660.

Fourteenth-century Scotland's Exchequer remained an audit office, more like the exchequer of any contemporary bishop or magnate than the one which sat at Westminster. Although it generated record rolls in its accounting sessions, it had no regular terms like the English Exchequer and might not meet for several years at a time, and, when a commission did sit to consider the accounts, its location depended on who was chairing it. As a result the Scottish Exchequer developed none of the great offices and regular judicial activities that Westminster's did. In fourteenth-century Scotland, the chamberlain customarily ran finance from the royal household and travelled with the king. Even after James I's reforms in the 1420s and the appointment of a treasurer, no central financial office emerged in Scotland, probably because there was never thought to be sufficient business for it; the estate and customs revenue of the king of Scots in the later fourteenth century was about the same as the landed revenue of the English duke of Lancaster, around £7,000, though both had additional sources of revenue.

Bureaucracy does not of itself generate power within and for the state, as England as much as Scotland illustrates. The real power of a medieval king's government depended on things other than its hierarchy of pen-wielding bureaucrats, most notably on the king's own personality and his ability to use the resources and advantages his bureaucratic machinery could generate. The English state machinery at Henry III's disposal in 1235 might in theory have been the most formidable in Europe at the time, but the strain of its attempt to meet the king's requirements to finance his sister's imperial marriage rapidly led to the monarchy's effective bankruptcy. In the hands of a different king, such as Edward I, the state bureaucracy could mobilise the resources and manpower to conquer Wales and wage simultaneous wars in Scotland and France, though the strain in the end even here proved too much to meet the king's demands. Periodic financial crises brought on by royal over-ambition in war and peace revealed the true nexus of power in the nation, and it lay outside the royal household and its state offices. In England, Ireland and Scotland, and indeed briefly in Wales, the political fulcrum within the state came to be balanced on councils and Parliament, because in all the British realms the ruler was usually at a disadvantage in the face of his subjects' opposition.

Fragmentation of Authority

The king's own decisions sometimes conflicted with the centripetal force of centralising bureaucracy. For instance, by Henry I's reign a third to a half of the hundred courts of England had been in effect privatised, given to aristocrats and prelates to administer in the king's name and take their profits in return for a rent. No Norman or Plantagenet king considered taking them back into royal hands, as these 'franchises' were private property subject to inheritance and their possession could indeed be contested in common law courts. This meant that much of one level of public justice in the realm had been privatised, and for a variety of reasons kings were even willing to concede to subjects the next level, in certain cases. The governance of Cheshire had been conceded to its earl before 1100, and many of the shire courts of England were resigned to military earls by King Stephen during the crisis of 1138–1140. Though these concessions were largely quashed after 1154, for reasons of family politics Cornwall remained a private shire whose sheriff and court answered to its earl for long periods of time and, since the earl of Cornwall was also lord of Rutland in the thirteenth century, the same applied to that tiny shire. The earl of Salisbury was hereditary sheriff of Wiltshire so, although he answered to the Exchequer (and indeed a countess of Salisbury did in the thirteenth century), the administration of the shire was in the earl or countess's hands until the extinction of the earldom, and the same also applied to Worcestershire, whose sheriff-dom was and remained the fief of the Beauchamp family (earls of Warwick after 1268) into the fifteenth century. Even though Cheshire reverted to the Crown in 1237, its administration remained separate from the rest of the kingdom.

More pernicious than these ad hoc decisions of patronage proved to be the tolerance of the Angevin kings towards the rise of exemptions on noble estates from the jurisdiction of the king's legal officers. Great magnates, such as the earls of Gloucester, Leicester, Pembroke and Surrey, were routinely excluding the king's bailiffs and sergeants from their 'liberties' in the 1220s, not just from the private hundreds they controlled. They claimed the right on their manors to do justice through their own bailiffs just as they did in their hundred courts. The refusal of King Henry III to confront his earls and barons on the matter of their liberties led to a situation in which in Yorkshire in the 1260s, for instance, the sheriff was unable to act in well over half the manors of his huge county, but had to count instead on the bailiffs of the archbishop and chapter of York, the bishop of Durham, the abbots of Whitby, York and Byland, and the earls of Lincoln, Aumale, Richmond, Cornwall and Surrey to execute royal commands. Nor was it just magnates and prelates who claimed and got exemptions: the bailiffs of the city of York and borough of Scarborough could also exclude the sheriff of York from their bounds. All the sheriff could do was to ask private bailiffs to do his job for him, pass on royal writs and then all too frequently write back to Westminster complaining that nothing was done about them.

In the fourteenth century this idea of the 'liberty' went a large step further, when the earl (from 1360, duke) of Lancaster secured an enhanced liberty in 1351, which turned all his estates into a 'palatinate' entirely run by his administration and answering only to the Crown, on the model offered earlier by Cheshire. Privileged towns too gained a corresponding exemption. Already in Norman England, London elected its own sheriffs. The right to consider themselves as self-governing counties was later conceded to Bristol (1373), York (1396), Hull (1440) and (briefly) Scarborough (1483). In such circumstances, the king himself can be seen to be conspiring to undermine the potential power of his own bureaucracy. It is probable that he had little choice. When the government of Edward III grappled with what was perceived as local corruption and disorder in the country, it had to turn to county knights and issue special commissions to local leaders to try cases. These evolved after 1361 into a 'commission of the peace' whose members (justices of the peace) heard the cases that did not make it to Westminster, though they came to be supervised by touring professional lawyers, the king's sergeants, who sat with them in their assizes. Nonetheless, making the local gentry responsible for justice had its dangers: many of them were beholden to magnates, in whose affinities they were enlisted. In the most extreme case, the later medieval English palatinates, it was the dukes of Lancaster, Cornwall and York, and the bishops of Durham and Ely, who appointed their own justices of the peace.

The other realms of Britain had even less centralisation to contend with. In Scotland, the fourteenth-century territorial earldoms were generally conceded the pleas of the Crown that were so jealously guarded by the king in England, and even contested in Ireland. They were therefore on a par with the English palatinates in that respect, though the great earldoms and liberties of Scotland covered nearly two-thirds of its area, while the palatinates covered barely a tenth of England. Until 1426 the idea of Scottish Common Law was compromised by a willingness to allow a distinct territorial law to as large an area as Galloway, and even a personal customary law that was a privilege of the members of the MacDuff family, former earls of Fife. There was also reckoned to be a special legal zone along the border counties of England and Scotland, where the law of England and Scotland came into collision and special arrangements had to be made. In 1248 Englishmen and Scotsmen who were accused of offences in the other country had to answer for them on their side of the March between England and Scotland according to customary laws fixed by a commission of sheriffs and knights from either side of the border.

In Wales, the former lands of the houses of Gwynedd and Deheubarth were consolidated into a territorial principality with its own administration and bureacracy which appointed sheriffs and justices of the peace, and answered only to its prince, who was for most of the period after 1282 not the king of England, but his eldest son. The rest of Wales, the March, was an anomaly. All 'regalian' rights there were in the hands of the lords of each of its liberties, some of them as large as English counties, such as Pembroke, Glamorgan and Brecon. They operated miniature facsimiles of the English bureaucracy, with exchequers, chanceries and sheriffs. Glamorgan even called its county court a 'parliament'. The law that operated for English speakers in marcher courts was not the Common Law of England, which at least was still the law administered in the palatinate courts. The Welsh March had its own customary laws, which varied even between lordships. Welsh speakers had their own native law. What connected the March to England was the rights the king had over its lords as his tenants: he could take possession of under-age heirs and summon the marcher lords to his military service, but he could not tax them or interfere in their internal administrations. On at least one occasion an unfortunate royal messenger was forced to eat a royal writ he had brought into the March, seal and all.

The Community of the Realm

The truest measure of the reality of the medieval states of Britain lay elsewhere than in bureaucratic machinery and legal jurisdiction, however apparently impressive. This was the idea of the 'commune' or 'commonalty' of England and the English, and indeed a 'community of the realm of Scotland' as the Declaration of Arbroath put it in 1320.

The strength of this idea and its relationship to and (occasionally) distance from the king who was set over the community were the source of the self-conscious ideology of the medieval state, for the commune of England included all its naturalised inhabitants, who were subject to its king and its Common Law, at least in civil matters. Already by the later thirteenth century there was a legal concept of membership of this community, and a process by which a foreigner could be granted 'denizenship': that is, the rights of a freeborn Englishman, with the ability to buy English property and access to courts and commerce in England. Arguably, this idea of community appeared within the period of this volume. King Edgar of England (959–975) accepted that the Danes under his rule in England were not of the same community as the English, any more than the Britons and Gaels he believed were tributary to his crown in other parts of Britain. By the time of Æthelred II's wars in the early eleventh century this was no longer the case and the former Scandinavian colonists were Englishmen. The Danes Æthelred fought were the invading armies of Swein Forkbeard and Cnut, and his ealdorman Byrhtnoth was depicted by a contemporary as rallying the English troops against them before the fatal battle of Maldon (991), urging them to safeguard 'this country, the land of Æthelred my lord, people and soil!' The reality of this community is further indicated by the fact that the king occasionally felt the need to talk to it, as a body wider than the great magnates and prelates who populated his court and council. The Danish King Cnut of England (1016–1035) made a point of proclaiming to his new subjects that he would put right the previous abuses to which their kings subjected them, particularly in the matter of taxation: the grit in the nation's oyster, which eventually produced Parliament.

Throughout the twelfth century the king was obliged (often reluctantly) to concede that his subjects had a voice, and at times he actually sought a conversation, though in general he used his magnates as interpreters. For the better part of the twelfth century the rule of England was principally delegated by an absentee king to his queen or more often to his most capable and trusted magnates, lay and ecclesiastical, with the support of their fellows. So in that way the government of England was a shared enterprise with the king's leading subjects. It was in John's reign (1199–1216), when the king was no longer an absentee lord, that a king first went one step further and appealed to his people over the heads of his council and magnates. It was John who had ended the long-standing conciliar form of government. He tried to ignore anyone else's views and opinions after 1200, but at one point in 1213, as concerns and complaints mounted and conspiracy threatened amongst the sidelined and ignored magnates, John, looking for a different dialogue, summoned to Oxford representatives of the local elites, the county knights, 'to speak with us concerning the affairs of our realm'. What was asked of them and what was said we do not know, but one of the most significant features of the political world in England after Magna Carta was how far down the social scale went an awareness of politics at the centre and how rife was the nation with rumour and opinion about the government of the realm.

The very existence of widespread political rumour is evidence of an insatiable national thirst for news. Letter books of Henry III's reign contain copies of Magna Carta for reference of magnates and abbots but also for the use of local knights; Oxford students heard reports of the discussions on taxation the king's council had in the 1230s, and they, as much as the magnates, were easy prey to highly coloured rumours of the king's determination to snatch back the liberties conceded the realm in 1215. However, political awareness went even deeper into society than that. All adult males on occasion were obliged to go to local assemblies and swear loyalty to the king, especially in times of national stress as when in 1205 a French invasion seemed imminent. When the definitive crisis of the realm occurred in 1258 with royal government in collapse and the king pitted against the 'community of the realm', it is remarkable how the peasantry of England, free and unfree alike, appeared not only aware of the policies at issue, but willing to enlist in the struggle for liberty, oppressed as they were in their townships by the local bailiffs of king and magnates.

It was out of this idea that there was a community of the realm that the Parliament of England grew as a formalised voice in a dialogue with the man who sat on the throne. England was not by any means the only realm in dialogue with its prince at the time. Since medieval rulers customarily asked the advice of their magnates as itself an exercise in good kingship, a form of dialogue was inbuilt in medieval political culture. Meetings between kings and assemblies happened across Western Europe in the early thirteenth century. In England the dialogue, as elsewhere, focused on money-raising. The difference between England and (for instance) France was that the *'parlement'* (discussion) between the two parties was unbalanced towards the king's subjects. It was unbalanced because of what King Henry I did to establish his rule after 1106. His ambitions to buy the loyalty of his magnates depleted the huge landed base of royal lands enjoyed by his father and elder brother. It was a deliberate binge of grants out of royal assets: manors, boroughs and forests which were squandered for a short-term purpose. It was not even a sell-off, the king wanted loyalty from the recipients in return, not cash. Henry went even further, issuing generous exemptions from England's ancient land tax, the geld (on which more below), to the officials of the Exchequer and favoured allies, crippling its returns so that the geld was scrapped in the 1160s. The English royal estates were never to recover from Henry's reign, and King Stephen, his successor, found himself unable to repeat the strategy on his accession, to the discontent of some of his magnates. In contrast, Philip II of France (1180–1223) acquired and fiercely hung on to a vast landed base of estates and cities in Picardy, Normandy and the Loire valley, which was to finance the pre-eminence of his previously poverty-stricken dynasty throughout the thirteenth century. A Parlement grew up in Paris, but the Capetian kings used it as a legal tribunal, not a place for debate or as a source of consent from his subjects for taxation. Unlike the Plantagenets and England, if Capetian kings spoke with the community of the realm of France it was by their own choice, not through necessity.

Taxation

The king's problem in England was clearly recognised as early as 1235. In a literary exercise of around that time, an Oxford student imagined the magnates of England responding to a demand for taxation to meet Henry III's foreign expenses thus: 'If the marriage portion of your sister has taken most of your wealth, why then do you resort to us, when you have rents and farms with which you might enrich your treasury?'[3] The king had just held a great council seeking financial support through a desperate expedient: asking for a one-off feudal aid, even though custom and Magna Carta did not allow such a thing for the marriage of a lord's sister, only his eldest daughter. King Henry's traditional revenues from lands and rights of wardship barely provided £15,000 in a year, rather less than the dowry of £20,000 he had promised the emperor. The king had to reassure his vexed subjects that he would not use their consent as a precedent on any future occasion, and meet their concerns about incompetence in his administration by a dismissal of sheriffs and distrusted favourites. This was to be the recurring pattern over the next two centuries. Kings embarrassed for funds had to seek subsidies from a sometimes grudging and suspicious community of the realm through its representatives, whether council of magnates or a parliament of **estates**, and offer concessions over policy or personnel to get them, as well as be forced to listen to complaints of mismanagement of what they had. Just the same analysis was expressed by Sir John Fortescue (died 1479) in his famous tract *De dominio regale et politico* (generally known as *The Governance of England*) where he expressed the view that mismanagement and consequent poverty were the root cause of the political problems of the Lancastrian monarchy in the 1460s.

On the other hand, the community could not deny the king had a right to demand its financial support. England had a long history of being taxed, going back to the highly effective land tax of the geld which was a major source of finance for the king in 1000, and remained so until undermined by exemptions offered by the Norman kings. Yet it still brought £2,400 to the king in 1130 (around 10 per cent of total receipts at the Exchequer), and in view of the subsequent losses of the king's estates, in 1162 (the last year it was exacted) it made up around 20 per cent of the king's annual receipts at the Exchequer. It was well enough embedded a tax that it survived the dislocation of Stephen's reign, when it was still apparently collected, but for whatever reason Henry II and his council decided to look for better options. One option was to attempt a new land tax assessed on a revised valuation. This eventually produced the carrucage, levied in 1198, but doubts about the fairness of the assessment and the value of its return made it a short-lived experiment, lasting only one generation.

The Angevin king's government simultaneously hunted around for new sources of revenue, and as early as the 1160s it began to focus on the king's rights as a feudal landlord, not on his ancient rights as lord of the land of England. It was the custom that the French brought to England that a lord could demand financial support from the people of his manors and towns in his lordship: the right of tallage, a right which in the king's case extended to the Jews of England, who were classified as a type of royal serf and so liable to his taxation at will. The king could also ask for support in cash in lieu of military service, a payment called scutage, which became in essence a war tax. King Stephen had used it systematically, perhaps because he found the geld difficult to collect from his dissident subjects and troubled realm. So King Henry II and his advisers experimented in shifting the burden of taxation away from the land and on to individuals under his lordship, the holders of knights' fees and other estates. By the end of his reign, Henry and his advisers had gone one step further along this route, on the theory that a lord at need could ask his men for support in more general terms and expect them to respond. The result was the 'aid' (*auxilium*) which applied the idea of tallage more generally: asking all the tenants of property across the realm for a fraction of their expected annual income in a cash payment.

Such aids were levied in 1166 and 1184. That of 1188 was the one which had long-term consequences. It asked an entire tenth with the pious excuse of the financing the king's oath to go on crusade to liberate the beleaguered kingdom of Jerusalem (and so was called the 'Saladin Tithe'). It began the long medieval tradition of national resistance to taxation. Commissioners went out and assessed the incomes to be expected by all England's landholders on their livestock and crops, and the totals were eventually fixed, though not on the basis of lists of individuals but on the totals which might be expected for each basic unit of English administration: the **townships** (*villatae*) which made up the hundreds and wapentakes of England and through which the aid was collected. So, by a devious sleight of hand, a new tax evolved in England which had the potential to produce rather more than the old geld had done, if on a different basis. The difference was that since it was theoretically levied on individual tenants' incomes and movable goods it could be levied only with their consent, because by the French tradition from which it was derived it was a voluntary gift in aid to the lord. So the Saladin Tithe had first to be debated and authorised by a great council of the king's tenants-in-chief, which was held at the royal residence of Geddington in Northamptonshire. It was on this fracture point of social history that rested much of the political instability that periodically troubled later medieval England.

The mechanism of the aid agreed in Henry II's reign was too potentially profitable a source of revenue for the king to ignore. He could negotiate a fraction of the notional income of his tenants: a fortieth, thirtieth, fifteenth, thirteenth and tenth were all demanded at various times in early days. Eventually it settled down to a combinations of fractions, a fifteenth from rural estates and a tenth from towns, such as that asked for by Edward III to finance his Scottish campaign in 1332, which brought him a useful £37,500. The aids produced substantial sums, dwarfing other forms of income. The heavy assessment of an entire thirteenth in 1207 brought £57,000 into King John's grateful hands as he planned to launch a seaborne attack on his Capetian enemies to recover his lost French provinces. In the early days the king could even use personal pressure to negotiate up the fraction with individual magnates on their lands.

The need for consent to this highly desirable form of taxation added an impulse to the expansion of Parliament beyond the council of magnates and prelates. If Parliament became the body which consented to this sort of feudal taxation, which it was by 1235, then it made sense to include within it representatives of the local elites who actually collected it on the ground: the knights of the shires and the patricians who ruled the towns and cities of England, as occurred for the first time during the reforming baronial regime in 1258–1259 when knights were asked to join the barons and prelates to contribute their experience and voice. The reform movement based its appeal and authority in its claim to speak for the community of the realm. So the already well-embedded idea of the community was further affirmed in a dialogue which demanded consent from all the governed, and the curious thing was that the re-energised regime of Henry III and his son Edward did nothing to reverse this expansion.

 ## The Potential of Parliament

It was Edward I's wholehearted adoption of the expedient of a parliament of several estates, including the Commons, which inaugurated a new phase in the development of the English state. The parliament of estates was accepted by the king as the authentic representative of his realm and a channel for its voice. It needs some explanation as to why an authoritarian monarch such as Edward I was the one responsible for accepting this state of affairs, for he was something of an enthusiast on the subject. In part it had to do with his youthful embrace of the reform movement of 1258, which was framed around the idea of the realm exerting itself to rein in a wilful and wasteful king, who happened to be Edward's own father. But his perpetuation of the idea of a parliament of estates after the crisis of 1263–1266 was over can only be because he found it to be a congenial way of ruling. Confident amongst his magnates (the greatest of whom were actually his loyal kinsmen), respected by Church and commoners as a crusader, jurist and formidable soldier, Edward I could face the assembled estates with no trepidation at all. It was a splendid stage for the kingship of such a man, and it was natural to extend the idea to the three estates of his other realm of Ireland, which acquired a parallel parliament in Dublin during his reign. When a respected king and his respectful estates were in harmony, Parliament amplified the bass note of his authority rather than shrieking in discord. It is not surprising that Edward made the most of Parliament's potential, as that other self-possessed warrior-king, his grandson Edward III, would do in turn.

This change in emphasis in rulership had happened even before Edward became king. From the Parliament at Marlborough in 1267 a parliament of three estates became a common (though not yet invariable) form of meeting between king and community, which might happen more than once a year, as it did in 1268, when it began to grapple with the financing of the Lord Edward's crusade. Once he was king and back from the Mediterranean, Edward rapidly consolidated the use of Parliament in his government in deliberate pursuit of a realm where public peace and consensus reigned, as it had not in his father's day. For most of Edward's reign it met twice a year while the king was in England, mostly in Westminster. It was at the time of Parliament that the king staged great public occasions, dynastic marriages and chivalric ceremonies; he set out policy statements, asked advice and secured consent for both war and peace. As with the Capetian version, Parliament had a legal dimension. It became the stage for high-profile prosecutions (such as the show trial of Prince Dafydd ap Gruffudd of Gwynedd in 1283); it was also the place where the king received humble petitions for justice from individual subjects and issued his great statements of law. In 1275 Edward told Pope Gregory X that the principal business of Parliament was no less than 'the common welfare of the people'. So central had Parliament become to the English state by his death in 1307 that during Edward's son's reign people could not conceive of an England without it, and assumed that it had existed in its fourteenth-century form since before the Conquest.

Perhaps the most potent and attractive function of the later Plantagenet parliament was the ability it gave the king to mobilise his nation for war, especially through expanding his tax-gathering powers, such as its highly significant concession in 1275 that the king might take indirect taxes from trade, particularly duties on wool and leather. Twelfth-century kings had waged war principally by employing paid companies of cavalry and infantry out of their own revenues, stiffened with the elite households of their magnates. This proved insufficient when Capetian pressure engineered the collapse of Angevin hegemony in northern France in 1203–1205, which is why new sources of taxation became so pressing. Under Edward I the English government found ways of financing what has been called a 'war state' through loans and taxation, and Parliament was at the heart of national mobilisation, for its consent to taxes was binding on the community it represented. There was, however, a price to be paid. In return for its money, the estates often succeeded in pushing their own agenda. From the later 1270s until it got its way in 1290, the Commons pushed for the expulsion of the Jews from England, as the county knights represented the group in society most prone to suffer the consequences of Jewish moneylending.

Sometimes the agenda of Parliament went well beyond the king's wishes, however. Between 1294 and 1302, Edward I had to raise at least £60,000 a year to keep his armies in the field, and direct taxation granted by Parliament accounted for only £282,000 in that period. New forms of indirect taxation filled much of the gap, notably an unprecedented new tax on England's most lucrative export, wool, levied with the excuse that it was sanctioned by the king's ancient right to requisition goods for his own use. A levy of £2 on a sack yielded around £116,000 to the treasury in the most intense period of warfare between 1294 and 1297. By 1297 the strain was too much for the country, and resistance to taxation, direct and indirect, naturally focused on Parliament, where a small cabal of armed and hostile earls led the resistance to new and unprecedented levels of taxation in the name of 'the community', waving the usual banner of Magna Carta. Organised and united resistance led to the king's capitulation, including the curtailing of his claim to levy indirect taxation without parliamentary consent.

This was the pattern of political life that was repeated frequently over the next century and more. Incompetent and divisive kings had the most to fear from this new political world. Parliament could certainly enhance but was also able to debilitate the king's executive power, as even Edward I eventually discovered to his cost. Under a compromised king in bad times, Parliament could be a wayward force, too easily influenced by cabals of hostile magnates. So Thomas of Lancaster in 1315 used Parliament to place himself at the centre of resistance to his cousin, the king, and used it to reinforce and sanction the reforming Ordinances imposed by the magnates on the king in 1311. By 1321 a hostile and insurrectional Parliament was claiming the right to make laws and to indict and exile those it considered public enemies, such as the king's Despencer favourites. Eventually in 1327 it was to be Parliament that proposed and enacted the deposition of Edward II for, although it was the magnates who engineered the coup against the king, the national community had to sanction such an extreme political revolution, and this could be done only through proposing it to Parliament. So in a crowded Westminster Hall, lords, prelates and Commons heard the articles alleging Edward's unfitness to be king and, after a sermon urging the deposition by the archbishop of Canterbury, the whole assembly shouted its consent and hailed the new king, his son. Edward III's experience with Parliament exceeded the success of his grandfather's and for the same reasons. The king was a master of the stage-managed state occasion and, after 1332, a successful young warrior. But rather more than Edward I he succeeded in entirely domesticating his nobility, dominated by his loyal war-captains and close relatives. It was not until his declining years that an aristocratic party emerged which had the power to manipulate Parliament, and that was led by his own youngest son, the duke of Lancaster.

The Parliamentary Century

The English experience of parliament was not the only one that Britain offers. As has been said, many European realms generated representative assemblies in the thirteenth century, and Scotland was no exception. Therefore it would be going too far to see the

Parliament of Scotland as another instance of the diffusion northwards of English political practice, but rather part of a common European experience. Just as in England, the earliest Scottish assemblies were made up of gatherings of magnates, though there is no proven instance of the use of the French word for it until 1290. The first hint of such a body comes in the time of Alexander II, who called an assembly (*colloquium*) in 1235, the same year we catch a first glimpse of parliamentary debate in England. All we know of the Scottish assembly of 1235 is that one part of its proceedings was to produce a binding settlement to a legal dispute between the abbey of Melrose and a local knight.

The 'Parliament of Scotland' (as it was called in 1290), just like the Parliament of England, became prominent when the will of the community of the Scots needed to be expressed, so it played a central part in the succession crisis of 1290–1291. It was probably the English domination of the crisis that led to the word *parliamentum* being applied to the Scottish assembly. The same English influence shaped the institution, for like the English Parliament its Scottish equivalent met more than once a year, though unlike the English Parliament it did not as yet include Commons as such, though knights must have attended as members of the king's council. Lesser landowners, knights and free tenants, were summoned to Scottish parliaments under the Edwardian regime, as in the one Edward I held at Berwick in 1296 when he wanted the community of Scotland to do him homage and put the Balliol years behind it. It is at least significant in this period that Edward felt the need to address (and intimidate) a community of Scotland, though perhaps he would not have rated the Scottish Parliament as any different in standing to the Parliament held in his name in Dublin, which was also subordinate to the Parliament of England. Indeed in 1305 a meeting of Scottish knights at Perth was convened to select ten representatives to join the English Parliament, a first tentative step towards what would have amounted to a British parliament. As with Ireland in 1305, a number of English magnates were also great lords in Scotland, so the second estate at least was briefly connected across all the three British realms.

It is not therefore surprising that, even after the failure of Edward's grand project of conquest, the Parliament of estates of King Robert I (1306–1329), whose father had himself been summoned to the parliaments of Henry III as an English baron, show a marked similarity to those held at Westminster. The necessity for the Bruce to summon a parliament to express the common will of the Scottish people was an inheritance from England, as it certainly did not mirror the French experience. The famous Declaration of Arbroath (1320) could have been enacted only in a parliament to give it the authority that it had in speaking for the whole realm of Scotland. The competence of the Scottish Parliament after the Edwardian crisis mirrored that of England: it functioned as a legal forum and a place to propagate assizes; it was a place where his subjects could petition their king; and it was also a forum for the king to enter a dialogue with the community of his realm, and so magnify his kingship. Most importantly, from at least 1326, the Scottish Parliament complete with borough representatives was asked to grant national taxation. There were of course differences too. The idea of a baron or a bishop requiring an individual summons to a parliament (already an ancient idea in England in the fourteenth century) was not customary in Scotland until after 1428. Another difference was the idea that leading freeholders of the sheriffdoms, landholders who were not magnates or even royal tenants, had a right to attend the Scottish Parliament, which widened its social composition and the strength of its consent to any proposal made by the king. But it also meant the magnates and landowners had a much stronger influence on debate in Scotland than did the urban members of Parliament (MPs), who were not just marginalised; they did not even have seats in the parliamentary sessions until the later fifteenth century. Nonetheless, Scotland as well as England had its parliamentary century after the time of Edward I, a time when the assembly was a vital political theatre and treated as such.

Events consolidated the importance of the Scottish Parliament in the fourteenth century, as the minority of King David II, his exile in France and his period of captivity in England, and the weakness of his two Stewart successors made its voice and support all the more important in a realm besieged by warfare, internal dissent and insecure dynastic succession. Parliaments were the instruments by which aristocratic factions marginalised Robert II (1371–1390) and Robert III (1390–1406). Scottish kings had to learn to manage Parliament, and against his own inclination David II found he had to acquire the skills of manipulating the assembly to his own advantage, skills he might well have acquired from observing the consummate parliamentary artistry of his nemesis, Edward III of England. So we find James I in 1428, in the process of toppling the power of the MacDonald Lord of the Isles, attempting to copy the Plantagenets by imposing shire commissioners who would manage parliamentary selection in the royal interest; but the experiment failed. The fifteenth-century Stewarts, strong and ambitious kings though they were, could not escape the need to enlist the political community of their realm, and in 1445 the young James II found he had little choice but to swear before Parliament that he would do nothing 'touching the common profit of the realm without consent of the three estates'. His son, James III (1460–1488), as a result prefigured the Tudors in developing a theory of his untouchable imperial status as king, an intellectual vent perhaps for the frustrations of dealing with an embedded political community which continually thwarted his executive power.

In the meantime in England a similar gulf of unease gradually opened between the executive power of the king and the community he ruled, which had its means of protesting through Parliament. Parliament was in fact geared to protest, for the Commons' role in Edward III's reign became one of petitioning the king about contentious issues (the petition was called a 'bill') to which the king's magnanimous response was to approve a legislative act in Parliament. The last years of Edward III brought this potential for conflict to a head. The year 1376 saw the king ill, confused and plainly not long for the world; his son, the Black Prince, was on his deathbed; the government was chronically short of money; the French wars were unaffordable; and Parliament was mobilised against the king's younger son, John of Gaunt, on the matter of taxation. Parliament was willing to attack not just the king's ministers, but also his mistress Alice Perrers, who was drawing a couple of thousands of pounds from public revenues for no obvious benefit to anyone apart from herself. It found a new weapon to assert its discontent, a process called impeachment (from the French verb *empescher*: 'to accuse, prosecute').

Impeachment was in fact a development of something that English shires, liberties and hundreds had been doing on a local scale for many decades, since indeed the reform movement of the 1250s: using local juries to 'present' or indict people suspected of corruption. Edward's government had itself encouraged this local process in the 1350s as a way of meeting national discontent about misgovernment and corruption. Now Parliament let loose the process on the king's unpopular ministers to devastating effect. In this so-called Good Parliament the Commons unsurprisingly took the lead under its newly elected Speaker. In session under the high vault and plate tracery of the chapter house of Westminster Abbey, the body discussed and compiled a catalogue of abuses, presenting a grand petition for the magnates to endorse and pass on to the king. It was an emotional, crisis session; the child-heir Richard of Bordeaux, in a mourning suit of black for his recently dead father, the Black Prince, was presented to the Parliament to rally feeling for the sick king, whose threatened councillors were in the meantime trying to convince him that he was in the position in which his father had been in 1327. After eleven weeks of fevered activity the Commons got its way, and secured the dismissal of the most objectionable members of the king's household, though they stopped short of impeaching the chief officers of state. Since it would not vote money, the Parliament was eventually dismissed with no response to its petitions. John of Gaunt chose not to attend the usual farewell dinner.

For Victorian historians of the age of Gladstone, who operated on hindsight, the Good Parliament became a milestone on the way to 1688 and the Glorious Revolution. It was the first intimation of the potential for an insurgent Commons to challenge the executive power of the king. Though it deserves the notice it has got from historians, the crisis of 1376 does not look nowadays so revolutionary, but more of a consequence of the way two Plantagenet kings, Edward I and his grandson, had mobilised and exploited the idea of a community of the realm. Had anything created the crisis, therefore, it was ultimately the decisions the king himself had taken, knowing full well what it was he was doing. If any further demonstration of that was needed, it can be found oddly enough in Wales. The same tensions of military failure and over-taxation which produced political discontent and crisis in England in 1376 destabilised the conquered principality of Wales, where the native aristocracy was marginalised and the Welsh peasantry heavily exploited. The last male representative of the house of Gwynedd, Owain ap Thomas, Llywelyn ap Gruffudd's great-nephew, supported as an exiled prince in Valois France where he became a notable mercenary leader, had been assassinated by an English agent in Poitou in 1378.

Deprived of any leadership, or the vent of Parliament by the fragmented and decentralised government of the principality and the March, the Welsh gentry turned to dissent through fostering treasonous prophecy favouring a native uprising in the face of oppressive taxation both from the king and the duchy of Lancaster, which one contemporary estimated as having squeezed a remarkable £60,000 from the Welsh populace in the reign of Richard II (1377–1399). Problems were particularly severe in the northeast, where the earl of Arundel was a harsh and exploitative landlord. Marcher lords were leading figures in the English political crisis of 1399, and a number of the most prominent of them fell victim to the violent removal of Richard and the usurpation by Henry Bolingbroke. The collapse of marcher leadership and the noble affinities that went along with them ignited a rebellion in 1400 led by a Welsh gentry figure with a direct descent from the princes of Powys, Owain ap Gruffudd Fychan, lord of several manors centred on Glyndyfrydwy in Merionethshire. He was not merely successful in a military campaign which turned the principality and several lordships into a Welsh-ruled enclave between 1402 and 1408, Owain 'Glyndŵr' as self-proclaimed prince of Wales attempted to erect a Welsh state to give his insurgency a more permanent basis. The significance in the context of this chapter is the way that he expressed this through the summoning of a parliament in 1404 at Machynlleth, near Aberystwyth, to give himself the legitimacy of a Welsh prince in dialogue with his own national community. Owain, a former student at the Inns of Court and a soldier with links to the Fitz Alan and Lancaster **affinities**, was expressing Welsh national identity in a political language he had acquired in Plantagenet England. Another indicator of this was his adoption as prince of Wales of the heraldry of the ancient princes of Gwynedd, though his heraldic descent lay elsewhere. The arms of Llywelyn ab Iorwerth (1197–1240) were adopted in the fifteenth century as a symbol which expressed Welsh statehood and legitimacy. In this, Owain was doing no less than had the first Bruce king of Scotland, who had adopted as king the arms borne not just by Alexander III but by the ineffectual John Balliol before him.

 The Late Medieval State

The deposition of Richard II carried out in 1399 echoed uncomfortably closely that of Edward II at the beginning of the century (see pp. 306–7). It demonstrated the continuing and inescapable problem of placing executive power in the hands of a monarch without the personality or skills to work with the representatives of the community of the realm. The crisis was paralleled in Scotland with the marginalisation of Robert III by his close kin and aristocracy, who much preferred to work with his queen in the management of the kingdom. Rather than being deposed, Robert was more considerately allowed to go into internal exile. The fact that both British realms experienced similar and simultaneous problems, in which national parliaments played a key role in legitimising the emasculation of royal power, tells how fundamental was the weakness which lay at the heart of the late medieval British states. It was fundamental because the theology of kingship meant it was difficult, even impossible, to ignore an inept and divisive king who was nonetheless the embodiment of his realm and central to its political system. Unfortunately for such a king, custom and long practice allowed the magnates and their parliamentary allies to claim a right to act for the community in solving the problem, if necessary by force.

The balance of power in the realm in both Scotland and England favoured the magnates in any contest of power, and in both realms the creation of great appanages for cadet princes of the royal house in the fourteenth century gratuitously added to the instability. In Scotland in 1399 the Stewart duke of Albany was king in all but name, wresting full power for himself as 'prince and governor of Scotland', while in England the Plantagenet duke of Lancaster simply seized the throne rather than submit to a capricious and unbalanced king, his cousin, who was brutally done away with the next year. So in England we find an anomaly where the political system could exalt and further the rule and resources of kings such as the young and vigorous Edward III and Henry V, but destabilise and ultimately destroy compromised kings such as Richard II or Henry VI. Long-term hostility between England and France and its costs arguably further destabilised the political community of England through the demands periodically made on it by its king as war-leader and by the failure of his captains. Scotland's luck in the fifteenth century was the distraction the Anglo-French conflict imposed on England and the eventual coming to power of a series of capable and politically alert Stewart kings.

A popular poem of 1413 pithily describes the balance of power within the state as the new century commenced. It stressed the interdependence of the realm's estates: lords, Commons and clergy all of one mind ('all at one assent') under the king but, of them all, the Commons were the 'fayrest flour' of the royal crown. Contemporaries such as the political poet John Gower (died 1408), a man who had lived through the great days of Edward III and the bad times of Richard II, viewed the king as overseeing the realm rather than ruling it, and subject to the consensus of generations as to his rights: 'Do away with law, and what is a king?' It is a perfect echo across a gulf of two centuries of the views of the London chronicler in King John's days: kings who ignore customary restraint are no kings. There is a poignancy in the earnestness of these political sketches. In fact, the last medieval century was no different from its predecessors in the outbreaks caused by the structural instability of the state, which all too often pitted the executive power of an inept king and his coterie against the suspicious political community. It saw in both England and Scotland the unrolling consequences of that instability as it had developed in parallel at either end of the island of Great Britain. Scotland to a large extent was the beneficiary of this, and England was the loser.

The extended political crisis caused by the brutal usurpation of the Lancastrian line by the Plantagenet branch of York in 1460 demonstrated quite how unstable the state had become in England. England's anarchic succession practices and the consequences of military reversals in France had their part to play, but they merely magnified the problem. The fifteenth century is remarkable in that writers recognised the instability of its own political society and produced some notable essays on its inadequacies. It is also remarkable in the way that thinking about the balance of power between king and community was better articulated (see pp. 347–8), and kings began to express their own frustration in aggressive terms. This is best seen in Scotland. James III of Scotland (1460–1488) found his magnates and Parliament too much of a check on his executive authority, so he began his adult reign by stressing his imperial authority within his realm; an act of his in 1469 declared that Scotland was an 'empire' and so implied he had the untouchable prerogative of an emperor (see p. 325). To emphasise the point, his imagery on his coinage adopted the closed imperial crown. Rather like Richard II of England, James ended up losing his life for his revolutionary beliefs, in James's case more respectably (in medieval terms) fleeing from battle at Sauchieburn, a martyr to his subjects' suspicions and discontent with his divisive style of kingship. He too was blackened by posterity, with rather less justification than Richard's posthumous vilification. This was the situation which the incoming Tudor monarchy in England had to find a solution to, and it is no surprise that ultimately it was also the imperial grandeur of their crown that the Tudors chose to appeal to, and so exalt their executive power beyond any interference from the estates.

 POSTSCRIPT

The development and change in the scope and understanding of the state form one of the most gripping themes in the medieval centuries in Britain, the consequences of which we still live with. We find a continuing debate down the centuries ignited by John's abandonment of the compromise his Norman and Angevin predecessors had engineered to make England governable. The community of the realm found a voice in the thirteenth century and was listened to by the executive king, not just in England but by royal mandate in Ireland. It was a development equally in evidence in Scotland, which was responding to similar stresses. This did not necessarily weaken the royal power; in fact it arguably strengthened it even if the reason it came about in England was the shift of the balance of poweer between king and magnates. The story of the state in medieval Britain is one in which a people under a king explored and tested the idea of how government could work, and the forces that shaped it. The *next chapter* deals with a force which stood outside politics and borders, and how a king and people accommodated it, that of faith and Church.

KEY TEXTS

Brown, A. L. *The Governance of Late Medieval England, 1272–1461* (Hodder Arnold, 1989), a comprehensive and clear guide to a complex subject. • Harriss, G. *Shaping the Nation: England 1360–1461* (Oxford University Press, 2005), a more detailed and very authoritative study. • Maddicott, J. R. *The Origins of the English Parliament, 924–1327* (Oxford University Press, 2010); more than just a history of an institution, it is a wide-ranging look at medieval political culture. • *Parliaments and Politics in Scotland, 1235–1560*, ed. K. M. Brown and R. J. Tanner (Edinburgh University Press, 2004), a well-assembled range of studies and unusually successful in the way they come together to give a coherent picture of the English state's northern counterpart.

FURTHER READING

Allen, M. 'The Volume of the English Currency, c. 973–1158', in *Coinage and History in the North Sea World, c. AD 500–1200: Essays in Honour of Marion Archibald*, ed. B. Cook and G. Williams (Brill, 2006), 487–523. • Carpenter, C. 'War, Government and Governance in England in the Later Middle Ages', in *The Fifteenth Century*, VII, ed. L. Clark (Boydell, 2007), 1–22. • Carpenter, C. *The Wars of the Roses: Politics and the Constitution, c. 1437–1509* (Cambridge University Press, 1997). • Carpenter, D. A. 'English Peasants in Politics, 1258–1267', *Past & Present*, 136 (1992), 1–42. • Davies, R. R. *The Age of Conquest: Wales, 1063–1415* (Oxford University Press, 1987). • Duncan, A. A. M. 'The Early Parliaments of Scotland', *Scottish Historical Review*, 45 (1966), 35–58. • Goodare, J. 'The Estates in the Scottish Parliament, 1286–1707', *Parliamentary History*, 15 (1996), 11–32. • Grant, A. *Independence and Nationhood: Scotland, 1306–1469* (Edward Arnold, 1984). • Green, J. A. 'The Last Century of Danegeld', *English Historical Review*, 96 (1981), 241–58. • Harriss, G. 'Political Society and the Growth of Government in Late Medieval England', *Past & Present*, 138 (1993), 28–57. • Holt, J. C. *Magna Carta* (2nd edn, Cambridge University Press, 1992). • Holt, J. C. 'The Prehistory of Parliament', in *The English Parliament in the Middle Ages*, ed. R. G. Davies and J. H. Denton (Manchester University Press, 1981), 1–28. • Maddicott, J. R. 'Magna Carta and the Local Community, 1215–1259', *Past & Present*, 102 (1984), 25–65. • Mitchell, S. N. *Studies in Taxation Under John and Henry III* (Yale University Press, 1914). • Molyneaux, G. *The Formation of the English Kingdom in the Tenth Century* (Oxford University Press, 2015). • Pryce, H. 'Owain Gwynedd and Louis VII: The Franco-Welsh Diplomacy of the First Prince of Wales', *Welsh History Review*, 19 (1998), 1–28. • Reynolds, S. *Kingdoms and Communities in Western Europe, 900–1300* (Oxford University Press, 1984). • Richardson, H. G. and G. O. Sayles. *The Irish Parliament in the Middle Ages* (University of Pennsylvania Press, 1952). • Stacey, R. 'Parliamentary Negotiation and the Expulsion of the Jews from England', in *Thirteenth-Century England*, VI, ed. M. Prestwich (Boydell, 1997), 77–101. • Stacey, R. *Politics, Policy and Finance Under Henry III, 1216–1245* (Oxford University Press, 1987). • Stephenson, D. *The Governance of Gwynedd* (University of Wales Press, 1984). • Stringer, K. J. 'States, Liberties and Communities in Medieval Britain and Ireland, c. 1100–1400', in *Liberties and Identities in* the *Medieval British Isles*, ed. M. Prestwich (Boydell, 2008), 5–36. • Taylor, A. *The Shape of the State in Medieval Scotland, 1124–1290* (Oxford University Press, 2016). • Vincent, N. 'Why 1199? Bureaucracy and Enrolment Under John and His Contemporaries', in *English Government in the Thirteenth Century*, ed. A. Jobson (Boydell, 2004), 17–48. • Walker, D. M. *A Legal History of Scotland*, I (T. & T. Clark, 1988), II (T. & T. Clark, 1990). • Watt, J. A. 'Dublin in the Thirteenth Century: The Making of a Colonial Capital City', in *Thirteenth-Century England*, I, ed. P. R. Coss and S. D. Lloyd (Woodbridge, 1986), 150–7. • Watts, J. 'Looking for the State in Later Medieval England', in *Heraldry, Pageantry and Social Display in Medieval England*, ed. P. R. Coss and M. Keen (Boydell, 2002), 243–67.

NOTES

1. Regesta Regum Scottorum, 2, *Acts of William I*, ed. G. W. S. Barrow (Edinburgh University Press, 1971), no. 39.
2. C. M. Turnbull, 'Cyril Northcote Parkinson', *Oxford Dictionary of National Biography*.
3. *Lost Letters of Medieval Life: English Society, 1200–1250*, ed. and trans. M. Carlin and D. Crouch (University of Pennsylvania Press, 2013), 127.

6 Establishing the Church

OVERVIEW

Medieval Europe was in many ways a more unified place in cultural and spiritual terms than it is today, at least for the lettered elite. In part this was because of its inheritance of literature and philosophy from Rome, which was as living and vital in Poland and Spain as it was in Scotland. The growing European influence of French culture and aristocratic ideals also played a part by the twelfth century. But, even more so, 'Christendom' was united in a shared faith and devotion, and with the rise of the power and influence of the papacy in the eleventh and twelfth centuries this faith was overlaid into a demand for obedience in its expression to Rome, which became a political as much as a moral and religious force, and one to which even emperors had to listen. Britain and its rulers found themselves accommodating structures and demands from outside, and a supranational power with ambitions of its own. The challenge for the Church, on the other hand, was how to educate and discipline its clergy and fulfil its pastoral duty to its people, an enormous task in the diverse realms of Britain, let alone in a Christendom that spanned Europe.

An Island of Minsters

Eleventh-century Britain was an ancient Christian land, with a rich heritage of saints and spirituality. The English owed their very name as a people and nation to a seventh-century decision at Rome that the Germanic people it was dealing with in Britain were the Angles (*Englysc*), not the more dominant Saxons. In 1000, some of what was characteristic of the Church in later medieval England was already established. The two archbishoprics of Canterbury and York divided their authority at the river Trent, though they had not yet decided their tussle for supremacy, and their claims over the British Isles beyond the kingdom of England remained as yet undefined. As England was defined by its shires, so the English Church was defined by its territorial **dioceses**, most of whose boundaries were coterminous with those of shires. Great Benedictine monasteries were already then important in the South and Midlands, though none was yet to be found in the North. Three of the great cathedrals, Canterbury, Winchester and Worcester, were staffed by monks (something all but peculiar to England), but the rest by communities of priests under their bishops. Elsewhere, the picture was not so familiar to the modern eye. England, let alone Wales and Scotland, was not yet a patchwork of village-based parishes, each with their church and priest, which remains a defining image of the English countryside even in these latter days. The religious structure of the eleventh century was, as it long had been, based on the minster.

A 'minster' (Lat. *monasterium*) is a word which has become attached to the dominant form of religious organisation in English Britain before 1150, an area which included Lothian and Fife. It is shorthand for what were actually quite diverse institutions, but which all had this in common: they were large central churches serving many dependent settlements, run by communities of clergy. They were funded by the profits from the minster's own estates and from church taxes (often called 'church-*scot*', though there were a lot of other local names for it). Many of the minsters were run as family enterprises, father succeeding son as the minster head; others were in the gift of bishops, earls and kings; some seem to have been quasi-monastic institutions following a rule of sorts; others resembled more formal communities of cathedral canons. Some minsters were ancient, others more recently formed from subdividing older units (what are called 'secondary minsters'). Quite a number of them, such as Marton in Warwickshire or Howden in Yorkshire, served an area coterminous with an administrative hundred which had once perhaps been the ancient estate it was originally built to serve; that at Stow in Lindsey was the central church of a lost Anglian sub-kingdom (see Fig. 6.1). This pattern of church organisation extended into Anglian Lothian, where a typical great Northumbrian minster could be found at Coldingham, north of Berwick. Further north and west were ancient and wealthy churches at Whithorn, Culross, Glasgow, Hoddom, Melrose and Abercorn, founded under the rule of Pictish, British or Anglian kings.

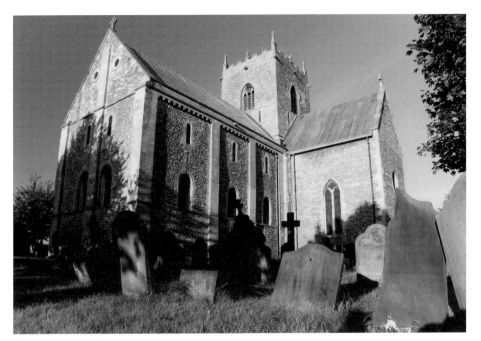

Fig. 6.1 Minster at Stow, Lincolnshire. The ancient and wealthy minster church at Stow, the chief church of the province of Lindsey, still retains the impressive stone nave, lower tower and crossing as rebuilt by Bishop Eadnoth II of Dorchester (1034–1050) in the 1040s with the support of Leofric, earl of Mercia. Work was still going on at Stow at the time of the Norman Conquest.

Curiously, much the same form of organisation can be found parts of Britain where English kings never ruled, notably in Wales. Here churches called *clasau* were dominant in the eleventh century, where communities of priests (*claswyr*) served churches on which depended large territories, not hundreds this time, but large multiple estates or sub-kingdoms. Well-documented South-East Wales in the eleventh century shows a minster pattern similar to England: some *clas* churches were ancient and distinguished, like Llancarfan, once the seventh-century monastery of St Cadoc, or St Gwynllyw (modern Newport), mother church of the region of Wentloog. Even within Wentloog there were other significant churches. That at Bassaleg was so ancient it gets its name from the fact it was once called a *basilica* by its people, in days when Latin was still a spoken language in Britain. The rather less ancient *clas* at Llandaff, with its stone church and ecclesiastical precinct, was very much a family enterprise, run by a group of interrelated Anglo-Welsh priestly clans. A comparison with what happened to British Cornwall indicates that parts at least of Wales were experiencing ecclesiastical change in the tenth and eleventh centuries, where many of the original minsters – each with its own particular saint and protector – were sinking in importance as a few amongst them increased in influence. Llandaff, for instance, was originally a minor church, but it was emerging into greater importance because the local bishop of Glamorgan decided to settle there during the course of the century and made it the centre of a regional **cult** of St Teilo, the patron of his ancient diocese. Much the same can be found at the eleventh-century community of Mynwy (St Davids) in Pembrokeshire, once the monastery of the great David, where an Anglo-Welsh community of *claswyr* had become the home of the bishop of Deheubarth.

We know something of the extent of the intellectual activity going on at Mynwy from the survival of its poetry, hagiography and historical writing. The community at Llandaff was perhaps less distinguished, but in the 1120s it still possessed an archive of episcopal and ecclesiastical documents which went back to times when Herefordshire was a British-ruled province. The difference between Wales and England lay in the lack of any regular episcopal administrative structure and the often unhappy state of relations between churches and the local kings. The Welsh churches, since the time of Alfred the Great's biographer, Bishop Asser (a Welsh favourite on whom the king had bestowed a number of English minsters), had looked to England for friendly support, which must have been what brought Welsh ideas of church organisation into line with those beyond Offa's Dyke. The eleventh-century community of Llandaff apparently made a practice of sending its youngsters to study at Worcester. In default of royal support, the Welsh bishops looked to powerful episcopal cults to intimidate their enemies: as a result the eleventh-century bishop of Glamorgan was often called 'the bishop of St Teilo' and the bishop of Deheubarth, the 'bishop of St David'.

A similar situation to Wales is found in Brittonic Galloway, dominated by the ancient church and community of St Ninian at Whithorn which was the base for a bishop of the Galwegians, and which looked to Northumbria and York for support and leadership in the eleventh century. Elsewhere in Scotland the church was organised differently. The Scots developed religious communities reacting to the inspiration of the Irish Church. In this case these were quasi-monastic communities in a tradition called *Céli Dé* (Anglicised as 'Culdees') which spread and developed across Alba in the ninth century, offering a simpler form of religious life than that of powerful religious communities like Armagh or Iona, with widespread authority and royal connections. An exception was the house of *Céli Dé* established at St Andrews in Fife which had close connections with the Scottish royal house and like Whithorn became the seat of a bishop. Most *Céli Dé* lived in diverse and modest houses, some living to a rule, some being communities of priests who recognised a priestly obligation of celibacy and some who tolerated marriage. What made them different from the major monasteries such as Whithorn and Iona was their lack of territorial attachment to kingdoms and sub-kingdoms. Their responsibility was confined to their own community. In their diversity they resembled more the *clasau* of Wales and indeed shared their fate, many of them being converted after 1100 to small regular monastic priories of monks or canons.

Church organisation across Britain in 1000 therefore had a British dimension and a common character, focused on the idea of the central minster church. This can ultimately be traced back to the Irish-influenced missionary Church in England, Pictland and Alba in the seventh century, as it penetrated the island of Great Britain from its base in the community of Iona in the Inner Hebrides and Iona's offshoot of Lindisfarne on the Northumbrian coast. Minsters in England were initially district mission churches under royal protection and based in royal townships. In turn they were to offer the organisational model for the emerging dioceses of the eighth century (see Map 6.1). The evolving Church in the Gaelic and Anglian kingdoms that were to become Scotland drew on the same model, each in their way. It even appears to have influenced the political chaos that was Wales. The Welsh Church assumed an English shape despite having its own unbroken Christian tradition since the Late Empire, as Welsh clergy looked to England for support and inspiration in default of any native royal protection.

The Managerial Revolution in the Church

As well as being a land of minsters, Britain was also in 1000 a land of bishops. The fall of Rome did not eliminate these former imperial officials in the lost British provinces. Bishops may even have survived in the corners of emerging Anglo-Saxon England which still remained under British rule. They certainly lived on in Cornwall, Wales and Ireland, though the post-Roman British bishop of the Celtic lands had little in common with his imperial predecessor other than his command of Latin and his sacramental office. By 1000 the English archbishops and bishops had reinvented their former role as officials linked to the state. They were now appointed by the king, gathered in councils under his presidency and ruled dioceses whose limits were set by him. The English episcopate of Edward the Confessor was cosmopolitan: it included bishops from Lotharingia in the Empire and from northern France. As in continental Europe, some English bishops had the superior rank of archbishop and metropolitan and ruled over provinces, at Canterbury in the south and York in the north, so in its upper ranks the English Church was very much part of the European Latin mainstream even before the Conquest.

The bishops of Scotland and Wales were not so conventional. Welsh bishops before 1100 had dioceses but their authority was defined by the prestige of the cults of episcopal saints focused on their chief minsters (*clasau*) as much as the kingdoms where they claimed primacy. They lived at episcopal communities or monasteries but had no cathedrals as such. They had no archbishop as their superior other than ill-defined claims by Canterbury and York to be supreme over them, bolstered by the tendency of the Welsh clergy to look to their English colleagues for schooling and support. Their appointments arose out of the communities of which they were part, rather than by any royal fiat. Scotland likewise had in 1100 no national church as a doppelganger to

Map 6.1 Dioceses and Provinces of Britain

the imperial state, no archbishop and no urban cathedrals. Indeed some of its dioceses, such as Whithorn, were not dissimilar to those of the Welsh: episcopal communities tied into a relationship with the English to the south. The Isles by contrast depended on the Norwegian see of Nidaros (modern Trondheim) across the North Sea.

By 1200 much of this ancient structure had disappeared, and the Latin pattern of dioceses in a close relationship with the state had been established throughout Britain. Circumstances and papal ambition, as much as the policy of kings, made it inevitable that it should. A good instance is the policy of King David of Scotland (1124–1153). In pursuit of his aim to erect Scotland as a state on the Anglo-French model he imposed an episcopal structure from the top down, beginning at Glasgow and extending it as his influence spread even into the far north, with sees and cathedrals established in Aberdeen, Moray (Elgin), Ross (Fortrose) and Caithness (Dornoch). The eccentric community King David found at the church of Brechin (a lay 'abbot', a priestly community of *Céli Dé* in an informal association with a bishop) seamlessly became a regular cathedral town with bishop, chapter and canon prebendaries by the time of Alexander II. But in Wales it was the bishops themselves who Latinised their status, since they had no one else to do it for them. The enterprising Bishop Gwrgan (Urban) of Glamorgan (1107–1134) enthusiastically placed himself in submission to Canterbury, built a cathedral, appointed canons and archdeacons, and constructed a historical dossier proving the antiquity of his diocese under the patronage of St Peter, sending a copy to Rome to make sure his standing was accepted at the Holy See and following it there in person to argue territorial claims against his fellow bishops.

The progressive concentration of population on villages and hamlets in England from the ninth century onwards had a major impact on minsters, whose communities saw new settlements appear or old ones expand within their jurisdictions. These rising villages had lords and tenants who sometimes had the ambition to have their own church and priest within their manors. If the minster had a secular patron who also wanted to redistribute the community's resources then it could not resist such pressure. By the eleventh century, the ecclesiastical landscape was changing under all sorts of influences. Some minster communities fought back and attempted to impose themselves on the churches intruding themselves within their broad jurisdictions. Endless compromises had to be made about church revenues: the scot, mortuary dues and burial fees, which had previously been the minster's prerogative. This was occurring as much in Wales as in England. Bishop Herman of Ramsbury, while in Rome in 1050, reflected on the ecclesiastical building boom going on in his day in rural England to the pope. The clerical biographer of King Gruffudd ap Cynan of Gwynedd (died 1137) likewise rhapsodised on the churches rising in the new villages of his prosperous realm in the 1120s and the proprietary chapels the king himself had raised in his residences. Gruffudd, however, continued to honour and support the major *clas* churches of Gwynedd: Holyhead, Penmon, Llanarmon, Dinerth and others, not to mention the episcopal community at Bangor, where he was buried. Along with this multiplication of churches in England and Wales went a rise in demand for ordained priests to offer mass on the increasing number of altars, a demand that new schools were beginning to cater for.

The progressive localisation of the Church's pastoral structure therefore had very little to do with the arrival of a new Norman order in England in 1066. Perhaps the principal contribution of the new French aristocracy was an enthusiasm for regular monasticism that its English predecessors had not had. Many of the old minsters were appropriated after the Conquest to French monastic communities, as was the ancient Warwickshire minster of Wootton Wawen. It became the site and endowment of a priory to the Norman Benedictine abbey of Conches soon after coming into the hands of the Tosny family, patrons of the mother house. The rising number of **Augustinian** and **Cluniac** monastic communities in Henry I's reign did well out of minsters, which were made instantly more respectable by conversion to regular houses. The minster of Daventry in Northamptonshire was one of dozens which became a house of monks, where before 1107 it was a minster community of four priests, called secular canons. Likewise the prosperous Yorkshire minster of Bridlington was converted to a major Augustinian priory by its incoming French lord, Walter de Gant, around 1114, its canons given the option of retirement to country churches or entry into the new monastic community.

However, the new French aristocracy was not automatically hostile to native minsters. Normandy itself had parallels in major collegiate churches of secular canons living a common life by a rule, such as those at Aumale (Seine-Maritime) and Mortain (Manche). In England, wealthy urban minsters at Warwick, Hastings and Leicester and in London at St Martin-le-Grand, found noble patrons who did not turn them into monasteries but regularised them in a different way, promoting them as collegiate chapter churches of canons under a dean, rather like miniature cathedral churches, each with its own constitution and prebend. The energy and investment behind this process, and the source of it in manorial lords, can be found in the eleventh-century evidence of Domesday Book and even more evocatively in the sundial inscriptions over the new Romanesque doorways of Northern churches, such as that of St Mary le Wigford (Lincolnshire): 'Eirtig had me made and endowed with possessions to the glory of Christ and St Mary.'[1] Curiously, in these monuments names of English landowners feature more than Norman ones even in post-Conquest rebuilt churches. The process was particularly intense in cities such as Winchester and London, where patricians were as likely to raise proprietorial churches in the precincts of their urban hall-complexes as were rural landlords in their villages. By 1200, London had 110 stone-built parish churches, a number of them, such as St Mary Aldermanbury, originally being domestic chapels. It was the landowner too who financed the priests who served these parish churches, setting aside tithes (tenths) of agricultural produce for their support and offering also some land the priest himself could work or rent out.

The fragmentation of local church organisation and the rise in clergy numbers were a major disciplinary challenge to any bishop in the eleventh century. But even before the Conquest there are signs that English and Welsh bishops were rising to it, even seizing it as an opportunity. With the inability of minster communities to manage the increasing clerical population, bishops had to find ways to monitor subordinates who were dependent not on them or on minsters but on the manorial lords who had given them their livings. One response was to get managerial. At least once a year, in Holy Week (the week before Easter), priests had to gather before their bishop to receive the consecrated oil or 'chrism' that was a feature of several church sacraments. This occasion could be turned into a synod, where the bishop could issue regulations, give consciousness-raising addresses and even preside over tribunals. The admirably efficient Bishop Wulfstan of Worcester (1062–1095) was apparently doing something like this before the Conquest. Another response was to increase control by erecting a bureaucratic hierarchy for the diocese. In both Wales and England some bishops had already appointed senior clergy as 'archdeacons' before the Normans appeared. Their only function would have been to monitor discipline, as archdeacons did not possess the high liturgical functions of a bishop; some were probably not even priests. The office of archdeacon had not appeared much earlier in Normandy than it had in Britain, so archdeacons were not a consequence of Conquest, simply a response generated within Latin Christianity to a common problem. But the new Norman hierarchy was keen to systematise what they found in England. The Council of Windsor in 1070 declared, a little ambiguously for our purposes, 'that bishops ought to institute archdeacons and other ministers in holy orders into their churches'.[2] But its pronouncement hints at an enforced standardisation of the organisation we already find appearing in ecclesiastical structures. All the eight archdeaconries of the huge diocese of Lincoln were functioning by 1090, perhaps in a response to the enormous organisational problems faced by its bishop, who administered a diocese stretching from the Humber to the Thames.

By the early twelfth century, another level of managerial responsibility appears with the office of dean, usually called by historians the 'rural dean' to distinguish him from the dean of a chapter church. Where dioceses in 1000 had been a network of varying minster jurisdictions, they were subdivided by 1150 into archdeaconries and deaneries, with officers having direct responsibility for the conduct of all clergy within their bounds, and an obligation to discover if candidates for livings were suitably qualified. The organisational picture was not quite as simple as this brief sketch may sound. Some groups of churches claimed immunity from the local bishop, as the churches of the bishop and chapter of Durham in Yorkshire did from their archbishop. The archbishop of York's church of Hexham in Northumberland claimed the same immunity from the authority of the bishop of Durham. Complicated ways sometimes had to be found round these anomalies, but the end result was still that there was always someone responsible for the conduct of parish priests and their underlings. Archdeacons and deans were not only responsible for the incumbents of parish churches; they also monitored the numerous ecclesiastical proletariat called 'chaplains', priests who found a living in the households of those same incumbents, who paid them salaries and fees for their services. Any large parish in Britain was likely to have anything from two to half a dozen of these junior clergy, even by 1200.

Moral Reform

As power accumulated in the hands of archdeacons so did the potential for corruption. By the mid twelfth century, archdeacons were carrying out tours of inspection on their archdeaconries on the lookout for evidence of sexual transgressions and other irregularities by their clergy. When they found it, some were reputed to have taken bribes to look the other way. Others were alleged to have invented groundless charges by which to blackmail the innocent. King Henry II of England, in his sardonic way, observed around 1158 that archdeacons and deans were extorting more money from his subjects with false allegations of adultery than the king himself was able to extract from them. There were other complaints by 1200 that archdeacons imposed themselves on their clergy by demanding expensive hospitality for themselves and their numerous households of clerks and servants as they toured the localities, enjoying a luxurious lifestyle at the expense of their inferiors.

It is curious, though very human, that a concern for probity and right conduct could be turned into a basis for corruption, but so it was. The roots of this problem are found in the circles of Pope Leo IX (1049–1052) where an agenda was formulated for the moral reform of the clergy. The original idea had been to impose celibacy on the clergy, but the agenda of reformers had increasingly included the sexual behaviour of the laity as well. Much of the effort of the reform movement was focused on the regulation of sex through monogamous marriage. In England, the Church was well on its way to imposing its view of marriage, and its control over marital litigation, by the second half of the twelfth century. Sex outside marriage was condemned as adultery, a sin identified with the mortal sin of 'luxury' (sensual self-indulgence). It was also an offence that was actionable in church courts. Originally the word 'adultery' covered all sorts of sexual misconduct but, in the legalistic world of the twelfth century, adultery came to be defined more narrowly by canon lawyers, and by 1190 it meant sex between a single or married person and someone else's spouse of the opposite sex (though there was a misogynistic argument at the time that in fact only women could be adulterers).

This reforming agenda was at odds with the long-established way of life in all parts of Britain where priests took wives and had children, to produce the sort of respectable clerical dynasties which controlled some of the minsters of England and Wales, and which also provided any number of bishops and abbots. So St Ailred, abbot of

Rievaulx (died 1167), was a son of Eilaf, the head of the wealthy minster of Hexham (Northumberland), the offspring of a senior English clerical dynasty associated with the communities of Hexham and St Cuthbert since the tenth century. Two consecutive archbishops of Canterbury, Lanfranc (1070–1089) and Anselm (1093–1109) – both monks – presided at church councils which condemned clerical marriage in increasingly intolerant pronouncements. Nonetheless, Richard de Beaumais (1152–1162), bishop of London, was one of no fewer than six sons and nephews placed in the chapter of St Paul's Cathedral as canons, dignitaries and archdeacons by his namesake and predecessor. How could an archdeacon like Henry of Huntingdon (died *c.* 1157) prosecute with a straight face his clergy for fornication and nicolaitism, when he had inherited his archdeaconry from his father (who bore the highly suitable name of Nicholas)? Yet he too went about producing a son and grandsons who followed him in his family property at Little Stukeley (Cambridgeshire). But, nonetheless, clergy were imperilling their prospects in the Church by taking a wife in the twelfth century. The historian Roger of Howden (died 1202) followed his father Robert as head of the family's Yorkshire minster around 1171, but not before he had to use the favour of the archbishop of York to override a prohibition on his institution by Pope Alexander III. Likewise he had to withstand the peevish mockery of celibate clerical colleagues, such as Gerald of Wales (died *c.* 1225), who told scurrilous tales of Roger's wife's humiliation, glued by her buttocks to a shrine in his Yorkshire living by an act of divine disapproval of her husband's way of life.

Witch-hunts of clergy in sexual relationships and even of lay people indulging in adulterous liaisons were well under way by the reign of Henry III (1216–1272). In 1240 the statutes of the diocese of Worcester ordered archdeacons and their 'officials' (legal deputies) to identify clergy who cohabited with women. The penalty for those who were detected in liaisons would have been deprivation and excommunication until proper penance had been performed. A different sort of punishment was the possibility of blackmail both by neighbours and by corrupt church officials. Bishop Robert Grosseteste of Lincoln (1235–1253) was nonetheless eager to extend the same inquisitorial methods employed against clergy to the laity of his diocese, and commissioned friars to actively seek out adulterers and apprehend them. Matthew Paris tells us that a backlash amongst the aristocracy led to the king ordering Bishop Robert to call off his unauthorised inquisition, the only time such an extreme moral intervention was to happen in medieval England. Sexual adventuring by married men was a risky business, not least because an offended husband was not punished if he caught and mutilated any incautious lothario caught *in flagrante delicto*. In 1289 the official of the archdeacon of Ely wrote to the sacrist of the abbey of Bury St Edmunds, notifying him that an adulterous couple were causing scandal in his jurisdiction. The surviving letter requests the sacrist to have the pair publicly denounced as excommunicates who were to be shunned by their neighbours until they had been absolved by the Church.

Religious Life: The Mass, Office and Confession

Britain fully shared in the extraordinarily rich liturgical and spiritual life that developed and flourished across eleventh- and twelfth-century Northern Europe. Not one part of medieval Britain escaped it. The British Isles were united with the rest of Christendom in the devotion of the mass, the central Christian act of witness (see Fig. 6.2). The early thirteenth-century layman was expected to take communion once a year, though some aspired to receive it weekly. Partaking of communion was one thing, however, and attendance at mass was another. It was daily for some, possibly for many. William of Malmesbury around 1126 makes some comment on the deficiencies of pre-Conquest English religious practice as compared with the exemplary behaviour of the contemporary Norman court. He condemned the pre-Conquest English nobles who failed to go to church in the morning 'in the Christian way' but who would impatiently and inattentively hear a hastily garbled mass in their chambers. William the Conqueror by contrast devoutly attended daily mass and for good measure heard mattins and vespers sung by his chapel clerks. Even as he criticised the English, William of Malmesbury nonetheless betrays that he thought the nobility before 1066 at least viewed hearing a daily mass as a duty. Daily attendance at mass was probably in reality more a thing to be desired than practised. It was only in towns where there were many altars or where households contained priests as chaplains that attendance at a daily mass was likely to occur. But the wealthy aspired to it at least. Twelfth- and thirteenth-century literature is full of instances of its aristocratic characters rising at dawn to go first to hear mattins and the mass before they sought the 'break-fast' table.

A particularly popular use of the mass was as a means of intercession for the dead. Aristocrats had the resources with which to finance the multiplication of masses for their departed family and friends when it became a noble practice to do so. When magnates had begun the ambitious foundation of Benedictine monasteries in Normandy in the 1020s, one of the principal purposes of such abbeys and priories was to pray for the souls of the founder and his kin and offer a magnificent *anniversarium* mass on the days of death of the members of the lineage. The second wave of foundations which occurred in the first half of the twelfth century which brought new Cistercian, Augustinian and **Premonstratensian** monasteries multiplied the opportunities for masses of intercession. In time, people found ways of making such masses more their own. The first moves towards detaching them from cloisters and commissioning new institutional altars in large churches occurred late in Henry II's reign, when we begin to find masses for the souls of dead aristocrats and members of the royal family being endowed at particular altars in chapter churches. John of Mortain, the future king, gave away the collegiate church at Bakewell (Derbyshire) to Lichfield Cathedral in 1192 in return for a daily mass for his health when alive and for his soul's salvation when he was dead. The concern to endow appropriate daily masses had spilled down the social

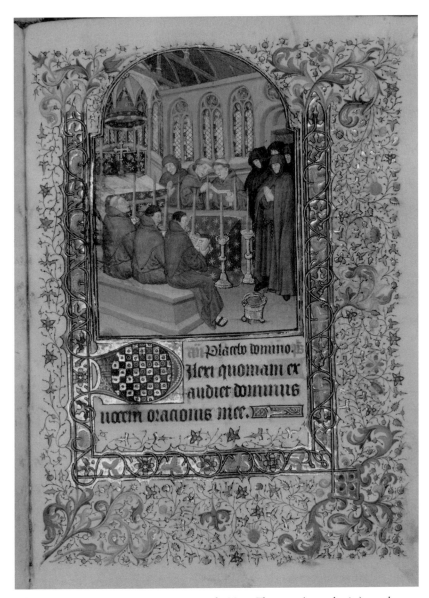

Fig. 6.2 Fifteenth-Century Illumination of a Mass. The mass (or eucharist) was the central Christian rite, celebrated daily in most churches. It was also celebrated on a multitude of occasions, notably marriages and funerals. This illumination depicts a funeral mass. Friars of the three main orders are present to assist, holding tall candles (torches), and lay mourners are swathed in black cloaks. A brass bucket holds holy water with which to sprinkle the body, laid out under a pall in front of the high altar.

scale by the time John himself was king. It is not long after 1200 that we find knights and urban merchants endowing chapels and altars, where priests would say perpetual daily masses for their souls and those of their family and friends. Henry III's reign saw a rapid multiplication of examples of this privatisation of the mass. The definitive later medieval practice of the foundation of perpetual chantries was well under way in the second half of the thirteenth century.

There was a range of devotional practices available to lay people apart from those centred around the mass. The first was an engagement with the daily office, the daily round of prayer laid down for clergy and marked by the canonical hours of the day (prime, tierce, sext and nones, vespers and compline). The daily office was not supposed to be for the laity, but nonetheless some of the more well-heeled laity became caught up with it as a vehicle for the expression of their own devotions. In the 1220s the 'Ancrene Riwle', a rule of life intended for a group of aristocratic English ladies living in an informal religious community under guidance, asked the women it addressed to undertake to follow the daily office said for them by a clerk, though they were not supposed to join him in saying it. Did this enthusiasm have a starting point? There has been a temptation to see lay spirituality taking a leap forward following the publication of the canons of the Fourth Lateran Council (1215), principally because they are the first source which has much to say on the subject of lay devotion. But the idea that devout lay aristocrats followed the clerical daily office can plausibly be traced back well before 1200. The possession of a psalter (the book of psalms) is one indicator, for the recitation of a course of the psalms was one of the principal components of the canonical hours. Earl Robert II of Leicester (died 1168) might by that indication have had some aspirations to follow the hours of the office. He and his wife left their own personal copies of the psalter to Leicester Abbey at their deaths; the psalters were still to be seen in the abbey's library in the fifteenth century. Since Earl Robert is known to have been literate and to have employed a large clerical household, he would certainly have been capable of following the hours in his own chapel.

This level of piety was more widespread in Britain than England. When talking of that exemplary queen, Margaret of Scotland, William of Malmesbury said she would hear triple mattins in Lent – hearing offices of the Trinity, the Cross and the Virgin, and reciting the psalter. We have the account of the devotions of her son, David, given by his friend and sometime household officer, Ailred of Rievaulx, who says that the king, on his deathbed, followed the recitation of the office being said by the clerks of his chapel. He restrained them if they went too fast, so that he could hear every word and respond appropriately to each versicle. The survival of books of hours from the 1240s onwards is testimony to the fact that many amongst the laity were by then pursuing a regime of prayer in their homes, and reading in Latin a stripped-down version of the daily office. Around sixty such books survive from before 1300, which is no mean total in view of the accidents of survival. Books of hours encouraged meditation on the office of the dead and the penitential psalms, and they particularly focus on the figure, the joys and the sufferings of the Virgin Mary.

It is more than likely that the users of such books were undergoing regular 'auricular' confession (that is, individual and spoken confession into a priest's ear, rather than the general confession of sins made by the congregation in every mass), which was a feature of lay spirituality throughout our period. The ladies to whom the 'Ancrene Riwle' was addressed were supposed to undergo directed confession 'each week'. This was not itself new. A concern for private confession and subsequent penance can be glimpsed as far back as the time of Henry I of England, and it is unlikely to have been a new feature even then, either in England or in France. Before 1095 Queen Margaret of Scotland made frequent confession to the senior cleric who wrote her *Life*, as he tells us. The Conqueror's half-brother, Count Robert of Mortain, apparently confessed to Vitalis of Savigny in the 1080s, and on one occasion stripped to receive a flogging from the abbot as a token of his penance for sins that otherwise could not be amended. The practice of confession was certainly a prevalent form of spiritual discipline and education in the court of Henry I, with Queen Matilda (died 1118) taking the prior of her Augustinian foundation of Holy Trinity, Aldgate, as her 'father for confessions'. He is said to have turned her towards the relief of the poor as part of her penitential regime. Her wider influence on the court can be seen in the sheriff Gilbert of Surrey, who we are told was a particular friend and follower of hers, and was likewise devoted to confession and poor relief.

Henry I himself undertook some sort of confessional regime. Robert of Torigny tells us that Aethelwold, Augustinian prior of Nostell and bishop of Carlisle in 1133, was 'the man to whom he was accustomed to confess his sins'. Carlisle was a diocese offered around 1186 to a later royal confessor, Paulinus of Leeds, confessor of Henry II. Peter of Blois, archdeacon of Wells and later London, who may have been another confessor of King Henry II, was the author of more than one work on confession and penance. The sudden appearance of such works at the end of the twelfth century tells us that the practice of confessing publicly before a bishop or senior priest on Maundy Thursday, the Thursday before Easter, in a crowd of others (as we know happened in Norwich in the 1140s) was not enough now for many people. They wanted individual moral counsel and well-instructed confessors, the personal trainers of the twelfth century. Alan of Lille's handbook on penance has some positive ideas about the spiritual thirst which laymen might suffer and the ways it might be satisfied. Alan had encountered lay people whose spiritual striving included not just the giving of alms (pressed on the laity by other writers), but fasting, prayerful vigil through the night, disciplined meditative prayer and biblical instruction.

Lay Piety

Simon de Montfort, earl of Leicester (died 1265), is perhaps the thirteenth-century lay person whose spirituality we can approach most nearly, though it is undeniable he had very much an individual outlook on devotional practice that did not necessarily match those of his peers and contemporaries. He was literate in Latin and the vernacular and capable of reading widely in theology and works of devotion. His devotional practices would have been developed in his youth in France, in a family closely engaged with crusade and the defence of orthodoxy from Cathar heresy. He did not arrive in England until he was in his twenties. Yet he was in sympathy with religious expressions he found in England, and struck up close friendships with English churchmen, notably Walter de Cantilupe, bishop of Worcester (1237–1266), and the pair of West Country friends, Robert Grosseteste and Adam Marsh, a Franciscan friar. It was these two whom Simon made co-supervisors of his will in 1259 in so far as it concerned its dispositions for the poor on his estates, 'and particularly the *gaaneours* whose goods I have many times acquired, and whom I suspect that in some people's eyes I have wronged'.[3] Montfort was deeply involved in the debt market, and it clearly preyed on his conscience. Simon's acute introspection on the subject of his sins and obligation to the poor was due to a confessional regime, as is testified by his possession of a copy of a confessional hand-book, which his son passed on to a **Dominican** convent near Paris. Later tradition at St Albans and amongst the Franciscans had it that Montfort undertook mortification of his body, wore a hairshirt, and always appeared in plain and unassuming dress as a sign of his humility before God.

Lay society was avid to possess relics of sanctity. The aristocracy was distinguished by the greater number it could afford, and the greater range of its ability to find them. This was as true of the pre-Conquest period as after 1066. The collegiate church of Waltham, founded by Earl Harold of Wessex, received a prodigious collection of relics from its patron, many apparently deriving from Rome, Flanders and the Rhineland. Earl Leofwin of Mercia seems to have been another pre-Conquest contributor. Norman aristocrats were also collectors. Some hint as to the richness of English relic collections in the twelfth century is given by the list of 242 relics accumulated by Reading Abbey between 1121 and 1193, many deriving from as far afield as Rome and Constantinople, which had travelled to England in some cases well before the abbey's foundation. In the 1120s, William d'Aubigny, a royal butler and leading magnate of Norfolk, gave to his priory of Wymondham on the day of his wife's funeral 'grieving and in tears' a silver cross inlaid with splinters of wood from the True Cross and Christ's manger, as well as fragments of the tomb of the Virgin Mary at Ephesus. This very precious relic had claims to have been put together from materials collected all over the eastern Mediterranean, and must have been commissioned some time before its use, with this purpose in mind. It had mementos of the birth and death of Christ as well as His mother, who had been assumed into heaven immediately after death. What more suitable relic to reassure a bereaved man, 'looking to the salvation of the departed and her prospect of endless punishment'?

Twelfth-century aristocratic chapels seem to have been stacked with such objects, and they had their uses other than devotional. Around 1141, the Winchester merchant

Ralph fitz Picard acquitted himself by an oath at Gloucester on Earl Milo of Hereford's gospel book and the relics of his chapel. The earl of Pembroke's handsome chapel at Caversham in Oxfordshire in the early thirteenth century had not just a mass of relics allegedly brought back from the Holy Land by Robert, the crusading duke of Normandy (including the head of the lance that pierced the side of Christ on the Cross), but also a miraculous statue of the Virgin Mary. There are few inventories of such things, but there are some indications of what might have been collected in a list made by Tewkesbury Abbey in 1239 of the furnishings of the chapel of Countess Isabel of Gloucester, which she left to the abbey in her will. It included ecclesiastical furnishings: a silver chalice, gospel book and thurible, silk copes, chasubles, dalmatics and tunicles for a high mass with priest, deacon and subdeacon. But she also had a large collection of relics, including ones sent her from Rome in a silver phial by the pope, including relics of Ss Cornelius and Damasus, popes, and bits and pieces of a horde of Roman martyrs.

We have already seen from the surviving thirteenth-century books of hours how the person of the Virgin Mary was by the 1240s a powerful focus of lay devotion. It is not easy otherwise to trace the penetration of Marian spirituality into lay aristocratic life. A chronicler tells us that, trapped in sanctuary at the church of St John at Devizes in 1233, Hubert de Burgh, earl of Kent, 'devotedly prayed for the help of the Blessed Virgin'. When he was later escaping the king's troops with the help of Earl Richard Marshal's military household, hiding in a wood on the Gloucestershire shore of the Severn estuary while loyalist troops from Bristol closed in on them, Hubert again prayed to the Virgin, and heard a voice saying repeatedly, 'Fear not, the Lord will deliver you!' Apart from the chapel at Caversham and its statue, there are some other and earlier twelfth-century instances which indicate that aristocratic devotion to the Virgin was not new in the 1190s. The canons of Laon Cathedral brought their outstanding collection of relics of the Virgin to England in 1118 and toured the south of the kingdom, meeting devotion from lay people of all stations in the process, and collecting a large sum of money for the rebuilding of their cathedral. Aristocrats were the part of lay society most able to undertake pilgrimage as an expression of their piety, and collections of miracle stories depict a remarkably mobile population in search of shrines, indulgences and cures. Philip, prior of St Frideswide, Oxford, around 1190 records a blind, deaf and partially paralysed knight called Hamo de St-Ciry, who rode to Canterbury in his nineties looking for a cure for some of his ills at Becket's tomb, before travelling on to Oxfordshire to find relief at St Frideswide's intercession.

The dominant spirituality of the biblical books of Wisdom, the ostentatious and austere *contemptus mundi* ('the repudiation of worldly vanities'), moved some knights to the hermitage, the crusading orders and the monastic cloister. Asceticism in religious practice was a byproduct of an outlook which regarded the world and all its joys as mere distracting vanity, and it has been suggested that this inspired and was paralleled by a knightly cult of embracing denial and suffering, particularly in the practice of crusade. But even if such a limited approach tends to ignore the great range of options which defined aristocratic spirituality, *contemptus mundi* had its undeniable impact. Even if it did not lure aristocrats to the regular religious life or the heroic self-denial of the religious orders of knights, it still coloured a distinctly aristocratic spiritual life and devotion, where denial of the world was an especial virtue in those to whom the world had given most in material terms. So Stephen de Rouen meditated gloomily in his lament for that most fashionable and elegant of aristocrats, Waleran II, count of Meulan and Worcester (died 1166), a literate man and indeed a writer of Latin verse. 'Wealth melts away, honour is trodden down and the world's glory is one day remembered, the next forgotten, and once forgotten is gone forever. Count Waleran himself saw that he would be earth, worms and dust: he dreaded eternal punishment and he strove to enter heaven. He gave away, dispersed and thought little of his goods and he took the easy yoke of Christ upon his body with a pious heart.'[4]

Monastic Expansion

One of the most extraordinary manifestations of medieval religious life was a direct response to the feeling of despair at the possibility of salvation in a materialistic and immoral world. The origins of monastic life lay in the wilderness of Egypt in the fourth century. The impulse to withdraw from the corruption of the cities and seek an exclusive relationship with Christ continued to act on society across Europe for many centuries, and all over Britain and Ireland led to individuals and communities seeking their own – very different – wildernesses as early as the sixth century. Classic Benedictine monasticism, as it developed in the Frankish empire in the eighth and ninth centuries, was by no means the only form of monasticism, but it was the one destined to define for ever what European monasteries should be and how they should function. In 1000 the idea that Benedictinism was the only form of religious life worth pursuing had only recently come to dominate the minds of the elites of Church and State. King Edgar (959–975) gave his backing to a number of aristocratic bishops who wanted to impose the continental Rule of Benedict on England's unconventional miscellany of minster communities. By Edgar's death thirty or so male and seven or eight female monasteries had been re-founded on new lines, mostly in Wessex. But the subsequent reigns brought few further foundations, though the Confessor's abbey at Westminster is a major exception.

The incoming Norman regime therefore found in England thirty-seven of the sort of large Benedictine abbeys they were already familiar with from their own monastic renaissance in the early eleventh century. The fact that Canterbury, Sherborne, Winchester and Worcester were cathedrals run by monks might perhaps have struck the French as somewhat unusual. But William the Conqueror would have found the arrangements at his new residence of Westminster not dissimilar from his Norman home at Fécamp, where his seaside palace was in close proximity to a great Benedictine house under his direct patronage, in which his ancestors lay. The abbey at Westminster was constructed in just the way a Norman would have expected, though those churches they encountered elsewhere in England might have looked on the ramshackle and antiquated side, with their multiple buildings, peculiar rotundas, porticos and turrets, such as the complex which survived at St Augustine's Abbey in Canterbury.

The Normans soon applied themselves to putting this architectural eccentricity right, and by the middle of Henry I's reign every one of the surviving English abbeys had experienced major rebuilding on the northern French model. An impressive number of new abbeys and priories had also been added to the architectural bonanza which was reshaping the townscapes of England. No more dominating example of this can be found than Durham, whose formidable cathedral-priory still rises dramatically on its promontory above the river Wear as it has done since 1093. Within twenty years, such was the dynamism of the period, it had already been rebuilt by Bishop Ranulf Flambard, a building remarkable in European terms for the stone rib-vaulting it pioneered, a precondition for the great Gothic churches which would begin to appear across Northern Europe within half a century. In the meantime, in the North of England and Scotland, Benedictine communities were founded to restore Northumbria to the shining beacon of monastic life it was imagined to have been in the days of Bede, sometimes at places Bede had praised, such as Whitby, Jarrow, Lindisfarne, Coldingham and Tynemouth, and sometimes at entirely new sites, such as Selby, York and Dunfermline.

But this late Benedictine boom was modest in comparison with the monastic expansion of the first half of the twelfth century. During Stephen's turbulent reign (1135–1154) on average nine new monasteries were being founded in England every year. Between 1100 and 1170, in three human generations, organised monasticism was revolutionised, in large part by aristocratic investment, whether of a great earl, wealthy prelate or local knight. New monastic orders with a strong reform agenda found patrons across Britain: the Augustinian black canons, whose intention was to take in hand existing minsters and their secular (non-monastic) priests; or the Cistercian white monks and their Premonstratensian imitators, the white canons, whose intention was to offer a purer and more spartan monasticism, which did not deploy its resources of wealth and prayer in the pomp of elaborate liturgy and architectural splendour of which the movement found the Benedictines and their offshoot, the Cluniacs, guilty. The Cistercians in particular brought regular monasticism to the parts of the British Isles where it had never been known, especially in Wales and Scotland. They embraced the original monastic ideal of seeking God in the wilderness, and were more than willing to take up the opportunities offered by a new generation of patrons to found abbeys in Welsh valleys, Yorkshire dales and Scottish glens rather than in or near urban centres. So abbeys arose in what Cistercians fondly liked to call 'the desert' but which were in most cases simply existing agricultural landscapes remote from towns.

Initially the movement attracted hundreds of choir monks and lay brothers, and on their labour and the generosity of the aristocracy some of these abbeys became great and famous, not least the Yorkshire houses of Rievaulx, Fountains, Byland and Jervaulx, which found themselves as a result pitted against the established Benedictines and the archbishop, whose supervision the Cistercians evaded, as they did all episcopal oversight. Not all these abbeys prospered. Another Yorkshire Cistercian house, Sawley, did not do at all well, set as it was 'in a cloud-wrapped and rainy area where crops did not ripen for harvest and as often as not rotted on the stalk, where for over forty years the community was diminished because of poor supplies and lack of amenities, and the depth of its poverty inspired contempt and distaste'.[5] The founder's daughter, Matilda de Percy, chose to refound it on a more secure basis as a point of family pride. It is a reminder of quite how dependent the monastic expansion was on its aristocratic sponsors.

The twelfth-century monastic expansion fed back into the wider Church in the British Isles. The Cistercians in particular, being an international order and exempt from oversight and, it also claimed, taxation, naturally identified with the agenda of its promoter, the papacy. The Cistercian order played politics. Though King John of England's one monastic foundation was Cistercian (Beaulieu, Hampshire), the Cistercians were in conflict with him on more than one occasion in his reign. Elsewhere, in Wales certain Cistercians identified more with their patrons, the Welsh princes, than the marchers. Their houses at Strata Florida and Aberconwy from the 1170s fostered a native Welsh historical tradition and the dynastic identity of the house of Gwynedd. Abbots might become bishops, and the first two Norman archbishops of Canterbury were leading Benedictine abbots before they were promoted. Two of the most politically influential twelfth-century English bishops, Henry de Blois of Winchester and Hugh of Avalon of Lincoln, had begun their careers as monks, the one a Cluniac, the other a Carthusian. Bishop Henry retained the abbacy of Glastonbury which he held in conjunction with his bishopric.

But well before 1200 the monastic enthusiasm was waning. Its patronage depended too much on the participation of aristocrats, with founders requiring burial and perpetual commemoration in return for their generosity, however religiously sincere it was. When the founding family died out, as the Mandeville earls of Essex did in 1187, a foundation like their Walden Abbey could find itself in conflict with the successors. Walden was humiliated and victimised by the new earl, Geoffrey fitz Peter, who bullied the monks into subservience and reclaimed lands they thought were theirs. Likewise, it was not unusual for the descendants of a founder to regret their ancestor's generosity, and launch lawsuits to reclaim lands and benefices from what they considered over-endowed monasteries, which clogged the business of thirteenth-century courts.

New and sometimes distinguished monasteries might be founded on occasion in later centuries, not least for the admirably austere and scholarly **Carthusian** order, but by 1220 aristocratic patronage and religious enthusiasm had generally moved elsewhere.

Church Against State

A huge international movement unrolled over the centuries dealt with by this book. It did not originate in Britain, though some of its great dramas were played out in these islands. This was the papal **curia**'s embrace and vigorous pursuit in the eleventh century of what is called the 'Gelasian' principle in relations between the pope and the emperor. Pope Gelasius I (492–496) may not have occupied the chair of St Peter for very long but he set out a manifesto in his conflict with the Emperor Anastasius which was continually to energise and dog relations between Rome and the imperial courts of Europe thereafter. Faced with a heretical emperor demanding his obedience, the pope retaliated by asserting that his status as the successor of Peter gave him authority over the Church in East and West, and primacy in his office above that of the emperor. The rivalry for supremacy between pope and emperor was brought to a nexus by the papacy itself, when Pope Leo III (795–816) awarded the status of emperor to the king of the Franks in 800. This was an act intended to recruit an ally against the pope's Lombard oppressors, but also to end once and for all the problem with the Eastern emperors and indeed demonstrate papal supremacy in a new way. In the long term, however, it set up a new and more dangerous rivalry with an emperor who was on the papal doorstep, and whose control was not easy to evade. It ultimately led to generations of subservience by a domesticated pope who was all too often an imperial nominee, subject to the emperor's appointment and sometimes removal. The eleventh century saw a reaction to this state of affairs, even at the curia of Pope Leo IX (1049–1054), himself a German aristocrat and an imperial nominee. He set out a moral reform agenda for the Church and pursued it with an energy that defied even imperial opposition. His household attracted young and radical clergy, the most influential of whom proved to be an Italian cardinal by the name of Hildebrand, elected pope as Gregory VII (1073–1085).

One aspect of Pope Gregory's agenda which came home to Britain was the item of his epic struggle with the Emperor Henry IV in which he insisted that no lay ruler had the right to 'invest' bishops and abbots, that is, to select them and grant them the symbols of their office. The Conqueror was a dutiful son of the Church and had sought the backing of the papacy in his invasion of England, receiving a banner as a token of Rome's support. Duke William, being a lay ruler of exemplary piety and deep conviction, was particularly anxious to place his conquest within the realm of divine providence, and a papal legate followed him to England in 1070, with the intention of asserting a new moral force in the rule of the English Church, backed by Rome. William indeed was happy to accept his crown from papal legates in his Easter crown-wearing at Winchester that year. But none of this was intended as any change in the position and power of the English king in relation to his nation's Church, and William as king presided over several councils in the 1070s as English kings had long done.

In the meantime, Gregory VII had become pope, and a new mood was becoming evident in the higher echelons of the Church. At various points in his reign Gregory would excommunicate the Emperor Henry IV and King Philip I of France. Nor did he ignore England. One of William's leading Norman abbots entered Gregory's household and gave him ready access to intelligence about the Anglo-Norman realm, as can be seen in the close personal interest the pope took in senior appointments in the Norman church. The most fraught episode, however, came in 1080 when the king received a papal letter complaining that the ancient tax owed Rome by England called 'Peter's pence' was in arrears, and suggesting that its existence obliged William to acknowledge that he was a vassal of the pope as king of England (a position that Gregory adopted against every ruler in Christendom). William promised to pay up, but rejected vassalage, saying there was no historical precedent for the claim. With other matters more pressing, Gregory seems not to have pursued the matter further. That he pursued it at all, however, was a straw in the wind from the **Lateran**.

Gregory's agenda long outlived his rather sad end, and it became the banner for radical and reforming clergy in many nations thereafter, men who consequently and inevitably were seen to be more loyal to Rome than to their king. This was especially so in the days of Archbishop Anselm of Canterbury (1093–1109). Anselm was a remarkable theologian and an exemplary priest and monk, but he was not at the time of his election a Gregorian, so he innocently accepted his archiepiscopal cross and investiture from King William Rufus. It was probably not until he was at Rome in 1099 in his first period of exile from England that he even became aware that he had transgressed Rome's view of what was right and proper in relations between lay rulers and the Church. When he came back to England in the aftermath of Henry I's seizure of the throne, Anselm knew better. His protector and patron, Pope Paschal II (1099–1118), took a close interest in Anglo-Norman affairs; indeed, one of his cardinals (John of Telese) had been Anselm's monk at Bec-Hellouin.

Anselm returned to England in 1100 determined to pursue the investiture issue with the king, and he returned on the condition that the issue would be addressed. But, once secure on the throne, Henry ignored both his archbishop and a papal missive from Rome on the subject. The pope's position was that the king had no part in the process of election to high clerical office, could take no fees in the process nor demand homage from the incoming prelate. The attack on his traditional prerogatives deeply angered Henry, a king with a very strong sense of what was owed to him, as we have seen. Delegations to Rome failed to get the pope to budge on the issue of investiture, though he relaxed his opposition to homage somewhat. By 1103 Anselm's position was impossible, and he took the road to Rome initially to represent the king's views but in reality as an exile, for he got no further than Lyons on his return. It was not until 1105, when the king was in the throes of conquering Normandy, and needed all the moral authority he could get, that the situation shifted. He and Anselm met at Laigle on the Norman frontier and there ironed out a compromise: the king would surrender the right to invest prelates, though he would be allowed to take homage from them for the lands they held of the Crown.

Relations between kings and their archbishops in England were rarely so adversarial, and Anselm himself was not that eager a controversialist. But the tide of events pushed Anselm into conflict, like it or not. Those tides grew stronger in the twelfth century as the papacy slowly transformed itself into an international body with real power and ambitions which inevitably conflicted with those of lay rulers. One of its manifestations was the papacy's rise to be a supreme tribunal to Christendom for a range of issues, developing its own international law on the basis of papal pronouncements or decretals, which came to be called 'canon' law. Already in the 1130s numerous English and Welsh people were making the trek as far as Rome to state their cases at the Holy See. Kings were uneasy about this, perhaps, but generally did not refuse litigants access to Rome.

Papal legates increasingly travelled outwards from the papal court, dressed in the garb of the pope himself and demanding his prerogatives. They settled the affairs of provinces, arbitrated wars and disputes, and held councils imposing Rome's view of church organisation on doctrine from Norway to Sicily. Things were managed carefully so as not to be too open a challenge to royal authority, for no legate could enter a kingdom without its sovereign's permission. It also became the practice to be less aggressive in the use of the legate by awarding commissions to favoured native bishops to exercise, as happened in Stephen's reign (1135–1154) when legateships were held by Bishop Henry of Winchester and Archbishop Theobald of Canterbury. The swamping of the papal courts by litigants also had its inconveniences. The answer was delegation, as the pope referred cases back to panels of local clergy (known as judges delegate) to hear them in the pope's name and impose a verdict from which there was no appeal. Nonetheless, by the 1160s the pope was indisputably the most potent figure in Christendom, and the clergy's loyalties were no longer strictly focused on their king, but demanded by the head of their order at Rome. So, when the power of the state became as manifest and coherent as it did in England in the twelfth century, there was bound to be conflict, and the most spectacular instance of it in Europe occurred at Canterbury, where the radical archbishop, Thomas Becket, was assassinated by a noble cabal acting in the king's interest in 1170.

The Becket Affair

The case of Thomas Becket thoroughly bemused twelfth-century England and indeed all of Christendom. The protagonist was the son of a London patrician family, born in a house on the north side of Cheapside, on the edge of the cosmopolitan Jewish quarter. He was sent to board for his early education amongst the Augustinians of Merton priory, which was then the fashion. Curiously, the only English pope, Nicholas Breakspear (the later Adrian IV) seems to have been schooled at the priory some years before Thomas. From Merton, young Thomas was removed to the grammar schools of London as a teenager. Such were his family's connections and wealth that young Thomas was brought up with aristocrats in aristocratic style. He was sent to finish his education in the schools of Paris, though not, it seems, with the intention of his becoming a master of any academic discipline. In fact Thomas's expensive high life in the city may have brought his stay there to a premature end. Social connections led to his employment in the household of Theobald archbishop of Canterbury around 1146 as a junior clerk, where he found a good deal of favour from the archbishop, though he also seems to have made some powerful enemies, not least the future archbishop of York, Roger de Pont l'Evêque.

Making devoted friends and powerful enemies was a talent the young Becket seems to have had in abundance. His social confidence and ease made him a talented diplomatic agent, and it was these talents that earned him promotion to the archdeaconry of Canterbury and the wealthy provostship of the chapter church of Beverley in 1152, as well as several benefices granted him as retainers by interested noble patrons. His position inevitably involved Thomas in the negotiations to end the civil war and in 1153–1154 he must have often been in the vicinity of the young duke of Normandy, finally adopted as his heir by King Stephen. His emerging reputation and energy brought Thomas to the duke's notice and, early in 1155, within a month of his coronation as Henry II, he appointed Thomas chancellor of England. Their subsequent friendship had a lot to do with mutual sympathy and intellectual liveliness; both were avid gamblers and hunters, and Thomas developed a taste for military campaigning. He also developed a taste the king did not have, a delight in extravagant display and entertainment, a reaction perhaps to the uncertainties in the early career of a self-made man.

Such was the unlikely man King Henry II selected as his new archbishop of Canterbury in 1162, on the death of Theobald. Becket as archbishop continued some of his earlier traits, employing a huge clerical and secular household at vast expense and entertaining lavishly. He did not immediately abandon secular clothing, much to the distaste of the monks of Canterbury, who disliked him intensely. He also proved to be a harsh litigator in enforcing his new property rights, which earned him other enemies. But before 1163 something surprising emerged. Thomas had a crisis of identity, throwing himself into a life of religious discipline, even taking up the study of theology after a long gap. If he was going to be an archbishop it appeared that he wanted to be a great one, and so he identified with the more radical aims of the Church against royal authority. Since in England royal authority was developing in a new way, gathering to itself ultimate legal jurisdiction and developing the royal courts as a centre of justice, King Henry II was on a collision course with the ambitions of the papacy to remove the

Church from all lay authority. So Becket deliberately placed himself in the way of the express train of history, and was consequently smashed. In 1163 he began leading the opposition to the king's reform programme, a degree of ingratitude that appalled and then infuriated Henry II, whose plan was to bring clergy within the jurisdiction of the Crown for criminal offences with no exemption because of their order. Becket stood alone, for none of his colleagues saw any point in a confrontation with their formidable royal master.

The crunch came in 1164 when at Northampton Becket was isolated, abused and threatened not just by the king but by his magnates, who ominously denounced the archbishop as a traitor to the realm. In a rather Putinesque way, Becket was charged with embezzlement as a way of bringing him down, rather than his true offence of opposing royal authority. He promptly fled for the Capetian realm and sought the protection of Louis VII. He remained in exile as a guest of the Cistercians of Pontigny, and there he had years to improve his education and learn austerity. He found Pope Alexander III (1159–1181) less than supportive, for the pope on viewing Henry II's legal proposals declared he could see the point of some of them. But slowly Becket gathered support despite himself and the violent opposition to his standpoint by many of his own bishops. In 1169 the king was sufficiently embarrassed by papal pressure to begin to relax his demands, and settlement became possible, though Becket's grim determination to punish his subordinates for their disobedience to their archbishop was a new problem, alongside an emerging paranoia about the king's intentions towards him. When a formal settlement was eventually reached in Normandy in July 1170, it was Thomas's vengefulness and suspicion which subverted it. Returning to England and Canterbury, he ignored the settlement and excommunicated his enemies. When news of this reached the royal court, there was uproar and, in response to the king's open rage against his archbishop, four of his barons, offended on their king's behalf, left the court for Canterbury. On 29 December 1170, after denouncing Thomas as a traitor and pursuing him through the palace and cloisters, they assassinated him in the north transept of his own cathedral as the choir monks were finishing the office of vespers.

By placing himself in the way of oncoming danger, Becket succeeded in entirely derailing the king's ambitions to limit the autonomy of the Church within his realm. His death, hailed as a martyrdom, brought Henry II to the lowest point in his reign and validated Becket's cause. Even his bitter enemies, of which there were many, had to accept his being in the right. Interdicts on Henry personally and on his lands followed in response to the universal horror at the murder. A cult developed rapidly around the archbishop's tomb, pilgrims flocked there and miracles in plenty proclaimed his sanctity. He was canonised in 1173, and the king himself visited his tomb to receive discipline and repent in 1174. Such, however, was the canniness of Henry II that he could make something even out of his own defeat. He had the deviousness to adopt his dead former friend as the patron of his own cause. His sensational victories over his enemies that year were claimed to be the result of the favour of St Thomas the martyr. In 1179 Henry II even appointed himself tour guide to King Louis of France and several other French princes when they too came to the tomb seeking the saint's favour.

Becket became England's patron saint, and his image featured on the seal of his native London. A crusading order of English knights was founded in his name, with its chief priory in his former family home on Cheapside. London bridge was rebuilt in stone in his memory. For the rest of the middle ages, pilgrimage to his tomb-shrine at Canterbury was one of the chief acts of devotion in Britain, not just England. The long-term significance of his career was to enable an extraordinarily privileged status for clergy in England, who were beyond the reach of the secular criminal law, because of the 'benefit' their order gave them. But more significant yet was the pattern he set for his successors at Canterbury, such as Stephen Langton (whose seal exhibited the martyrdom of Becket), St Edmund Rich (who died in exile at Pontigny) and John Pecham. All three set themselves in open opposition to their king and defeated him, following Becket's road to exile in two cases. It was for this inheritance that in 1538 Henry VIII had Becket's tomb destroyed, his government specifically prohibiting the cult, declaring Becket to have been 'a rebel rather than a saint', and that 'there appears nothing in his life and exterior conversation whereby he should be called a saint, but rather esteemed to have been a rebel and traitor to his Prince'.

 The Bureaucratic Church

The power of the papacy continued to grow, not least under Innocent III (1198–1216), the pope against whom King John set himself and suffered a defeat almost as catastrophic for royal power as Becket had inflicted on his father. In this case the fight was over the king's right to nominate to the principal ecclesiastical offices of his land, in particular to the see of Canterbury, to which the pope appointed Stephen Langton over his head, which eventually brought on a damaging interdict (1208–1214) and indeed the formal deposition of the king by the pope in 1212. It was to Innocent that John surrendered his realms of England and Ireland, to receive them back as papal fiefs. One inheritance of that struggle was the peremptory right of the pope to 'provide' nominees to any and every benefice in England, which was a source of almost comical corruption and incompetence in the later medieval Church. Later popes in their search to reward adherents and courtiers would issue letters awarding cardinals, papal chaplains and chamberlains, or indeed anyone with influence in the curia, the next vacancy to bishoprics, archdeaconries and cathedral dignities in England. If they secured them, the lucky beneficiaries would never visit, but have their revenues channelled back from papal agents and **farmers** in London if they were resident in Italy.

Provision gave rise to scandal and endless lawsuits, as lay patrons and chapters fought to delay or circumvent papal letters. It began to be perceived as an abuse in both England and France in the 1240s when the number of such provisions was still relatively few and when the right was principally exercised to decide contested elections. But by 1342 papal ambition to control appointments had generated a bureaucracy bestowing 100,000 offices across Europe in a single year. It may be true that many of the disputed offices were 'graduate entry' appointments to which little or no pastoral responsibility attached, but it ended in eroding religious life and leadership in England's major churches to no one's benefit. Opposition to it was already growing in England in Edward I's reign, when in 1306 Parliament legislated against Church income leaving England. In 1351 an act forbade papal appointments within England, while in 1353 the first of a series of acts known by the Latin word 'Praemunire' (from the opening word of the royal writ or order to enforce it) halted all legal cases going to Rome which could not otherwise have been dealt with in English courts. The papacy was significantly unable to offer any resistance to such rebuffs, being already deeply compromised and curbed within the kingdom of France.

A characteristic of the Church in both England and Scotland from the later thirteenth century was its colonisation by career bureaucrats, all men with a remarkably similar background. This was not something unknown in the twelfth century, when already in Henry II's reign archdeaconries and canons' stalls were increasingly being filled by clerks of the royal chapel, who might very well hold not just these in plurality, but also a range of rectories of parishes. The lucky beneficiary would enjoy the combined revenues of these offices until (for some) they attained a bishop's throne, when it was customary to surrender all lesser benefices. The only cost for these men was to appoint subordinates to do the actual work, though without effective supervision such deputies often turned out to be incompetent. It was more or less universal in Britain to find aristocratic fathers furthering sons through church office and patronage, so we find Rhys ap Gruffudd prince of Deheubarth (died 1197) bestowing thirteen rectories in his gift on his clerical son Maredudd, and pressuring the bishop of St Davids to appoint him to the archdeaconry of Cardigan. Although he was exceptional, the most extreme and notorious case of such a pluralist was the unpleasant Bogo de Clare (died 1294), a younger son of Earl Richard de Clare of Gloucester (died 1262). In his seedy and astonishingly litigious career beginning from the age of seven, Bogo secured or disputed more than thirty benefices across Ireland, England and Wales along with prebends in six cathedrals and the great prize of the treasurership of York, one of the most lucrative ecclesiastical offices in Britain. Bogo had a palatial residence with a warehouse of luxury goods (or wardrobe) at the east end of Cheapside and lived in as lavish and aristocratic a style as the earl his brother. As a papal chamberlain, he was exempt from any episcopal oversight and used the privilege ruthlessly. One contemporary verdict on him in a notice of his death was that, 'God only knows if his life was worthy of praise, but no-one thought it worthy of imitation.'

A much more common type of pluralist in the thirteenth century was the rising class of bureaucrat. Unlike Bogo, such men were mostly from gentry families with just enough resources to afford a university education for a son. On graduation they looked to solicit episcopal or royal patronage as household clerks. Bishops and kings could and did use the benefices in their gifts in lieu of salaries for their clerical employees. The clerks of the Exchequer, the Chancery and the Royal Chapel were by 1300 almost all from this sort of background, men patiently amassing and exchanging rectories and prebends while working in their lord's interests in his accounting office or in his courts as a justice or delegated official. Most were respectable enough men, and many were sincerely religious, though the more ambitious of them always had an eye on the main prizes, the deaneries and sees of England, Ireland, Wales and Scotland, for the same class of cleric was just as evident north of the border. Such a man was an Oxford-educated Welsh cleric, canon lawyer and careerist, Dr Adam Usk (died 1430), whose chatty chronicle intersperses national events and marvels with a meticulous register of when precisely he acquired his many rectories and prebends and from whom, though he was in the end disappointed of the bishopric he actively sought.

This sort of common background and education in its nominal leaders produced a fourteenth- and fifteenth-century ecclesiastical hierarchy very different in its aspirations from that of the twelfth, when quite a number of able and sometimes saintly theologians, philosophers and scholars occupied the bishops' bench. Indeed King Stephen (1135–1154) made a point of seeking out such men for the sees of England and Wales, to his universal credit at the time because, for all his faults as king, no one denied his exemplary piety. It does not seem, therefore, that the rise of higher education in Britain increased the calibre of clergy; in fact it appears to have done no more than homogenise and domesticate them as careerists. With such men as the leadership of an institution that had once pitted itself against lay power and subdued it, the old Gregorian ideals were subverted and the Church became what has been called 'monarchical', meaning that the national monarchy now had the chief say in its direction. It was not unique in this, for the Church in Spain and France was likewise squarely under the king's thumb. But in England this subservience did not produce a Church leadership willing to oppose its reformation by a monarch and the radical Protestant clique of advisers to whom his political needs would one day open the door.

There are many parallels between the late medieval Church in Scotland and in England, which is not surprising in that the clerical world and its relationship with monarchical power was common to Western Europe beyond the British Isles. Their bureaucratic structures were similar and indeed there was an occasional interchange of personnel between them until the thirteenth century. The similarity did not end after 1306, though Scots students thereafter resorted more to Paris, Orléans or Louvain for their higher education than to Oxford and Cambridge. It was not until 1412 that the foundation of St Andrews university offered the possibility of an indigenous education to that level. The Scots too had to deal with the problems caused by papal provision which at Glasgow, according to its bishop in 1363, was disrupting the administration of the diocese. King James I (1406–1437) promoted parliamentary legislation to curb the practice, which brought on him the anger of Pope Martin V (1417–1431). The relative poverty of Scottish benefices made them less worth the effort of securing at Rome, however, so the problem was not so central as it was in England.

It was not until 1471 that there was a Scottish equivalent of the Statutes of Praemunire, when the imperial king James III secured legislation strictly limiting papal taxation, legal appeals and appointments within his realm, which in itself raised the authority of Parliament in Scotland above that of the papacy, much to the annoyance of Pope Sixtus IV. Scotland's Church was as national and monarchical as that of England, and this was recognised outside Britain. Perhaps this was most evident when the papacy erected archdioceses at St Andrews (1472) and Glasgow (1492), which once and for all extinguished any claim of the English or Norwegian archbishops to any primacy within Scotland and so respected the Scottish royal agenda. But long before that, when Edward II of England maintained to the pope that he had the right to appoint to Scottish bishoprics, he was given short shrift at Rome. The late medieval Scottish Church experienced much the same impulses as those elsewhere. There was a parallel fourteenth-century rise in chantry foundation, though in Scotland they were known by the French term 'chaplainries' (*chapellenies*). The erection of major collegiate churches by the higher aristocracy was likewise parallel to that in England, while the friars and Carthusians likewise acquired the bulk of lay patronage directed at regular clergy. Lollardy reached Scotland through at least one English missionary, James Resby (burned in 1407). There was sufficient unease about the infection of heresy in Scotland for the duke of Rothesay in 1399 to promise to uproot it from the realm, and it was seen, as in England, as a threat as much to the State as to the Church. The 1425 Parliament directed bishops to seek out Lollardy in their dioceses, though it does not seem they found any. In part this may be because there is less evidence in Scotland amongst the laity of that deeply emotional **pietism** which was found in England in the fourteenth century, and which set itself against ecclesiastical authority.

 Enthusiasm and Heresy

The thirteenth century brought with it a new form of more popular piety. The medieval Church was always uneasy when the poorest and least educated of its flock became enthused over doctrine, and for good reason. There is no one more stubborn and fixed in his views than an autodidact. There was, however, little in the way of outright heresy to be found in Britain in the eleventh and twelfth centuries. The one instance was the arrival in England in the early 1160s of a mixed group of uneducated missionaries from the Low Countries, who went about preaching that the Church's sacraments were not valid. Their beliefs seem to have echoed those of the Cathars, hostile to the power structures of the Church. There was initially very little idea what to do with them. But in 1166 twenty or thirty of them were rounded up, along with their single English convert, and they were tried and condemned before a Church council at Oxford. On their refusal to recant, their punishment was to be branded, beaten and cast out of society naked, excommunicated from all contact with their fellow men. The group is said to have died of exposure and starvation on the roads. Drastic action may have cauterised any immediate influence their heresy had, but it seems they found no general dissatisfaction with traditional Catholicism in England that they could exploit in any case. Thirteenth-century religion likewise found channels for enthusiasm, notably in the intelligent and occasionally ecstatic preaching the new orders of friars brought to Britain, and which appealed alike to commoner, university student and aristocrat.

The friars gave an additional impulse to the sort of introspective religion already established in Britain the previous century in royal and noble circles, which focused very much on sin, its confession and its penance. Both Franciscans and Dominicans achieved great influence within society across Britain in towns and at the courts of thirteenth-century Gwynedd, Westminster and Scotland. Their enthusiasm beguiled many of the scholars of the new universities into joining them; as a result the quality of their preaching was high. Some among their confessors grew powerful enough to defy any control by diocesan bishops. It was not a position their orders lost for the rest of the middle ages, bolstered by the willingness of some friars to attack even the Church for its perceived failure to live up to its ideals. By 1300 we find lay people deeply involved in their relationship with God through Jesus Christ, and willing to explore their own humanity and pain through His, and that of His mother, Mary.

Such a form of religion wanted to go further than what doctrine offered and drifted out into the mystical, where visions and ecstatic emotion counted as much as words. This was the spiritual world of Margery Kempe (died c. 1438), a citizen of Bishop's Lynn, whose intensely personal conversion to faith was accomplished by a vision of Christ, who sat on the end of her bed and talked her through the mental trouble of postnatal depression. She had in the end thirteen children and struggled to come to terms with daily life, but in 1413 fled into her own internal world of high emotion and ostentatious faith, consulting about her experiences with the renowned female mystic Julian of Norwich (died c. 1416) and travelling widely, even to Palestine and Rome. Often charged with heresy but treated sympathetically by the bishops she came before, however rude she was to them, she embarrassed people wherever she went with her tears, bawling and emotional demands. Her overmastering compulsion to give witness of her faith produced the first autobiography in English, which shows her to have made a wide acquaintance with visionary writers, male and female. Being illiterate, she managed all this through amanuenses and sympathetic clergy who would read to her.

It was only in the later fourteenth century that England bred up its own heretical movement. It came not from the streets but from the university. The movement gathered inspiration from the Oxford theologian, John Wycliffe (died 1384), who in the 1370s began preaching challenging sermons about the nature of papal authority and the priesthood as against the authority of princes. What he had to say was noticed in court circles. Edward III had been the first king of England to move to limit papal authority in England since Henry II, when in the 1350s he allowed Parliament to exclude the pope's direct authority from England. It was a pragmatic decision on the king's part, the prelude to heavy taxation of the Church to support the war effort. Not surprisingly, therefore, Wycliffe found a powerful patron in the king's son, John of Gaunt, when he preached that the Church's wealth and privilege forfeited any spiritual right for it to pontificate against lay power. For Wycliffe, power and authority depended on righteousness alone, a perilous position which opened the same door the Cathars had, which was that priesthood and spiritual leadership were open to those who felt justified before God, not just to those the Church authorised by ordination. Wycliffe in fact embraced principles which would one day be part of the Protestant programme that would divide the Western Catholic Church. On a political level his preaching opened a rift between the Church and the State, and awarded primacy to kings. On a spiritual level he deprived the Church of the right to say who was or was not saved, which was a decision open only to God and a man's conscience. The Church's sacraments he believed of little importance to salvation, which could only be attained by living up to the precepts of the Bible, so for him preaching was far more important than the witness of the mass, whose miraculous significance as a Christian rite he denied.

Wycliffe's teachings were condemned even in Oxford, and in 1382 the archbishop of Canterbury pronounced his teaching heretical, but support by an aristocratic clique allowed him to carry on his defiance and counter-attacks with a singular stubbornness. He died still unexcommunicated and in possession of his livings in 1384. His radical views gathered disciples, though he did not himself seek to set up any sort of movement. There were plenty of educated laymen in the aristocracy and gentry of England of his day who could appreciate his standpoint, and for a while they even had influence at court. His radicalism intrigued and attracted academics, who conveyed his views in their preaching. The most significant achievement of this clique was the translation of the **Vulgate Bible** from Latin into English, an enormous undertaking centred on Queen's College, Oxford, in the 1390s, resulting in the appearance of a usable 'Wycliffite' text by 1401, thus making the central authority of the Bible available to those not educated in the schools. It was accompanied by the publication of a wide range of tracts on Wycliffe's teachings addressed to the literate public, with the deliberate intention of creating a demand for reform amongst a wide range of people.

Slowly the Wycliffite movement provoked a reaction, with Archbishop Thomas Arundel of Canterbury (1396–1414) sponsoring the death sentence for stubborn heretics in 1401, and in 1406 energising the government to shift responsibility for apprehending such heretics to justices of the peace. The adherents of the heresy were known derisorily as Lollards (probably from a Dutch word for 'babblers', which was applied to any sort of heretic). Their radicalism became perceived as a threat by the royal government. The first serious clampdown occurred under Richard II in the 1390s. His successor Henry IV was less keen to weed out Lollard sympathisers from Parliament and the court, and so prosecution of its adherents fell to Archbishop Arundel, who forced Oxford to burn Wycliffe's books at Carfax in 1411 and drove out his remaining adherents from the university, many leaving for Bohemia, where their teachings were already making dramatic headway and ultimately led to the overthrow of the Catholic Church in that kingdom. In England the target then became the secular followers of Wycliffe and the Lollard preachers who ministered to them. King Henry V (1413–1422) redefined Lollardy as a threat to his own authority as much as to the Church, and between 1414 and 1417 a roundup began which culminated in the burnings of a number of high-profile adherents (which almost caught Margery Kempe in its trawl). Under relentless persecution and without leadership Lollardy dwindled, though it was still perceived as a sufficient threat for Pope Martin V to have Wycliffe's heretical bones disinterred and burned in 1428. Tracts and copies of the English Bible might continue to resurface, but Lollardy was already by then a spent force and, though historians have suggested that secret undergound Lollard cells lingered into Tudor times and provided the seedbed of popular Protestantism, this is nowadays seen as highly unlikely. It never had sufficient popular attraction to derail traditional Catholic spirituality. Its austerity and intellectuality had little immediate appeal in a realm where abuses in the Church were not so offensive for Lollardy to energise mass popular protest, and where the Church had been so domesticated into the State that to challenge the one was to challenge the other.

The Inheritance of Medieval Education

When pondering the inheritance left us by the middle ages, it may well be that its most significant legacy was what it achieved in higher education. The twelfth and thirteenth centuries saw – generation by generation – greater investment and ambition in academic studies to a degree unknown since the ancient world, and in part inspired by it. The twelfth century is credited with a 'renaissance': a renewed and intense look at the classical Latin inheritance first investigated by the talented scholars associated with the court of the Frankish kings in the eighth century. Scholars from Britain played a major role in both the eighth- and twelfth-century renaissances, and so it is not perhaps surprising that higher education developed as rapidly in England as it did in Capetian France and northern Italy. Just after 1200 a focus of educational endeavour was found in the university, a community of self-governing scholars licensed to teach a student body, men whose specialised studies were advanced by publication and debate. It was a concept unknown in Western society until its appearance in England, northern Italy and France at the beginning of the thirteenth century.

It is less easy to credit the middle ages with progress in basic literacy in lay society than it is with advances at the very pinnacle of studies. There is some evidence to indicate an expansion of literacy in the course of the twelfth century, when the English royal government increased the volume of written instructions issued to its regional officers and demanded back from them more in the way of (written) information. The argument is that these men (if previously illiterate) had to acquire the functional skills of literacy to know what was required and communicate it. So by this theory it became necessary for knights to learn to read if they had any ambition to have a career in administration. But the theory may overstate the impact of increasing bureaucratisation in royal government and probably underestimates the existing extent of literacy amongst the laity. Casual social correspondence (in Latin) can be proved to have been frequent in the twelfth-century upper classes even between lay people. Literacy was certainly a skill established as desirable in every social class in England by the early thirteenth century, and probably by the late twelfth. Rather than see Western society as on an upward trajectory towards literacy and modernity in the middle ages, we ought to see it as finding new uses for skills it had inherited from an earlier world.

We can glimpse before 1100 the way that literacy was acquired in Britain and how education became more ambitious. Most towns already had schools, which were run as enterprises. In some towns at that date, as in Warwick for instance, the grammar school was under the control of the earl, who licensed its masters but who eventually granted the privilege on to the collegiate church he founded there. The school in Hastings was already under the control of its minster at the beginning of the century, and its schools did not just teach grammar, but also tutored boys in music so their voices could be employed in its services. The great churches of Wales, notably St Davids and Llanbadarn, developed reputations for learning which must have attracted students, though we know that before 1100 the younger members of the priestly families of Llandaff were packed off to the school of Worcester for their education.

There was already in 1100 a demand for education greater than established schools in minsters and monasteries could offer, and we find evidence that masters, such as Robert de Béthune (died 1148), who was to become bishop of Hereford in 1131, made a substantial living by running their own boarding establishments charging fees. Noble households employed live-in tutors for their young, and we occasionally hear of their names. Earl Robert of Gloucester, son of King Henry I, employed the eminent philosopher William de Conches to tutor his ward, Henry Plantagenet, in Bristol in the 1140s. The earl himself had acquired a wide knowledge of the liberal arts when a boy in Normandy in the 1090s confided to the household of the senior cleric, Samson of Douvres, who later became a bishop in England. Some schools by 1100 offered rather more than the elementary education needed by the younger child or the more advanced education the 'high school' (*magna schola*) offered the adolescent. These were to be found in northern France, where the famous cathedral schools of Laon, Chartres and Paris attracted a new, arrogant and competitive form of master: true academics of whom the defining type was the famous controversialist and grammarian, Peter Abelard. These schools attracted ambitious students from far afield, from England and the Empire, some of whom became recognised in turn as 'masters' (*magistri*), a title given to a student who had completed an advanced course of study which qualified him in turn to teach.

None of England's schools had as advanced a reputation in the twelfth century as the northern French ones, but some offered specialised teaching, not least the schools of Oxford which acquired a reputation for teaching civil (Roman) and canon (Church) law in the 1170s and even attracted a few foreign students, as well as reputable teachers. Before 1200 three English towns possessed schools which were reckoned centres of advanced education, with large student bodies and associations of masters, the other two being Northampton and Cambridge. A generation of turbulence within John's reign culminated in a diaspora of scholars from Oxford in 1209 to the other two schools after trouble with the civic authorities of the town. When the dust settled, two academic colonies had consolidated at Oxford and Cambridge, which by 1220 had defined themselves as self-governing universities offering a wide range of liberal studies beyond law and theology. In the early years their student bodies were drawn from the middling classes in society, and were intended for ordination, the jumping-off point for careers in Church and state administration. It would not be until the fifteenth century that greater aristocrats sent their sons to university. But, nonetheless, the universities received patronage from the great, particularly great ladies, willing to endow halls and their chapels in return for the prayers of the masters and scholars, as Devorguilla, lady of Galloway, did in Oxford in 1266 and so began Balliol College (named after her late husband). Most such benefactors were, however, alumni who had ascended to high posts in Church and State, such as Walter Merton, chancellor of England, who gave his name to an Oxford hall that same year. Eight colleges in the two universities were founded by bishops. In the fourteenth century kings and queens too set up halls, Edward II of England (1307–1327) leading the way. Monastic houses built halls for their own monks, as Gloucester Abbey and the monastic cathedrals of Canterbury and Durham did. These halls took more than young monks, however; Durham Hall offered a number of free university scholarships to poor youths living on the priory's estates in the North of England.

The medieval university was not a place of research and the advancement of knowledge, as we understand modern universities to be. It was seen rather as a school to produce a learned and orthodox elite to fill the higher ranks of the Church, who would in the course of things also fill high official posts in the royal government. It was certainly a place of debate, where rhetoric was taught as a high civil art to equip men to argue in the civil and Church courts, and sometimes to frame arguments to justify the king's ambitions at home and abroad. Universities trained minds to be useful, as the middle ages looked at it, and over the decades study at a university became the experience which was common to the leaders of England's administrative class, rather more so than the limited administrative and common law education offered by the London Inns of Court, which had also come into being before 1300. For this reason later medieval Scotland felt the need for places of higher education, all the more necessary after 1330, as English universities were not attractive or welcoming to Scots, and those of France and the Empire were a long way away. The new colleges that appeared in Scotland in the fifteenth century (St Andrews, 1412, Glasgow, 1451 and Aberdeen, 1495) drew on the models of Paris and Cologne, where Scots had previously studied. The Scottish universities taught both canon and civil law, and offered theology and the liberal arts, the characteristic medieval curriculum.

Scotland grew its own universities, but what it failed to provide were the schools of vocational study in law and administration for the laity which the London Inns offered to the sons of the English gentry. This need is principally responsible for the remarkable act of 1496 in the Scottish Parliament, which directed that the eldest sons of the landed classes should be set to learn their letters (in Latin) from the age of eight up to their attaining a high school standard, when they should graduate to higher studies in the university faculties of law and the liberal arts. It made education a legal requirement for one class of children (admittedly, a very small and privileged group) and is naturally seen as a consequence of the rising humanism of the fifteenth century, though it could also be argued that it was making good on opportunities long available to the corresponding English elite. As in the London Inns, the motive was vocational, so the boys could be trained as landowners and magistrates learned in property and criminal law. Scots and English alike had long recognised the career value of a liberal education, and in the final medieval century were consolidating it. We should perhaps be cautious of theories of a 'rise in literacy' in any historical period, but what the middle ages certainly did was to prove the usefulness of an advanced education, a remorseless logic which later periods did not contest and which indeed in the nineteenth century eventually extended the advantages imposed on the sons of the fifteenth-century Scottish gentry to all British children.

POSTSCRIPT

Though the middle ages knew that Church and State could be forces opposed to each other, and indeed defined them that way, it was not the case that they were locked in struggle for the allegiance of the people. Henry II of England might well have seen the Church as thwarting his ambitions for his kingdom, but he was not anticlerical: his ambition was to bring true justice to his realm, and he derived that ambition from an oath sworn in a cathedral in words constructed by theologians out of Scripture. Far more bishops agreed with him than with Becket. It is difficult for the post-Enlightenment, postmodern mind to appreciate quite how saturated in faith and its practice the medieval mind was. On the other hand, it is also not the case – as eighteenth-century humanists sneered – that this was something that stifled intellectual curiosity and promoted credulosity in medieval Europe. It may be a Purgatory to read and follow their tracts and glosses on Scripture, but you can only be impressed by the sheer energy and meticulous argumentativeness of multilingual medieval intellectuals. A culture that created the world's first universities, two of which were in Britain, was destined in the end to further the human spirit and its achievements.

KEY TEXTS

Barlow, F. *Thomas Becket* (Weidenfeld & Nicholson, 1986), a masterpiece of intellectual biography. • Blair, J. *The Church in Anglo-Saxon Society* (Oxford University Press, 2005), an original and persuasive rewriting of five centuries of Christian history in Britain, which fully states the author's 'minster thesis'. • Duffy, E. *The Stripping of the Altars: Traditional Religion in England, 1400–1580* (Yale University Press, 1992), an undoubted classic of religious history, still the fullest appreciation of late medieval spirituality. • Knowles, D. *The Monastic Order in England* (Cambridge University Press, 1941); though now venerable, this is a book whose ability to evoke the life and ideals of the medieval cloister remains unmatched. • Rubin, M. *Corpus Christi: The Eucharist in Late Medieval Culture* (Cambridge University Press, 1991), an imaginative and broad look at the foundation of medieval religious life.

FURTHER READING

Anglo-Norman Durham, 1093–1193, ed. D. Rollason et al. (Boydell, 1994). • Atkinson, C. W. *Mystic and Pilgrim: The Book and the World of Margery Kempe* (Cornell University Press, 1985). • Aurell, M. *Le Chevalier lettré: savoir et conduite de l'aristocratie aux xiie et xiiie siècles* (Fayard, 2011). • Bernard, G. W. *The Late Medieval English Church: Vitality and Vulnerability Before the Break with Rome* (Yale University Press, 2013). • Brett, M. *The English Church Under Henry I* (Oxford University Press, 1975). • Burton, J. *The Monastic Order in Yorkshire, 1069–1215* (Cambridge University Press, 1999). • Clanchy, M. T. *From Memory to Written Record: England, 1066–1307* (2nd edn, Oxford University Press,

1993). • Cobban, A. *English University Life in the Middle Ages* (Ohio State University Press, 1999). • Colish, M. *Medieval Foundations of the Western Intellectual Tradition, 400–1400* (Yale University Press, 1997). • Cowley, F. *The Monastic Order in South Wales, 1066–1349* (University of Wales Press, 1977). • Crouch, D. 'The Troubled Deathbeds of Henry I's Servants: Death, Confession and Secular Conduct in the Twelfth Century', *Albion*, 34 (2002), 24–36. • Follett, W. *Céli Dé in Ireland: Monastic Writing and Identity in the Early Middle Ages* (Boydell, 2006). • Hill, P. H. and D. G. Pollock. 'The Northumbrian Church at Whithorn', in *Medieval Europe VI: Religion and Belief*, ed. J. Grenville et al. (University of York Press, 1992), 189–94. • Hudson, A. *The Premature Reformation* (Oxford University Press, 1988). • Jamroziak, E. *The Cistercian Order in Medieval Europe, 1090–1500* (Routledge, 2013). • Jamroziak, E. *Survival and Success on Medieval Borders: Cistercian Houses in Medieval Scotland and Pomerania* (Brepols, 2011). • Logan, F. D. *University Education of the Parochial Clergy in Medieval England: The Lincoln Diocese, c. 1300–c. 1350* (University of Toronto Press, 2014). • Maddicott, J. R. *Simon de Montfort* (Cambridge University Press, 1994). • McFarlane, K. B. *John Wycliffe and the Beginnings of English Nonconformity* (Penguin, 1972). • McFarlane, K. B. *Lancastrian Kings and Lollard Knights* (Oxford University Press, 1972). • Murray, A. 'Confession Before 1215', *Transactions of the Royal Historical Society*, 6th ser., 3 (1993), 51–81. • Oram, R. *Historic Whithorn: Archaeology and Development* (Council for British Archaeology, 2010). • Oram, R. 'Prayer, Property and Profit: Scottish Monasteries, c. 1100–c. 1300', in *Scottish Power Centres from the Early Middle Ages to the Twentieth Century*, ed. S. Foster et al. (Cruithne, 1998), 79–99. • Orme, N. *English Schools in the Middle Ages* (Routledge, 1973). • *Pastoral Care Before the Parish*, ed. J. Blair and R. Sharpe (Leicester University Press, 1992). • Southern, R. W. *Robert Grosseteste: The Growth of a English Mind in Medieval Europe* (2nd edn, Oxford University Press, 1992). • Southern, R. W. *Saint Anselm: A Portrait in a Landscape* (Cambridge University Press, 1990). • Stringer, K. J. 'Reform Monasticism and Celtic Scotland, c. 1140–c. 1240', in *Alba: Celtic Scotland in the Middle Ages*, ed. I. B. Cowan and R. A. McDonald (Phantassie, 2000), 127–65. • *Studies in Clergy and Ministry in Medieval England* (Borthwick Studies in History, 1, 1991). • Swanson, R. *Church and Society in Late Medieval England* (Oxford University Press, 1989). • Thomas, H. M. *The Secular Clergy in England, 1066–1216* (Oxford University Press, 2014). • Turner, R. V. 'The Miles Literatus in Twelfth- and Thirteenth-Century England: How Rare a Phenomenon?' *American Historical Review*, 83 (1978), 928–65. • *Twelfth-Century Archidiaconal and Vice-Archidiaconal Acta*, ed. B. R. Kemp (Canterbury and York Society, 92, 2001). • Veitch, K. '"Replanting Paradise": Alexander I and the Reform of Religious Life in Scotland', *Innes Review*, 52 (2001), 136–66.

NOTES

1. J. Blair, *The Church in Anglo-Saxon Society* (Oxford University Press, 2005), 417.
2. *Councils and Synods with Other Documents Relating to the English Church*, ed. M. Brett, F. M. Powicke, C. R. Cheney, D. Whitelock and C. N. L. Brooke, pt I: 2 (Clarendon, 1981), no. 87.
3. C. Bémont, *Simon de Montfort*, trans. E. F. Jacob (2nd edn, Oxford University Press, 1930), 277.
4. Stephen de Rouen, *Carmen elegiacum*, in *Chronicles of the Reigns of Stephen, Henry II and Richard*, ed. R. Howlett (4 vols., Rolls Series, 1886–9), II: 768.
5. *Monasticon Anglicanum*, ed. J. Caley et al. (8 vols., Record Commission, 1817–30), V: 512.

7 The Wealth of Britain

OVERVIEW

It was not until the very end of the middle ages that we find any inkling amongst contemporaries that nations and regions possess economies that exerted influence on the lives of their inhabitants. The idea that there were invisible forces – other than spiritual – that formed human affairs had to wait until the eighteenth century. But medieval people were very much in favour of accumulating wealth; they were alert to ways that it could be done and imaginative about exploiting them. Governments too were keen to tap into the wealth of the country, especially in times of war, though when they did their ham-fisted and directive methods could produce disastrous and unintended results. Britain had a few valuable commodities which contributed to its overall wealth and England's sterling silver currency was a strong one throughout the middle ages. The fact that the Scottish silver penny was tied to sterling parity for most of the middle ages tells us that, though the English economy was dominant within the British Isles, economic activity was very much a British phenomenon.

Wool and Wealth

Britain was perceived as a wealthy island in the eleventh century, and Scandinavian pirates and armies had been liberating that wealth to their own advantage for generations. The national land tax of pre-Conquest England was called the Danegeld for that very reason. England was far and away the economically dominant area of the archipelago in population, resources and markets. The fact that the English currency was so well monitored and exploited by the West Saxon monarchy was as much to the advantage of the kings themselves as to the merchants who needed a standard national currency in which to deal. Kings were also able to profit from imposing charges on trade at ports. Whether perception of England's great wealth matched reality is less clear. Were Vikings raiding England because it was so notoriously rich in silver and treasure, or was it because it was just a wealthier place than where they lived? There is a theory that it was the export of wool from England to the continent that produced a long-term beneficial balance of trade which attracted streams of silver into the islands and generated constant surpluses. Those who like to see economics as the mainspring for historical events would point out that the wealth of England would have been another reason for the Conqueror to invest so much prestige and resources in a risky bid for its throne in 1066. One thing that is clear, however, is that England had long possessed a vibrant market economy in 1000, one which allowed the kings to raise considerable sums from their subjects and their economic activity.

Wool is by far and away the best-known medieval commodity associated with the British Isles and its reputed wealth. Recent studies have emphasised that the wool trade with the continent was flourishing well before the eleventh century. Domesday Book demonstrates quite how much money the rural economy of England could, even then, generate for its landlords, and also that it was not arable farming which was their primary source of wealth. As early as the reign of Edgar (959–975) standardised weights and measures were imposed across England as a way of regulating but also assisting the marketing of unprocessed wool. Production of wool was generated in the eleventh century principally by smallholders in places like the open wolds of Lincolnshire and Yorkshire, though any area of open commonland might pasture large flocks belonging to a variety of peasant landholders, particularly on fenland during the drier months of the year. The raw wool was accumulated at market centres by agents who then dealt with the export merchants who shipped their cargoes principally to the Low Countries, where there was only poor-quality wool but the technology and the manpower to process it into high-quality cloth. Some idea of the key importance of English wool to the medieval economy of the Rhineland and Low Countries is the way English sterling pennies circulated as valid currency in the region from late in Henry II's reign through to the end of the thirteenth century, while the coinage of Brabant and other principalities took English designs as their model. England in effect had constructed an international 'sterling zone' on the basis of its 'wool-backed' currency. Scotland too shared in the wealth of the trade, exporting perhaps as much as a fifth of what English growers did at the peak of the market in the later thirteenth century, much to the benefit of its king's customs revenues. Scottish wool was a valuable commodity in the Low Countries, and the trade probably benefited from the fact that English sterling circulated as freely in Scotland as it did in Flanders. English and Scottish pennies had parity in value until the 1360s.

The wool trade expanded after 1100 for a number of reasons, including a growing population and an increasingly safe carrying-trade across a far less piratical North Sea. Even before 1200 there is evidence for selective breeding of sheep with the finer-quality fleeces available in Lincolnshire and the Welsh Marches, whose rams were sold on to landlords across the country, which gave some competition to the famously fine wools that came from Spain. The great twelfth-century monasteries of England (not to mention Wales, Ireland and Lowland Scotland) are famous for pasturing major flocks on the land they reclaimed or cleared and ranched as 'granges'. But they were not by any means the only major exploiters of the market; earls and barons could be quite as alert. Large estates, whether ecclesiastical or aristocratic, were by the thirteenth century entering into advance contracts with merchants for the delivery of their fleeces which were yet to be shorn. The merchants dealt with shipping agents to accumulate the cargoes at the ports of exit and ship them to fulfil contracts they had made with the weaving shops of the cities of Flanders, Holland and Brabant. In the case of wool we can see that throughout the period of this book a network of contacts and credit latticed together producers, middlemen, merchants, buyers and manufacturers across Britain, the North Sea and the Low Countries, which when taken in total was quite spectacular in its complexity and potential to generate wealth. It also attracted international capital, as merchants from Italy and Provence engaged with and exploited the trade in the thirteenth century.

Wool was so important to the economy of north-west Europe by the late twelfth century that the Angevin kings of England were able to use their control of the trade to influence relations with Flanders and the Western Empire. Of course this worked both ways: the ransom for King Richard in 1192 was calculated by the emperor and his advisers on the basis of their estimate of the value of the annual wool trade with the continent: 50,000 sacks or 6 million fleeces. The close economic bond was one reason why the counts of Flanders were time and again obliged to take the English side in the king of England's disputes with the king of France, though the west of their county was a French fief, not an imperial one like the rest of Flanders. It was the bad relations between English and French which eventually persuaded Flemings to drop out of the supply market by the 1270s and concentrate their capital on the actual production process, which resigned the commodity trading to Italians, Brabanters and English agents.

English kings did not help the trade, for efforts to exploit it usually met with negative and unintended consequences. The most catastrophic example was in the 1290s when Edward I's desperation for money caused him impose the infamous 'maltolt' between 1294 and 1297, when he levied a heavy additional export duty on wool. The merchants protected their profits by offering less money to the producers, thus bringing the price for fleeces down to a level at which most of it would not sell. The trade with the continent was halved as a result. Uncertainties and the collapse of Italian banking houses were all factors in what became in effect a catastrophic Plantagenet nationalisation of the trade. Edward III likewise meddled in the wool trade, treating it as a royal monopoly to help fund his expensive campaigns in the Low Countries between 1337 and 1341, with equally bad results. Thereafter he took the less contentious option of relying on high duties on wool exports to raise money.

Already in 1313 the Flemings had fixed on St-Omer as the central commodity market to deal in wool, to which all merchants must resort, the 'Staple' as it was called. The English adopted the same practice of designating staple towns in England in which export wool was to be warehoused and where English middlemen were given financial advantages in dealing with agents. Foreigners were then squeezed out, to the advantage of associations of English merchants who were given control by the king of the levying of custom. The export of wool declined after the boom years of the thirteenth century. Wool exports nonetheless remained the foundation for the prosperity of Kingston upon Hull and several ports in East Anglia. The export in raw wool remained around or below 10,000 sacks a year from the 1390s to 1500, but it was only about a quarter of what it had been before 1300. Much more wool after 1300 stayed in Britain, to fuel the rise of a domestic cloth industry. So the decline in exports was more than made up for by domestic demand, and wool remained king. Royal policy gave its management over to the merchants of the Staple – predominantly Londoners – who from 1400 ran it as a near-monopoly from what became their base at the English town of Calais and who worked hard to exclude foreign interlopers. They were willing to make regular loans out of their profits to needy fifteenth-century kings in order to maintain their control. They also used their monopoly to push up prices to foreign manufacturers rather than antagonise the English producers, who had a means of expressing their dissatisfaction through their friends in the Commons. The Calais mint as a result became a very important instrument of English fiscal control over currency from the 1420s to the 1470s.

English sterling currency was maintained at a high quality throughout the middle ages, and inferior foreign coins with debased silver content had to be melted and recoined as English sterling at an Exchange. Any foreign merchant had to pay in English coin and so ended up paying for his wool at a discount, while the mint's profits helped the king pay for the Calais garrison. It was good news for large English merchants and the Crown, but bad for Flemish merchants who found the price for wool rocketing in real terms. Many went out of business and the cloth trade abroad shrank accordingly. So the story of England's only great commodity trade in the middle ages is therefore one of over-exploitation, clumsy management and market regulation, leading to a decline which had remarkably far-ranging economic consequences for foreign markets and industry, though its mismanagement had one beneficial consequence of giving a massive stimulus to the home cloth industry (for which, see below).

British Commodities

The British Isles had few natural resources that the continent was interested in, other than its wool. One exception was, however, the scarcer metals, notably tin, but also to an extent lead (especially for the silver it contained). Thoughtful commentators in England were well aware of this, as a tract on the nation's wealth noted in the mid fifteenth century: 'For Spain and Flanders are as brothers and neither may live well without the other. But they may not maintain their importance without our English commodities, wool and tin.'[1] The mining and export of tin were ancient practices in Devon and in particular in Cornwall, going back to prehistoric times. Until 1300 England was the only source of tin in Europe, which made its mining highly profitable, for it was an essential component of all sorts of alloys, notably bronzes and pewter. Lead was mined in Cumberland, and both commodities were organised as royal monopolies in the twelfth century. Tin was particularly well regulated as a mining enterprise. Even with the opening of tin mines in Saxony and Bohemia after 1300, the price for English tin rose steadily in the fourteenth and fifteenth centuries, and the annual value of the commodity was around £10,000 in 1400. The 'farm' of tin mines (or the 'stannary') was a significant source of income to the king, and (when they were occasionally conceded it in the twelfth and thirteenth centuries) to the earls of Cornwall and indeed in later centuries to the duke of Cornwall, who was also prince of Wales. Ore was strip-mined under the regulation of the stannary court, or it was panned from streams and rivers. The smelted ore was cast into ingots and exported from West Country harbours to the continent principally by way of ports in the Low Countries or Plantagenet-ruled southern France

Lead was mined in a variety of places in Britain at different periods, but particularly in the Derbyshire Peak, Cumberland, Yorkshire, North Wales and the Mendip Hills. It was not a particularly profitable trade for export, and it was the presence of silver in the ores which made it at all worthwhile. It was the silver that made it occasionally economic to dig shaft mines to recover the ore, which was an expensive and hazardous process. A total of 385 tonnes of lead was mined in England and Wales in 1400 and 625 tonnes in 1500, which is hardly a huge output, but it was at least sufficient to mean that the British Isles did not need to import the metal, which had a widespread use in roofing, windows, cisterns, domestic utensils and pipes. Lead was also used to stamp the medals pilgrims collected from shrines and in glazes for pottery. Lead was a component with copper in the alloy called pewter, which was being used to cast vessels as early as 1000 in England. Pewter was perfect for the casting of medals as well as for cheap domestic and ecclesiastical chalices and flagons. Large-scale production of pewter objects began in England in the fourteenth century, and had a major centre in London, where 200 pewterers were working in the mid fifteenth century and where a guild regulated the trade from 1348. Pewterware was being exported from England by the reign of Edward II (1307–1327) and by the fifteenth century was the second most profitable exported article after cloth.

A far more common metal as a commodity, and less profitable as a result, was iron. Accessible it might have been in Britain, but medieval England still imported quality ingots of the processed metal from Spain and Sweden. Iron ore occurs in many parts of the British Isles, but there were particular centres where ore was mined and smelted in the middle ages, of which one of the most productive was in the southern March of Wales, notably in the Forest of Dean and the Wye valley where the limonite ores were extensively mined and processed as early as the beginning of the twelfth century. This region had particular advantages: the accessibility of ore, nearby forests to provide charcoal for the furnaces and a substantial river to offer both a source of cooling and a means of shipping the ingots to the coast. Monmouth was a particular centre for smelting in the twelfth century, with bloomeries (primitive furnaces) and forges for smelting wrought iron lining the bank of the Wye downriver of the town. The town's river meadows are to this day underlaid by acres of waste slag from the medieval processing. A particular interest of the Forest of Dean is the way that the local industry was managed and exploited at the time by local barons and monasteries. Excavations in the Wealden iron fields of Kent have revealed a continuous process of technological improvement in iron smelting throughout the middle ages, introducing water power, mechanical bellows and bigger furnaces producing bigger yields. Blast furnaces had been known in continental Europe since the twelfth century, but the technology did not spread to England until the end of the fifteenth century. When it did appear, it allowed the production of high-carbon pig iron which was worked to produce quality bar iron and steel in quantities, and we then enter the world where heavy industry was possible.

A medieval commodity which is difficult to assess and characterise was fish. East Coast fisheries began an abrupt rise around 1100 when the North Sea gradually ceased to be a highway for pirates and the potential of its migratory herring shoals became evident. Fishing ports multiplied rapidly down the east coast of Scotland and England (and indeed all around the North Sea down through the Channel to Normandy) during the twelfth century, providing a major economic impetus to new boroughs such as North Leith, Hartlepool, Scarborough and Yarmouth. Their annual fairs were held at the time when the coastal shoals of 'land' herring were passing the ports and the population surged from the nomadic fleets following the fish. Herring, salted and smoked for preservation, was a commodity which might well be sold to Baltic merchants and exported, as well as traded widely inland as far as Nottingham and Coventry. There was certainly a huge and constant demand for it, particularly in the seasons of Lent and Advent, which gave these boroughs a constant level of prosperity denied the trading ports. It also explains the willingness of London fishmongers to invest in the deep sea fleets, because there was a guaranteed return. The fleets of the east coast ports expanded to exploit the deep sea fisheries of 'winter' herring, and their larger vessels fared out to the Icelandic fisheries. Some indeed may have been fishing the Grand Banks off Newfoundland generations before Columbus reached the Caribbean. A hint as to the profitability of this trade can be found in the tithe records for the port of Scarborough, from which the fishing industry in 1416 can be calculated to have had an annual value of £1,555, which easily rivalled the returns for wool exports. Herring and the Icelandic fisheries went into decline in the fifteenth century, in part due to devastating losses to the Iceland fleet due to storms in 1419, though in compensation new deep sea ones opened nearer at hand in the shallow waters of Dogger Bank, where cod spawned.

 The Peasant Economy

The great majority of the population of Britain throughout this period was engaged in the production of food, through either arable or pastoral farming. Even what we would call urban areas were engaged in farming. Inhabitants of towns and cities generally had plots of land in the fields that lay outside the town walls or suburbs which they would use to pasture their own animals, and sometimes lease for cultivation and market gardening. Urban pigs wandered the streets to forage. There was in fact little of the urban–rural divide in medieval Britain except for the very greatest of its cities: London. London (and its satellites of Southwark and Westminster) was a special case, as its exceptionally large resident and transitory population and its many elite households and religious communities needed to be fed, often in style. Not only that, but fuel in great quantities was needed for its fires, and fodder was demanded for its beasts of burden. Recent studies have shown in great detail how even in the thirteenth century the agricultural production of the region surrounding London was geared to generating a surplus to feed the great city, whose impact was noticeable not just in Surrey, Bedfordshire and Essex but for its livestock needs out as far as Northamptonshire and Oxfordshire. For instance, the Thames valley before 1300 specialised in production of crops of rye, which was in great demand to produce the cheap bread to feed the large numbers of London's poorer inhabitants, while market gardening and dairy production dominated the fields for miles around the City. Since the City's demand for wood for its fires could not be satisfied from its region, a long-term shift was made to shipping

Northumbrian 'sea coal' south for its hearths and kitchens as the conurbation reached its peak population of around 100,000 in 1300, with long-term consequences for its air quality.

For most of the population of England, however, their lives were lived in their hamlets, villages and the nearest market town. At the beginning of the period of this book, agricultural workers came in remarkably varied groups of status, which in part reflected the disruptions of the Scandinavian invasions. There were slaves in England, in the sense of servants owned by their masters who might be traded. A large part of the profits of the Viking pillaging of Northern Europe was drawn from the enslavement and sale of human beings, and the practice had been for centuries ingrained in Anglo-Saxon and Welsh society. In 1086 this lowest level of status was still a reality in society, and it has been suggested conjecturally on the basis of Domesday Survey that up to 12 per cent of England's population were still then slaves. There were reasons to keep slaves, who tended to be specialised workers such as ploughmen, but also it was regarded as a charitable act for landowners to free them, which was a perverse reason to keep them. It may well have simply been this sort of illogicality which led to the rapid disappearance of institutionalised slavery from England around 1100. Certainly the historian William of Malmesbury believed in the 1120s that previous Norman kings had been urged to suppress the slave trade by the Church and that in his day slavery was a regrettable characteristic of the more primitive Celtic societies of the British Isles. There is little evidence, however, that slavery was any more prevalent in Wales and Scotland than it was in pre-Conquest England. Its rapid decline in Britain was likely to be part of more universal economic and social changes.

The people we call peasants were no simple and uniform group of poor rustic labourers. The idea that they were comes from the medieval elite itself, who despised all agricultural workers as uneducated, uncultured and crude, the very opposite of what they were in fact. The agricultural workers we find in Domesday Book were very varied. Those of the North and Midlands were more likely to be free cultivators of their own lands, for which they generally owed a cash rent. They are seen to be a consequence of the colonisation of those areas by Scandinavians in the ninth century. Such men might well have been called 'villeins' though the pejorative nature of the word masks what might have been quite well-off tenant or even **freehold** farmers, the ancestors of the later medieval **yeomen** and franklins. But even in the North and Midlands there were peasants who were closer to slaves than freemen, tied to particular estates with extensive obligations to the landlord. The lowest went by the French name of 'bordiers', men without access to ploughteams and field strips, little more than low-status labourers, though at least having smallholdings of an acre or two to farm in their village. 'Cottars' were probably also smallholders who had some share in a ploughteam as well as their cottage garden. Both these groups may have included people whose immediate ancestors in 1086 may have been slaves. As well as these, there were very likely peasants with no land, subsistence wage labourers, who are certainly very evident in the later medieval sources, though barely noticed earlier. Unfree peasants likewise farmed Scottish estates, though thirteenth-century sources indicate they mostly worked the land in return for short leases, without the heavy obligations to work on the lord's own demesne, which was a less significant element of the Scottish rural estate, or 'toun', the equivalent of the English 'township' or settlement.

Manors

This was the mix of agricultural labourers, tenant and free farmers who made the strangely complex world of the medieval manor possible. The word 'manor' comes ultimately from the Latin verb *manere*, and simply means a 'dwelling', though the manor became more than that. England, and for that matter lowland Wales (where the Welsh word *maenor* meant the same thing as 'manor' did in England, or rather had the same meanings) and Anglian Scotland, were already largely manorialised by 1000. It was a development associated with rising population in the ninth and tenth centuries, when landowners moved to concentrate population and rationalise production and rents on core villages, many artificially created for the purpose. In England, the village's fields were a communal enterprise, cultivated in strips owned or rented by individuals, but all sowing the same crops, with types of crop being rotated on a two- or three-year cycle and fields periodically rested as 'fallow' for the soil to recover some of their lost nitrogen from animals pastured on them. The manor developed as a cash-generating enterprise for its lord. Its field strips were worked by peasant tenants for rents, shares of crops and a set amount of work on the lord's own reserved acreage (his 'demesne' or home farm). The lord built mills (increasingly wind-powered after the end of the twelfth century), where he had a monopoly of milling his tenants' grain, which was done for fees (see Fig. 7.1). He expected other payments for allowing pigs into his woodland in season to graze acorns and beech mast. By the twelfth century (and in England quite possibly before the Conquest) lords had found another way of generating cash and status from their manors by holding a court (often called in English a 'halmote'). They collected money there from free tenants for a variety of reasons, such as fines simply for not attending, and they exerted a low level of justice over peasants: adjudicating disputes over land and judging public order offences, 'affray' being a common one, which of course brought in more fines. Lords would also charge fees to allow the lowest level of tied or bonded peasants to succeed to their tenures, to buy beasts or just to marry off themselves or their children.

This was the 'classic' medieval manor, but the reality was often more complex. A manor could easily be divided, for instance, when it was left by a lord to his several

Fig. 7.1 **Medieval Post Windmill**. The new technology of the windmill was developed in the lowlands of the Netherlands and eastern England in the 1180s, where there were no fast-running streams to power watermills effectively. They were erected on top of artificial mounds to increase the size of the sails to turn the heavy stones in the cabins. They were an early sign that medieval technology was beginning to transcend that of the ancient world.

children, and the shares then became smaller manors in their own right: which could easily produce a village subdivided between several lords and manors, with acreage dispersed across the fields and with rival mills and courts. Before 1100 this might be resolved by simply building new settlements as cores for the smaller manors and their fields, and abandoning the old one. The easier alternative was for one heir to buy out the shares of the others. New manors were still being created out of former wasteland or by new grants out of old estates well into the thirteenth century, so the medieval landowning map was by no means static. In some areas the land *outside* the open arable fields was more important to the lord, as when it contained extensive meadowland and pasture, such as in upland and wolds areas which specialised in ranching cattle and sheep.

Likewise, lordship had its limits and, like the king, a manorial lord had sometimes to negotiate with his tenants and engineer compromises. This would principally be over access to common land where the peasants' own animals were pastured: though it might technically belong to the lord, it was often managed communally through the halmote. Lords too had to offer something in return for lordship, such as for instance maintaining the drainage ditches and lanes of the manor, and keeping its church in repair. There were other, sometimes large, stretches of England which had no single proprietor but were managed communally by the surrounding lords and freeholders.

Such was Wallingfen, a huge wetland area of the East Riding of Yorkshire which offered fishing, peat-cutting and common pasture on a large scale to the people of more than fifty surrounding townships, and was run by an elected council of lesser gentry and yeomen from at least the thirteenth century until it was inclosed in 1781. It was in fact owned by no one.

The position of the lower level of dependent bonded peasant within these manors was not enviable. It is not by any means unusual after 1100 to find named individual peasants, their services and 'their brats' (Lat. *sequela*) granted away by lords to favoured individuals and monastic houses in a way that hardly distinguished them from outright slaves. There is a general belief amongst historians that the position of the custom-bound peasant in fact worsened during the twelfth century, and if so it was because his customary obligations to his lord began to be discussed and defined in common law courts. It may also be that rising population put free peasants at a disadvantage, causing their holdings to be subdivided to their progressive impoverishment (though the up-side would be that some peasants with the cash resources could accumulate bigger holdings by buying others out). Free peasants were reduced to servitude in all periods, and the process of impoverishment is certainly visible in twelfth-century records. The trend in the social standing of the peasant may have been generally downwards, as the Latin word *villanus* changed its Domesday Book meaning of simple 'peasant' to 'low-born serf' in the twelfth century.

Aggressive lords would seek to maximise their profits from the townships they controlled, and lawyers were useful and ruthless allies in the process, especially when it came to imposing objectionable labour services. The Angevin government helpfully provided in the 1160s a judicial order which allowed landholders to reclaim anyone alleged to be their peasant, forcing the burden of proof of freedom on the accused. The increase in record keeping was another way of tightening control: ecclesiastical and lay landlords were generating lists of peasants and their obligations already in the twelfth century (and in some cases before) to make sure village reeves and manorial stewards knew exactly what was owed the lord and by whom. The practice was universal by the thirteenth century. Such records meant that, when bonded peasants chose to argue away their status, the case for their 'naifty' could be argued from the written evidence as much as through local jury verdicts. There was certainly a movement in the thirteenth century to evade onerous peasant obligation, and not a few village communities banded together to hire lawyers to argue before the justices that at one time or other in the past their village had been owned by the Crown, because peasants on the king's manors were by definition freeholders. The burdensome nature of peasant tenure was just as evident in Scotland. Significantly, in 1305 the peasants on Scottish Crown manors petitioned Edward I for the same rights as those in England.

Change in the Manorial Economy

The condition of the peasant labourer in England changed after the Black Death of 1348–1350. When as much as half the population was lost, the remaining rural work force was obviously in a different position from its predecessors. Where labour is scarce it becomes expensive. Women experienced some of the benefits of this, as they rapidly found new job opportunities as weavers in the textile industry (though unsurprisingly they did not get equal pay with men). Within a decade of the pandemic's end, land-owners were being obliged to recognise the new state of affairs, despite a rear-guard action mounted in Parliament to impose statutes in 1351 to freeze pay to what it had been in 1348. The old labour-intensive and coercive practices were in collapse by 1380. The manorial court lost the ability to enforce some of the more objectionable labour customs, and by the early fifteenth century its control over succession to peasant ten-ures became increasingly nominal, no more than a fee paid on a property transfer. The manor courts in fact gained a new and more useful role as the court of record for certain type of landholding, **copyholds**, which still paid some vestigial fees to the manorial lord.

The countryside began to take on a new shape in the fifteenth century. Peasant holdings which were vacated and unfilled were consolidated by landlords into parcels of land to be leased ('farmed') for terms of years, which allowed the consolidation of 'farmholdings': taking land out of the communal system of open fields and introduc-ing a new flexibility in land use, not to mention a degree of entrepreneurship amongst the former peasantry. Where villages had been surrounded by two to four prairie-like open fields before 1400, in places where pastoral farming was more profitable the fields could be divided up, inclosed and hedged. It was perhaps not so much that the peasants rose in revolt in 1381 because the landlords were attempting to reimpose unsustaina-ble practices on the poor, but that both lords and peasants knew agricultural life was changing and peasants were deeply irritated and alienated by the fact that the Common Law and its practitioners simply could not react to radical change in the countryside fast enough. In 1381 it was the judicial officials and lawyers who were employed to enforce the one-sided provisions of the 1351 statute who fell to the swords and clubs of the peasant rising, not so much the landlords, and revolt happened in those areas where legal constraints and traditional practices were most deeply entrenched before the plague and harder to reimpose. The peasants took care where they could to burn manorial records, a tactic which historians might deplore, but whose intelligence can-not be denied. Serfdom was not abolished as a result of the rising of 1381, but it was already dying as an institution, and individual and local decisions led to its effective extinction within two generations.

In Scotland the situation was instructively different. The objectionable labour ser-vices that were demanded of English peasants were not so significant to the economy of Scottish manors, and though Scottish 'neyfs' were their lord's property, it is evident that landlords had lost interest in the more arbitrary features of peasant status even before 1300. This has been put down to population increase and a shortage of cultivable land, which allowed lords to hire cheap labour to work their own fields and pastures without imposing on their peasant tenants. The unfree peasant was an agricultural irrelevance in Scotland already by the time of the Black Death, and serfdom disappeared there without trace or complaint well before 1400. What did survive of the manorial world, as in England, was the way the lords exploited their monopoly on milling and the jurisdiction of their courts so as to raise revenue. As in England, later medieval village townships became stratified into societies of husbandmen and lower-class wage labourers. Husbandmen controlled small estates, sometimes mixed freeholds and customary tenures which were easier to accumulate after the loss of population in 1348–1350, and they had access to their own ploughs, or part-shares in teams. The wage labourers or cottars rented cottages with gardens, and they got by farming a few acres or working for husbandmen. In England, these labourers and servants generally made up the majority in each rural township. It was doubtless the dispossessed and poverty-stricken lower end of these communities that fuelled the movement of indigent paupers on to the roads of Britain, which is increasingly evident in the fifteenth century.

The agrarian economy was beginning to shift at the end of the period of this book. The lowland countryside of 1100 characterised by manorial estates and open fields, communally farmed by bonded serfs, was shaken by the population loss of the fourteenth century. Open fields did not of course disappear, and working examples were not uncommonly to be found across Britain even in the last half of the nineteenth century. But gaps opened up in the old way of life. Well before 1500 entrepreneurial yeomen were finding ways of abstracting lands by lease and purchase from the village fields and setting up the mixed holdings we would recognise as farmsteads, deciding their own crops and mixing forms of agriculture: with gardens, orchards, coppices, arable closes and (particularly) pasture for the keeping of profitable livestock. These were the men who began the process of inclosure of the landscape into smaller hedged closes. They were naturally hostile to the common rights which were so valuable to peasant cultivators and labourers but which limited their own opportunities.

Poverty

A further and allied characteristic of the later medieval economy was a rise in poverty and vagrancy. The poor of course were perpetual in medieval society, and the Gospels confirmed they were part of God's plan. They were indeed valued by the wealthy, as charity towards the unfortunate provided opportunities for salvation: they were often called 'Christ's poor'. Monks indeed categorised themselves as a class of poor deserving society's charity and protection above all others, in a rather curious and ironic reversal which much amused nineteenth-century Protestant historians. Most towns and cities opened one or more hospitals in the twelfth century for the benefit of the poor, where food and board were offered under the supervision of clerics and chaplains who led their little communities of men or women (they were usually segregated) in a form of monastic rule. Great lords and bishops were particularly engaged in this form of charity before 1200. Quite often these houses were to be found at town gates, because the biblical poor customarily begged at the gates of the rich. These, however, were for the respectable poor, those who had no resources but did have influence and connections to gain them places in such houses. There were still well over 500 of them in England and Wales in Henry VIII's reign and perhaps as many as 50 in Scotland at the end of the medieval period. Many of the older hospitals developed in the later middle ages into what we would regard as almshouses, rows of subsidised housing for those with little or no income, whose respectability and obligatory prayer for the founder were supervised by a warden. The fifteenth century produced in fact a vogue amongst the urban wealthy for founding such institutions (often called by the French name *Maisons-Dieu*) for the benefit of their deprived fellow citizens.

The indigent and rootless poor were a different matter entirely. Such people fuelled the clamorous crowds at church doors while funeral masses were going on within, waiting in hopes of a distribution of clothes and pennies under the terms of the last testament of the departed. They would also drift around at harvest time looking for casual work and frequent the hatches of monastic almonries seeking bread and shoes. Twelfth- and thirteenth-century monasteries maintained a generally good reputation for supporting the indigent, particularly in times of famine. But an increasing hostility to the poor begins to be evident after the crises of the fourteenth century, when many began to blame the poor for their own troubles, not least in asserting that their misfortune was the consequence of their own sinfulness. The decent agricultural poor peasant working hard to make ends meet on his smallholding might still be admired by writers, but the beggar was a social danger. Those who secured a place in an almshouse were specifically forbidden from begging on the streets. Marginal, roaming characters were blamed for the crime and assaults that would always occur on the unpoliced roads of medieval Britain, even though most violence that was recorded in medieval sources happened between angry, armed and confrontational males whose verbal disputes got out of hand but who knew each other well enough to hate. The rootless certainly increased in numbers in the later middle ages, but they did so because the terms of the labour market became harsh in their flexibility, with the poor labourer becoming mobile in search of work and truculent in negotiating terms with resentful and miserly employers. No wonder so many gravitated to the towns, where there were more opportunities for casual labour but less sympathy for the indigent, to whom the established inhabitants were not bound by any ties of neighbourly feeling.

Towns and Trade

As has already been said, there was not a clear line between urban and rural life in the middle ages, when even a sizeable town in medieval terms might have a population of only around 3,000 and be set in its own field system. Nonetheless there was a proportion of the population of Britain whose occupations were not rural and whose life was centred on the guilds and markets of cities and towns. Towns grew in the first three centuries covered by this book, though not in any explosive way. If there was an urban revolution it happened in Wales and Scotland, whose urban life and commerce before 1100 were non-existent. The lack of towns and trade was in fact one of the reasons the twelfth-century English found to despise their British neighbours. David I of Scotland (1124–1153), however, founded fifteen royal burghs in the east and centre of his kingdom, offering the citizens the privileges of Newcastle upon Tyne. He was followed in doing this by his magnates and bishops. In Wales it was the marcher barons who deliberately created towns at the centre of their lordships, such as those founded at Chepstow, Cardiff and Pembroke, which often received the customs of Hereford (derived ultimately from the Norman town of Breteuil). These little towns had to offer good terms to attract the migrants from England who formed their populations. Welsh lords were slow to follow suit, though where they took over new towns, as they did at Caerleon and Cardigan, they maintained them. In 1100 Britain had 100 towns and 10 per cent of its population living in urban centres. By 1300 there were 830 towns and 20 per cent of the population lived in them in England. In Scotland it is unlikely that urban centres ever included more than 10 per cent of the population. Most of these towns were small, and the further west and north you travelled, the smaller they were. Scottish and Welsh towns almost all fell into the range of 1,000 to 2,000 inhabitants, whereas the more prosperous English Midland market towns and its east coast ports might well fall within the range of 3,000–5,000.

The greatest of Britain's cities was undoubtedly London, which then as now had no peer in the British Isles in terms of population and commercial opportunity and indeed in north-western Europe was surpassed only by Paris. Even though there is little evidence about it in Domesday Book, which barely mentions it, London certainly had expanded into suburbs beyond its Roman walls before 1066. By 1200 London was the centre of a large conurbation, with Southwark growing south of the bridge over the Thames, and the suburb of the Strand swallowing the former Middlesex village of Charing (around about where Trafalgar Square now is) to link with the rising borough of Westminster. Even by the 1050s great magnates and bishops had properties close to the royal hall of Westminster. By 1200 all the lords and bishops, and some great abbots, had halls in the vicinity of London and Westminster. By 1250 the greatest of them, such as the Clare earl of Gloucester, had developed these into 'wardrobes' where luxury goods and commodities were acquired and stored by their agents. The earl of Leicester's twelfth-century hall on the Strand was progressively developed and added to and, having come in the 1260s into the hands of the king's son, Earl Edmund of Leicester and Derby, became a full-scale palace which took the name of the Savoy: a noble precinct which was an expression of the great power of the princely house of Lancaster which Edmund founded. By 1200 London had more than 100 parish churches, and its population has been estimated in the thirteenth century as then approaching 80,000 residents. The greater conurbation of Southwark and Westminster would have added perhaps a further 10,000–15,000. The description of London in the 1170s by its native son, William fitz Stephen, already talks then of the crowded City, its fortifications and great churches, its schools and markets, its cookshops and bath-houses, and the high standard of living of its urban elite, who lived as grandly as aristocrats. He also talks of the fires that occasionally swept through the streets, lined principally with timber houses.

Urban elites were already in the twelfth century running their cities and towns through control of the councils (generally called 'guilds merchant') as unapologetic oligarchies based on individual wealth. This meant a deliberate marginalisation of the poorer citizens, who on occasion rose against the rich in times of civil disorder: Edward II's reign was particularly notorious for urban riots and risings. London as ever was a class above this again and its urban politics occasionally had national consequences. This was never more noticeable than at the time of disputed royal succession, when Londoners maintained, as they did in 1066, that they had a formal right to be consulted. The most notorious example of London's national influence was in 1141 when its warring factions first lurched to accept Matilda when she was in the ascendant, and then turned against her when she failed to reward their adherence, driving her out of Middlesex. On that occasion London determined that England would not have a ruling queen. The City attempted the same in 1216 when it rejected the Angevin dynasty and opened its gates to Louis of France, whom the Londoners hailed as king, though on that occasion it backed the loser.

By 1300 cities and towns were fostering civic identities. They took coats of arms and had corporate seals. They invested heavily in the great churches which honoured their patron saint and which housed chantries for the commemoration of the souls, not just of dead citizens who could afford it, but of the entire town. Urban religious guilds might well recruit local aristocrats as much as citizens. Great processional feasts of the Church were attended by the mayor and 'commonalty' (the community of citizens) and the trade guilds, who offered entertainments and pageants. A fair of several days might occur on and around the feast day of its patron saint. Towns in the twelfth and thirteenth centuries undertook civic projects, and not just the defences of battlemented walls and gates, which still survive in some towns, of which York remains a fine example. Towns and the monastic houses within them undertook major engineering projects, most of which are now lost. But the remarkable and impressive extent of the subterranean aqueducts which piped a water supply into medieval Exeter are still there below its modern streets. Civic authorities also erected market halls, gaols, tollbooths, common halls for justice and (in the case of ports) quays and locks. Towns may in general have been small, but they had ways of appearing big in the social landscape.

Towns also overshadowed the commercial landscape. They provided a network offering markets and specialised trades to rural communities within six or seven miles around them, and traders moved from one town to the other on their designated market days. But there were national as well as local networks. Working from London or the bigger cities such as Bristol and Norwich, greater merchants would market their luxury goods to their customers. Already around 1200 City merchants were taking bulk orders of wine and fabrics from their wealthy aristocratic customers by letter, sometimes on credit, leaving the customer to pick up the expense of transporting the goods. As has already been said, the cannier aristocrats therefore opened depots for the receiving and storage of goods in their London mansions. Lesser people might still get the benefit of the luxury market from the stalls City merchants set up at the major regional fairs, already important at St Ives (in Huntingdonshire) and Boston (Lincolnshire) in the twelfth century, but itinerant traders in luxury goods could conduct a similar trade by travelling from one to another of the fairs held annually in market towns across the kingdom. There is some evidence that horse thieves and pickpockets did the same, though without the intention of paying for what they acquired.

The Black Death was arguably a bigger economic setback for Britain's towns than it was for the countryside. It hit urban concentrations of population hardest, as the emerging evidence of London's plague pits spectacularly demonstrates. The population collapsed from the 80,000 the City had housed in 1300 to 50,000 in 1377. London did not recover the population density it had experienced in 1300 until well after 1500, and though the great city began a recovery in the later fifteenth century Britain's small towns in general did not. Winchester, with a population of 10,000–12,000 inhabitants in 1300, had declined to 4,000 in 1520. The most vulnerable small boroughs simply disappeared as urban centres, which was the fate of more than a dozen Welsh and Scottish towns. There were exceptions, such as Kingston upon Hull, a late thirteenth-century new settlement which could draw on its importance not just as a wool-exporting port, but also as a base for a major North Sea fishing fleet exploiting the fisheries of Iceland, and later the Dogger Bank. But much of its prosperity was sucked from declining rivals such as Grimsby and Ravenserodd and by the collapse of York as an inland port and industrial centre. Something of the same sort happened to Edinburgh, which came to dominate the trade in Scottish wool with the loss of Berwick to the English, and which under James III gained the additional advantage of becoming the fixed centre of royal administration. By 1500 Edinburgh was rising into a different class of town than Aberdeen and Perth. Trade everywhere declined, as the fall in population did not affect just Britain, though a consequence of this was that London's place in the export and import of goods rose as merchants concentrated their activity there. The prosperous English east coast ports of the thirteenth century withered in the next, affected by their exclusion from the Baltic trade by the German Hanseatic ports. Scottish ports were less handicapped, having the benefit of the more adroit diplomacy of the fifteenth-century Stewart kings, James III and James IV, who became major players in North Sea maritime politics.

The Rise of the Cloth Industry

The Low Countries dominated the manufacture of European textiles through much of the period of this book, and until the fourteenth century Britain's place was to provide the raw material to service the looms of Flanders and Holland. There was always an insular cloth-making trade, however, and there is even some famous evidence of export of English cloaks to the continent in the eighth century. Wool, hemp and flax were processed into thread for weaving into textiles on a local basis in 1000, but the activity remained domestic and dominated by women until male artisans began to take it up on a larger scale in twelfth-century towns. Industrialisation in the cloth industry began with the invention of treadle-powered looms in the eleventh century in north-eastern France. Weavers became an occupational group in English towns during the course of the twelfth century, sometimes organised into regulatory guilds, though not on any scale able to compete with the industry in Picardy and Flanders. Most of their output was for local use, but the growing ambition to produce cloth for the market can be seen in the way that water-powered fulling mills become commoner in the sources before 1200. These thrashed and beat the woven cloth in a pit full of a bleaching clay to remove grease and soften the cloth. Originally it had been done manually with hammers or by treading it by foot in a pit (hence fullers were often called 'walkers').

Towns acquired areas called 'tentergarths', open ground where the fulled cloth could be stretched out on fences in the sunlight to complete the bleaching process. The processing of woollen cloth went further, with the teasing out of the cloth by carding, and then shearing it back. This produced a velvety broadcloth, the finest luxury type of which was called 'scarlet' (which had nothing to do with its colour, though it was often dyed with expensive imported kermes for a rich red colour to enhance its value further). Colour was added by dyes, of which saffron, woad and madder could be grown in Britain (though they seem generally to have been imported). Clothworking towns such as Beverley and Norwich had their own dye-houses where vats, wells, tubs and furnaces were set up. The finished product was checked for quality and length by guild and royal officials, and stamped for a fee. Despite the formidable competition in the

Low Countries, the English domestic cloth industry was visibly expanding as early as the twelfth century.

The early English cloth industry competed on the grounds of quality rather than quantity. The ready supply of fine wool in Lincolnshire and Yorkshire allowed a well-regarded native industry based on a Stamford–Lincoln–York axis producing specialised luxury cloth, such as scarlet, while the East Riding became famous for its quality multicoloured cloth. Fine linens were produced in Hampshire and Dorset. All the factors were in place, therefore, for expansion into an export industry. Before 1300 small-scale export of English cloth was already under way. This was given a major boost by social unrest in Flanders and political tension between England and France, which led to a short-term prohibition of cloth imports from Flanders in 1326. The Hundred Years War was decisive in shifting wool production away from export and into feeding the domestic looms of England. Cloth imports fell with the beginning of mass production of high-value English broadcloths. As profits grew, the industry developed in new regions outside towns, such as the dales of the West Riding and Lancashire, and the Cotswolds, close to supplies of quality wool and water power for fulling. The new Cotswold entrepreneurs were clothiers who contracted out to a cottage industry of weavers, fullers and finishers and then marketed the result. Yorkshire mass-produced cheaper cloth for a different market and on the basis of family enterprise. The cloth industry in towns concentrated on the most valuable and specialised luxury cloth. By 1500 England and Wales had become a major European producer of woollen cloth, with exports reaching the Mediterranean and Eastern Europe. Export of cloth therefore more than balanced the collapse of wool exports in the fourteenth century.

Manufactures

The workshops of London were more than capable of producing luxury goods to match the expensive tastes and demands of the lay and ecclesiastical elites. Although gold was rarely used for coinage in medieval Britain, it was much valued in the form of plate and jewellery. There were some native sources of gold, most notably in west Wales and south-west England, but they produced little. Most gold was either recycled or came from melting down imported gold coins (called 'bezants' from their reputed source in Constantinople or Byzantium, though most were in fact Arab or Moorish dinars). As has been said, silver was a more plentiful metal in Britain than gold though much of it came as a byproduct of the smelting of lead and copper. Manufacture in precious metals and jewels was carried out by the trade group called 'goldsmiths', and the Goldsmiths Company was unsurprisingly one of the most wealthy and influential of the City companies of London, responsible from 1300 for the assaying of the silver value of the currency and of silver plate in general amongst other things, regulating it with 'hallmarks', as it still does.

The busy work of early London goldsmiths can still be seen in the wax impressions of the fine silver dies they were creating for the seals of barons, knights and ecclesiastical dignitaries in the first half of the twelfth century. Little else of their work survives, though what does can be spectacular in both quality and design. They drew on the world's riches for their source material: diamonds, rubies, sapphires and many other gems, even the valuable curiosities of ostrich eggshells and coconut husks, which somehow reached Britain from India and Africa. Pearls at least were home grown by fresh-water mussels in the rivers of Wales, Cumbria and Scotland; indeed 'Scotch pearls' are found in the inventories of the crown jewels of both England and France. Great magnates and princes accumulated in their wardrobes stocks of unworked precious metal and stones, ready to pass on to craftsmen to work into the precious objects they commissioned.

The royal wardrobe accounts are remarkable testaments to the commission and accumulation of luxury fabrics and objects by the kings of England from the second quarter of the thirteenth century onwards, as well as to their demanding tastes. Silk was greatly prized in Britain, though it would not be until the seventeenth century that it was produced here. Nonetheless there was much silk in circulation in medieval Britain, whether derived from the eastern Mediterranean or later from manufactures in Italy, Spain and France, and the demand produced the supply that embroiderers needed to fashion luxury fabrics. Few patrons were more demanding than Edward III. Just for one jousting event in 1334 he equipped himself, his household knights, musicians and thirty-five squires with luxuriously embroidered broadcloth fur-lined suits and hoods, some of cloth of gold, more than two dozen different suits for himself, with specially tailored robes for his particular friends, as well as several sets of complete harness and armour for the action. On every major state festivity and often on minor ones he seems to have ordered elaborate and sometimes fanciful new suits, masks and headdresses for himself, his wife, children and courtiers in which they could enjoy the elaborate court dances and masques. The jewels, pearls and gold might well have been recyclable, but the endless commissions must have kept entire workshops in London busy. His accounts mention the commission of hundreds of items of precious jewelled and enamelled plate: cups, basins, ewers (water jugs), bowls and salt cellars. Little of this gorgeous argosy of royal treasure has weathered the sea of time, though one stunning exception is a jewelled gold coronet probably commissioned in Edward III's last years, which came into the hands of the Electors Palatine by marriage with a daughter of King Henry IV and can still be seen in the Schatzkammer of the Munich Residenz. It is lasting testimony to the beauty and imaginative craftsmanship available to discerning medieval patrons in the workshops off Cheapside.

A more widespread form of medieval workmanship, of which thousands of instances can still be seen, is the output of the workshops which from the thirteenth century produced alabaster and brass monuments in considerable quantities if not quite on an industrial scale. 'Brasses' – cast and inscribed plates of a flexible brass alloy called 'latten' set in a stone slab – commemorating and (often) portraying the dead begin to be manufactured in England in the 1270s in a process imported from Flanders. The latten sheets had to come to England from the continent throughout the middle ages (see Fig. 7.2). The manufacture was dominated from the first by London workshops, though at its beginning there were also regional urban producers at Newcastle, York, Lincoln, Exeter and elsewhere, though only the York workshop survived the Black Death. Some of the products were remarkably ambitious specific commissions, even including incised portraits of the deceased, and obviously expensive. In the industry's latter days cheaper mass-produced brasses spread the practice further down the social scale, to townsmen and rural yeomen, some coming from new local and regional workshops. The translucent gypsum called alabaster, which is quarried across the north Midlands of England, made a similar industry possible. Relatively easy to cut,

Fig. 7.2 Medieval Brass. Effigy of John Desford, canon of Hereford (died 1419), set in a limestone matrix. The legend calls the reader to pray for his soul. Such brasses were developed following a metallurgical breakthrough in a new sort of flexible bronze alloy (called latten) in the early thirteenth century, probably in Flanders. By the 1280s there were workshops engraving them all over England, though the centre of the craft remained London's East End.

smooth and polish, it was a fine material for tomb effigies, and workshops in or near quarries in Nottinghamshire and Yorkshire were producing sculptured effigies for elite tombs at the beginning of the fourteenth century: King Edward II's at Gloucester is an early instance of their art. Alabaster workshops continued to produce effigies to the end of the sixteenth century. In the middle ages their production also included delicate and fine devotional panels and statues, of which many examples somehow survived the Reformation.

The most common products of medieval industry are the ones which barely now survive other than through recovery by archeological digs. Mass production of wheel-thrown pottery at established centres of the industry in eastern England occurred in the tenth century, requiring workshops, specialised kilns and warehouses for drying and storage. Production also required ready access to fuel for the kilns, wood and peat being commonly used. In the eleventh century pottery was a well-organised and urban-based industry in England producing high-quality glazed bowls, vessels and jugs, with known centres of the industry at St Neots and Stamford. Judging by the Domesday evidence the industry was at the time still very profitable, which makes its collapse during the twelfth century rather difficult to account for. But by 1200 wheel-thrown, quality ware was being produced only in London, Stamford and York, while most of the local production had devolved to low-paid potters who worked their material by hand and probably made their living by a variety of means, not just their trade. This collapse can be understood, since towns were not necessarily the best places to produce pottery, as the clay and fuel usually needed to be hauled from elsewhere. The availability of cheaper wood-turned bowls and cups, and the depression of peasant income may have also had something to do with the decline.

The revival in the quality and quantity of pot-making in the fifteenth century has been related to rising peasant income and a consequent rural demand for higher-standard wares. As domestic pottery declined in the twelfth century, other uses of fired clay created related industries. Commercial tile-making for roofs was a widespread activity in the south-east of England as early as the twelfth century, though slates and oak shingles were a cheaper alternative in Wales and the west. Occasionally monastic houses set up their own tileries not just for their own use, but for commercial purposes. Battle Abbey's excavated tilery at Wye in Sussex had ten kilns and is known to have produced 100,000 tiles in the year 1355. Glazed two-coloured floor tiles were in general use across Britain by the thirteenth century, and their impressive effect and quality can still be seen in the excavated (and occasionally extant) floors of the great medieval houses and churches of England, Wales and Scotland. The production of floor tiles goes back in England before the Conquest, and it remained a large-scale enterprise centred on monasteries through to the end of the medieval period.

POSTSCRIPT

Economic forces can be seen at work in medieval Britain, and indeed the British economy was a real thing, itself influenced by the needs and greeds of European neighbours. There was wealth to be made and once accumulated to be invested in property and the loan market. Agriculture may have been the dominant activity, but there was a slow growth of urban centres and industries despite the reverse administered by the fourteenth-century mortality crisis, which itself led to major economic changes in the life of the peasant. Technology barely changed, other than in small ways, such as the use of wind power in mills from 1180 across Britain. Even in 1500 there was little sign as yet that the economies of Britain were poised to shift up a step in modes of production and capital, other than in the evidence we have for adaptation and openness to novelty in the population.

KEY TEXTS

Dyer, C. *Making a Living in the Middle Ages: The People of Britain, 850–1520* (Yale University Press, 2002), a comprehensive exploration of economic activity and society across Britain by the leading historian in the field. • *English Medieval Industries: Craftsmen, Techniques, Products*, ed. J. Blair and N. Ramsay (Hambledon, 1991), an encyclopedic and well-illustrated treatment of the commodities and industries of England. • Postan, M. M. *The Medieval Economy and Society* (Penguin, 1972), a game-changing book in terms of medieval scholarship on economic history, which has not lost its edge. • Sawyer, P. *The Wealth of Anglo-Saxon England* (Oxford University Press, 2013), a book which analyses and argues whether early England's economy was as exceptional as has been suggested.

FURTHER READING

Allen, M. 'The Volume of the English Currency, 1158–1470', *Economic History Review*, 54 (2001), 595–611. • Bailey, M. *The Decline of Serfdom in Late Medieval England: From Bondage to Freedom* (Boydell, 2014). • Bell, A. R. *The English Wool Market, c. 1230–1327* (Cambridge University Press, 2011). • Bolton, J. L. *The Medieval English Economy, 1150–1500* (Everyman, 1985). • Bolton, J. L. *Money in the Medieval English Economy, 973–1489* (Manchester University Press, 2012). • Britnell, R. H. *The Commercialisation of English Society, 1000–1500* (Cambridge University Press, 1993). • *Coinage in the Low Countries (800–1500)*, ed. N. J. Mayhew (BAR International Series, 54, British Archaeological Reports, 1979). • Campbell, B. M. S., J. A. Galloway, D. Keene and M. Murphy. *A Medieval Capital and Its Grain Supply: Agrarian Production and Distribution in the London Region, c. 1300* (Historical Geography Research Series, no. 30, Institute of British Geographers, 1993). • Dyer, C. *Standards of Living in the Later Middle Ages: Social Change in England, c. 1250–1520* (Cambridge University Press, 1989). • Faith, R. *The English Peasantry and the Growth of Lordship* (Leicester University Press, 1997). • Faith, R. 'The Structure of the Market for Wool in Early Medieval Lincolnshire', *Economic History Review*, 65 (2012), 674–700. • Galloway, J. A., D. Keene and M. Murphy. 'Fuelling the City: Production and Distribution of Firewood and Fuel in London's Region, 1290–1400', *Economic History Review*, 49 (1996), 447–72. • Hyams, P. R. *Kings, Lords and Peasants in Medieval England: The Common Law of Villeinage in the Twelfth and Thirteenth Centuries* (Oxford University Press, 1980). • Keene, D. 'Medieval London and Its Region', *London Journal*, 14 (1989), 99–111. • Lloyd, T. H. *The English Wool Trade* (Cambridge University Press, 1977). • Saul, N. *English Church Monuments in the Middle Ages: History and Representation* (Oxford University Press, 2009). • Whyte, I. *Scotland Before the Industrial Revolution: An Economic and Social History, c. 1050–c. 1750* (Longman, 1995).

 NOTE

1. *The Libelle of Englyshe Polycye*, ed. G. F. Warner (Oxford University Press, 1926), lines 86–90 (c. 1436), English modernised.

8 The Organisation of Society

OVERVIEW

It was not just the Church which provided a cosmopolitan
and supranational force in the life of Britain; so also did the
aristocracy, whose culture and pursuits were European, not
parochial in the middle ages. 'Society' was a concept medieval
people understood and even analysed within their limits; they
knew that it was a subdivided unity and that there were social
levels within it. Medieval society was not unsophisticated
because it was medieval. In fact it was a complex interlacing of
communities and structures, which ambitious and intelligent
aristocrats could orchestrate to their own advantage. It could
be a violent world, where grudges and enmities were pursued
relentlessly and where the deficiencies in royal control could be
exploited and subverted, since the king generally relied on local
elites to actually administer the regions. This is not a story of
progress. British society got more violent and corrupt rather than
less in the period of this book.

Visions of Society

The medieval peoples of Britain had a view of society as a thing to which they belonged and in which they each had a place, though not an equal one. In the view of one twelfth-century poet: 'Everything that the rich achieve – king, count and magnate – is paid for by the poor: the rich of this world squabble but it's the poor who foot the bill.'[1] It was not by any means beyond medieval capacities to visualise a nation or the human race as a social entity and to go on to analyse it. It was all the easier since medieval people knew that they were all one under God, and both the Old Testament and the Gospels said that there were seventy-two nations, one for each of the disciples Jesus sent out (Luke 10). The English, the Welsh and the Scots were known to be three of these, and each had centuries of history behind them, in the case of the Welsh allegedly going back to Trojan times. Medieval intellectuals most frequently used theology to explain how society worked and interacted. By the tenth century English thinkers, including King Alfred the Great, had absorbed a Frankish idea of society as tripartite: divided between those who fought (and ruled), those who prayed and those who laboured. Each of the three ought to support and protect the other in a harmonious relationship, and therefore – obviously – each must know its place, even though some of the serried ranks had clearly got out of step with the rest.

Around 1002 the Benedictine Ælfric of Eynsham used the idea of the Three Orders to criticise those clerics who got so confused in their ideas of the right ordering of things as to lead troops in the field as if they were warriors. The idea of three interlocking orders was passed on to the laity as the way things ideally ought to be in society. Stephen de Fougères, Henry II's court chaplain, used it in his preaching in the 1150s. He wagged his finger at the generic peasant not to get above his station, but encouraged his like by saying that 'knight and clerk assuredly depend on the result of his labour'. The Three Orders, or estates, continued to hover in medieval British consciousness. It was proverbial in the later middle ages that 'no good can come of a knight without sword, clerk without book or labourer without tools'. Mostly it comes out when knights encounter clergy who tell them what to do. So the force commanded at Falkirk in 1298 by Bishop Anthony Bek of Durham is said to have ignored his commands as his business was liturgy, not swordplay.

But, that said, the idea of the Three Orders is useful to us only in demonstrating the insight medieval people had acquired from Scripture, that any human society was a subdivided unity. The symbol of the king as head of his nation said much the same (see p. 91), and the medieval coronation procession made that vision manifest in the streets of Westminster. The Three Orders was not by any means the only medieval perception of society, and certainly not the most important one. As a theological scheme, it visualised society organised by function. Yet there is plenty of evidence that medieval people more commonly perceived society as a unity ordered in a hierachy of status, from the greatest to the least. Here the organising principle was not function but degrees of wealth and nobility, and the level of power and responsibility that went with each. The period of this book saw this secular idea of society grow and mutate into something immensely powerful: the idea of the nation as a community united in a common purpose, with each of its members responsible for the whole so far as their different capacities allowed them. Before 1500 and even as early as 1200, there is a lot of evidence that thoughtful people were pledging their allegiance to this abstract ideal, rather than to the person of their king, who might even be perceived as a threat to the greater good of the realm. This was the idea of the commonwealth, which rose within the scaffolding of both the British monarchies. Kingdoms were progressively defined as communities of interest, not the personal property of the king as their lord.

A Supranational Nobility

In fact, kings always tacitly acknowledged that their realms were not their own to dispose of at their whim. They had no choice. Kings had to deal with two powerful interest groups who also thought in terms of the realm, and indeed beyond it. The first and most powerful, because of its moral authority and connections with the universal power of the papacy, was – as we have seen – the Church. Less obvious, but more immediately deadly, was the group on whose military and administrative support the king depended, his magnates. Magnates ('great men') is a term the middle ages well understood. Chroniclers were alive to the doings and opinions of these men, and kings ostentatiously included them as assenting to their written acts and proclamations. The most astute of kings took great pains in building up support and friendships amongst the magnates, for when properly and sensitively employed they could much magnify the power of any king. They could deliver him effective military support and docile provinces. As early as the twelfth century magnates did not think it beneath them to occupy government or judicial offices, and they were always ready to participate in royal rituals of state, especially as they usually collected handsome fees for any inconvenience involved. It was because of committed magnate support that kings such as Henry II (1154–1189) and Edward III (1327–1377) could enable the kingdom of England to punch far above its weight: to execute the conquest of Ireland in the late twelfth century and challenge the dominant power of France in the mid fourteenth.

Certain magnates were wealthy and ambitious enough to see themselves operating on a grander stage even than just England or Scotland. The twelfth century in particular was a time when aristocrats often migrated, holding lands in several realms. Britain was then an important part of a Francophone world with an international aristocratic culture. English and Scottish aristocrats can be found as habitués of the tourneying grounds of northern and central France. So in the summer of 1166 the young King William the Lion of Scotland 'with a numerous company', on a visit to his sister, the duchess of Brittany, joined in a major tournament on the border of the French counties of Maine and Blois where they encountered English and Norman knights as well as the local aristocracy. The twelfth-century Scottish aristocracy included magnates with origins in Normandy, Picardy and Brittany, as much as Galloway, Alba and Lothian. The greatest of magnates had to craft their policies and ambitions accordingly. The political world of Waleran II of Meulan (died 1166), whose family was of Norman origin, included the semi-independent county in the French Vexin from which he took his principal title; the entire Marais quarter of the city of Paris; large estates in central Normandy, where he ruled as the king's lieutenant between 1136 and 1141; ancestral manors in Dorset which had been his family's since the Conquest, and an English earldom of Worcester he had secured from King Stephen. To this he later added the wealthy lordship of Gournay-sur-Marne east of Paris, as a marriage gift from King Louis VII. Waleran had to operate within three distinct realms, which were sometimes realms at war with each other, and he did so with a surprising adroitness.

This sort of supranational Francophone aristocratic culture remained a fact throughout the middle ages, though the possibilities it opened up became increasingly limited as the thirteenth century progressed and the king of England's influence retreated to the British Isles. Nonetheless, as late as 1232 an earl of Pembroke ruled estates which encompassed castle lordships in the Pays de Caux of Normandy; the Breton border lordship of Dinan; large and profitable manors spread across the south of England; the Welsh marcher castle-lordships of Striguil, Usk and Pembroke; and, greatest of all, the liberty of Leinster in Ireland with its cities, ports and fortresses. No wonder that the earls of Pembroke had to maintain a war fleet in the Bristol Channel to help control communications across their scattered domains. The projected marriage alliances of Earl William Marshal II of Pembroke in 1220 included unions with the ducal family of Brabant, the Capetian cadet house of Dreux and the Scottish royal house. He eventually married King Henry III's sister.

Such international opportunities may have become rarer, but did not end even with the Treaty of Paris (1259) by which Henry III resigned the lands his dynasty had once ruled north of the river Loire. The dukes of Brittany were also earls of Richmond in Yorkshire for most of the period up until 1399. The notorious Peter Gaveston (died 1312), who found a career at the court of Edward I and attained the earldom of Cornwall, was of the Gascon noble house of Marsan, which had been involved with the Angevin court since the 1150s. Edward III was willing in 1366 to grant the earldom of Bedford to the great northern French lord, Enguerrand de Coucy, and offer him his eldest daughter as his wife in pursuance of his political ends in France. The appearance of the order of the Garter in England (1348) provided an institutional framework for this sort of international chivalric association at the highest level of society. Though the Garter had a diplomatic function (being awarded to sovereigns as far away as Portugal and Poland), it also deliberately included militarily distinguished 'stranger' (that is, foreign) knights associated with the Plantagenets, thirteen of them in the later middle ages: Gascons, Hainauters, Flemings, Dutch, Portuguese and Germans.

A quite different dynamic encouraged connections between aristocratic Scotland and France in the later middle ages. The young King David II's upbringing in his Norman refuge between 1334 and 1341 under the protection of Philip VI of France was an early instance of the political necessity that so frequently drove the Scots into the arms of the Valois monarchy. Along with the young king's household came two Douglas boys: the elder, William Douglas (died 1384), earl of Douglas and Mar, grew to manhood in France and enjoyed the large lordship of St-Saens in Normandy. He fought with his lord, King John II of France, against the English at Poitiers in 1356. His cousin Archibald 'the Grim' (died 1400) likewise spent many years in France, and it was his son and namesake, the fourth earl of Douglas, who began a long military association with King Charles VII, culminating in his creation as duke of the Touraine in 1424 with the office of lieutenant-general of France, though his death at the hands of an English army at Verneuil a few months later meant he did not enjoy his unique and exalted status for very long. It was not just Archibald Douglas who gravitated to the armies of France. His son, the earl of Wigtown, and the earl of Buchan both independently enjoyed estates in the Touraine and Berry from the gift of the dauphin Charles.

It is worth mentioning that the Anglo-French wars gave similar opportunities to Welsh aristocrats, and not merely those Welsh mercenary spearmen and archers who had long been the backbone of the infantry of English armies. Owain ap Thomas ap Rhodri (died 1378) was the great-nephew of Prince Llywelyn ap Gruffudd of Wales (died 1282). Though a landowner in several English counties and son of an Anglo-Welsh county knight, Owain's family's high claims enticed him into French service as early as the 1350s, where he became a distinguished commander going by the name of 'Yvain de Galles'. In 1369 and 1372 the French financed expeditions by which Owain attempted to assert his claim to the principality of Wales, where a party had formed in his support. In 1378 he was assassinated by an English agent in Gascony because of the military and political danger he now represented.

§ Cross-Border Nobility

The French-speaking magnates of medieval Britain belonged to a broader world of Western aristocracy, but they also had their own domestic British reservations within it. The period from the 1120s to the 1290s was one of particularly strong links between the magnates of England and Scotland, for whom the Tweed was no barrier to their ambitions and activities. Cross-border connections had quite a history even before the reign of David I of Scotland (1124–1153). The long-lasting dynasty of the earls of Dunbar and March – descended from Uhtred, earl of Northumbria (died 1016) – migrated north from English Northumbria in the 1070s. Earl Gospatric fell out with William the Conqueror in 1072 and found refuge with King Máel Coluim III Cenn Mór. He and his descendants continued to call themselves earls, eventually taking as their title the fortress granted them by Máel Coluim. Since Gospatric's son was rehabilitated at Henry I's court and was restored to many of his family's former English estates, the Dunbars were able to control a formidable cross-border estate until as late as 1335. They were magnates as much at home in Lothian and the Merse as they were in Northumberland, patrons as much of Durham Cathedral priory as of Melrose Abbey. It was a consequence of this link that, even as late as 1314, Earl Patrick V (died 1368) might covertly assist Edward II of England's escape from the disaster of Bannockburn.

King David I, Henry of England's brother-in-law and earl of Huntingdon before he was king of Scotland, was the man chiefly responsible for increasing cross-border links. He actively recruited Anglo-French barons to populate the Scottish court and Lowlands. From this period comes the settlement in Scotland of the likes of the Norman lords of the Yorkshire region of Harterness (the Bruces, who took their name from Brix in the Cotentin) and the Balliol lords of Bywell in Northumberland (from the Ponthevin lordship of Bailleul-en-Vimeu, which they still enjoyed in the fourteenth century). An informed English commentator could say in 1212: 'The present kings of the Scots represent themselves more as Frenchmen in their descent, behaviour, language and devotions. They have reduced the Gaelic Scots to the lowest level of society and employ only Frenchmen as their household knights and officers.'[2] This was overstating things, but it was a matter of ease in the reign of Alexander III (1249–1286) for the great nobleman Roger de Quincy (died 1264), earl of Winchester and constable of Scotland, to operate in Leicestershire, Northamptonshire, Galloway or Fife, where he ruled the lordship of Leuchars. He issued charters indifferently to English and Scots beneficiaries, and knights of either realm populated his large retinue. It is worth noting that it was by a Scottish office of state that he chose to dignify his formal style.

Such links were not much challenged by the episodic warfare between the kings of England and Scotland in the twelfth and thirteenth centuries. They may even have helped moderate problems between the kingdoms. There is every reason to see the Anglo-Scottish magnate as a stabilising anchor in relations between the kingdoms right up until the watershed of the reign of Edward I. Even indigenous lords were drawn into this world. Fergus, ruler of Galloway (died 1161), married a daughter of Henry I of England. His grandson Lachlan (died 1200) preferred to be known by the Franco-Breton name of 'Roland', hero of the great foundational epic of French literature. Roland of Galloway's marriage into the Anglo-Scots Morville family brought him estates in Lothian and England. His son Thomas was brought up at the English court where he was acknowledged and treated as a cousin of the king, and he used his contacts to acquire estates in Ulster. There is more than a little reason to think of the court of the early Angevin kings as being quite as much British as English in its drawing power for magnates.

By contrast, Welsh magnates did not make so decisive a crossover into the Anglo-French aristocratic world. The Welsh 'magnate', as I have used the term here, is not in fact that easy a creature to find. Since Wales was not politically united, it had no recognisable national aristocracy as England and Scotland (and eventually Ireland) did. Welsh kingship depended on military force and not on the consent and counsel of any community of landed aristocrats. Major landowners who were not kings might in fact be of rival royal descent themselves, and most Welsh kingdoms were too small and poverty-stricken in any case to generate substantial cadres of non-royal aristocrats. It was only with the rise of Gwynedd into an embryo Welsh state in the thirteenth century that something resembling a Welsh magnate appeared. It happened at much the same time as we find stirrings of Welsh cultural interest in the dominant Francophone aristocratic culture of the day, when Welsh adaptations of French romances and a translation of the iconic epic, the *Song of Roland*, appeared.

An identity of Welsh aristocracy might be externally imposed. The English Chancery and chroniclers of the 1230s were convinced that there was a class of 'Welsh barons' whose allegiance belonged by right to the prince of Gwynedd, and Henry III had them do homage to the new prince, Dafydd ap Llywelyn, at Gloucester in 1240. But these 'Welsh barons' were in fact men whose view of their place in the world was not far removed from the prince they were supposed to serve: men ruling fragments of their former kingdoms of Deheubarth, Morgannwg, Maelienydd and Powys. It was only in Gwynedd itself that there eventually emerged the sort of aristocrat who operated within the framework of a state as stalwart supporter and counsellor of his prince. The Welsh magnates of Gwynedd played their brief part in their prince's resistance to the Edwardian conquest, and then disappeared into the tenantry of the royal demesne that North Wales subsequently became. Curiously, however, Wales did generate two brief English dynasties of magnates of Welsh descent. The former Welsh princes of Powys Wenwynwyn appeared as barons in Edwardian parliaments under the surname 'de la Pole' (i.e. Welshpool). So also did the banneret Sir John Abadam (died 1311), a Welshman of Gwent and, by descent, the hereditary steward of the kingdom of Glamorgan. He had inherited a Gloucestershire castle, and so was naturalised into English society.

Titles and Dignity Across Britain

English and Scots magnates shared the same political world as their king, and took a similar outlook on its affairs. This was implicitly recognised from the beginning of this period in the councils of magnates and bishops who surrounded and supported their king, which are considered elsewhere in this book (see pp. 125–32). The solidarity of the magnate group was increasingly sanctioned by signs of status throughout this period. Already in 1000 England and Scotland awarded titles of high (but non-royal) status to the greatest magnates. In Gaelic Alba, there were dynasties of magnates called mormaers responsible under the king for the governance and defence of provinces such as Moray, Fife, Strathearn and Atholl. In England a similar group, called ealdormen, served the West Saxon monarchy. These great lords were equated in Latin to the continental dukes (Lat. *duces*) of the former Frankish realms. In the wake of the Danish conquest of 1016 the title 'ealdorman' gave way to the new style of 'earl' (a word with connotations of high dignity in both English and Danish). When the Normans conquered England a half-century later, the earl was demoted by 1070 to be the equivalent of the continental counts (Lat. *comites*, Fr. *comtes*) of northern France, but nonetheless the earl was still a magnate title of high dignity. Earls made up a small group at the very apex of society totalling between seven and forty in any medieval reign depending on the accidents of inheritance and the policy of the king, in whose gift the title ultimately lay.

By the 1170s the status of the Scottish mormaer too had been equated to the Anglo-French 'earl', a development helped along by the existence of a dynasty of English earls at Dunbar on the Scottish side of the Tweed and the fact that the Scottish royal family itself enjoyed English earldoms (Northumberland, Huntingdon and, briefly, Chester). Scottish earls made up a relatively large group amongst the Scottish magnates, with the earl of Fife for long the greatest of them; as Scotland's premier earl he had the right to present the king for his inauguration at Scone. The ancient Gaelic dynasties of Alba, such as Fife, Strathearn and Atholl, survived on into the age of the Bruces and Stewarts. So also for a while did two ambiguous dynasties, those of the Gaelic lords of Galloway and Argyll, both of whom still had royal pretensions in the twelfth century. The rulers of Galloway eventually chose the title 'lord' (*dominus*), a word whose vagueness could support a range of claims; the king of England after 1199 was 'lord of Ireland'. Somerled (died 1164), the ruler of Argyll and the Isles, could be called *regulus* ('kinglet') in Latin and *rí* ('king') in Gaelic sources, but he gave rise to the MacDhomnaill (MacDonald) dynasty whose leaders called themselves 'lords of the Isles' in the fourteenth century, though they also went on to secure status as earls of Ross within the emerging Scottish peerage. Their fourteenth-century rivals in the West, the Caimbeulach (Campbell) 'lords of Argyll', likewise secured earldoms, of Atholl and Argyll. The earldom of the Lennox (*Leamhain*) is a variant on the same story. The Gaelic lords of the isthmus between the firths of Clyde and Forth, who traced their descent all the way back to Irish royal forebears, and who came to rule from their fortress of Balloch over the originally British lordship of Dumbarton, were accommodated within the new Scotland with an earldom by King Alexander II, at the same time as in 1238 he abstracted Dumbarton from them, and installed his own sheriff there. The earls of the Lennox did not fight the changes; in fact they installed English knightly tenants in the Lowland parts of their lordship. By the time the Stewarts took the throne, the Scottish earldoms and their possessors – whether of French, English or Gaelic origin – were conventionally European in the way they expressed their status. And, as in England, the title of earl became increasingly commandeered and domesticated within the royal family as **appanages** for the king's children and grandchildren, legitimate and illegitimate.

The later middle ages saw the greater magnates become more concerned with the expression, exaltation and differentiation of their dignity, aided from time to time by the king himself; Edward III (1327–1377) and Richard II (1377–1399) are famous for multiplying titles and secular ritual. By 1300, English earls were beginning to imitate dukes and princes in wearing gold coronets in public, though the practice was not allowed them at the royal court. In 1337, a new step was taken when Edward III created his eldest son duke of Cornwall, citing Arthurian precedents for such an innovation in his realm. Edward later created several dukes within his family, including his third cousin (once removed), Henry of Grosmont, as duke of Lancaster in 1351. Henry's distance from the throne was sufficient to reckon him as the first non-royal duke. But royal cadets increasingly occupied duchies as the fourteenth century progressed on into the fifteenth: York, Clarence, Hereford, Exeter, Bedford and Aumale. These new greater titles undeniably passed outside the royal family when Richard II created his very noble friend Earl Robert de Vere of Oxford marquess of Dublin and then duke of Ireland. By the end of Henry VI's reign, a ladder of dignity had been created for the English peerage, with hereditary barons, viscounts, earls, marquesses and dukes gathered around the throne each with their distinct regalia and robes. Even within the ranks there was differentiation, with Henry de Beauchamp, earl of Warwick, recognised by Henry VI as 'premier earl' of England, with the right to wear a coronet in the king's presence.

The same process is visible in Scotland, with the erection of duchies for royal cadets in 1398, when Robert Stewart (died 1420), son of King Robert II, was created duke of Albany, and his nephew David Stewart (died 1402) became duke of Rothesay. In England, the king's eldest son and heir presumptive had the superior title of prince of Wales; north of the Tweed the king's eldest son went by the title of 'the prince of Scotland'. The slow filtration of new titles from the south combined to create a similar graduated peerage by rank to England, including by 1500 a marquess, though not yet a viscount. The parallels of the emergence of a Scottish peerage with that of England are unmistakable, though it is not always easy to say whether the respective aristocracies were simply forming in the same circumstances or whether there was diffusion of English ideas into Scotland. England and Scotland both expressed their political life in the fourteenth and fifteenth centuries through parliaments, where the king sat among and above his magnates and prelates. It would be natural therefore for a common idea of a national peerage to appear in both, though the Scots had a different idea of how far the right to sit among the lords went down in society, distinguishing 'lords of Parliament' from possessors of freeholds called baronies. Likewise the appearance of Scottish dukes and marquesses could have been as much to do with the influence of France as of England. In both kingdoms (and indeed also in Ireland) a titled peerage, its privileges, attributes and ceremonies of investiture were a central part of court life, and they shared this with every other royal court in Western Europe. By 1500 it was inconceivable that a princely court could be without the precedence, coronets and robes of its dependent titled nobility, some of them enhanced by bearing the titles of ancient household offices, high constable, high steward and marshal.

Magnates and Power

Great men expressed their greatness by the number and quality of their followers, as much as by the sparkle of gems and sheen of scarlet, silk or gold wrapped around their persons. As early as the eleventh century we can see just how they recruited followers. The earls of Edward the Confessor's England founded their power on their office. It gave them control of major estates in their shires reserved for the earls. When this was added to their personal family estates such earls were very considerable men, and they used their presidency of the shire court and administration to recruit local landowners into their interest. Pre-Conquest earls also recruited households of paid professional warriors (sometimes called *huscarls*) but the basis of their local power was their official influence, not military intimidation. Their personal estates tended to be scattered across several shires, and they had no castles, as great men on the continent did. They therefore did not have the ability to create miniature principalities on which to found the sort of hereditary local eminence found in contemporary France and Germany. This lack of military infrastructure did not mean that the power of eleventh-century English earls was by any means derisory just because it was dependent on the king's will and transitory office. It was on his widespread network of retained local thegns and his control of several shires that Harold Godwineson seized the throne in alliance with his brothers in 1066.

Eleventh-century aristocratic power in Wales was organised as differently from that of England as England was from that of France; power here was the point of the spear. Any great Welsh magnate, king or otherwise, founded his influence almost entirely on military force, his 'household' (*teulu*). His warriors were mercenaries with little cachet of the noble culture which was beginning to gather round the continental knight, though they did have a warrior ethic of heroic sacrifice. Intimidation was the sole mechanism of local power in Wales, which accounted for much of the political instability and violence of its society. Little kings pieced together dominance over districts called commotes and cantrefs, because that would give them the right to exact the food rents that supported the retinues which safeguarded them from their rivals. They gave little in return for what they took from their people.

The Norman Conquest led to one major social change. William of Normandy brought with his army the continental expectation of his counts and barons that hereditary castle-lordships were the normal way society was organised. From the tenth century, France and Germany had seen a narrowing of power on the magnate class, expressed through the building or acquisition of formidable fortresses and the garrisoning of them with mobile forces of professional cavalrymen, the knights. England knew nothing of this apart from an attempt in the 1050s at castle-building in Herefordshire by Ralph of Mantes – a French count made earl of the West Midlands by Edward the Confessor, his cousin. But as soon as immigrant French magnates were established on their new estates in England they instituted practices familiar to them from their lives across the Channel. Some of them proceeded to build castles for which royal permission was neither sought nor expected. Few of these new castles were of the scale of the royal fortresses erected in London, Canterbury, Rochester, Colchester or York, but formidable **seigneurial** castles such as Striguil (Chepstow), Cardiff, Bristol, Pleshey, Richmond, Arundel and Lewes were a message to the English (and indeed the Welsh) that a new form of social organisation had reached their shores with the Norman conquerors. These castle-lordships (or castellanries) were not drawn on a blank map. The estates which constituted them were sometimes the continuation of pre-Conquest English lordships given to a new French lord. But when the Conqueror bestowed entire shires (like Cheshire, Cornwall, Shropshire and Herefordshire) or regions (like Holderness or the rapes of Sussex) on incoming Frenchmen, he was duplicating French conditions in England at a stroke.

French ways of expressing local power had their impact on Scotland too, but here the native aristocracy assimilated the new continental model rather than becoming a victim of it, as we have already seen with the example of the earldom of the Lennox. Change in Scotland was slower and more episodic than in England, though it has to be said that English-speaking Lothian had long been open to southern influences, and Gospatric of Dunbar's interests spanned the Merse and Northumberland in the Conqueror's reign. The reign of David I (1124–1153) saw extensive colonisation of Lothian and Clydesdale by Anglo-French aristocrats who were expected to bring with them the castles, knights and aristocratic culture to be found in the south. Change came later in other regions, though Anglo-French immigrants had settled in Galloway and the Lennox by 1200.

A fine case study of how Europeanisation was extended across Scotland is offered by Earl David II of Huntingdon (died 1219), the grandson of King David I. Around 1179 he was given many estates down the east coast of Scotland between the river Tay and Banff by his brother King William, of which the largest component was the lordship of Garioch in Buchan, north-west of Aberdeen. His appanage was assembled out of much older Gaelic estate-centres, all now gathered under his authority, as in England, where ancient large estates were assimilated into the new aristocratic honors. But Earl David's French-educated mind built a continental superstructure on them. Just like many of his Scottish fellow earls, he erected castles and patronised adjacent burghs as estate and commercial centres on his Lowland estates; in his case Inverurie was built as a northern focus in Garioch, and Dundee on Tayside in the south. Dependent on his seigneurial castles were the estates of knights he established in the surrounding regions, some of whom built their own fortified manors. Insensibly, Earl David, proud descendant of the Gaelic kings of Alba, replicated the social structure of northern France in an entire region of Scotland quite as thoroughly as the Conqueror's French magnates had done in England. Where he led others followed. Even in the remote north of the realm, in Caithness, where Scandinavian earls ruled a mixed Gaelic–Norse populace, Earl Haraldr Maddaðarson (died 1206) resisted King William, his overlord, from his castle of Thurso in 1196, and had ambitions to acquire the royal burgh of Inverness.

 ## Power and Castles: The Honor

Where they were built, the new castles were the centres of a novel form of social entity for England (and later Scotland): the complex of estates called by contemporaries (in Latin and French) an 'honor'. Honors did not by any means always have central castles; some simply had residential lordly halls. The honor's principal expression was social, not architectural. It had an honorial court where the lord administered justice on his tenants in his own name, not the king's. His court was an expression of his personal grandeur, and he might hold festivities in his castles and other residences at the principal religious feasts of the year – Christmas, Easter and Pentecost – and there be attended in state by his household knights, body squires, chamberlains, butlers, seneschals and dependants, as we know happened in the early thirteenth-century honor of the earl of Warwick. When household accounts appear in some numbers in the later middle ages, we begin to see quite how grand and expensive were such events. The aristocratic year was dominated by the Church calendar, its feasts and fasts. The grand festive banquets, orchestrated by stewards and their staff, rich in courses, music and entertainment, were preceded by periods of abstinence which perhaps made the high feasts all the more notable and enjoyable. They were certainly crowded events. The household of Eleanor, daughter of King John, countess of Leicester and Pembroke, in 1265 exceeded 200 persons; that of Earl Thomas of Lancaster (died 1322) exceeded 700 in 1318. But these were exceptionally grand households of aristocrats at the height of their influence. Between 100 and 200 was perhaps a more likely total for any later medieval English magnate, particularly since there was a marked decline in the level of household staffing in the fourteenth century, which had peaked around 1300. A great

Scottish earl such as Archibald Douglas (died 1424) seems to have deployed a similar size of household to his English peers. Hospitality was extended to the lord's guests and pensioners, who could double the mouths which needed feeding on even an ordinary day at the two customary large meals of dinner and supper, particularly if the lord were resident in or near London and the royal court. Musicians, trumpeters, heralds and a staff of clergy, even choirs, were retained by the great to add grandeur to the liturgy and state of their appearances.

The honor also had a parallel financial structure, with, from the mid twelfth century, an office of receipt and account (an 'exchequer' or 'chamber') where the lord's officers would receive his rents and issue receipts. The honor was a community of interest and a major factor in English social life for at least a century after the Conquest. The singular thing about England, however, was that the honor never became the sole form of social organisation, as it was in most of northern France, where interventionist royal government was confined to the vicinity of Paris. In England, the honor was grafted on to a society where there were alternative ways for magnates to influence and be influenced by their neighbours. These were the communal county and hundred courts, which remained for over a century after the Conquest what they had been before 1066: the centres and expressions of local communities which, though less significant than they had been before 1066, were still vigorous and popular institutions.

Power and Neighbourhood: The Affinity

In England magnates found that they could dominate lesser neighbours who were not their tenants by making common cause with them or, if finesse was either not required or beyond the capacities of the individual magnate, simply by intimidating them. Lords could in this way extend their influence beyond the core of landowners who were linked to them by tenure and homage, which paradoxically could make them potentially more influential and ambitious than magnates might be in France. A parallel and complementary form of organisation to the honor existed in England, which historians call the 'affinity'. It was individual to the magnate who created it, and not a hereditary community of property-holders as the honor was. The honor might be the starting point for the affinity, but the affinity also included neighbours attracted to a particular magnate because they wanted his protection and patronage. It might include clergymen, royal civil servants, lawyers and financial agents as much as landowners.

The affinity became increasingly important to magnate power throughout the twelfth and thirteenth centuries, when the established honors went into a slow decline as communities of interest. For instance, the political newcomer Simon de Montfort (died 1265) constructed an affinity in the neighbourhood of his great castle of Kenilworth from the 1240s onwards, helped by a political vacuum caused by the eclipse or extinction of the earldoms of Warwick and Chester. Leading bannerets (that is, superior knights who led other knights), knights and clergy, needing a patron, enlisted in his interest and gave him political dominance of Warwickshire and Leicestershire. Kenilworth became the redoubt of his cause during the rebellion of 1264–1265, which cost him his life; alongside him on the field of Evesham died many of the closest members of his affinity, loyal to the bitter end.

Honors and affinities both penetrated north into Scotland with the Anglo-French barons and knights who moved there. Though the exclusive and concentrated castellanry was more common in Lowland Scotland than it was in England, and indeed Scotland better resembled the Welsh March in its network of honorial jurisdictions, it is possible to find later medieval Scottish magnates operating political affinities more widespread than their estates, just like those of England. The knightly family of Douglas began their rise to greatness in the retinue of King Robert I, where James Douglas (died 1330) became one of the Bruce's principal military followers. In 1372 William (died 1384), the first Earl Douglas, issued the first-known Scottish military indenture, to his kinsman, the lord of Dalkeith. In 1400 William's first cousin Archibald (died 1424) inherited the earldom. He had married Margaret, daughter of King Robert III, in the 1380s. This great man, who was to die as a French duke and general in Charles VII's service, sat at the centre of an extended political affinity in his Lowland lordships in Clydesdale and Annandale, where local lords not tied to the Black Douglas by tenure still nonetheless solicited his friendship and alliance and resorted to him for arbitration. Sheriffs and local knights took on his livery and the status of squires of his household and filled his council, which included retained lawyers and clerics, just as in English contemporary examples. In 1409, to avoid tension with the governor of Scotland, the duke of Albany, Archibald entered into an indenture with the duke to regulate their regional relationship, especially the tensions between their rival affinities. Earl Archibald had already reduced to impotence his most dangerous regional neighbour, George, earl of March, so as to assume ascendancy over Lothian and the March and advocacy over the great borderland monasteries. Presumably Archibald did not feel in an entirely alien social world when he travelled south of the border and was living in his rented London mansion, or travelling to Canterbury to visit the shrine of Becket, which he and his countess not infrequently did.

We can see the political world of the affinity in fifteenth-century Scotland quite as well as we can in England and it forms a useful parallel. We find a Scottish society which used indentures in much the same way as those issued by English magnates to their dependants in the time of the duke of Albany and Earl Archibald early in the fifteenth century. Money fees paid to his followers by Albany, as ruler of Scotland, can be traced through the Scottish Exchequer. This sort of society operated in much the same way in the Lowland south as it did in the Highland north and west. It continued to flourish and even expanded its scope. From the 1440s links between lords and followers were established by a new and popular form of indenture called a 'manrent', from an Old English word which had survived in the north Anglian dialect, meaning 'to enter into dependency'. The surviving records of the earldom of Argyll give a glimpse of how widespread these bonds of dependency were in Scottish society. Earl Archibald (died 1513) in his day commanded an affinity of 54 local lairds and 116 lesser landowners: his kinsfolk, servants and friends. The rise in this sort of social bond may have a lot to do with the extinction of the ancient Gaelic territorial earldoms in the fourteenth century. A more mobile and volatile society succeeded it, in much the same way as the English affinity had expanded with the decay of the old landed honorial community two centuries earlier.

Affinities often had to be built from scratch, and with difficulty. When Richard Neville (known as 'the Kingmaker') became earl of Warwick in 1449 through marriage, he found himself competing for local influence in a west Midlands already well populated by influential magnates. He struggled to maintain the hold on Worcestershire that his Beauchamp predecessors had enjoyed. He was a young outsider, with his dynastic roots in the North of England. He had to devote money, time and some pains to reclaiming the allegiance of the former Beauchamp affinity and to allying with and subordinating the magnates who had intruded on his political playground. His success depended on the ability to subordinate one key local personality, William Mountford, and to come to a living arrangement with a rival, the duke of Buckingham, a great magnate in north Warwickshire and east Gloucestershire. Neville failed to do either. His progress towards his eventual success was punctuated by setbacks, local violence and criminality in the early 1450s, when restive local gentry lurched into conflict with Buckingham, hoping for Neville's support. He was unable to gain any hold on the sheriffs or MPs of Warwickshire. It was not until 1454 that the earl began to gain some grip on the local community, assisted by an adroit compromise with his co-heir to the Beauchamp lands, the earl of Wiltshire. The result was a more peaceable locality, which began to unite around Neville's interests and leadership.

The affinity was the characteristic form of social organisation in later medieval England, when the honor was only a survival, merely by then a means of milking money from those linked to magnates through legal customs on lands held by knight service. Affinities were not by any means standard. They might be recruited for a variety of purposes. As early as the thirteenth century, a great lord might assemble followers for several different reasons. William de Valence (died 1296) was a tournament buff, and he retained many followers because of a shared interest in the sport. Most affinities had a local dimension, such as that of Guy de Beauchamp, earl of Warwick (died 1315), which was engineered so as to dominate early fourteenth-century Worcestershire and Warwickshire. Sometimes local links were made on a grand scale. The affinity of successive dukes of Lancaster, Henry of Grosmont (died 1361) and John of Gaunt (died 1399), was recruited to offer the dukes connections throughout the realm and at court, so widespread were their landed interests and possessions: the Lancastrian livery badges and robes could be found everywhere (see Fig. 8.1). The king himself might copy his cousin of Lancaster, as Richard II did in recruiting his own national network of knights, based not at court but in the localities.

It was on the Lancastrian and Yorkist affinities that much of the real power of the fifteenth-century monarchy rested and much of the social instability too. Historians in general do not have much good to say about the affinity, and it is easy to see why. Its discoverer, K. B. McFarlane, decried it as a corrupting influence on later medieval justice and public life. It has been argued that the emergence of the affinity as the principal means of exerting magnate power in the aftermath of the Barons' Wars (1215–1217) produced a more volatile society in England. The honor was a community of local landowners with a vested interest in civil peace. The only interest retained knights had was in keeping their lord's favour and, if their lord was vengeful, vindictive and rebellious, there was little incentive for them to restrain him. When lords of affinities competed, as in the Warwickshire of the 1450s, violence and uncertainty followed. The affinity could cut magnates free from local opinion and social responsibility and was always potentially disruptive to peace and justice.

Fig. 8.1 Livery Collar on the Tomb of Sir Thomas Arderne (*c.* 1400). Retainers of noble affinities would wear robes and badges presented to them by their lord. The most famous of these was the golden 'Collar of Esses' presented by the dukes of Lancaster to their chief followers and officers. They were later presented by the kings of England to the likes of chief justices and the lord mayor of London.

Gentry

An affinity was possible only because it could be erected on a local aristocratic society, like a tower on an elephant's back. There were counties in England where there were no active magnates, such as fourteenth-century Gloucestershire, a county where monastic landowners were dominant. The only meaningful resident magnate connection there was the minor one of the Berkeley family, whose members generally followed greater men in the thirteenth and fourteenth centuries. So it would be going too far to characterise medieval England as a land everywhere dominated by its earls and barons. Reconstructions by historians of local societies can run hard on to the intellectual sandbank of family studies. Generations of historical study have revealed the astonishing medieval complexity and dynamism of such societies: local families rising and declining, intermarrying and feuding, seeking or evading local government office, linking themselves with urban-based elites and recruiting new members from the emerging professions of the law and estate management.

Magnate dynasties could rise out of this milieu, just as the De la Poles rocketed up after 1300 out of a mercantile and landed base in Hull and the East Riding to become earls, dukes and potential contenders for the throne in the fifteenth and sixteenth centuries. Local gentry were the recruiting ground for the judiciary, higher clergy, civil servants and many of the great captains of medieval England. Such local communities were not, it seems, happy places, as local tensions and resentments spilled over into enmity and sometimes assassination. They could become nightmares to live in if they were corrupted by entrenched dynasties of lawless thugs, as southern Leicestershire was by successive generations of the Folleville clan from the 1260s to the 1330s: the Doones of the middle ages, intimidating, kidnapping and murdering their neighbours; gangsters encouraged by magnate protection who exploited periods of civil unrest.

Local Leadership and Community

Giving meaning and structure to such local communities is even harder than reconstructing them. Did they think in terms of the community of the shire, the ancient divisions of England, imported later into Scotland and Wales? There may well have been a consciousness of a shire in England as a social entity in the middle ages, with its own customs and manner of speaking English, as we know was the case for Norfolk and Cheshire as early as the twelfth century. Such local patriotism did not, however, produce anything much in the way of political strength and direction, especially with the slow decay of shire courts in the thirteenth century. Historians of the English middle ages tend to characterise the leaders of county society as 'gentry', but they fail to agree any definition of what such a social group was, or how, when and why the gentry became important in England. However, sometimes contemporary evidence helps. The early Angevin kings plainly perceived a social group prominent in local society and focused in 1170 on the knights, as being the most identifiable amongst them. Henry II made them responsible for local order in their counties while King John summoned representative knights of the shires to the royal presence to lecture them and sound them out on national affairs. It is on these county knights that historians tend to fix when they discuss early manifestations of the gentry. The problem is that the numbers of knights fell away drastically as a result of social changes in the early thirteenth century. To erect reconstructions of local gentry on just the knights is to build an igloo on an ice floe travelling south.

By 1300 there had long been a consciousness that 'gentility' was not just the property of knights in the localities. Indeed, this had long been the case. Already in the 1240s there are statements that non-knights could be noble, a realisation prompted by the fact that families which had previously sought knighthood no longer did so, put off by the office and expense which went with the distinction. Likewise it could hardly be denied that the brothers and children of men who were knights, even if not themselves knighted, could claim the same distinction of descent that knights enjoyed. Already, then, the rank of esquire was emerging in England, as it had emerged in northern France. Esquires aspired to the same pursuits and even some of the trappings of a knight, and by 1300 were taking the local offices knights had once occupied and competing alongside them in tournaments and jousts. But even lesser families had some claim to a share in the community of common interest with knights and esquires within any locality or shire. Fitful attempts were made in the later medieval centuries to accommodate such an understanding, though it was not until the Statute of Additions (1413) stipulated that indictments should explicitly mention the precise social status of any defendant that social distinctions began to solidify. This led ultimately to the emergence of the idea of a 'gentleman' as a level of status appropriate to a landed person of estate and education, if not noble lineage, like an esquire or knight. But it can hardly be said that the fifteenth century came to much of an objective definition of what that status was.

A county society like that of fifteenth-century Warwickshire could include men who were not much distant in standing from the magnates. Sir William Mountford (died 1452) was a man derived from a distinguished lineage which can be traced to Viking Normandy, even if his grandfather had been born illegitimate. His family had been established in the county since the eleventh century. Sir William was a prominent retainer of the Beauchamp earls and had been knighted on campaign with Henry V in Normandy. He cultivated personal links with the Lancastrian court as well as holding all the major local offices, being the earl's deputy as sheriff of Worcestershire. The primary focus of his interests remained in north Warwickshire where his manors lay. It can be difficult to pin down how such a man might have understood his world. Ambition and marriage could take a man well away from what appears to be his estate centre. From the early thirteenth century we can see Warwickshire knights might well also be Oxfordshire, Gloucestershire and Staffordshire knights, because they had significant estates which spilled into those shires. There were many gradations of landed income below such a man as Mountford, and one would assume the less the income, the less influential the family. But importance depended on context.

The spectrum of propertied families went down to people historians call 'parish gentry': estate stewards with legal training, small landowners or clergy with family lands and rents, who may not have been of great importance in the theatre of the shire, but who were considerable enough in their own villages. They might even have some lineage and a history behind them going back to the Conquest. An Englishman called Thurkil son of Fundu was granted a small landed estate amounting to around 120 acres near Kingsbury in Warwickshire in Henry I's reign. His successor William consolidated his holdings with other small grants and was a low-ranking witness in many local documents around 1200. The family remained locally notable into the reign of Edward II in the vicinity of Kingsbury, seat of the much more important gentry families, and indeed we happen to know that each of its generations expressed its feeling of belonging by burial in Kingsbury church. The Fundu family had some pretensions to elite behaviour, laying out a small park in its Kingsbury estate during the thirteenth century and maintaining a small archive of property deeds, but no Fundu ever went so far as to aspire to knighthood, and none appears regularly in the retinue of any local magnate, though they were tenants of the earldom of Chester. But Fundus do appear regularly in gatherings of the county court of Warwickshire for well over a century, which is a confirmation of their localised eminence and their allegiance to their shire.

 ## Kinship and Society

The less land a man had, the more local his interests, or at least so one would assume from the case of the Fundus. So how local a society was medieval England? One possible answer is that society was more local in England than Scotland, and in this way. In England neighbourhood could be defined as an intermarried association of local landowners with similar interests. In Scotland, as in marcher Wales, locality was generally defined differently, by lordship boundaries. On the Scottish border was the earldom of March, which was co-terminous with the lordship of Dunbar and made up most of Berwickshire. The border district called the Merse therefore looked up the property chain to its universal landlord in his great castle at Dunbar. The lowland areas of Wales and Scotland were less of a local community of interest than a family enterprise. In upland Scotland and in indigenous Wales it was often the *toisech* and *pencenedl* who had local authority as head of a kin and arbiter of its land, in ways that had no parallel in Anglo-French society. The bureaucratisation of Gwynedd by its native princes in the thirteenth century and the power of the castle-lordships of the March eventually repressed the importance of such patri-archal characters in Wales. The most considerable Welshmen became in the four-teenth century members of the landowning Welsh gentry (*uchelwyr*) who populated the new shires of the royal appanage and liberty that was now the principality of Wales. They carried on much like the Anglo-Welsh squirearchies of the neighbour-ing marcher lordships.

Older conditions still held good in Gaelic Scotland, however. In mid thirteenth-cen-tury Carrick, Earl Níall (died 1256) based his authority on being head and arbiter of his clan as its *cenn ceneóil*, a social office which was still much in evidence in fourteenth-century Galloway. The idea that 'heads' (*capitanei*) of kin with rights over extended family groups and local territories persisted even in the Lowlands in 1490, when the Scottish Parliament legislated against this in what was by then English-speaking Carrick. In the Highlands, the chief of the kin remained the centre of local organisation into the days depicted in Sir Walter Scott's *Waverley*. Here in 1447, Ranald Malcolmson of Craignish and John Alexanderson of Melfort in Argyll could define their 'country' (*patria*) and 'clan' (*natio*) as subordinated to them as *toisech*, an office and territory in which they and the elders of their 'kin' (*parentela*) expressed and exercised a shared interest. Regional magnates in Gaelic Scotland, such as the Campbell and Macdonald lords of Argyll and the Isles, had to base their political and military authority on the concurrence, 'manrents' and contractual bonds of these kin-chiefs, not on making common cause with any self-identifying community of landowners.

Local Identity

There is no medieval example of the identity of a shire attracting any local patriot-ism in Scotland, but numerous instances, going back to the twelfth century, of shires doing so in England. In the twelfth century, men wrote tracts to explain what was dis-tinct and superior about Cheshire and Norfolk and their people: the *Cestrenses* and the *Norfolchienses*. Already in Angevin England a 'country' (*patria*) was something to which you belonged, in which you associated and to which you had an emotional allegiance. This was not necessarily a shire; it might be defined as a region like the Warwickshire Arden, west of Coventry, or it might be a hinterland focused on a conurbation, such as Bristol, York or – most notably – London. 'Londoners', 'Yorkies' (*Eboracenses*), 'the Cinque Ports' and 'Bristollians' all feature in twelfth- and thirteenth-century records as communities with common interests and characteristics, the Bristollians and the mar-iners of the Cinque Ports both being seen as piratical and violent.

The important point was that localism was focused on a geographical and historical entity, not a personality. And in the case of a shire or a chartered borough, there was an institutional framework of courts and offices which further defined the local community. The sheriff and his subordinate officers were major players in English local life already in 1000, as they continued to be after 1100. Indeed the need for and importance of such people and institutions were so obvious that they were exported from England not long after 1100. There was a shire and sheriff of Glamorgan in Wales by the time Henry I was king. 'Pembrokeshire' was constituted as a shire with a sheriff not long afterwards. The northern regions of England, which had so far escaped them, were shired as Cumberland, Westmorland and Northumberland in the reigns of Stephen and Henry II. By then much of Scottish Lothian had also been shired: the administrative innovation of David I. Just as in England, the Scots focused their shires on a central borough. Hardly surprising therefore that, in Ireland, English Leinster, Meath, Munster and Ulster were all shired in the generation after 1200, with Dublin possessing a sheriff a generation earlier. The English, Anglo-Irish and Anglo-Scots could not conceive of localities organised without such a framework to express it.

Sheriffs

There were offices within the shire which were rallying points or objectives for members of the community. Principal of these was the sheriff, which, as we have seen (see pp. 104–5), was increasingly important as the local responsibility of the earl for public order became no more than a relic in the reigns of the Norman kings. The disposal of the office of sheriff was of deep concern to the king and the Exchequer well into the thirteenth century, a time when a large amount of royal income was derived from local demesnes, forests and rents, and the shire court was a vital local forum for justice and communication. As a result kings were reluctant to let the office remain within particular families. Devon, Gloucestershire, Surrey, Cambridgeshire and Bedfordshire were all retrieved before 1165 from families that may have thought they had staked a hereditary claim to them. Even so the shrievalties of Wiltshire and Worcestershire did become the prerogative and power base of many generations of particular magnate families, and Worcestershire's shrievalty remained attached to the Beauchamp family from the early twelfth century into the mid fifteenth. Likewise, we find very few twelfth- and thirteenth-century examples where dominant local magnates were allowed to intrude their own followers into the office, other than in Stephen's reign when an attempt was made to revive the idea of earl as local military governor, and the brief episode when Count John, King Richard's brother, was given control of six shires for much of the period between 1189 and 1199.

When Angevin sheriffs were appointed, they were very often men close to the court. A defining example of such a 'curial' sheriff is Ranulf de Glanville (died 1190). He was a member of a prominent Norfolk family who had already acquired some reputation in legal affairs by 1160. In 1163 he was appointed as an outsider to Yorkshire with a brief to reform its administration, an office he was obliged to surrender in 1170. At the same time he was also employed as a justice in the Exchequer, and appeared in the king's entourage on the continent. He was employed as sheriff of several other Northern counties up until 1180, and was also on occasion a captain, justice-in-eyre and ambassador. In 1180 he was promoted to be justiciar of England, a post he held until 1189, during which time he was entrusted with the education of the king's son, John. He was efficient and remorseless, both in administration and in the enrichment and promotion of his own family. But he was only the greatest of many similar Angevin careerists. Such sheriffs remained for nearly two centuries what they had been before 1066: the king's pre-eminent local representatives, working in his interest and at the behest of the Exchequer. But with the decline in the importance of the shire court and also in the income from royal estates under the early Angevins, a 'curial' interest in appointing sheriffs became less pressing.

This loss of the king's attention had two consequences for sheriffs. From the thirteenth century, the appointment to some shrievalties was allowed to fall into the hands of great magnates. Cheshire had always been an exception, though its possession had returned to the king in 1237 and so its sheriff became a royal officer (indirectly). The king's brother, the earl of Cornwall, however, was conceded direct control of the sheriffs of both Cornwall and Rutland in the 1230s. The earl of Lancaster, another royal brother, was given the same privilege in the 1260s. The shrievalties of both Cornwall and Lancashire were thus tacitly attached to two earldoms (which later became duchies) as part of their extensive privileges and evolution into privileged 'palatinates'. The other consequence was that, from Edward I's reign onwards, sheriffs became diminished in status to local functionaries selected from a small pool of experienced men of affairs of established gentry families, the same group which provided magnate seneschals, knights of the shire and other local officers. From 1300 the king strikingly demonstrated his indifference to the office by being willing to allow shires to elect their sheriff if they so chose. Most did not, probably fearing trouble if local magnates pressed their own candidates into office. Around 1330 Gloucestershire petitioned that Thomas, lord of Berkeley, had prejudiced law and order in the shire by intruding his clients into county offices. Counties preferred as sheriffs local men of business and property who would not hold on to the office too long, with all the problems long tenure might bring. In 1371, Edward III's council agreed to an annual turnover of office as an answer to local concerns. In practice this tended to mean the circulation of the office around a small committed gentry group within each shire. In the south such pools were bigger, but in the north the small number of substantial gentry willing to do the job meant that it fell into very few hands. By the fifteenth century sheriffs throughout the kingdom were increasingly selected from a very narrow interest group amongst the gentry elite.

Local Officials

There was a large slate of late medieval local offices: deputy sheriffs, hundred bailiffs, justices of the peace, sergeants, coroners, deputy coroners, tax collectors, clerks and escheators. They had begun to grow up as early as Norman times, when there was already a hierarchy of deputy sheriffs, coroners and bailiffs, and these surged in numbers in the 1280s as Edward I's government began to multiply special commissions for taxation and local justice and appoint local knights to their panels. The lesser shire posts were generally filled by local gentry, a group which got an increasing hold on such commissions from the end of Edward II's reign. By the fourteenth century a man could pursue something of a shire-based career if he had ambitions to occupy public office, and such a man could feed back into national life when nominated as MP for a county or borough. Sheriffs generally had a background in lesser county posts or in Parliament before they were appointed, though that should not be taken as indicating that men worked their way up a career structure to the top. Quite a few were appointed with no known previous background in administration. If anything preceded appointment as sheriff in the later middle ages it was previous experience in Parliament. Such men had an acquaintance with the big picture and enjoyed contacts in Westminster. More than a third of knights of the shire in the second half of the fourteenth century also served at some time as sheriffs. Of course, such careers attracted only a minority of local gentry. The majority had other concerns, or operated within the interest of magnates, not the king. But nonetheless the existence of a local official elite insensibly added to the feeling of local identity throughout England because such men were conscious of and articulated local interests and ambitions.

Local Life

It is not easy to gain access to the world of the gentry, even in England, other than by the painstaking tracing of property accumulation and careers. Sometimes large collections of deeds and accounts survive for certain families, and so we can at least put dates to their lives and reconstruct the shape of their families, but medieval muniment chests do not quite get us to the heart of local life. However, on occasion the veil lifts and such people can speak to us. The sample letter books of the mid thirteenth century conjure up local communities where a man's neighbour was as important as his lord. Local knights, freeholders and ambitious peasants associated, lent each other stock, asked for help in legal cases, complained about their servants, looked for education and career openings for their children, and planned to raise new residences, barns and mills. They discussed national politics, particularly their suspicion of the king's intentions in relation to the liberties of the realm and his obnoxious demands for taxes. They were also convinced that crime was a growing problem in their society. The great magnate or ecclesiastical prelate was for these people a potentially dangerous intruder in their world, demanding hospitality, inconvenient military service and loans, and liable to intimidate them through his local seneschals and the menace of his mortal enmity. The sexual conduct and misdeeds of one's neighbours were as vital a topic of interest then as now. Gossip, far-fetched stories and innuendo were the currency of social discourse in medieval halls and chambers.

As in Henry III's England, so in Henry VI's. The world of the landowner and gentleman, John Hopton of Blythburgh, Suffolk (died 1478), seems from the records he has left us little different from that of eight generations earlier, though England itself had by then changed in its position in the world, in its agriculture and population and in the way its society understood itself. But still in John Hopton's day relations with the dominant local magnate were a factor in any career, and John attracted the notice of William de la Pole, duke of Suffolk, through whom he briefly obtained a minor court office. He occupied local positions: returning officer for elections, an assessor and a member of the commission of the peace for Suffolk. He had Yorkshire interests which lifted him out of his narrow neighbourhood and made him less typical of his peers. Other than that, he farmed and improved his land through his bailiffs, maintained a degree of style in his entertaining and residence, and added to his rentals and estates where opportunity arose. He was ambitious for his eldest son, who indeed rose higher than he did in public life, and solicitous about his children's education. He loved his wife (he married twice) and married his daughters into other local gentry families. He inspected his livestock, hunted his woods, fished his streams and entertained his fellow justices of the peace in his manor house. When he died, he was buried in a chantry he had founded in the church at Blythburgh, which he had spent a good deal of money on improving: an unexceptional and very local life amongst neighbours and family, with the world of the royal court and the magnates at a social distance, if not entirely unconnected to his.

POSTSCRIPT

The social structures of the medieval period show it at its worst. The ambitions of magnates and the inadequancies of local government produced at times in places something very like gangsterism, wrapped in furs and gold chains. Periods of civil conflict in England such as those of 1215–1217, 1265–1267 and 1318–1322 caused lasting disruption and eroded confidence in just government. Outright violence and feud were not perhaps the normal state of affairs, but even in stable and peaceful communities medieval society looked to magnates and local elites for leadership, which expected deference and favours in return. There was a structure of local government and justice but it operated by the grace of the rich and powerful and it was implictly corrupt. The saving grace of the medieval political world was that the reality of corruption was continually highlighted against the strong ethical and moral sensibility its aristocracy was taught by the Church, and the ancient world whose authors it venerated. Medieval people therefore had a strong sense of what a just society ought to be and, though corruption may have been implicit in their daily lives, no one ever believed that it was either right or the way life should really be.

KEY TEXTS

Coss, P. R. *The Origins of the English Gentry* (Cambridge University Press, 2003), a work which gives answers to questions about the nature of medieval local society and being middle class in the middle ages. • Crouch, D. *The English Aristocracy, 1070–1272: A Social Transformation* (Yale University Press, 2011), a study which for the first time put English ideas of aristocracy in its European context, which has generally been ignored. • Crouch, D. *The Image of Aristocracy in Britain, 1000–1300* (Routledge, 1992), one of the few studies of the meaning of aristocracy across British society, focusing on material culture. • McFarlane, K. B. *The Nobility of Later Medieval England* (Oxford University Press, 1973), a book which brilliantly laid bare the structures of power in late medieval England and launched the concept of the affinity.

FURTHER READING

ENGLAND

Acheson, E. *A Gentry Community: Leicestershire in the Fifteenth Century, c. 1422–c. 1485* (Cambridge University Press, 1992). • Carpenter, C. 'The Beauchamp Affinity: A Study of Bastard Feudalism at Work', *English Historical Review*, 95 (1980), 514–32. • Carpenter, C. *Locality and Polity: A Study of Warwickshire Landed Society, 1401–1499* (Cambridge University Press, 1992). • Coss, P. R. *Lordship, Knighthood and Locality: A Study in English Society, c. 1180–c. 1280* (Cambridge University Press, 1991). • Crouch, D. *The Beaumont Twins: The Roots and Branches of Power in the Twelfth Century* (Cambridge University Press, 1986). • Crouch, D. 'From Stenton to McFarlane: Models of Societies of the Twelfth and Thirteenth Centuries', *Transactions of the Royal Historical Society*, 6th ser., 5 (1995), 179–200. • Collins, H. E. L. *The Order of the Garter, 1348–1461: Chivalry and Politics in Late Medieval England* (Oxford University Press, 2000). • Given-Wilson, C. *The Royal Household and the King's Affinity: Service, Politics and Finance in England, 1360–1413* (Yale University Press, 1986). • Gorski, R. *The Fourteenth-Century Sheriff: English Local Administration in the Late Middle Ages* (Boydell, 2003). • *Lost Letters of Medieval Life: English Society, 1200–1250*, ed. M. Carlin and D. Crouch (University of Pennsylania Press, 2013). • Powell, T. E. 'The "Three Orders" of Society in Anglo-Saxon England', in *Anglo-Saxon England*, XXIII, ed.

M. Lapidge et al. (Brewer, 1994), 103–32. • Richmond, C. *John Hopton: A Fifteenth-Century Suffolk Gentleman* (Cambridge University Press, 1981). • Saul, N. *Knights and Esquires: The Gloucestershire Gentry in the Fourteenth Century* (Oxford University Press, 1981). • Walker, S. *The Lancastrian Affinity, 1361–1399* (Oxford University Press, 1990). • Woolgar, C. M. *The Great Household in Late Medieval England* (Yale University Press, 1999).

SCOTLAND

Barrow, G. W. S. *The Kingdom of the Scots: Government, Church and Society from the Eleventh to the Fourteenth Century* (Arnold, 1973). • Boardman, S. *The Campbells 1250–1513* (John Donald, 2006). • Boardman, S. 'Lordship in the North-East: The Badenoch Stewarts I. Alexander Stewart Earl of Buchan', *Northern Scotland*, 16 (1996), 1–30. • Brown, M. *The Black Douglases: War and Lordship in Late Medieval Scotland, 1300–1455* (Tuckwell, 1998). • Brown, M. 'Regional Lordship in North-East Scotland: The Badenoch Stewarts II. Alexander Stewart Earl of Mar', *Northern Scotland*, 16 (1996), 31–54. • Crawford, B. E. 'The Earldom of Caithness and the Kingdom of Scotland, 1150–1266', in *Essays on the Nobility of Medieval Scotland*, ed. K. J. Stringer (Edinburgh University Press, 1984), 25–43. • Crawford, B. E. 'The Joint Earldoms of Orkney and Caithness', in *The Norwegian Domination and the Norse World, c. 1100–c. 1400*, ed. S. Imsen (Tapir Academic Press, 2010), 75–98. • *The Exercise of Power in Medieval Scotland, c. 1200–1500*, ed. S. Boardman and A. Ross (Four Courts, 2003). • Grant, A. 'The Development of the Scottish Peerage', *Scottish Historical Review*, 57 (1978), 1–27. • Grant, A. 'Earls and Earldoms in Late Medieval Scotland (c. 1310–1460)', in *Essays Presented to Michael Roberts*, ed. J. Bossy and P. Jupp (Blackstaff, 1976), 24–40. • Grant, A. 'Franchises North of the Border: Baronies and Regalities in Medieval Scotland', in *Liberties and Identities in the Medieval British Isles*, ed. M. Prestwich (Boydell, 2008), 155–99. • Grant, A. 'Scotland's "Celtic Fringe" in the Late Middle Ages: The MacDonald Lords of the Isles and the Kingdom of Scotland', in *The British Isles 1100–1500*, ed. R. R. Davies (Edinburgh University Press, 1988), 118–41. • Hamilton, E. *Mighty Subjects: The Dunbar Earls in Scotland, c. 1072–1289* (John Donald, 2010). • Oram, R. 'Castles and Colonists in Twelfth- and Thirteenth-Century Scotland: The Case of Moray', *Château Gaillard*, 22 (2006), 289–98. • Stringer, K. J. *Earl David of Huntingdon, 1152–1219: A Study in Anglo-Scottish History* (Edinburgh University Press, 1985). • Wormald, J. 'Bloodfeud, Kindred and Government in Early Modern Scotland', *Past & Present*, 87 (1980), 54–97. • Wormald, J. *Lords and Men in Scotland: Bonds of Manrent, 1442–1603* (Edinburgh University Press, 1985).

WALES

Carr, A. D. *Owen of Wales: The End of the House of Gwynedd* (University of Wales Press, 1991). • Davies, W. *Wales in the Early Middle Ages* (Leicester University Press, 1982). • Stephenson, D. *The Governance of Gwynedd* (University of Wales Press, 1986).

NOTES

1. Walter of Arras, *Ille et Galeron*, ed. Y. Lefèvre (Classiques français du moyen âge, 1988), lines 1353–58.
2. *Memoriale fratris Walteri de Coventria*, ed. W. Stubbs (2 vols., Rolls Series, 1872–73), II: 206.

9 Life Experience

OVERVIEW

Modern media portrayals of the medieval past delightedly home in on the (to us) weird practices and squalor of medieval daily life, and so have fostered as false an image of its backwardness and dark superstition as the Enlightenment did. Medieval daily life was as humdrum as that of the modern or any period, and focused on a daily routine of work, domestic cleaning, food preparation and socialising. The middle ages did not in fact differ markedly in its beliefs about gender and family roles, childhood, education and sexuality from those of British society up until the nineteenth century. Nor were its physical conditions and the challenges of illness and mortality it faced much different from those of the succeeding period. Its attitudes to coping with widespread early mortality could be argued to be in some ways more advanced and effective than those of early modern and modern society, which has only recently rediscovered ways of confronting, accepting and accommodating the inevitability of death.

Expectations on Women

The middle ages had its views on how each person should conduct him- or herself, and they were not as unrelenting or restrictive as some twentieth-century scholarship might suggest. It would be fair to say that acceptable male and female conduct was mostly *understood* by medieval people, rather than *imposed*. But correct conduct was a more central feature of medieval life than it is for us, and there were reasons for this. Not least was the fact that everyone who learned to read did so from the ages of seven to seventeen from standard Latin texts whose principal subject matter was conduct and morality. Medieval people were also constantly advised to look to the conduct of others: to admired characters in history and literature for clues as to what was moral or not. Proverbial sayings were collected and memorised for their moral content. And always, just as now, people were alert to the reactions – both positive and negative – of those around them to their choices and words. Men and women of any sensitivity were in a constant, silent dialogue between themselves and this 'habitus', testing what they did and said against how the world reacted to it. Since prosperity and opportunities depended on the degree of social success their behaviour attracted, this medieval fixation on conduct was a pragmatic one.

There was a good deal of literature available to tell the medieval reader how a man and woman, adolescent or mature, should ideally behave, and it survives from as early as the first half of the twelfth century. It had more explicit things to say about how women should conduct themselves than men: not surprisingly perhaps, as females were supposed to be by their nature wayward and in need of control. The first conduct book in French appeared before 1150 in what would soon be the continental domains of Henry II of England, and it was devoted to desirable and undesirable female behaviour. More and more such tracts appeared as the century progressed, and from the 1180s more and more of it was in the vernacular, intended for a wide audience who needed to know about table manners, deference, and dress and speech appropriate for every occasion. By the 1220s tracts appeared which taught a more particular kind of conduct specific to the man who wished to be perceived to be noble above all others, tracts we call 'chivalric'. These portrayed a conduct so deeply moral and restrained as to be almost unattainable by any mortal short of a saint. Their true intent was more to provide a rationale for why it was that male aristocrats – all of whom embraced knighthood (in French, *chevalerie*) – had to be deferred to as superior beings beyond the restraints of lowlier men.

Expectations of gender came less from handbooks than from the unwritten way things were done in society. It could be quite forgiving at times. This explains how Matilda, the daughter of King Henry I, might make a bid for the throne in 1135 and almost succeed in taking it in 1141. There was no law to say it could not be done, and there were enough people willing to accept that Matilda was not transgressing the bounds of acceptable behaviour in her ambition. The middle ages had a clear enough idea of gender difference, however. We encounter it mostly through popular theology. Adam and Eve were the mother and father of all, and their disobedient behaviour in Eden was the basis of a lot of sermon literature which conveys gender expectations. Much of what it said tended towards the conclusion that males should be by their nature more in control of themselves. William of Conches, the Norman philosopher and tutor of the boy Henry Plantagenet in his education at Bristol in the mid 1140s, provided an early summary of medieval gender difference in his *De philosophia mundi* ('On Natural Philosophy'). He taught in his theory of elements that women were composed of the same elements as men, but of lesser purity, so women were unbalanced and more extreme in what they did. By this view, it was a matter of debate who had most responsibility for the original sin: Adam or Eve. Eve may have been weak and disobedient, but more was expected of Adam. Stephen de Fougères in the 1150s had a similarly low opinion of the frailties of women: their flirting, their vanity and their uncontrollable sexuality (which might lead to orgies with servant lads, shameless lesbian encounters, sorcery and abortion). However, in the end, his strictures on women ended with this surprisingly positive conclusion:

We lost the Celestial City which was our inheritance, but of that offence we were pardoned when God took human form. When God lowered himself to descend to Earth to take the form of man in the body of a woman and to undergo death and give up his life, we can think well and reflect that God raised woman above man, even indeed over St Peter in Rome; the lady is now with the angels who let evil into the world with an apple.[1]

Any negative portrayal of Eve as an archetypical woman was balanced by the positive medieval role model offered by the Virgin Mary, through whose obedience the original sin of Eden was more than redeemed. The example of Mary offered a powerful ideal of feminine virtue and status, especially as images of her coronation and enthronement next to God and her Son were everywhere to be found in churches and books of hours. Medieval female seals from as early as 1100 depicted their noble owners in a pose modelled on that of the Virgin, sometimes holding the chaste lily that was her particular symbol. As the middle ages progressed, the figure of the Virgin loomed ever larger over society. Her example was made more and more relevant to the female life-cycle. The eleventh-century Virgin was the serene empress of heaven, virtuous and untouchable: a source of protection but not a being any mortal female could approach. But the thirteenth century wanted to know more of the human Mary, her joys and griefs. French vernacular poetry celebrated these and meditated on them, and they became the basis of the reflections to be found in many of the magnificent books of hours of the ladies of gentry and patrician families. Here female readers would find real encounters between themselves and a woman who experienced the pain of childbirth and stood by powerless at the premature and hideous death of her Son. This was the Mary whose intercession was frantically sought by women during the sickness of a child or at the point of bereavement. It was permissible to pray to her Son through her, for He was supposed to remain the child of her womb, though himself God. As the English female mystic, Julian of Norwich (died *c.* 1415), observed, Mary was the human being most nearly involved with Christ and his sufferings, and therefore it was a woman who experienced the fullness of love. More even than that, when Mary stood faithful and grieving at the foot of the Cross, she embodied the entirety of Christian believers, which made her, not Peter, the founder of the Church.

Expectations on Men

By contrast, it is surprisingly hard to say what was the expectation of being a man in the middle ages. No one tried to define masculinity for us, the way they defined femininity. So how can we approach it? The condemnation of unmanly behaviour is one way into the mystery of medieval masculinity. There is a temptation to define male as 'not female', and treat the genders as opposites. There was indeed a critique of defective masculinity based around the idea of effeminacy, which implies that a woman might sometimes be taken as the opposing concept to a man. Clerical writers were likely to attack objectionable men by crediting them with a liking for effeminate dress and long hair, displaying womanly weakness or, at worst, indulging in sexual relations with other males. So the poisonous pen of the Norman monk Orderic Vitalis (died *c.* 1142) defended the virtue of his hero, King Henry I of England (1100–1135), by denigrating his rivals and brothers, William Rufus (1087–1100) and Robert Curthose (died 1134), as sybarites who were happy to harbour sodomites openly at their courts and adopt their queer fashions and discourse. However, in the middle ages, men who wished to be seen as mature were as likely to define themselves against ideas other than womanliness: ideas such as 'immature boys' or 'the irrational and uneducated'. Richard II's critics sneered at him as a 'boy' whereas his rival, Henry of Bolingbroke, was a 'man', despite the fact that Richard was in his thirties when his throne was usurped. Another factor that needs taking into account was the constant pressure for medieval men to assert their masculinity. Medieval masculine status was something that was acquired at the point of coming of age. Once acquired, it had to be constantly asserted against other males, or be lost. Femininity was acquired at birth and was a constant factor in the possessor's life: expectations of both girls and mature women were so low as not to need asserting.

Male behaviour must then as now have depended to some extent on hormones and brain organisation, though it is not clear as to how dominant a factor physiology is in conduct and expectations even in modern times. But testosterone-driven competitiveness was undoubtedly a characteristic of all medieval masculinities, whether amongst clergy, academics and knights, or even peasant farmers. This does not always amount to outright aggression, but it is to be seen in the construction of masculinity as being that of a man against other men (on tournament fields or in academic debate). 'Heroic suffering' is characteristic of several medieval male types, whether a knight triumphing over exhaustion and wounds in battle or on crusade, or by a monk starving himself by fasting or other acts of mortification. There was no shortage of such characters in medieval Britain. One was the English baron, William Longespée II (died 1250), who was vaunted by subsequent generations for his valiant martyrdom in pursuing a hopeless battle against the Mamelukes in Egypt. Another sort of heroic masculinity was provided by the ascetic model of St David of Wales, whose medieval Lives and devotional verse portrayed him as a monk of excelling austerity. As a fourteenth-century Welsh poet put it: 'But one food entered his mouth: cold bread and cress and black water the whole length of his lifetime.'[2] Under the name of 'hardihood' (Fr. *hardiz*), this was a recognised component of the chivalric model of noble male behaviour.

A difference between the genders in the middle ages was that a man's masculinity was reckoned to be radically different from a boy's, rather more so than was a woman's from a maiden's. Little more was expected of a mature woman than of a girl (who could be married and a mother by thirteen). If there was a point of transition, it was the biological one of menarche, when menstruation first happened. But a mature male was viewed as very different from a boy, and expectations shifted accordingly. Medieval boys and male adolescents were expected to be by their nature biddable and heedless, thus sharing several feminine characteristics. This condition ended at the point when they were reckoned to have come of age, which from the beginning of the thirteenth century for most males of the landowning classes in England and Scotland was taken as the twenty-first birthday. It might be later for tradesmen emerging from their apprenticeship to journeyman status, or it might be earlier for a cleric when he received the first of the higher orders, that of subdeacon, or at the point when he achieved his university degree.

Coming of age for a male of a gentry or knightly family involved a ceremony associating them symbolically with other males, through their investiture with the insignia and equipment of war and tournament, the principal theatres for medieval masculine display. Indeed, most knighting ceremonies were followed by the chance for the new soldier to advertise his masculinity in a feat of arms. After that the new adult male was expected to aspire to the ideal of mature masculinity represented by the character known in French as the *preudomme* ('man of worth'). To be praised as such a man was the desire of every aspiring male in public life, whether noble or commoner. It meant that a male was respected for his self-control, self-possession, sound advice and knowledge. The *preudomme* arose out of French society in the eleventh century and was a constant measure of masculinity throughout the middle ages. Written acts of the king of Scotland customarily addressed themselves to all the *preudommes* of his land from the 1150s onwards. He was a creature of proverb. That a *preudomme* was supposed to do this or that was one way that masculinity was defined in the French-speaking world throughout the middle ages. There also emerged the *preudefemme*, as an ideal of mature, discreet and self-controlled womanhood, though the expectations on her were much lighter. One medieval proverb defined the *preudefemme* as a woman who did not call her maidservant a whore when she was annoyed.

The Shape of the Family

Human organisation is based on the family. It is a constant factor in all societies and periods, though its shape is not fixed or standard. The medieval family is often misunderstood because of the evolutionary model of family development produced in the 1870s, which early social philosophers devised as a key to explain what they saw as radical changes in their own society. Victorians saw themselves as living at the end result of a process by which the extended kin-groups of biblical pastoral peoples narrowed down under the economic pressures of urbanisation and industrialisation to the 'nuclear family' of nineteenth-century Europe and the USA: that is, a small economic unit comprising parents and children alone. The model was self-consciously evolutionist (that is, it drew its intellectual inspiration from Charles Darwin): it saw the family as a social organism mutating to fit environmental factors (especially changes in economic activity, such as agriculture and urbanisation). It also saw the nineteenth-century family as the foreordained end of a process which Victorians linked to human progress. The middle ages was a key period by this model, the time when patriarchal clans gave way to lineages, when strong monarchy and law courts broke the dominance of violent, feuding kin-groups. The Victorians liked to see the middle ages as a time when primogeniture, the concentration of inheritance on the eldest son, was established. Primogeniture supposedly allowed individuals to acquire major concentrations of wealth, rather than have to compete for scraps of resources with the other members of their kin-group: modern capitalist society was believed to have evolved from such an all-important change in family structure.

Since the 1950s sociologists have seen the family as a more complicated thing than the Victorians were willing to contemplate, and as having a simultaneous variety of shapes within the same society. The medieval families in Wales, Scotland and England analysed in modern studies are not in fact that different from modern ones. They followed a generational rhythm: small at the beginning, as a man and woman became a couple, often still dependent on the resources given them by the generosity of their parents. Then families expanded as the couple had their children and made further links through the marriage of their offspring. Finally families contracted as the parents aged and children moved away from the home to set up their own family units. Looked at in this generational way, the family of the middle ages was little different from today's, at least in terms of the way it divided economic resources. Indeed, from the eleventh century, we can clearly see that parents throughout Britain worked to make sure that all their children were provided for decently. Sons could usually expect some share of their parents' lands, and daughters could expect some sort of marriage-gift to take with them to help set up their own family unit. Generally the eldest son – if there were several of them – got the most in any division. Often a second son was given the lands his mother had brought into a marriage, or acquisitions made by his father in his own right, rather then inherited lands. The idea of strict primogeniture (with the eldest son taking all) seems to have been invented as a legal ideal in the judicial circle around King Henry II (1154–1189), perhaps following the king's own policy statement devised to preserve military tenures. Primogeniture was never enforced by English courts until the mid thirteenth century, and when it was fathers found ways to evade it by giving away lands to younger sons in their lifetimes, or making unbreakable testamentary provisions devised by lawyers to divide their estates. The marriage contract drawn up to endow estates on daughters and their offspring existed as early as the middle of the twelfth century, and the female was never threatened by the concentration of resources on one child which primogeniture would in theory threaten as regards males.

Looked at in terms of resources and generations, a medieval family was not too different from that of today. But it was not in fact a modern family. Primogeniture is not entirely a myth. Though few aristocratic fathers were so mean as to confine all their inheritances to one son if they had several, they did rather cherish the idea of their lineage (that is, families perceived as being on a vertical track through time) and its consequent dignity, which had to be supported by appropriate wealth. This naturally favoured the eldest son in any generation. A greater consciousness of the way nobility was projected through blood lines appears during the twelfth century, drawing on the more ancient idea that the claim to royalty depended on descent (see pp. 76–8). Society came to the conclusion that the more ancient the blood line, the more noble it was. A great man like Earl Roger de Quincy of Winchester (died 1264), who could trace his maternal blood line back to the Emperor Charlemagne, might spend his last years in a state of depression because after three marriages he had only daughters and his name was going to die with him. He found solace in obsessively hunting his many parks and forests throughout England, and other people's too if he could get away with it.

Ancestry and Kinship

By the fifteenth century, the heraldry of the noble class alluded to any speck of lineage, whether derived from father or mother, quartering and subdividing the shield to marshal the armorial bearings of each noble line that produced a particular individual.

For all this obsessiveness, medieval noblemen may not have carried an encyclopedic knowledge of their forebears around in their heads, however. For instance, so great a man as William Marshal II, earl of Pembroke and brother-in-law of the king (died 1231), had little idea of his ancestry beyond that of his grandfathers, and did not even know the fate of some of his uncles. But such gaps in memory allowed opportunity for falsification. As a result, we find fourteenth-century nobles of obscure origins, such as John Norwich, whose father made a name as a lawyer, daring to have an appropriate pedigree manufactured for him, which traced a fictitious lineage back to a companion of the Conqueror. Research and fiction made up for aristocratic memory in the middle ages as much as in later centuries, but the fact that such gaps had to be filled tells us not to overestimate lineage as a medieval obsession, for all its obvious usefulness to a man's place in society.

As well as vertical lineage, the middle ages cherished a simultaneous horizontal view of family, rather more developed than that of the present day. Medieval people perceived family broadly across a generation. They called this dimension in French a 'parage' (that is, as a group of contemporaries linked by common ancestry), a concept close to what modern sociologists would call a 'kin-group'. It was a more vital and usable idea than the idea of 'cousinship' is in modern Western society. Parage arose in part out of economic realism. It might help make a man's fortune, because kin were more likely to assist his career and offer help than pure strangers. Around 1158, the influential Anglo-Norman baron, William de Tancarville, offered support, career opportunity and education to his maternal second cousin, the twelve-year-old William Marshal, and provided a marriage-portion to another young cousin, Beatrice. So the monk Samson of Bury St Edmunds found himself besieged by 'a multitude of new kinsmen' seeking employment from him on securing the abbacy of his wealthy house in 1182. His dilemma was not unique. King Henry I and King Henry II both explicitly forbade the abbots of the royal houses at Reading and Waltham from rewarding their relatives with lands and offices belonging to the abbeys. A jaundiced twelfth-century proverb ran: 'The more your wealth and treasure, the more numerous your kinsfolk!' Another, even more world-weary, commented sardonically, 'People prefer a crook who is a kinsman to a decent fellow from another family.'[3] It is the parage idea that gives rise to the still current saying that 'blood is thicker than water'. It is a social mechanism by no means entirely dead within today's more meritocratic society, even after the appearance of job interviews and competitive examinations in the nineteenth century. This extract from a sample letter of the thirteenth century is an insight into how it happened, with a father writing to a personal connection seeking an open-ing for a son: 'Since we have the greatest confidence in your friendship, we send our beloved son to you, asking that, for my love and service, you receive him into your employment, knowing for certain that he is of good character, and prompt, ready, and loyal for every kind of service.'[4]

People had to be conscious of their parage for other sorts of pragmatic reasons, even though most of its members were outside the warm zone of affection. From the middle of the eleventh century the Church defined marriage between cousins as incestuous and grounds for annulment (see p. 236). In Henry I's England it was still expected that both the paternal and maternal kin of a man accused of murder would take responsibility for clearing his name and making compensation to the bereaved relatives. Less formally, when a state of mortal enmity was declared by one man against another, the offended man's kin would be expected to take his part, and the offender's kin would share in the hostility visited on him. A man whose parage was small and undistinguished would have to be very cautious of people he might offend. This continued to be the case throughout our period. A chief justice of Henry III's reign, Henry of Bath (died 1260), while not himself well connected, had married into the powerful allied families of the Bassets and Sandfords, dominant at the royal court by then for several generations. When Henry found himself in trouble in 1251, accused of corruption by a personal enemy amongst the baronage, it was his wife's Basset kin who used their influence with the king to bail him out.

Medieval people were not necessarily happy with the use of a wealthy and noble parage for personal advancement. It drew criticism and sarcasm in England, where voices were being raised as early as the twelfth century in favour of a more meritocratic approach to public life. We can see a strand of rising discontent from the comments of the Benedictine academic Alexander Neckam in the 1190s about the undeserved eminence men claimed in society through their noble blood, to the popular preaching Froissart reported of the friar John Ball in the 1370s: 'If we all spring from a single father and mother, Adam and Eve, how can they claim or prove that they are lords more than us?' But, in medieval Britain, needs must. In the poorer societies of Wales and Scotland, where there were fewer opportunities for advancement, the exploitation and assertion of kinship were more deeply rooted in political and social life. Just as with the English, the affective family was generally restricted to the three-generation nuclear model. A tenth-century Welsh school text (the 'Colloquy') defines the people one should care for as grandparents, parents, brothers, wife, children, aunts and, of course, personal friends. Uncles and sisters must be an oversight. The pre-Conquest Welsh made similar use of kin for protection and furtherance as the English. In Welsh customary law, the kin (*cenedl*) took responsibility for a homicide or the obligation of debt amongst its members. But there was more urgency to the link than in England. Kinship ties in Wales were most important in the right they brought to a share in a piece of property, which was vested not in an individual but in a group of common descent through the male line (*yr gwely*). This was the case throughout the middle ages in Wales, but more particularly after Welsh customary law was defined and encoded during the twelfth century, as lordship and landholding became more territorial, organised and exploitative. So a knowledge of one's place in a kin-group was more pressing for a Welshman than for a contemporary Englishman. This perhaps explains the vital importance of bards in later medieval Wales, with their encyclopedic resources on genealogy, both oral and written. Scotland nursed a similar model of empowered, extended kinship. In thirteenth-century Carrick, the chief of the Kennedy family occupied a similar place to the 'head of kin' (*pencenedl*) found in Wales. In fourteenth-century Atholl, the cadet descendants of the extinct line of earls maintained power in their province under the guise of the extended 'Clann Donnachaid', with whom newcomers had to reckon.

Family Love

Did medieval people love their family, whatever its shape was? The measure of affectivity in the middle ages has been disputed. An old tradition in scholarship is that medieval people did not invest much affection in their offspring, and were expected to be cold-hearted, even brutal in their treatment of their children. In part this was because twentieth-century historians, looking at the high mortality rate of children in the middle ages, came to believe that medieval parents dared not invest too much love in them, because the odds of their children's survival were so grim. Keeping an emotional distance contained the potential damage. But investigation has proved that medieval parents were quite as likely to adore their children as modern ones, despite the tragedy of early death and the emotional risks that went along with it. The affective nuclear family, that which demanded cherishing, was no different from today's, as has been said above. It embraced three generations and extended little further than first cousins. When push came to shove, cousins were perfectly capable of working against their relatives. So in 1163 the Norman baron Robert de Montfort engineered the treason trial and destruction of his cousin's husband, the royal constable Henry of Essex, in an unsuccessful bid to recover property in Suffolk his father had lost. A large proportion of the property litigation in England and Wales which came before the courts of Common and King's Bench throughout the later middle ages was between siblings and cousins, who clearly did not like each other particularly.

But before we get too caught up in the family dysfunctionality exploited by medieval lawyers for their living, we have to note the contrasting abundance of evidence of normal love and affection within medieval families. There was even an archetypical functional family to which all could make reference; this was the Holy Family (Mary, Joseph and the young Jesus) idealised in sermon and in many medieval paintings, where we can see Joseph at work in his carpentry shop and Mary at her loom, while they look affectionately at the infant Jesus at play between them, occasionally scooting around the floor in a wheeled 'baby walker' in fifteenth-century depictions. A symptom of the attractiveness of the image is that medieval theology improved on the deficiencies in the Gospels by filling out the entirely invented identities for Jesus's fond maternal grandparents, Hannah and Joachim, and composing fictional gospels which dwelt on engaging tales of Jesus's childhood which Scripture regrettably failed to provide, but which medieval people wanted to know about.

Medieval letters between husbands and wives are sometimes extravagantly affectionate, and it would be unduly cynical to doubt the reality of the emotions they avow and put their rhetoric of devotion down to convention (Fig. 9.1). In a competitive society where male weakness was punished, the sympathetic and wise wife who could offer disinterested advice and unconditional support to her beleaguered husband was an invaluable helpmate. Other correspondence shows the uses to which expectations of parental care and concern might be made by children. In a sample letter of around 1240 sent by an Oxford university student to his mother back home, we find homesickness, as well as manipulative emotional exploitation: 'You will know that I am well at Oxford, and as happy as possible, but I have been bare of clothing for a long time, and I am hungry because I have no money with which I may choose to allay thirst or hunger ... thus, may you look to my immediate welfare, so that I might visit you in a better state and stay for a longer time.'[5]

Medieval parents confronted the pain and grief of bereavement of their children as best they might. When a (probably) diabetic Yorkshire teenager, Orm, fell into a coma

(a)   (b)

Fig. 9.1 **Late Medieval Family Group**. The medieval equivalent of a family photo, in this case that of a merchant called Gerard Horenbout, painted on an altar piece for his domestic chapel. None of the children are of age, and were not believed capable of steady religious meditation, so they carry small bronze crosses to signify their prayerfulness before God.

in the autumn of 1124, we have the account of a local priest as to his parents' initial panic and then grief when they concluded he was dead. They carried the boy from place to place trying to ease his condition and then, in despair, his passage into the afterlife. Their astonishment and gratification when he made a temporary recovery are all the more poignant. The family nursed him tenderly until his death and had him buried next to a former playmate in the churchyard of Howden minster. Family love might transcend death. A Cornish family of Launceston in the 1160s was doubly bereaved by the simultaneous death of an infant daughter and a grandfather and so buried the little girl in the priory between her grandfather Jordan's legs. In such circumstances medieval parents made the most of the resources their faith gave them. Endowments were made for lights, prayers and masses for the soul of the departed child, and so parental care reached after them beyond the grave. When William, son of Edward III, died in 1348 aged three months, the body was coffined at Westminster Abbey, covered in cloth of gold, surrounded with a burning forest of candles, with black suits awarded to fifty poor to pray for the child's soul. Such measures can only have been a comfort to the parents, one largely denied to the modern world. They did not doubt that their children still loved them even though they had gone amongst angels. When a Cornishman called Æthelsige had a vision of the afterlife in the 1120s, it was his dead eleven-year-old son who came smiling to greet him and act as his guide through Purgatory and Paradise, where the boy now resided.

Marriage

The idea of marriage as contractual (approved by families and involving exchange of property), exclusive (both partners being monogamous) and consensual (both partners publicly and freely agreeing to go ahead with it in a church) only appears late in the middle ages (in the mid thirteenth century in its full form). This arrangement (called sometimes 'Christian marriage') is less than half as old as Christianity. The situation before 1100 has in fact some parallels with the present day. Couples entered a variety of relationships, with a contractual marriage seen as the apex of the arrangement – though this need not then have been exclusive, or even consensual. The earlier medieval world recognised a parallel non-contractual consensual relationship called by clerks 'concubinage', which like a contracted marriage produced legitimate children. William the Conqueror was born to such a relationship, and the legitimacy of his birth was not an issue in succeeding his father as a child in 1026. Concubinage would not be unlike the contemporary informal 'partnership' arrangement between couples.

What was distinctly early medieval was the widespread evidence of polygyny (male relationships with multiple women). Elite males might simultaneously have relationships with two or more women, even maintaining multiple households: the 'official' contractual wife and her children, and the concubine(s) and children. Thus King Henry I of England (1100–1135) had his contracted wives Queen Matilda II (1100–1118) and Queen Adeliza (1121–1151), the marriage with Matilda producing the children who became his heirs. Adeliza was childless by the king. The queens seem principally to have lived at Westminster palace and enjoyed the handsome estates traditionally held by the queen of England. But, from his teenage years, Henry conducted serial and possibly simultaneous relationships with young women from English and Welsh landowning families which produced more than twenty children. He maintained these women and their children in a variety of houses in the Thames valley, notably in his latter years the palace of Woodstock (Oxfordshire, now Blenheim Palace), furthering handsomely the careers and marriages of his offspring, by that date considered as illegitimate by the Church. The eldest of them, Robert of Gloucester (died 1147), was disqualified from consideration as his father's successor in the debates of 1135 because of his birth.

The papacy began to stake a claim for Church jurisdiction over sexual matters from the mid eleventh century, though initially the radical circle of theologians around the pope only aimed to regulate the sex lives of clergy. But there was already a basis for the Church to meddle in the lives of lay people, and the ambitions of Rome soon extended wider in society than the clergy. As early as the ninth century, Church authorities had been raising the question of incestuous sexual liaisons, basing its strictures on rules in the Jewish scriptures (the Christian 'Old Testament'). It tried to apply the rules it found there to men and women who were – it was said – too closely related (that is, cousins to the seventh degree). Society in general paid little attention to this radical new thinking on sexuality until the 1070s, when a prestigious, aggressive and powerful papal monarchy began to emerge with an agenda for the moral reform of society along biblical principles. Bishops throughout Europe were encouraged to enquire into family relationships, seek out prohibited marriages and put an end to them. One of the first to do so was Bishop Ivo of Chartres (died 1115) who was in the 1090s compiling detailed files on the descent and family connections of aristocrats in his diocese and beyond – including those of neighbouring Normandy – and vigorously disputing the validity of the 'incestuous' marriages his investigations revealed.

Surprisingly, aristocratic families often co-operated with these genetic witch-hunts. They did this for pragmatic reasons. They found the new regulations offered both flexibility and opportunity. They could buy dispensations to permit important marriages within the prohibited degree. They also found that if a man wanted to dispose of an uncongenial wife all he had to do was demonstrate she was his cousin, and the pair might well get a divorce (or rather 'annulment'), which allowed the unsatisfied husband to get rid of his wife while keeping the property which came with the marriage. Since medieval aristocracies were closely inter-related this was all too easy a scam. Realising that its radical moral idealism had left the Church vulnerable to exploitation, the papacy was obliged in 1215 to cut the prohibited degree of cousinship to four degrees from seven. But it had by then established its jurisdiction over human sexuality. Marriage disputes, adultery and claims of illegitimacy were becoming the routine business of Church courts by the 1150s, and it was already getting the reputation of being a crooked business. Henry II is said to have complained in 1158 that archdeacons and deans were extorting more money from his subjects with false allegations of adultery than the king himself was able to extract from them. In that same decade, his court chaplain was preaching against the scandal by which such men took money to forget sexual allegations against individual women: corruption built on corruption.

The Church, rather than the family, increasingly controlled the venue and ceremony marking a marriage, something it was working on in England as early as 1076. In part this was because it needed to ensure that declarations were made in public about cousinship and consent before the marriage took place. This was the reason that from 1200 it was required of priests to announce publicly in church an impending marriage for the three Sundays before it was due to take place, so as to give those who objected to it on grounds of kinship a chance to inform on the couple. The medieval ceremony was customarily performed before a priest at the church door, before the party went inside to hear a nuptial mass. Marriage in church allowed clergy to lecture the couple about the solemn nature of the sacrament (equated with Christ's faithful relationship with the Church itself). Under Pope Alexander III (1159–1181) canon (Church) lawyers established that no marriage could be valid unless both partners had declared that they entered into it freely. This was something new and benefited women, whose say in whether they wanted to be married or not was not always respected, though we find the necessity of a woman's consent before marriage discussed in King Cnut's law code of the 1020s. Consent was a major advance in Western women's status, though the Church had actually introduced it to stop women who wanted to enter monasteries being forcibly married off. In reality women perhaps often continued to be disposed of by their male relations or their father's overlord, like it or not.

Sex Outside Marriage

The Church preached faithfulness in relationships and exclusive sexuality, working hard to establish monogamy as the normal practice. But society itself remained tolerant of polygyny for quite a while. Elite males continued openly to take sexual partners (in French called *drus*: meaning 'mistresses' or 'paramours') other than their wives as is silently attested by the large number of illegitimate aristocratic children to be found in society in the later medieval period. King William the Lion of Scotland and his brother David, earl of Huntingdon in England and lord of Garioch in Scotland (died 1219), fathered and furthered numerous illegitimate sons and daughters, to whom they were uniformly generous. They did no less than their successors. Earl David's great-great-grandson, Robert Bruce, earl of Carrick and later king of Scotland (1306–1329), produced numerous illegitimate children who populated the fourteenth-century Scottish aristocracy. In the middle ages extramarital children were not the only consequence of sexual promiscuity. Signs of the ravages of syphilis have been found in a number of later medieval skeletons.

Heterosexual sex outside marriage was adultery, which was condemned by law codes and the Church throughout the period of this book. The church defined it as a major sin. The danger in adultery was as much physical as spiritual. Before 1100 it was allowed that offended husbands or fathers might kill their wife's or daughter's lover if caught in the adulterous act, without penalty or compensation to the lover's relatives provided it was done within a set number of days. By 1200 vengeance killing was illegal, but it was still permissible for the offended husband to castrate an adulterer without being accused of a crime, and indeed there are records of this happening. A pernicious side effect of the Church's control of marriage was the increasing stigmatisation of children born outside marriages it sanctioned as 'illegitimate' or 'bastard'. By the end of the twelfth century, such children had no right to inherit property from their parents, and indeed could not leave property they had acquired in their own right to their children. This created a large class of untouchables in society with inferior civil rights, regarded as tainted from birth by their parents' sin. Legal penalties on bastards in fact continued in England until 1976 in addition to the social ones.

The Church had notably less success in imposing its harsh views on Welsh society, where children conceived from what canon law regarded as irregular liaisons long continued to enjoy full rights of succession alongside their legitimate half-siblings. There was a conscious resistance to canon law marriage, including a carelessness as regards prohibited degrees of kinship which infuriated a succession of archbishops of Canterbury (in whose province Wales fell). Marriage remained contractual rather than sacramental in Wales, and Welsh customary law retained its easy attitude to the legitimate or illegitimate status of children to the end of the middle ages. It was only Prince Llywelyn ab Iorwerth of Gwynedd's attempt in the 1230s to exclude his elder illegitimate son, Gruffudd (died 1244), in favour of his legitimate child by Joan of England that opened the door to canon law. His ultimate failure demonstrated that it was a step the Welsh did not want to take. Llywelyn was succeeded by his grandson through Gruffudd. The harshness of the Church's position on bastardy was in fact often inconvenient to landowning parents in England and Scotland. Fathers found uses for their bastards as agents, knights and potential marriage partners for lower-status neighbours. It was even established by the thirteenth century that a child a father recognised as his own (even if he knew differently) was legitimate. Likewise children could be retrospectively legitimated if their parents subsequently married or if a decree was obtained from Rome. This happened as early as 1204 in favour of Philip II of France's bastards, and the case of the legitimation of John of Gaunt's bastards in the fifteenth century created several noble houses regarded as having claims on the throne of England.

Sexuality

In the middle ages, as now, sexual attraction was the most powerful, constructive and disruptive force in human society. It energised social relations, literature and music then, as it does today. Medieval adolescents apparently thought of little else after their hormones kicked in, and unregulated underage sex was seen as a problem in the middle ages. Medieval people were frank about sexuality and its indulgence. One version of the popular medieval instruction book for boys, *Facetus*, composed in the mid twelfth century, offers adolescents advice on how to seduce girls, gives practical hints on foreplay and sexual positions, and wise (if what we would regard as sexist) advice on avoiding prostitutes and emotional consequences. Its standpoint is not at all modern, for all the frankness. It assumes that, by their uncontrolled nature, all women are up for it and, if they would not co-operate, they were weak and you could take it anyway. However, since rape was a serious criminal offence in the middle ages, and was vigorously pursued, the 'rapist's defence' was not necessarily the medieval law's view. In fact this dichotomy is a reminder that medieval views on sexuality and its consequences were not monolithic but diverse and complex. The Church for its part regarded casual sex as fornication, and a sin to be repented of.

The sex act and reproduction were not separable processes in the middle ages as they are now. Recreational sex without consequences was not a medieval concept, as pregnancy would occur for the woman sooner or later, if she were healthy and well nourished. But the rate of children conceived outside marriage indicates that the risk did not stop the indulgence. The Church for its part held that sex was appropriate only in marriage and then for the purpose of procreation. There were seasons the Church thought intercourse more appropriate than others: certainly not in the meditative and penitential seasons of Advent (four weeks before Christmas) or Lent (the forty days before Easter) or on weekly fast days (Wednesday and Friday), holy (saints') days or Sundays. Sex with a woman during her menstruation or pregnancy was profoundly wrong (an inheritance of a blood taboo from the Jewish origins of Christianity). According to the Church's penitentials, sex was therefore permissible for less than half the year. It nonetheless happened illicitly. Its potential consequences were mitigated a little by the generally low fertility rate of the medieval couple. Infertility was not a consequence of obedience to the Church's requirements for abstinence but had a variety of possible causes: a generally poor diet leading to stillbirths; deliberate abortion; or avoiding risk of conception by copulating anally. There is evidence of some unsatisfactory medieval contraceptive practice, either through ejaculation outside the vagina, douching the genitalia after sex or primitive attempts to obstruct the passage of sperm into the fallopian tubes. One English physician, John of Gaddesden (died 1361), suggested hopefully that a violent sneeze or physical exercise might expel unwanted semen.

Sexual attraction could, as now, turn to intense and sometimes obsessive erotic love, that thing most difficult to describe but unmistakable to experience. Influenced by the classical love poetry of Ovid (Publius Ovidius Naso, *c.* 43 BC–AD 17) the middle ages produced a large and passionate genre of erotic verse, some of it all-time classics, like the *Roman de la Rose, c.* 1220. The language of these may seem to us sometimes over the top and tinged with too much religious imagery, while the male perspective dominates, but nonetheless there can be little doubt of the power of such feelings in medieval society for women and men alike. A lot of medieval poetry is unashamedly homoerotic as much as erotic, which confirms that the full range of human sexual desire was experienced by medieval people, and responded to by them.

Medieval England made a considerable contribution to the idea of romantic love, which remains dominant in Western culture. It derives its name from the 'roman' (a novel in prose or verse in the 'romance' or French language). The development of a novelistic, escapist genre of literature in the later twelfth century owed a lot to men and women writing in the realms of the king of England. In these novels typically a young (noble) man would encounter a young woman and they would fall desperately in love. After a series of adventures, the man would earn the right to take the woman as his wife, by making a reputation and a fortune. England and Scotland produced two popular and long-lasting examples of such romances, *Guy of Warwick* (*c.* 1199) and *Fergus* (*c.* 1217), both written in French verse. The later tales of the *Mabinogion* translate French romance tales into Welsh, for the benefit of intrigued thirteenth-century Welsh aristocrats. In this world of the romance, the pair would base their union on erotic attraction rather than an act of family policy organised by parents or guardians, as happened in the real world. It points up a difference between the longings of medieval people for erotic fulfilment and the hard reality of their society, a tension still evident in the Regency world of Jane Austen.

The great Jane's medieval predecessor was the female aristocratic poet, called ambiguously Marie 'de France'. In fact she was clearly of a French noble family with links to England and South Wales, a woman steeped in Arthurian literature. Her most likely identity is Mary, daughter of Waleran II (died 1166), count of Meulan in France and Worcester in England, himself a Latin poet. Marie's short stories (*lais*) tell of love reached through great pains, such as the tale called *Guigemar* whose eponymous hero found no woman to suit him until he encountered a queen imprisoned by her unworthy husband. Their stolen love was adulterous and dangerous. Though it was consummated, they were forced apart. Long separated, they endured the consequent agonies until reunited through great difficulties. It is not too much to see in Marie's tale of Guigemar an artistic echo of the tensions in a society where human impulses were thwarted at every turn by social and religious barriers.

There is a long tradition based on a nineteenth-century analysis of romance literature which proposed that erotic love was expressed and felt differently in the middle ages:

notably in the ideal of 'courtly love'. This was a form of love where the noble male would idolise the object of his adoration to the extent of humiliating himself at her will, as a way of demonstrating the transcendent power of his desire for her, which surpassed even his masculine impulses. The male lover would not expect sexual satisfaction; his restraint demonstrated his virtue. The ideal was almost masochistic in the self-abasement of the knight in his desire to serve his lady, and not in fact that complimentary to women. The relationship between Lancelot and Guinevere as portrayed in the 1170s by Chrétien de Troyes was the template for this idea, and Britain produced the parallel tale of Tristan and Iseut, where the young knight has to see the object of his affections daily at the mercy of a boorish and jealous king, her husband. The desire of the males in this model was directed at the untouchable wife of another man, and it does once more point to the erotic tensions at the heart of medieval society. But it is less than likely that the anaemic subservience of Lancelot's love for an imperious Guinevere had any other than a literary existence.

The Tyranny of Normalcy

Well before 1000 handbooks had appeared in Britain designed to help clergy decide on penance for sins committed, detected and confessed. They give a remarkable amount of detail as to what was considered unacceptable sexual behaviour, from masturbation to bestiality. They defined a state where sex was acceptable to the Church only when practised between a married couple, with the male on top (and not entering the woman from the rear), the woman not menstruating, and on days which should not otherwise be devoted to religious observance. All societies seek to establish what is 'normal' and acceptable within it, even in bed. Likewise, society has to grapple with aspects of human sexuality it does not want to approve of. The most unacceptable of these was homosexual desire. The origins of same-sex attraction have only recently been identified as physiological, originating in the level of testosterone at key developmental stages in the womb. Too little testosterone, and male foetal brains develop feminine traits of sexuality; too much and female foetal brains develop male traits. Homosexuality is not therefore a matter of choosing a life style (and there are in any case many homosexualities); it is an inborn sexual impulse, and has always been a natural consequence of the varying patterns of human development. Recent studies suggest the figure of 3–5 per cent of males and females being predominantly homosexual in their orientation in the modern world. It follows from this that there must have been a broadly similar proportion of homosexually inclined people in the middle ages as now, and the sketchy historical record indicates as much.

The middle ages offered no identity with which a homosexually inclined male or female might identify, other than the sodomite, which was hardly a positive one, and which in any case applied to anyone whose sexual practices diverged from the very narrow limits of acceptability the Church placed on sexuality by the eleventh century. Most homosexuals must simply have conformed to what was expected of them, denied what their bodies were telling them and endured the torment and emptiness. Identifying medieval homosexuals is therefore not easy, though there must have been scores of thousands of them over the medieval centuries struggling to express what they were. Literary historians have had to go looking in the spaces between words and intention to find 'queer' allusions in literature. There is something of an industry in trying to out medieval kings as homosexual, but plausible cases have only been made for William Rufus (1087–1100) and Edward II (1307–1327) on the hardly conclusive grounds of their patterns of behaviour. William Rufus's court was accused by hostile clerics of being a haunt of sodomites, while the king himself never married. Edward II was undeniably besotted with several male favourites, most obsessively with Peter Gaveston (exec. 1312) and Hugh Despenser the Younger (exec. 1326). Both Rufus and Edward were insinuated to be sodomites by contemporaries, though not until they were safely dead. Richard II – in whose reign the word 'deviant' first appears in the English language – was likewise close to male favourites, though in his case he was clearly also obsessed with his beloved wife, Anne of Bohemia (died 1394). So far as the case for Rufus's queerness is concerned, late marriage was the norm rather than the exception for males in the middle ages, so his lack of a wife does not convict him. Edward II fathered many children without trouble, and indeed had an illegitimate son, Adam, at a time when his relationship with Gaveston had begun and before his marriage in 1308. Gaveston himself had two daughters, one illegitimate. Seeking close dependency from a series of men was part of Edward's character which might indicate emotional insecurity and neediness as much as homosexuality. But it is the blind obsessiveness of Edward's devotion to Gaveston that gives the clue that it did indeed tip over into the homosexual. These questionable kings demonstrate the sexual and emotional complexity of the human condition in any historical period.

Medieval society was in general homosocial, and homosociality can shift towards homoerotic longings. Men then as now might form exclusive emotional bonds with other males, even if they are not sexually based or consummated, the phenomenon known nowadays ironically, even comically, as 'bromance'. If a male or female were homosexual, he or she was often in a situation of long-term closeness to other men or women. This was nowhere more so than in the enclosed world of the monastery, a medieval environment which generated some undeniably homoerotic verse and behaviour. The dangers of celibate clergy resorting to homosexuality and pederasty are frequently alluded to in medieval sources. But the same might also apply to the military households of kings and nobles, where men formed an emotional dependency on their male lord and male companions rather than on women. The intensity of male-on-male relationships can occasionally be glimpsed. That of William Marshal (died 1219) with his handsome and beloved 'dearest lord' the Young King Henry of England (died 1183) is described in homoerotic terms by Marshal's biographer. Marshal was a hero to the boy-king, seven years his junior, and the king was an attractive, engaging and beautiful youth. We know of English knights such as the courtiers and kinsmen Saher de Quincy (died 1219) and Robert fitz Walter (died 1235) who as tourneyers in the 1160s or 1170s and soldiers in the 1200s pursued a formal brotherhood of arms, their heraldry featuring on each other's shields in later life. Such relationships might conceivably have moved into the homosexual. It was not for fear of the dark that lights burned all night long in monastic dormitories.

Church penitentials from the early middle ages onwards show a graphic awareness of homosexual practices in men and women, much as they disapproved of them. They more or less expect heedless teenagers to engage in same-sex acts, judged by the relatively light penalty imposed on boys who pleasured each other: a flogging. Anal, intercrural, masturbatory and oral sex between homosexual men and women are all registered and described. The moral reform of the eleventh century identified same-sex practices ('the sin against nature') in detail and considered indulging them to be deeply sinful, deserving expulsion from office and punishment in chains and confinement for clergy. But such acts (stigmatised as sodomy) were perversions and did not identify their perpetrators as anything other than wilful sinners: they were not 'homosexuals'. As a matter of course, heretics were regarded as sodomitical, like the Templars of the early fourteenth century, which was a natural consequence of their extreme sinfulness. Medieval religious authorities were out to construct a view of what was normal and acceptable in sexual practice, and impose it on society. Their action amounted to erecting the tyranny of normalcy on their society, not the persecution of the gay, as we might be tempted to look at it.

The Widow

An anomaly in medieval society was the position of the widow, which allowed a degree of independence to a woman. On the death of husbands, wives came into full control not only of their own inheritances but of the lands given them on the exchange of the marriage contract. Medieval widows were not required to remarry, though many did. But those who did not could live an independent life, and society accommodated it. Matilda Bigod (died 1248), the eldest daughter of William Marshal, was freed to remarry around the age of thirty when her first husband Earl Hugh Bigod of Norfolk died in February 1225. She negotiated a stunning match with Earl William IV de Warenne, the king's close cousin and the principal rival to the power of the Bigods in East Anglia. It was a political coup of some magnitude, and it must have been negotiated by Matilda herself. Matilda's second husband was considerably older than she was, probably in his mid fifties by the time they married. She seems to have conducted herself with a degree of independence during this second marriage. She is found making purchases of land in Yorkshire in her own right. Her second husband died in 1240. Matilda, now in her mid forties, chose to live an enterprising single life. The countess, enjoying a third of the lands of two great earldoms, entered into an active career of litigation to secure her rights. In February 1242 she took at a rent from the king the keeping of her late second husband's honors in Yorkshire and East Anglia, which were interpreted also to include the rape of Lewes and town of Stamford, since the Warenne son and heir she had by him was underage. She was appointed castellan of Conisbrough in May 1242, making her undoubtedly the most powerful and wealthy woman in England from 1242 onwards. The death of her last surviving brother, Ansel Marshal, on 23 December 1245 brought her into an even greater position of potential power, as the eldest living child of William Marshal and an independent woman. One recognition of this was the king's allotment to her, as her father's eldest daughter, of the right to the title of 'marshal of England', a state office of some power and dignity. The division of the Marshal inheritance brought her the entire lordship of Netherwent, several large manors in England, and County Carlow in Leinster.

Noblewomen could maintain themselves happily in the later middle ages by employing their own legal counsel and stewards, even if they did not have the support of their sons and male relations. Serial widows (and the difference in male–female life expectancy and in age at marriage meant there were quite a few of them) became wealthier and wealthier, denying their inheritances to their sons, sometimes for decades. Lawyers could be allies as well as adversaries to women: for instance, the legal process of 'jointure' allowed a husband and wife to acquire estates and properties jointly, giving the widow enhanced control of her late husband's property. The law courts were ferocious in supporting widows' rights, awarding interim custody of disputed land before the verdict. Therefore widows were dominant landowners in medieval society. In England the politically ambitious Isabel de Forz (died 1293) acquired two earldoms and was so powerful that the king attempted the fraudulent takeover of her lands: she successfully resisted him until on her deathbed. An even more iconic widow was Margaret, the Countess Marshal, granddaughter of Edward I, married in her late teens to John Mowbray, Lord Seagrave, at such a high price to him that on his death in 1353 she enjoyed almost his entire estate, which she had received as her widow's jointure (or settlement on marriage). She denied her lands to John's daughter and heir, whom she outlived, as she long outlived her second husband. She was created duchess of Norfolk in her own right and died in 1399 as one of the wealthiest people in England, possessing her father's earldom and the bulk of her husbands' major estates. The position of women in the middle ages was not in general a happy one, but for some longevity brought compensations, as Chaucer's Wife of Bath happily witnessed in a literary context.

Medieval Childhood

A medieval child's birth was a time of danger for both itself and its mother. It is probably no coincidence that medieval midwives and parents would be quick to protect the child from a variety of dangers once the cord was cut and it was washed. Amulets of coral or amber were provided to protect the baby from supernatural dangers, such as the malevolence of spirits and the evil eye. The newborn was tightly swathed to keep it warm and secure, and not least it was taken promptly to the church to receive the baptism which would admit the child to the possibility of redemption and ultimately to paradise. The mother too had to undergo ritual purification before being readmitted to the community. The concentration of ritual at this point in the life-cycle has a lot to tell us about the anxieties that it inspired.

The view held since the 1990s is that the stages of medieval childhood should not be understood as being much different from early modern childhood, and that we should be thinking in terms of historical continuity in this area, not a discourse of 'progress', where education and child-care blossom as a result of the advances of industrial urbanism in the eighteenth and nineteenth centuries which supposedly invented the very idea of childhood and child-care. The affective nature of medieval adult–child relationships is increasingly stressed in modern works on past childhood. We have good medieval authority for this. The knight and social commentator, Philip de Novara, a statesman, writer and grandfather, in his *Four Stages of Human Life* (*c.* 1270) tells us that children are to be understood as the focuses of love. They bring it out of their parents, and particularly the mother who suckles the child. They are always the focus of attention and are made a fuss over by those who come into contact with them and, of course, they love those who love them, 'Such', he says, 'is the great love, which is placed within people as part of their humanity, and moves them to tend and to care.'[6] A modern child-care specialist could hardly put it better. Of course, medieval ideas about disciplining the child were somewhat more decisive than suits the modern stomach. But in a society where pain was regarded as an invaluable memory aid for a feckless intellect, the middle ages had a rationale for not sparing the rod. The ritual blow (*colée*) of the knighting ceremony was intended to fix the event in the unfixed mind of the youth who was receiving it.

Analyses of a wide range of sources (conduct books, saints' lives, medical textbooks, miracle stories and coroners' records) have come up with a similar picture of the understanding of medieval childhood across Europe. Children had to be understood on their own terms, and the middle ages was quite able to define for itself what those were. According to medical texts, children were characterised by the dominance of humours of heat and moisture; hence they were emotional, restless and wayward, stabilising the older (and drier) they got. The stages of medieval childhood are pretty well understood.

There was a time of nursing until the child was weaned in his or her second year. Children were expected and allowed to play through infancy until as late as the age of twelve. There were gender differences in that girls generally tended to stay in or near the home, while from the age of three or four boys roamed the neighbourhood (as we learn from the pattern of reported accidents of fourteenth-century London children). Boys liked to play in small gangs on the margins, on river banks, in timber yards and back alleys. Children of working families were not allowed near adult work until after twelve, as they were believed to be lacking in both physical strength and judgement, though both boys and girls might be trusted to run messages or draw water. Girls below the age of eight tended to be distinguished as 'maidens' (Fr. *pucelle*) as opposed to older girls up to twelve who were perhaps of more use round the house. Boys were just boys (the word is used for all stages of male childhood); the gendered term 'girl' was likewise used for all of female childhood. 'Infant' (*enfans*) applied to both genders until puberty. Medieval noble children were somewhat cloistered from their parents by nurses and the institution of fostering, the greatest of them being given their own households. Even so, their parents took an active delight in them, as Novara tells us. There is the curious fact that Henry VII of England (1485–1509) is recorded as losing 6s 8d at cards in 1498 to his son, the future Henry VIII, then aged seven.

Adolescence was a condition recognised by medieval people. The biological fact of puberty and the process of physical growth and bodily change that followed were too momentous to be ignored in the middle ages, especially as they had implications for family marriage strategies. The onset of adolescence was a dividing point for both male and female childhood. It was perceived as a time of rapid growth, high emotion, awkwardness and sexual experimentation, as acknowledged by medieval medical texts and conduct books. The words 'adolescent' and 'youth' were applied to twelve- to sixteen-year-old males, as well (in noble households) as the words 'valet' or 'squire', though those could be applied to youths as old as twenty-one. Philip de Novara's considered view of male adolescence dwells on the distracted state of teenagers, their animal spirits and energy and not least their sexual awakening, which they could not stop themselves from indulging, to their moral danger. He says wearily the same thing any modern parent might: 'There are many young people who are so arrogant that they think they know everything, can do anything and are infallible. But they very often get in a complete mess.' But he then adds what remains to parents the abiding delight of the teenager: 'The best thing about youth is that the young brim over endlessly with cheerfulness and affection, even if they think seriously about very little.'[7] Novara also has a view of female adolescence as a distinct stage of development, likewise sexually charged and over-confident, necessitating strict control of the girl by her parents. He recommends early marriage for their own moral benefit. Early marriage was indeed the fate of many adolescents of the upper class. Fifteenth-century English marriage contracts for child couples anticipate that the boy would be sleeping with his (often much younger) wife by the age of sixteen.

The end of childhood was well defined for boys, though it varied according to custom, social class and period. From the eleventh century, aristocratic boys would receive arms (be knighted) and thus become adult at any time between fifteen and twenty-one depending on where and when they lived, but in England the age of adulthood was generally fixed as twenty or twenty-one by the early thirteenth century, where it stayed fixed in Britain until 1967. A noble male would then be a *bacheler*, a knight on the path to achieving recognition as a mature 'man of worth' (*preudomme*). For trainee clergy the rite of passage was ordination (eighteen was the minimum age for the subdiaconate, the most junior of the orders with an active role in the mass), and for tradesmen it was finishing an apprenticeship and admission to a guild. Marriage was not necessarily an act proclaiming adulthood, at least in the higher social bracket (though it was for urban artisan classes). Marriage could happen at any age amongst the aristocracy, even in infancy (though not in the case of the lower social classes). Cohabitation did not generally occur until after fifteen in any case. The middle ages had no age for sexual consent, which was monitored through consent to marriage. There was no parallel rite of passage for girls, and so the age of transition to adulthood was unstated, other than by the biological fact of menstruation, whose significance was known to medieval physicians. Nonetheless, there was a consciousness of the difference between girls and women, represented by the ideal of the 'worthy woman' (*preudefemme*) or mature, responsible matron. Probably the key point was menarche, after which reproduction became possible. This could occur as early as twelve even in the middle ages, but was for most girls somewhat later than nowadays (currently it averages 11¾ years). Marriage (as opposed to betrothal) would not generally occur until fourteen, and with marriage came the woman's authority over the household, a transition marked by a change of address: the unmarried girl would be called *damoiselle* (Lat. *domicella*), the married woman *dame* (Lat. *domina*).

Life Expectancy

Average life expectancy at birth in Europe even before the Black Death (1348–1349) was around thirty-five years, a figure which is often misunderstood. For those who reached the age of twenty, it was not unreasonable to expect a further forty years and more of life. What the statistic meant was that medieval infant mortality might run in excess of 30 per cent; currently in Britain it is around 0.2 per cent. It might have been as much as, or more than, 50 per cent in the plague-ridden later middle ages. Surviving childhood and adolescence was the trick. If a child could reach adulthood, he might reach the age of sixty or seventy, which was not uncommon. Childhood was undeniably a time of high mortality, and higher in some areas and amongst the poorer social groups.

What impact did high mortality have on medieval parenting? The deep grief of bereaved medieval parents and constant fears for their young are testimony to emotional investment by them in their children, as much in girls as boys. There is no sign of refusal to engage emotionally with them as a defence mechanism, any more than high mortality led to emotional withdrawal of Victorian parents from their young. Boys tended to survive better than girls, as they were less likely to be nursed out of the household. The highest danger was in the first year of life, the lowest in the age group between ten and fourteen, but there were peaks of mortality around six and in late adolescence.

Like most agrarian societies, the middle ages valued male children for pragmatic reasons: males were economically more profitable to families. This preference for the male intensified during the twelfth century when the aristocracy began to invest more heavily in the idea of noble lineage as transmitted by males, for lack of a son thereafter meant death to the lineage. However, there is an abundance of evidence of how medieval fathers might idolise their daughters, and there are very few clear cases of wives being divorced because they did not produce male children. Infanticide was not unknown in medieval Britain; it shocked people and and was promptly investigated and punished. The deliberate killing of unwanted babies because they were female, which is found in the cities of Southern Europe, is not, however, evident in medieval Britain. Abandonment of newborns happened with both sexes of baby, and indeed more girls were abandoned than boys. But society had mechanisms for the care of 'foundlings'.

Anxiety and Disease

Medieval children were prey to many debilitating diseases, some – like rickets – the result of vitamin deficiency. Others struck quickly and often fatally, such as measles, whooping cough and enteric fevers. Medieval people who survived to adulthood were subject to the diseases we would call Third World, but also to those we associate with modern Britain. We can credibly reconstruct cases of cancer, hepatitis, tuberculosis, rheumatoid and osteo-arthritis, gout, influenza, typhus, diabetes and heart disease from the medieval historical record, as much as from the analysis of skeletal remains. A major medieval health danger, particularly for armies in the field, was dysentry, but it was just as dangerous to crowded and insanitary urban populations, prey to all sorts of vicious enteric infections.

The medieval life style introduced its own particular problems. The diet of the elites, lay and clerical, favoured fish and red meat and put either a low priority on vegetables or too much (in the case of the poor). Fruit was valued, but not easy to get hold of at certain seasons. The end result was a deficiency in particular vitamins, especially A, C and D, though the last would have been made up for by adherence to the preference for fish on fast days. The elite diet was excessively high in protein. Alcohol consumption too was higher than the modern average. The result for some would have been morbid obesity with the consequent possibilities of liver disease, varicose ulcers and late-onset diabetes. All three of the Norman kings of England were afflicted with obesity. There is a strong likelihood that it was his diet which killed the Conqueror in 1087.

In these circumstances the services of physicians were highly valued, though it was their consultative and diagnostic skills which were perhaps valued more than their ability actually to cure people. A twelfth-century proverb tartly observes: 'A good friend is better than a doctor, who can cure no illness.'[8] But anxiety trumped cynicism every time, and doctors with a good reputation were much sought after. William the Conqueror was so impressed with the Confessor's Lotharingian court physician, Baldwin of Bury, that he retained him in his service after 1066. The Italian medical expert, Faricius (died 1117), made a great reputation as a court physician in England following his attendance on Queen Matilda II in her first pregnancy. He was consulted widely by the aristocracy of his day and was nominated to the abbacy of Abingdon by his friend the king. His fame even led to consideration as a candidate for archbishop of Canterbury, which was scotched – according to his monks – by some bishops' prejudice against a colleague who had made a living diagnosing women's health from their urine. A *medicus* is often found amongst the clerical staff of great medieval nobles from the twelfth century onwards, which indicates a certain health anxiety amongst the leisured elite. It also attests to the widespread practice of the diagnostic examination of bodily wastes and regular blood-lettings (phlebotomies) amongst the aristocracy, by which the balance of physical humours and health was supposedly maintained. The poor were not so indulged, for medieval doctors lived by the fees they charged. The poor could only hope for the charity of the better-off. It was in the later thirteenth century that physicians and surgeons appear in Britain less as household retainers and more as professionals, touting their university credentials and living off fees, and London and the greater towns began to introduce regulations for their conduct in the next century, the less prestigious surgeons incorporating as a craft guild in London by 1376.

Behind the learned world of Faricius and his colleagues was one of folk remedies relying on superstitious beliefs about precious stones, magical charms, the water from certain springs or the more solid virtues of particular medicinal herbs. Purgatives offered by medieval apothecaries may not have been entirely worthless, and indeed the use is still made today of the aloes and rhubarb they employed for the purpose. The use of opium deriving from the fruit of the poppy as a sedative was certainly known to Western physicians from translated Arabic texts as early as the twelfth century, though there is no evidence for its medical use for pain relief in Britain before the sixteenth century. Most efficacious of all was believed to be the intercession of the saints. Much of the population on medieval roads was of people suffering long-term illness in search of cures at particular famous shrines, to the extent that cities and towns would appoint medically qualified men to keep their gates to diagnose whether the state of sick travellers trying to enter was a danger to public health. The administrators of shrines too kept watch, and publicised by their meticulous records the cures effected by their relics, so as to encourage further visitors and the grateful alms they were happy to offer.

The spread of leprosy (nowadays known as Hansen's disease) during the middle ages led to dramatic measures to accommodate sufferers of what could be an ugly and infectious bacterial disease, characterised in some strains by discoloured waxy skin, lesions, ulcers, crippling of hands and feet, skeletal malformation and loss of extremities. As a disease it was much feared in the middle ages, and consequently much studied and theorised about, and it was generally believed to be a disorder of the humours of the body caused by black bile, conveyed by fetid breath or by sexual activity involving menstrual blood. The eleventh and twelfth centuries were far from ignoring it. This period saw a remarkable degree of charitable donations by the social elites, and as a consequence lepers were offered the chance of entering monastic-style communities which grew up outside most main towns, and there be provided with food and medical care, and indeed as a way of offsetting the sin that was taken to be the root of most disease.

Distinct monastic orders grew up from the 1120s – such as the canons of Grand-Beaulieu lès Chartres and the leper-knights of the Hospitallers of St Lazarus of Jerusalem (with an English commandery at Burton Lazars in Leicestershire) – which were generously endowed with lands and revenues for the care of lepers. The twelfth century saw major investment in such hospitals across Britain, mostly erected as acts of piety by aristocrats and many dedicated to St Leonard, a particular patron of the sick. Some 300 were erected in England in the middle ages. Medieval lepers were not therefore shunned; indeed their hospitals and churches were often prominent buildings erected at the entrance to towns. Nor were lepers confined to their precincts. It was a point of pride for spiritually inclined aristocrats and bishops to patronise these communities of sick, who were called by such people 'my brothers and sisters in Christ, the martyrs of Christ'. Queen Matilda II of England (died 1118) and Hugh of Avalon, bishop of Lincoln (died 1200), were well-known advocates of this theological attitude. Visiting and even tending lepers became an act of high religious devotion, and some princes, such as Theobald the Great, count of Champagne (died 1152), the brother of King Stephen of England, were famous for it. In this case, religious duty and the example of Jesus's care for lepers countered any impulse to stigmatise them, however much their disease caused revulsion.

The virulence of leprosy ebbed during the later medieval centuries as that of other forms of tubercular infection increased. Former leper hospitals were wound up, took more general patients or simply devoted their endowments to the indigent poor. By the fifteenth century there was little trace of leprosy left in Britain, though it was still feared and studied obsessively, which left a historical legacy of some persistence in misinterpreting medieval attitudes to the sick. The disease did, however, leave a beneficial legacy in the ingrained medieval impulse, drawn from the Gospels, to offer a

wide, charitable support to the sick. The old leper hospitals had run popular frater-
nities which the healthy and well-off joined, so as to benefit from the prayers of the
afflicted, and they paid handsomely for the privilege. Much of this support in the later
centuries was ad hoc – the support of better-off family members for the chronically ill
and disabled. But the middle- and working-class urban religious guilds that grew up
within the greater parish churches in the fourteenth century often included amongst
their good works the financial support of afflicted members. Trade guilds too might
support members who suffered industrial or occupational injury. In some ways these
diffuse efforts made good the failure and decline of many of the twelfth-century general
hospital foundations.

Mortality Crises

Later medieval society experienced periodic mortality crises, when disease-related
deaths exceeded the capacity of the population to replace itself. Iconic medieval plagues
were not the only reason these occurred. The years 1150–1152 for instance seem to have
experienced an interlude of high mortality caused by a fatally protracted cold season
across north-western Europe in the winter of 1149–1150, which led to late germination,
depletion of food stocks, a catastrophically poor harvest and widespread starvation
over the autumn and winter of 1150–1151. The weakened populace had no resistance
to a variety of fatal diseases including widespread enteric diseases or dysentery, and
perhaps also influenza. The mortality in those years was unusually high amongst the
aristocracy. The inroads on the population were so drastic as to suspend hostilities in
the civil conflicts of England and northern France in 1151. We can detect familiar mortal enemies of human existence at work even in the medieval centuries. Influenza seems
to have been behind a series of visitations on Britain (called the 'sweating sickness') that
began in 1485 and led to a high seasonal mortality.

Episodic famines occurred throughout the later middle ages, and the rising population of England in the thirteenth century may have been partly to blame for the severity
of the famines in Edward II's reign. Other indigenous diseases, such as malaria (known
as 'ague') in the coastal and wetland districts, played their part in weakening the population. The population lived on the edge. Atlantic-dominated weather in 1315 brought
constant warm fronts and continuous belts of rain which flooded fields, preventing germination of crops, and inducing widespread famine. It affected Northern Europe across
Britain, France and Germany, which compounded the problem in Britain, as food was
unavailable to import. The winter of 1316–1317 was as bad, worsened by an early spell
of harsh freezing, and food prices rocketed. The cycle was repeated in 1320–1321 and
1321–1322. It was further compounded by simultaneous animal epidemics (murrains)
which ravaged cattle and sheep herds until the early 1320s. Border warfare between

Scots and English added local difficulties. Marginal peasants abandoned the land and migrated, or starved. The difference from 1150–1152 is that the fourteenth-century 'Great Famine' was not associated with pandemics, though it is estimated that 10 per cent of the population disappeared from the countryside.

The later medieval centuries experienced the most dramatic pandemic the human race has yet weathered, the Black Death of 1348–1350, whose long-term impact continued over two centuries. The agent was a form of bacterial infection of the blood, *Yersinia pestis*, from a family which has periodically visited several devastating plagues on humanity. Though characterised as bubonic plague transmitted to humans from fleas infesting rats, the transmission of the disease was probably more complex than that. The pathogen responsible is certainly offered a generous reservoir by black rats and infects their fleas, which would have passed the disease to humans. But to spread as it did, it must also have passed from human to human by proximity or by pneumonic means (that is, coughing), especially in winter when the infection was at its height, and there may have been possible reservoir species harbouring it other than rats.

The plague's virulence was extraordinary, killing between a third and a half of the population of the British Isles over two years. It was not an easy death, though it may have been quick for those who contracted the pneumonic variety. Symptoms included an initial malaise and headaches followed by fever, vomiting and a hacking cough which produced a red sputum as the lungs became infected. Medieval sources refer to swellings appearing on the nodes of the neck, the armpits and groins of victims as the pathogen exceeded the capacity of the body's defences to combat it. The blood-borne bacillus rapidly compromised the internal organs of victims, and death was through organ failure and septic shock. Four out of five infected died well within eight days of the symptoms appearing, and some (those infected with the pneumonic strain) died a lot quicker.

All major cities and many minor towns filled mass graves dug on their outskirts with the dead, and those who died in this traumatic event were not forgotten. A Cistercian abbey, St Mary Graces, was founded in 1350 on one of the London pits, that in East Smithfield, and a Charterhouse on the West Smithfield pit. At Scarborough on the east coast, a charnel chantry served by several priests was built on top of its cliff-top plague pit, whose skeletons continue to emerge and drop into the sea at intervals as the cliff erodes. The striking thing about the record for the terrible years 1348–1349 for our understanding of our ancestors is that, in all this, life went on for the living: animals were tended, crops sown, rents were paid, records were kept and courts met, though business was thin and labour scarce. The dead were collected and buried with decency, coffined or shrouded even in the plague pits. The clergy as a group seem to have been heroic in their devotion to their calling, which took them into extreme danger.

The Black Death reached England late in the summer of 1348. The population knew it was coming. On 17 August the bishop of Bath and Wells ordered penitential exercises on Fridays, the day of the Passion, 'to beg God to protect the people from the pestilence which has come from the East into the neighbouring kingdom'. France was intended. It may have appeared in Marseille as early as the autumn of 1347, progressing slowly north. As it approached, King Philip VI asked the University of Paris for an analysis of the new menace; the best the scholars could tell him was that it had been triggered by a planetary conjunction in Aquarius in 1345. Its access into Britain was the ports of the Channel coast, and cases were probably emerging in the coastal counties by July 1348. It had reached London by November. The plague raged in the south over the winter of 1348–1349. During the spring of 1349 several plague pits were set aside to take the overflow of corpses from the City of London's churchyards. They were planned and administered with some care by the City authorities. Excavation of the East Smithfield pit has found that the dead were stacked up to five deep in the trench burials; 2,400 corpses are estimated to have been eventually laid there, and a further 10,000 in its bigger West Smithfield counterpart. The current London Crossrail project has encountered previously unsuspected pits. Estimates are not possible of how many plague victims were buried in the City's churchyards before they were full, or closed, but that 20,000–30,000 victims died in London is perfectly credible, and thousands more would have perished in its large satellite settlements of Southwark and Westminster. Archbishops, bishops and abbots all fell victim, as well as aristocrats, though the lesser clergy, who honoured their duty to their flock, suffered worse: nearly half died, as opposed to just over a quarter of aristocrats, who could take refuge in their country manors. One member of the royal family died of plague, Joan, King Edward III's daughter.

The Black Death penetrated Wales by March 1349 and Scotland during the winter of 1349–1350. The sparser density of population in Wales and Scotland may not necessarily have led to any lower level of mortality than in England. At Llan-llwch near Carmarthen, eleven out of its twelve tenant farmers died. Lowland Scotland and its burghs can have suffered no less than the neighbouring northern shires of England. There is some reason to think members of the Scottish nobility took advantage of their remote Highland estates to find refuge from the worst of the plague. They certainly suffered less even than their English counterparts, and it is generally argued that Scotland suffered less population loss and more rapid replacement than England. Perhaps the worst thing about the Black Death was its periodic re-occurrences. The debilitated population, already in decline from the early part of the century, was subject to a second ferocious outbreak in 1361–1362, which killed off between 10 and 15 per cent of the remaining populace, particularly the young, and further depressed the replacement rate in population. Further outbreaks occurred in 1369 and 1375, and plague remained endemic, if localised, throughout Britain throughout the rest of the period of this study.

Ageing

Medieval people were not enthusiastic about getting old, and indeed a medical tract survives from later medieval England which offered advice on slowing the ageing process by the management of bodily humours. Its advice was probably no more useful than many of its modern descendants.[9] The fountain of youth was very much a wistful medieval fantasy, belief in the existence of which is found in the early fourteenth-century travel writings attributed to an English knight, Sir John Mandeville. Medieval people looked at approaching old age with stoicism at best and with little expectation of autumnal repose. Retirement was a concept unknown to the middle ages, not least because there was little financial support available for the aged. William Marshal, earl of Pembroke and regent of England, mounted horse and took up arms to lead his troops to victory at Lincoln in 1217. He was about seventy years of age at the time, but that did not stop him exchanging blows with a much younger knight. He had to be reminded to put on his helm by his household before he rode into action, however. He was not an exception. Several of the corpses from the burial pits associated with the battle of Towton (1461) were those of active veterans in their fifties, and possibly older.

The long-lived were not a tiny group proportional to the adult population in the middle ages, and with St Gilbert of Sempringham (died 1189) we have credible evidence of a medieval centenarian; he died at the age of 105 or 106, having still a role as head of his monastic order the previous year, before his final illness. Calculations of the age groups amongst the landed and ecclesiastical elites of the fourteenth and fifteenth centuries show that even in an age of plague well over a quarter of any adult cohort (those over twenty) would reach sixty years of age. Nonetheless, the middle ages set a limited economic value on the old. In the 1020s the compensation (weregeld) paid to relatives of murder victims dropped by more than a half for a victim who was over the age of fifty. Weregeld was set the same as for a ten-year-old for a man of sixty-five and a woman of sixty. Medieval society certainly believed that the age of sixty was a watershed, and it was all downhill physically and mentally from there. Osteoporosis in post-menopausal women, osteoarthritis in both sexes, bunions and gall stones were the painful trials medieval ageing inevitably brought. In the 1270s, Philip de Novara, a sexagenarian, advised those who passed eighty that they had best pray for death.

Unless entirely inhibited by physical and mental incapacity, the medieval aged remained active in the world for longer than we would expect today, with consequent distress to them. Then as now there was a degree of impatience with the old, their slowness and incapacity, as Daniel of Beccles observed in the 1180s: 'While you are in your prime as a servant to your lord you will have his affections, but when the burden of age tires you, saps your vitality, makes you slow and unresponsive, or perpetually stiff in your limbs, you will become distasteful to him.'[10] Kings, bishops and lords never had the prospect of a retirement, which made King Edward III's senescent last years rather pitiable and desperate. The bodily image of a kingdom with the king as its head meant that the debility of a monarch was reflected in his dysfunctional and decaying realm, the curse of the Fisher King. No less melancholy are the medical excuses for long-term non-attendance sent by numbers of parliamentary peers in the same centuries, citing inability to ride, crippling gout, poor eyesight, deafness and chronic illness. Septuagenarians were customarily allowed exemption from jury service in the fourteenth-century City of London because of their likely plea of incapacity. The septuagenarian citizens of much less populous York had to buy the privilege of retirement, which tends to indicate that the labour of the aged in medieval society was essential at several levels, and their retirement from public affairs was resisted, because it caused problems. The office of sheriff in England, for instance, was seen as one for the mature male. Once appointed, later medieval sheriffs might have to carry on in office for decades as the central government was all too conscious of the difficulty of finding replacements for the onerous job, which involved much stress, arduous travel and unpopularity for the superannuated sheriff, all for little return. Almost 40 per cent of later medieval sheriffs died in office or soon after chronic illness forced a retirement; the majority served into their sixties and seventies, quite a few after a career of four decades.

Did age bring any compensations in medieval Britain? Grandchildren of course were a delight, though medieval women, who married young and who lived longer than men on average, were more likely to encounter them than their husbands. The memories of the old were important, though later medieval culture was primarily a written one. In 1265, Henry III wrote to the octogenarian Loretta de Briouze, the widow of the last Norman earl of Leicester (who had died in 1204). She had been living as an **anchorite** in Kent since the 1220s, and was one of the few available resources on the rights and duties of the seneschalcy of England that went with the earldom, which the king was intending to confer on his younger son, Edmund. The period, however, did have an ideal of a contemplative and placid finale to life, where judgement and experience compensated for loss of physical pleasures and faculties. Cicero's essay on old age (*De Senectute*) was popular in the middle ages as an evocation of the quiet pleasure the aged might take in memory and gardening. It was by no means uncommon in the twelfth century for laymen and clerics active in the world to seek out the cloister to spend their last years in spiritual exercise and prayer, which was a Christianised version of Cicero's retirement plan. It was expected that children care for their aged parents, and those who failed in their duty, which had the authority of the Fifth Commandment (Ex. 20: 12), were condemned. It likewise expected old people to act their age, which meant behaving with dignity and restraint. For all the anxiety involved in ageing, and the distaste for its physical manifestations, a degree of attention and care was the right of at least the respectable old.

POSTSCRIPT

No one in their right mind would choose to have been born in the fourteenth century, were the choice given them. A wise player of the game 'What historical period would you like to have lived in?' would pick the twelfth. It was a time without pandemics and a period of expanding horizons, opportunity and economies, and people of the time seemed to be aware of their good luck. Medieval people had no hindsight, however, and each medieval generation played the hand they had been dealt as well as they could. One cannot but be struck with the fortitude with which they coped in sometimes quite horrible circumstances. The unchanging rhythm of the agricultural year and the Church calendar was a strong foundation for the sense of the normality of their lives, which was unshaken even by the frequent tragedy of early death. Another was the ability to enjoy what life gave them in diet, talent, amusement and sexual opportunity, of which we have an abundance of evidence.

KEY TEXTS

Binski, P. *Medieval Death: Ritual and Representation* (British Museum Press, 1999), a comprehensive study of medieval mortality and death culture, devised as a course book. • Gilchrist, R. *Medieval Life: Archaeology and the Life Course* (Boydell, 2012), an authoritative study arising from an archaeological study of life, diet, disease and mortality in Britain. • Harvey, B. *Living and Dying in England, 1100–1540* (Oxford University Press, 1993), a unique study of diet, illness and mortality derived from the copious records of the monks of Westminster Abbey, but with much wider conclusions. • Karras, R. M. *Sexuality in Medieval Europe: Doing unto Others* (2nd edn, Routledge, 2012), coherent and thorough study of medieval attitudes to the body and desire concentrating on the evidence rather than on theory.

FURTHER READING

FAMILY AND MARRIAGE

Betzig, L. 'Medieval Monogamy', *Journal of Family History*, 20 (1995), 181–206. • Brooke, C. N. L. *The Medieval Idea of Marriage* (Oxford University Press, 1989). • d'Avray, D. L. *Medieval Marriage: Symbolism and Society* (Oxford University Press, 2005). • Duby, G. *Medieval Marriage*, trans. E. Foster (Johns Hopkins University Press, 1978); revised in G. Duby, *The Knight, the Lady and the Priest: The Making of Modern Marriage in Medieval France*, trans. B. Bray (Peregrine, 1985). • Hareven, T. 'The History of the Family and the Complexity of Social Change', *American Historical Review*, 96 (1991), 95–124. • *Love, Sex and Marriage in the Middle Ages: A Sourcebook*, ed. C. McCarthy (Routledge, 2004). • Moore, J. S. 'The Anglo-Norman Family: Size and Structure', *Anglo-Norman Studies*, 14 (1991),

153–95. • MacQueen, H. L. 'The Kin of Kennedy, "Kenkynnol" and the Common Law', in *Medieval Scotland: Crown, Lordship and Community. Essays Presented to G. W. S. Barrow*, ed. A. Grant and K. J. Stringer (Edinburgh University Press, 1993), 274–96. • Murray, A. C. 'Theories of Germanic Kinship Structure in Antiquity and the Early Middle Ages', in *Germanic Kinship Structure: Studies in Law and Society in Antiquity and the Early Middle Ages* (University of Toronto Press, 1983), 11–32. • Peters, C. 'Gender, Sacrament and Ritual: The Making and Meaning of Marriage in Late Medieval and Early Modern England', *Past & Present*, 169 (2000), 63–96. • Scott, J. 'Gender: A Useful Category of Historical Analysis', *American Historical Review*, 91 (1986), 1053–75. • Sheehan, M. M. 'Theory and Practice: Marriage of the Unfree and Poor in Medieval Society', *Medieval Studies*, 50 (1988), 457–87. • *Wife and Widow in Medieval England*, ed. S. S. Walker (University of Michigan Press, 1999).

FAMINE, DISEASE AND PANDEMIC

The Black Death, ed. R. Horrox (Manchester University Press, 1994). • *The Black Death in England*, ed. M. Ormrod and P. Lindley (Paul Watkins, 1996). • Demaitre, L. *Leprosy in Pre-Modern Medicine: A Malady of the Whole Body* (Johns Hopkins University Press, 2007). • Fitch, Audrey-Beth. 'Assumptions About Plague in Late Medieval Scotland', *Scotia*, 11 (1987), 30–40. • Jordan, W. Chester. *The Great Famine: Northern Europe in the Early Fourteenth Century* (Princeton University Press, 1996). • Kershaw, I. 'The Great Famine and the Agrarian Crisis in England, 1315–1322', *Past and Present*, 59 (1973), 3–50. • Oram, R. 'Disease, Death and the Hereafter in Medieval Scotland', in *A History of Life in Medieval Scotland, 1000 to 1600*, ed. E. J. Cowan and L. Henderson (Edinburgh University Press, 2011), 196–225. • Rawcliffe, C. *Leprosy in Medieval England* (Boydell, 2006). • Rawcliffe, C. *Urban Bodies: Communal Health in Late Medieval English Towns and Cities* (Boydell, 2013). • Ziegler, P. *The Black Death* (Penguin, 1969).

GENDER

Bennett, M. 'Military Masculinity in England and France, c. 1050–1225', in *Masculinity in Medieval Europe*, ed. D. M. Hadley (Longman, 1999), 71–88. • d'Alverny, M.-T. 'Comment les théologiens et les philosophes voient la femme', *Cahiers de Civilisation Médiévale*, 20 (1977), 105–29. • Duby, G. 'Women and Power', in *Cultures of Power: Lordship, Status and Process in Twelfth-Century Europe*, ed. Thomas N. Bisson (University of Pennsylvania Press, 1995), 69–85. • Farmer, S. 'Persuasive Voices: Clerical Images of Medieval Wives', *Speculum*, 61 (1986), 517–43. • Hadley, D. M. 'Medieval Masculinities', in *Masculinity in Medieval Europe*, ed. D. M. Hadley (Longman, 1999), 1–18. • Hanawalt, B. A. 'Golden Ages for the History of Medieval English Women', in *Women in Medieval History and Historiography*, ed. S. Mosher Stuard (University of Pennsylvania Press, 1987), 1–24. • Kaeuper, R. W. *Holy Warriors: The Religious Ideology of Chivalry* (University of Pennsylvania Press, 2009). • Karras, R. M. *From Boys to Men: Formations of Masculinity in Late Medieval Europe* (University of Pennsylvania Press, 2003). • Mate, M. E. *Women in Medieval Society* (Cambridge University Press, 1999). • Phillips, K. M. *Medieval Maidens: Young Women and Gender in England, 1270–1540* (Manchester University Press, 2003). • Rubin, M. *Mother of God: A History of the Virgin Mary* (Penguin, 2010). • Stafford, P. 'Women and the Norman Conquest', *Transactions of the Royal Historical Society*, 6th ser., 4 (1994), 221–49, esp. 221–30.

LIFE STAGES AND MORTALITY

Butler, S. M. 'A Case of Indifference? Child Murder in Later Medieval England', *Journal of Women's History*, 19 (2007), 59–82. • Dyer, C. *Making a Living in the Middle Ages* (Yale University Press, 2002). • Gorski, R. C. *The Fourteenth-Century Sheriff* (Boydell, 2003). • Hanawalt, B. A. 'Historical Descriptions and Prescriptions for Adolescence', *Journal of Family History*, 17 (1992), 341–50. • Hanawalt, B. A. 'Medievalists and the Study of Childhood', *Speculum*, 77 (2002), 440–60. • *Old Age: Approaching Death in Antiquity and the Middle Ages*, ed. C. Krötzl and K. Mustakallio (Brepols, 2011). • Orme, N. *Medieval Children* (Yale University Press, 2001). • Rosenthal, J. *Old Age in Late Medieval England* (University of Pennsylvania Press, 1996). • Shahar, S. *Growing Old in the Middle Ages* (Routledge, 1997).

SEXUALITIES

Boswell, J. A. 'Revolutions, Universals, and Sexual Categories', in *Hidden from History: Reclaiming the Gay and Lesbian Past*, ed. M. Duberman, M. Vicinus and G. Chauncey, Jr (Meridian, 1989), 17–36. • Brundage, J. 'Let Me Count the Ways: Canonists and Theologians Contemplate Coital Positions', *Journal of Medieval History*, 10 (1984), 81–93. • Clarke, D. *Between Medieval Men: Male Friendship and Desire in Early Medieval English Literature* (Oxford University Press, 2009). • Federico, S. 'Queer Times: Richard II in the Poems and Chronicles of Late Fourteenth-Century England', *Medium Aevum*, 79 (2010), 25–46. • Jaeger, C. Stephen. *Ennobling Love: In Search of a Lost Sensibility* (University of Pennsylvania Press, 1999). • Payer, P. 'Early Medieval Regulations Concerning Marital Sexual Relations', *Journal of Medieval History*, 6 (1980), 353–76. • Poos, L. R. 'Sex, Lies and the Church Courts of Pre-Reformation England', *Journal of Interdisciplinary History*, 25 (1995), 585–607.

NOTES

1. Stephen de Fougères, *Le Livre des Manières*, ed. R. A. Lodge (Droz, 1979), cc. 287–89, p. 99 (my translation).
2. Iolo Goch (died c. 1398), 'A Pilgrimage to St Davids', in *Medieval Welsh Poems*, trans. J. P. Clancy (Four Courts, 2003), 240–3.
3. *Eracle*, ed. G. Raynaud de Lage (Classiques français du moyen âge, 102, 1976), lines 2797–8; *Ille et Galeron*, ed. Y. Lefèvre (Classiques français du moyen âge, 109, 1988), lines 852–3.
4. *Lost Letters of Medieval Life: English Society, 1200–1300*, ed. and trans. M. Carlin and D. Crouch (University of Pennsylvania Press, 2013), no. 78.
5. *Ibid.*, no. 82.
6. Philip de Novara, *Les Quatre Ages de l'Homme*, ed. M. de Frevile (Société des anciens textes français, 1888), c. 2 (my translation).
7. *Ibid.*, cc. 35, 56 (my translation).
8. *Eracle*, lines 4082–4.
9. *De retardatione accidentium senectutis*, attributed to Roger Bacon (died 1294).
10. Daniel of Beccles, *Urbanus Magnus*, ed. J. G. Smyly (Hodges, Figgis, 1939), p. 45, lines 1293–8.

10 Material Britain

OVERVIEW

The middle ages lives among us still in its material legacy, of
which there is a great deal. This is not just in the thousands
of medieval churches which remain the focus of many villages
and market squares, and in the great cathedrals which still
dominate the skylines of our cities. Street plans and many main
roads still follow the routes of their medieval predecessors, and
medieval timber frames and cellars often lurk behind later street
frontages. Medieval barns, homes, market halls, colleges, bridges,
mills and harbours can still be seen and are indeed still in use
today over a half-millennium later.

There is still a medieval core to modern culture, and an argument that it never in fact died but that we form a continuity with it. Medieval architectural styles did not go abruptly out of use in the year 1500. The peculiarly English Gothic style of stone construction known as Perpendicular remained popular from the fourteenth century until after the English Civil War, as what is called 'Gothic Survival', long enough indeed to move seamlessly into the Gothic revival of the later eighteenth century. Modern material Britain is undeniably and self-evidently shaped by the middle ages, as can be demonstrated as much by the towering Gothic canopy over the Scott memorial on Princes Street in Edinburgh as the grand frontage of Westminster Palace along the Thames. The urge to link with the middle ages is to be found in stone in several different ways: constitutionally, culturally, architecturally and symbolically. The appropriation of Gothic as the style of choice for academic buildings has an even wider legacy, as can be seen in the varied campuses of Princeton, Notre Dame, Yale and Sewanee in the United States.

Materials

One of the more subtle acts of cultural colonisation accomplished in the eleventh century was a symbolically material one. King William the Conqueror had limestone freighted from Normandy from the quarries of Ranville, north of his town of Caen, to provide the squared facing blocks for the White Tower of his massive new fortress in London. This was not because Britain lacked high-quality freestone of its own: the South West has fine golden oolitic limestones (the famous Bath stone), from which were crafted the magnificent late medieval church towers of Somerset and South Wales. The Midlands had the greyish, tough oolites from the Barnack quarries in Cambridgeshire (worked out by the 1450s) from which were built the great Fenland abbeys and the colleges of Cambridge. Yorkshire had its brilliant white Magnesian limestones available from quarries near Tadcaster, which were operated jointly for centuries as a large-scale business by the king and the Vavasour family, and which are still extensively worked for repairs to York Minster and other great northern churches. England even had Purbeck 'marble' quarried in Dorset, a fossil-rich, dark limestone which will take a polish, and which provided shafts for pillars in great churches all over England and material for sculpted tombstones made in London workshops.

Timber was, however, a much commoner material for building throughout the middle ages in both England and Scotland, though it obviously does not survive so well. This was true even in a great city like London, which was consequently often seriously damaged by fires. Before the conflagration of 1666 swept the medieval City away, it experienced almost as frightful a fire in 1212 when Southwark, London Bridge and much of the river frontage was consumed in a fire that left 3,000 half-burned bodies floating in the Thames, not to mention those that were completely consumed: a mortality much higher than that of the more famous Great Fire. It was as a consequence of such fires that around 1200 the City had imposed building regulations insisting on fireproof roofing materials and that party walls between tenements in the City should be of impervious stone. Timber was always the principal source of medieval building material, particularly oak crucks ('A' shapes) for the gable ends and hall bays of the better class of peasant houses. About 15 per cent of England was wooded in 1086, though there were few areas which might be called dense forest. Underwood was cropped by coppicing, which produced poles and withies for the infill of house walls as much as for flood defences along the coast and river banks. Bigger trees, particularly the oaks favoured for timber building, might be cropped after a growth of twenty to seventy years. The king might grant such trees from his greater forests in Gloucestershire at Dean or in Northamptonshire to favoured subjects for the purposes of building houses or windmills, which was no small gift. But Norway and the Baltic seem to have fulfilled a demand for imported timber for England and Scotland, both oak and conifers, which was greater than the insular supply could meet.

Brick and tile were building materials that had been used extensively in Roman Britain, and it is by no means unusual to find that they were quarried from ancient sites and employed in eleventh- and twelfth-century buildings, as for instance in the Norman hall-keep at Chepstow Castle in Wales in the 1070s. Indeed, standing Roman propylons and vaulted bath-houses at nearby Caerleon were apparently re-used as part of their residential complex by the Welsh kings of Glamorgan as a way of advertising borrowed grandeur, until torn down by their English successors in the lordship early in the thirteenth century. Brick was imported from the Low Countries in the thirteenth century, and is found used as packing in the vaulting at Coggeshall Abbey in Essex and Beverley Minster in Yorkshire in the first half of the thirteenth century. It was generally concealed in its earliest appearances in Britain behind plaster rendering, which made it look like more prestigious stone. However, by the fourteenth century native-fired brick was available as a material for building right down the east coast, and it was particularly used for large buildings in the North. The technique of firing in 'clamps' (kilns made up largely of unfired clay bricks) was imported into eastern England by the fourteenth century. Brick was used prominently in Hull's fortifications, houses and its great church of Holy Trinity at the end of the fourteenth century, and the brick-built early fifteenth-century gate at the North Bar of Beverley still survives.

Civic corporations at Hull, Sandwich and Beverley found it worth their while to maintain their own kilns and brickyards in the fourteenth and fifteenth centuries. The finer techniques of brick making introduced from the continent from Poland, Prussia and the Netherlands in the fifteenth century favoured its use even in royal residences, such as Henry V's Sheen Palace at Richmond (1414). It may have been a way of claiming some chic for the material that it acquired the name of 'brick' from France soon after

1400. Thereafter fine brickwork with specially moulded ornamental features such as window mouldings and chimney stacks, patterned in varicoloured brick or contrasted with freestone, flint and chalk blocks, was used openly and enthusiastically in buildings across England and came to a particular flowering in early Tudor England, of which Cardinal Wolsey's Hampton Court is perhaps the most famous surviving example, though there were many earlier substantial brick mansions of fine quality, such as the bishop of Lincoln's palatial house of the 1470s at Buckden in Huntingdonshire.

Glass was manufactured in England from silica sands and ash in the Wealden hills of Surrey and Sussex probably from quite early in the middle ages. Glassworkers were certainly mentioned in England in the twelfth century, though they may not necessarily have *made* the material they worked with. The sheets of glass necessary for the construction of windows were principally imported from Flanders and the Rhineland, but Burgundy and Normandy were other possible sources. Fourteenth- and fifteenth-century building contracts and accounts make it clear that imported glass was far better regarded for quality than that produced at home, even the white glass used for the diamond panes ('quarrels') of domestic windows, though the clear glass sheets produced in Surrey were of adequate quality and quantity for the purpose. The great coloured-glass windows which survived iconoclastic destruction in the Reformation, such as the vast east window of Gloucester Abbey (as big as a tennis court) and the remarkable theological windows at All Saints North Street in York, are a testament to the resources of the medieval glazier. There is every likelihood that Scotland also once boasted such artistic triumphs, particularly in the palaces and churches built and patronised by James I and James IV, but the Calvinist Reformation effaced them.

The Hall

One of the most symbolic of medieval buildings was the hall. The length and size of the great wooden halls of the pre-Conquest English royal compounds were in themselves a proclamation of status, while the scale of the hospitality and feasting within was a statement of lordship over men. The wife of a lord was a 'lady' (*hlaefod*) because her function was to be an accomplished hostess, which is what *hlaefod* meant, 'loaf-maker'. The Danes who invaded England in 1015 and the French in 1066 saw the hall in much the same terms, the focus of elite society and the warm centre of social life. There was little to distinguish between the early eleventh-century hall in England or Normandy. The main buildings of the royal residence of Cheddar in Somerset and those of Duke Richard of Normandy in Fécamp were much the same: the hall itself, a private chamber, kitchen and latrines were common to both, and a church was a feature of both compounds. The main difference was that the hall and church were stone-built in the Norman palace. Neither was fortified, though both had enclosure walls. We know that thegnly residences in England might well include a stout gatehouse tower, though they were not intended to be fortresses. Welsh society shared all these concerns, and its twelfth-century poetry goes so far as to make the cleanliness and repair of a hall a metaphor for its lord's standing.

Stone-built halls, roofed and floored with tile, became progressively more common in England and Wales after the Norman Conquest, and it was the second Norman king who in 1099 inaugurated a hall at Westminster so huge as to have no parallel in Western Europe as a statement both of his royalty and of his equally large ego. It had many subsequent imitators amongst the later aristocracy and prelates, though none as to its size. It also had a new sort of imitator. Pre-Conquest shire courts met in a range of outdoor and sometimes rather inconvenient sites: on hilltops, in meadows, heathland or churchyards. The new twelfth-century county courts of Cardiff and Rutland were, however, provided with purpose-built arcaded halls, on the model of Westminster, the first explicitly administrative buildings erected in Britain since the Romans left. Westminster Hall in the 1160s itself acquired a new executive function as permanent home of the Exchequer Court, and later of the King's and Common Benches of justice, a function it maintained long after the period of this book, thus restating its social purpose for a new bureaucratic age.

By the end of the twelfth century the high-status hall-complex had developed a generic plan, which reflected the needs of the households of the great. The royal palace of Clarendon near Salisbury, as it was redeveloped in the early 1180s, was a pattern for this. It sat within a great court, its rooms panelled and plastered, with separate apartments for the queen and a great chapel set with Purbeck columns. A particular new development (which may have been imported from France) was that annexed to the Great Hall and the kitchen were service rooms of buttery and pantry, where servants could be marshalled for the processions which brought in wine and the separate courses of the banquets. The pattern was endlessly repeated in the construction of medieval royal palaces and is found at their core not just in England, but also in Scotland, and is still evident in the magnificent residence at Linlithgow built by James I (1406–1437) in the 1420s (see Fig. 10.1). Later medieval hall-complexes built for the great across Britain followed this pattern throughout the middle ages, whether they sat in gardens in a country residence (as in the surviving example of Stokesay in Shropshire), or behind the street frontages of a city like London or York. They also formed the pattern for the buildings of the later medieval halls which were the core of Oxford and Cambridge colleges and the centres of trade guild life. Sometimes such hall-complexes sat within stone-walled enclosures, and might even feature ornamental towers and gatehouses with battlemented parapets, but they were not strategically sited, nor were they intended to be defended. Their military air was entirely due to the association of the medieval upper classes with warfare as a vocation.

Fig. 10.1 Linlithgow Palace. For all the political turbulence of fifteenth-century Scotland, the Stewart kings were capable of building innovative and luxurious residences. Linlithgow palace, between Edinburgh and Stirling, replaced an earlier castle, and was begun by James I in 1424. His inspiration was probably the impressive palace complex commenced by his mentor, Henry V of England, at Sheen near Richmond. James's courtyard hall and palace range were elaborated by his successors into a fine statement of Scottish monarchy.

The correct management of the lord's hall and its inhabitants is a notable theme in the early thirteenth-century Welsh law codes, an anxiety that aligns Welsh society with the European mainstream. The universal importance of the hall to medieval social life and advancement is evident enough in the anxieties the place inspired in those who attended them for dinners and receptions. From the twelfth century onwards, tracts appear which reflect morbidly on the way that conduct before a great person in the hall can sabotage a man's prospects by one false step or breach of manners. The correct way to manage food, drink and conversation in such sensitive situations inspires whole tracts from the late twelfth to the fifteenth centuries, and beyond, up indeed to the present day. Medieval people of any status had to be seen among their people to be truly appreciated to be as influential as they were, and the hall was where that could be most effectively done, associated as it was with the expense of public entertainment and hospitality. As early as the twelfth century lords and ladies were being advised to make a point of eating in public surrounded by their people, and told not shut themselves away in their chambers to dine. There was a concern even then to control access to them in public, which was done by erecting barriers of ceremonial as much as by closed doors.

In Welsh and Scottish as much as Anglo-French society, officers were employed to keep doors and control who might be allowed within the hall. Advice was offered as to how such officers should greet visitors of influence, how those permitted to approach the great should conduct themselves and speak, and how guests should dine without showing themselves to be less than urbane in the socially dangerous environment of the aristocratic household. Dining out in the middle ages was not a stress-free experience, even if someone else was paying the bill. Great people who had the burden of entertaining their retinue, neighbours and suppliants might well also not enjoy the experience very much, and wish to get out of the hall and public exposure as soon as it was decently possible. Escape routes were in fact offered, not least by creating inner chambers beyond the hall, to which only the private household was given access. At Winchester palace in Southwark, as it was rebuilt in the mid thirteenth century, where England's wealthiest bishop resided, a visitor had first to be permitted to pass through a massive gatehouse to an outer court, then gain admittance to an inner court surrounded by lodgings for the household, before he even got as far as the hall door. Once within the hall doors he would see the bishop only at a distance, and then only when the great man chose to leave his private chambers beyond the hall, where he had his bedchamber, library, private chapel and secluded privy garden to which very few had access.

The Castle

For many modern people, the definitive medieval building is the castle, a species of fortification which became a feature of the political landscape of France, the Low Countries and the Rhineland at the end of the tenth century. What made a castle distinctive was that it was a fortification designed with a degree of science, with earthworks, outworks and usually a central tower. It is this which distinguishes it from the 'fortified' hall which was customarily set within banks and an enclosure, but which had no pretensions to be statement of military power and strategic ambition. A castle was intended to be held by very few against many, and it was as readily built by the private enterprise of lords as by the public authority of kings. From its earliest days in the Frankish lands the castle was identified with the knights who garrisoned it in their lord's interest. A French count who attained the English earldom of the West Midlands built some structures that appear to have been intended as castles in Herefordshire in the 1050s, but in pre-Conquest England deliberate fortifications were otherwise public works surrounding strategic royal burhs.

Castles came to Britain (literally) in the baggage of Duke William's army, who apparently had prefabricated wooden sections shipped with his fleet ready to erect in the bridgehead he selected at Pevensey. The castle captured the attention of the conquered English when they wished to express the alien nature of the French conquerors: the Anglo-Saxon Chronicle borrowed the French word *chastel* to describe them, as English had no native word which would suit the bill. The Chronicle likewise coined a new term of 'castelmenn' for the knights who inhabited these alien structures which were promptly built in prominent sites in their great cities and towns. Strange, eye-catching and menacing though these structures were, there were not, however, that many of them built in the Norman period. The most impressive early examples were the castles with great stone keeps built by the Conqueror and his son, William Rufus. They were deliberately built to impress, using the style of great square donjon already established in northern France for generations as the centrepiece of the fortification, as in the still extant examples at London and Rochester, and in other now lost royal castles, such as Gloucester. Contemporary noble castles built in stone, as at Chepstow and Richmond in the 1070s and 1080s, were impressive too in their way, but they boasted castellated halls rather than donjons. It was not until the early twelfth century that the greater aristocracy began to copy the great donjon as a way of demonstrating wealth and power. The keeps of Kenilworth, Hedingham and Bristol Castles were constructed in that way by several of Henry I's officers and favourites to demonstrate they had arrived and could rival the king in their building expenses.

Already in the early twelfth century there were competing needs in the building of castles. Military defence and intimidation formed one purpose, but since most castles would never actually experience attack the investment of money and effort involved in their construction had to expect more of a return. So within the baileys of the great castle arose suitably prestigious residential complexes to house the lord and offer hospitality to his men, where the great hall and its associated domestic buildings were incorporated in a new context. Private castles such as Warwick, Wallingford and Leicester, as much as royal castles in London, Oxford and Dover, included within their walls collegiate churches staffed by canons to offer a suitable stage for the devotions of a resident lord. Hunting parks were laid out within a short ride of the castle for the lord to enjoy a suitably aristocratic recreation. By the 1120s castles were already rather more than military structures. Recent work by landscape historians has concluded that in their initial design twelfth-century castles were constructed as part of a reshaping of the local landscape to incorporate ornamental gardens and fishing ponds, and 'pleasances' where the castle might be seen to best advantage, hunting parties viewed and picnics offered. Within the castle, doors and stairways were arranged to allow for suitable ceremony in the approach to its lord and decorative stonework placed to best advantage.

However, castles were also military structures and had to respond to advances in military technology to be taken seriously. The devastating effect of the stone-throwing device known as the traction trebuchet, which came into use soon after 1100, rendered even stone castle walls insecure in the early twelfth century. It took a while, but castle architects abandoned the square donjon keep in the 1160s for rather more secure flanged or rounded keeps as still to be seen at Orford and Conisbrough. Where a donjon remained the centrepiece of the fortification as at the Tower of London, Kenilworth and Dover, architects provided concentric walls of fortifications or wide water defences to keep the deadly trebuchet at a safe distance from the castle core. It could be effective in demolishing stone walls only at the distance of a bowshot. The high point of castle design in Britain came in Wales in the reign of Edward I. The death of native lordship and English conquest produced a flourishing of military architecture unique in Western Europe. This involved not just the English king, but the prince of Wales and marcher barons such as Earl Gilbert de Clare, who was in fact responsible for the most impressive of the great castles: Caerphilly, a vast concentric fortress set within a lake built at improbable expense to demonstrate that he had terminated the Welsh lordship of Senghennydd north of his own lordship of Cardiff.

But the Welsh princes of Deheubarth, Powys and particularly Gwynedd were also capable in the 1250s and 1260s of raising stone fortresses and halls to demonstrate their own power, some of which (like the castle at Deganwy) were appropriated in due course by the Edwardian regime. The Welsh had in fact themselves been taking over or even building castles since Henry I's reign: fortification was one of the few aspects of Anglo-French culture that interested them. But the Edwardian conquest of Wales is rightly famous for the business-like and forbidding fortresses of Harlech, Conway, Criccieth and Flint (as well as the unfinished Beaumaris), which encircled conquered Gwynedd and intimidated the surviving Welsh aristocracy from contemplating any attempt to rise against English rule. They were not always successful. Despite the building of Caerphilly, the end of the Clare earldom of Gloucester saw a dangerous rising of the Welsh gentry in Glamorgan in 1316 which was suppressed only with difficulty.

The idea of the castle penetrated Scotland at much the same time as it had Wales, with a similar enthusiasm for the new military technology evident amongst its native rulers, who would first have encountered these structures in Cumbria and Northumberland. The first such castles, which are found in the early twelfth century, have unambitious timber walls and earth banks and mottes (artificial mounds). They do, however, appear in considerable numbers in Galloway and across central Scotland, and the incoming French colonists erected them as lordship centres. The advantages were equally plain to the native mormaers, and Earl David, the brother of King William, naturally raised a castle and neighbouring burgh at Inverurie on being granted the lordship of Garioch. Scotland underwent a remarkable period of stone castle-building in the thirteenth century which has left a sizeable architectural legacy. Since the active period of construction under Kings Alexander II and Alexander III was a time of peace and easy interaction between England and Scotland, it was not warfare which was the stimulus for this. For that matter, there seems to have been little impetus for ambitious structures amongst the great earls and the royal family (though the castle of the earl of Mar at Kildrummy is an exception), or the Anglo-Scottish noble dynasties such as the Quincys, Bruces and Balliols. It was the baronial families with interests in the west who invested heavily in stone: notably the Stewarts, as they extended their lordship over the Clyde valley and the Isles, or the Comyns at Badenoch and Lochaber in the north. The impressive southern castles of Dirleton and Bothwell were built not by great lords but by royal servants newly come to wealth and ready to advertise it in prestigious structures which may have been military in appearance but which had little military utility, much as had done the rising servants of Henry I of England more than a century earlier.

The later medieval castle across Britain shifted more and more into the mode of a high-status and prestigious residence. Kenilworth Castle in Warwickshire, for instance, had been formidably fortified and redesigned by King John, so effectively that the Montfortian rebels held out behind its lakes and concentric walls for well over a year in 1265–1266, defying the concentrated trebuchet bombardment of the royalists. It was subsequently acquired by the earl (later duke) of Lancaster. It was John of Gaunt who next redesigned it, and the Kenilworth he constructed in the later 1370s changed its emphasis to rich display. It was a palatial complex in two great courts, with a new great hall of considerable magnificence and state apartments fit for a duke who claimed to be king of Castile. The Lancastrian palace at Kenilworth trumped the castle and went on to dazzle future generations, up to the time of Elizabeth I. New fourteenth-century castles, such as the much-discussed Bodiam in Sussex and Duke Robert of Albany's castle at Doune, near Stirling, are more residences than fortifications, with the accent on comfort, though they all have the features of a military building. The invention of gunpowder artillery probably had little significance in this shift, though it did become increasingly effective as the fourteenth century progressed and was certainly far more dangerous to stone fortifications by 1400 than the trebuchet had been. Indeed, the possession of a highly expensive artillery train in Yorkist England and Stewart Scotland was one means by which the king asserted his dominance over the castle-owning aristocracy. It was by his artillery pieces that James II of Scotland brought low the Black Douglases in the 1450s, rapidly demolishing the fortifications of the Douglas fortress of Abercorn on the Firth of Forth. Nonetheless, the artillery of besiegers could still be offset by sufficiently thick walls and blockhouses for counter-artillery, so it was not in itself the reason for the retreat from the castellated residence, which had more to do with the reinvention of the hall-complex as the more prestigious Renaissance great house and the political strategies of the incoming Tudors.

Ecclesiastical Buildings and Their Characteristic Styles

Pre-Conquest Britain had stone buildings, some quite large, such as the major abbeys and cathedrals of Canterbury and Winchester, whose plans have been recovered by excavation. The massive masonry towers of tenth- and eleventh-century minster churches can still be seen at places like Barnack and Barton-upon-Humber. There is even evidence of eleventh-century pre-Norman stone-built churches in Wales at Llandaff and in Scotland at Dunfermline. But most of these early stone buildings were swept away by later eleventh- and twelfth-century stone replacements in a Romanesque style developed in northern France. The one exception was Westminster Abbey, which King Edward had already had constructed in a style derived from Jumièges Abbey in Normandy, though even that too was later rebuilt by Henry III in the 1240s. The surviving ecclesiastical buildings of the late eleventh and twelfth centuries, whether standing or in ruins, remain a considerable architectural heritage across Britain. The Romanesque of England produced churches grander and more ambitious than those of any other contemporary European realm. The Romanesque reconstruction of the parish churches of England, Scotland and Wales between 1070 and 1160 has left few areas of Britain with nothing to show for it. Though many churches saw substantial rebuilding in later centuries, even the renovated ones might still retain the old Romanesque tub font, the lower stage of the tower, the chancel arch or nave arcades. Great chapter churches and abbeys of the period might survive more or less intact (as at Durham, Kirkwall and Southwell) or retain at least the massive columns of their nave arcades (as at Dunfermline, Gloucester and St Davids). It may also be that it was in England around 1130 that the great technological advance of late Romanesque architecture took place, when masons at Durham suspended stone rib-vaults over the roof space above the choir and nave (see Fig. 10.2) instead of the customary flat timber ceiling (always a fire risk). They countered the outward pressure on the walls by means of well-placed buttresses. It was a device that spread rapidly through Normandy to central France within a single generation.

But even while some of the great Romanesque buildings of Britain were still on the drawing board, an architectural revolution was getting under way in the vicinity of Paris between the 1120s and the 1140s. At Sens and St-Martin-des-Champs, but particularly at St-Denis, a new style was evolving which increased internal space, window size and elevation because it depended not on the Romanesque round arch, but on the more structurally resilient pointed one. This is the style that became known to the Enlightenment mind as 'Gothic'. The architects who designed these new buildings did not, however, see themselves as heirs of the barbarians, but (as with most areas of twelfth-century life) as heirs of Rome, as can be seen in their copying (or even re-use) of classical columns and capitals for the pillars of their buildings. The new style spread through the Francophone world, producing distinct variants in the Plantagenet domains in France and Britain.

Fig. 10.2 Durham Cathedral Nave. Early medieval churches were prone to devastating fires (such as that which caused the rebuilding of Stow Minster in the 1040s; see Fig. 6.1). This was one of the main motives behind the daring innovation of suspended stone vaults of which the earliest surviving example is that of Durham Cathedral, erected around 1130. The concealed flying buttresses which made it possible are the first sign of the technological breakthroughs in masonry architecture which would produce the new Gothic style.

The twelfth-century buildings of Plantagenet Poitiers still exhibit a mixture of elegant tall Romanesque blind arcades and pointed vaults on multiple-shafted columns, which is to be seen in the spacious hall of the ducal palace and the cathedral of St Peter, a style which Henry II might well have transferred to his English royal halls, perhaps most likely at Clarendon and Winchester. A more Capetian style was employed in England for the rebuilding of the choir of Canterbury in the 1170s, where an architect from Sens was initially employed and which features an apsidal east end with ambulatory, as was the style of the Île-de-France. Thereafter, the influence of France is less obvious in the evolution of an English form of Gothic, which may itself have a lot to do with the political separation of England and Normandy in 1204.

The thirteenth-century English Gothic form (which acquired the appropriately insular name of 'Early English' from insular nineteenth-century Victorian devotees of neo-Gothic architecture) is a distinctive style characterised by groupings of tall lancets and the use of polychrome pillars, most strikingly demonstrated in the rebuilding of Lincoln Cathedral in the early thirteenth century and (though it is now in ruins) in the magnificent rebuilding of Rievaulx Abbey in Yorkshire in the 1220s and 1230s. It spread even further, for it is a style very evident in the cathedral built for the archbishop of Nidaros at Trondheim in Norway. Capetian France developed its own thirteenth-century national style in the form called 'Rayonnant', which emphasised height in its bays and apses and is characterised by overly involved window tracery. Its influence is (unsurprisingly) heavy on Westminster Abbey, reconstructed as it was by King Henry III, a man haunted and frustrated by his relationship with his royal cousin, Louis IX of France, who financed the remarkable examples of Rayonnant Gothic at Royaumont Abbey and the Sainte-Chapelle in his palace of the Conciergerie in Paris. The influence of Rayonnant was muted in later thirteenth- and early fourteenth-century England into a rather more subdued Gothic style, known to the English architectural historian as 'Decorated'. It favoured square-ended choirs and bays with huge geometrical traceried windows as in the rebuilding of York minster. It rejected the tall semi-circular apses found at the east ends of great French churches of the period. As a style it had its own reach within Britain, being employed in the thirteenth-century work at Glasgow Cathedral and at Holyrood Abbey in Edinburgh.

The summative English Gothic style called 'Perpendicular' was devised by the court architects of Edward III for his palaces and private chapels, and the beginnings of its characteristic rectilinear panelling could once be seen in the great collegiate church of St Stephen he rebuilt and refounded within his palace of Westminster in the 1330s and 1340s, and developed further in the simultaneous rebuilding of St Paul's Cathedral, both buildings now long lost but still recoverable through antiquaries' drawings and descriptions. It was called 'Perpendicular' by Victorian commentators for good reason, as it is instantly recognisable from its vertical and horizontal linear style, quite different from the curves of French Rayonnant and English Decorated. It is the style still to be seen in later medieval England's most magnificent survivals: in the chapels Henry VI had built for Eton College and King's College in Cambridge, and the major civic churches of English cities, such as Holy Trinity in Hull or St Mary Redcliffe in Bristol, or again in the grand country churches of Suffolk and Somerset. Of all the medieval architectural inheritances it was the most lasting, for it remained a building style employed in a variety of modes into the eighteenth century, not least in English college architecture. It was transmuted into modernity with the 'Gothic revival' style of the later eighteenth-century Romantic period, and as such it carries on to our own day and generation. The central tower of St Edmundsbury Cathedral was finished in 2005 in an early Perpendicular style. Its characteristic Englishness and association with the Plantagenet court doomed Perpendicular in Scotland (with the exception of Melrose Abbey in the 1380s). The new churches and chantries in the fifteenth century adopted a French late Rayonnant style (as at the flamboyantly sculpted Rosslyn chapel near Edinburgh) or in the academic embrace of a reinvented Romanesque form, recalling classical buildings and looking forward to the post-medieval baroque.

Domestic Housing

Most people in the middle ages looked at its architectural triumphs from the outside. They would never be allowed to penetrate the great churches beyond the pulpitum screen that closed off the choir, where only the servants of the sanctuary were allowed for the divine office. The humbler architecture of daily life has generally not survived too well as towns were progressively redeveloped with the expansion of population and economy after 1500. Most housing was timber-framed across the Midlands and South of England, though stone houses were more common in the North and Scotland, where timber was less available and stone therefore more economically possible. Timber buildings can last suprisingly well, but the growing prestige of red brick in the later middle ages offered a desirable replacement without the prohibitive costs involved in stone masonry, and progressive rebuildings destroyed the bulk of medieval housing in town and countryside. Even so, Chester's Rows and York's Shambles and Goodramgate remain splendid recollections of what a medieval townscape might have looked like. The villages of Herefordshire and Suffolk offer examples of standing fifteenth-century timber domestic buildings, and there are still many relics of earlier urban timber frames lurking in odd and surprising corners of modern towns, such as in the Bolts at Scarborough.

The bulk of the medieval population, over 80 per cent of it, lived in conditions we would now regard as pretty primitive even for the Third World. Accommodation across Britain from the eleventh to the fifteenth centuries for the rural poor was in 'long houses', simple thatched or slate-roofed timber-frame structures with an open vent for the hearth, and the livestock gathered in a 'lathe' or 'byre', an enclosure at one end of the house, sometimes balanced by a sleeping chamber for the family at the other end. Chimneys were a feature in England in prestigious houses in the eleventh century, but stacks and wall-built fireplaces did not become a feature of rural housing until the end of the period of this book, though they begin to appear in London housing from the fourteenth century. Early houses were so basic they were not infrequently disassembled, as we would a garden shed, and moved to new sites.

Occasionally whole villages migrated in this way when their fields were replanned. Rural housing only slowly grew more elaborate, with stone foundation walls becoming commoner after 1200, which may have extended the life of such a house to seventy years. There must have been a range of ambition in building domestic houses, depending on the resident. The wealthy free peasant or yeoman would have had bigger and more ambitious halls and a range of service buildings (stables, breweries and bakehouses) within an enclosure, which in some areas would have been enclosed by a deep rectangular ditch.

Water was hauled from wells or streams. Beds were communal. Sanitation involved buckets and little privacy, with pads of herbage used to deal with the consequences of evacuating. Rushes and straw were spread on the earthen floor for warmth and comfort's sake, though careless dumping of the used and stinking litter was a major cause of nuisance to neighbours and much resented. Furniture and utensils were limited to trestle tables, stools, chests and wood-turned plates. Nonetheless, as anyone associated with the excavation of medieval sites will remark, the internal walls of these homes were scrupulously whitewashed to keep the rooms light, their floors were swept clean and all rubbish removed (preferably to the midden) at a distance from the house. There was slow technological change over the years. Increasingly as the thirteenth century progressed rural buildings were erected or rebuilt with their timbers set on ground walls of rubble masonry, which cut down damp. The emerging freeholder class of yeomen required better-quality residences with multiple rooms, one designated as a 'hall', often the whole built within a banked enclosure. Larger houses, usually of two storeys, emerged in the fourteenth century for the more prosperous freeholder or cleric. The rising prosperity of the fifteenth-century lowland peasant led to what has been called a 'great rebuilding' and the gradual disappearance of the ancient long house from much of England, though it lingered in the poorer areas of Wales and Scotland for much longer.

Higher-quality housing existed for certain classes of people, and the middle ages evolved the idea of a style of building which was appropriate to people of a certain condition, such as the retainers of a great magnate, or the members of communities such as almshouses, university halls, and the colleges of vicars and canons. Such residences could be built around courtyards or constructed in rows, and all had a surprisingly uniform plan and appearance, which can still be seen whether in the Vicars Close at Wells Cathedral or in the courtyard of the residence built for John Holland, earl of Huntingdon, at Dartington Hall in Devon late in the fourteenth century. The houses are terraces of two storeys, a hall and parlour upstairs and utility rooms below, giving on to a small garden in some examples. Fireplaces were usually provided and sometimes latrines. Mostly destined for single men without families, such housing can still project an air of surprising comfort to the modern tourist, though it was one denied to most medieval people.

The best of medieval domestic housing – for those outside the upper classes – was to be found amongst the urban tradesmen and craftsmen. Their houses, mostly timber, generally incorporated halls and parlours, with bedchambers on the floor above. The kitchen, warehouses and workshops were at the rear, sometimes even a garden. If it was the house of a tradesman, a shop faced the street. In a city like London, houses might climb to three or four storeys, with a 'cock loft' in the gables that fronted the street, as land values increased the concentration of population and buildings maximised the value of their ground rent. A twelfth-century tall house of five storeys in stone was to be seen on London's Cheapside below the tower of St Mary-le-Bow until the time of the Great Fire. Twelfth-century stone houses were built for merchants in many towns, and Lincoln preserves fine examples of these.

A Medieval Environment

It is not that easy now to project oneself back into the medieval built environment, so much of which is lost, particularly in towns. What we now see is but a fragment of the whole. Because of the range of its documentation London perhaps brings us closest. Medieval Cheapside is a case in point (see Fig. 10.3). In 1300 this wide street, the best part of a half-mile long, ran from the precinct of the cathedral of St Paul, which towered up at its west end eastward to the large stone market hall of the Stocks in Poultry, London's main meat market. It was kept paved and swept, though not to most people's satisfaction, because it was unevenly maintained and some residents were not particular about dumping filthy domestic waste. Some 400 shops opened on to it selling a vast range of luxury goods, with many more commercial outlets in selds or covered bazaars opening off the great street. In this dense commercial area, with high property values, there was an incentive to build high, and the houses were already up to five floors by 1200. The road was crowded by traders, hawkers, shoppers, beggars, stray dogs, rooting pigs, horses and workers, and the rattling carts of rakers (street cleaners), with consequences in noise and stench from animal waste, though human waste was scrupulously confined to the cesspits and privies to the rear of properties.

London's water supply was from the 1230s piped east from the springs of Tyburn (the present Marble Arch at the end of Oxford Street) which ended in public conduits or public water fountains in Cheapside, from which watersellers might fill leather bags and retail it through the City, for those who did not have servants to send. Businesses which wanted to access the supply had to pay charges, and those who tapped the pipes illegally were severely punished. Poorer Londoners washed down by the Thames, though there were public bathhouses (the 'stews') which before 1300 had quite a reputation for immorality and the plying of the sex trade, allegedly in trafficked Flemish women. Cheapside was dominated by the belfry of St Mary-le-Bow, whose bells controlled the

Fig. 10.3 Cheapside. The medieval shape of London's main market and commercial street can still be glimpsed in this depiction from the time of Edward VI. The panorama shows St Paul's Cathedral on the right, and the church of St Mary-le-Bow on the left, with its multi-storey twelfth-century stone row of houses still facing the street. The great Conduit is in the centre of the street, which conveyed fresh water to the City along elm-wood pipes from springs at Tyburn.

rhythm of city life, but was lined by a further dozen parish churches and the hospital of St Thomas, headquarters of the crusading order founded in honour of Becket, who was himself a Cheapsider.

The great street was a public arena, its open space used for religious and state processions, tourneying events and pageants. It was also being used as a site where dogs might be set on bulls in the twelfth century, with consequent danger to the watching crowds from animals that broke free. Bow Church was itself home to the chief ecclesiastical court of the province of Canterbury and a centre of canon law, so lawyers and litigants thronged the street. At its east end was St Paul's Churchyard, with its open-air pulpit from which proclamations and state-sponsored preaching were made, while the yard itself was a book market, its soil continually opened in long trenches for the constant burials of City residents, whose bones were collected in due course and stored in the tall charnel chapel Becket's father had built in the centre of the yard in the 1150s. Life and death were very much cheek by jowl in such a medieval environment, which the modern Western world no longer has anything to match in its vitality, vileness and raw humanity.

POSTSCRIPT

Scholars can conjure up the lost music and dance of the middle ages and reconstruct its food, poetry and song. But we all live within its material legacy which still subtly shapes British streets, buildings, countryside and sometimes our aspirations. When in 1993 the entrepreneur brothers, David and Frederick Barclay, wanted to build a residence suitable to their wealth and aspirations on the Channel Island of Brecqhou they had acquired, they built a castellated multi-towered mansion. It seems we cannot even now shake off the medieval thought world.

KEY TEXTS

Liddiard, R. *Castles in Context: Power, Symbolism and Landscape, 1066 to 1500* (Windgather, 2005), a fine example of the broader and more imaginative modern study of the castle. • *The History of the King's Works*, ed. H. M. Colvin et al. (3 vols., Her Majesty's Stationery Office, 1963), the unrivalled catalogue and explanation of most of Britain's major historic buildings, whether standing or not. • Salzman, L. F. *Building in England down to 1540: A Documentary History* (revised edn, Clarendon, 1967), still the definitive work on building styles and materials. • Wood, M. *The English Medieval House* (Harper Collins, 1983), a comprehensive and standard work on domestic architecture, though with a bias towards standing structures, and of course England.

FURTHER READING

Avent, R. *Castles of the Princes of Gwynedd* (Her Majesty's Stationery Office, 1983). • Butler, L. A. S. 'Domestic Building in Wales and the Evidence of the Welsh Laws', *Mediaeval Archaeology*, 31 (1987), 47–51. • Brown, M. *Scottish Baronial Castles, 1250–1450* (Osprey, 2009). • Coulson, C. *Castles in Medieval Society* (Oxford University Press, 2003). • Creighton, O. *Early European Castles* (Bloomsbury, 2012). • Crouch, D. *The Image of Aristocracy in Britain, 1000–1300* (Routledge, 1992). • Cruden, S. *The Scottish Castle* (Nelson, 1960). • Gilchrist, R. *Medieval Life: Archaeology and the Life Course* (Boydell, 2012). • Grant, L. *Architecture and Society in Normandy, 1120–1270* (Yale University Press, 2005). • Rackham, O. *Trees and Woodland in the British Landscape* (Dent, 1976). • Rodwell, W. *The Archaeology of Churches* (History Press, 2005). • Schofield, J. *Medieval London Houses* (Yale University Press, 2003). • Simpson, G. G. and B. Webster. 'Charter Evidence and the Distribution of Mottes in Scotland', in *Essays on the Nobility of Mediaeval Scotland*, ed. K. J. Stringer (Edinburgh University Press, 1985), 1–11. • Smith, T. P. *The Medieval Brick-Making Industry in England, 1400–1450* (British Archaeological Reports, British Series, 138, 1985). • *Town and Country in the Middle Ages*, ed. K. Giles and C. Dyer (Society for Medieval Archaeology Monograph, 22, Leeds, 2005).

Part III

The Great Divorce

TIMELINE: 1217–1500

	England	Scotland	Wales
1221		Joan of England marries Alexander II	
1225	Reissue of Magna Carta		
1228		Destruction of the mac William of Moray	
1233–1234	War between Richard Marshal and Henry III		
1235	Debate over marriage aid for Isabel of England		
1240			Death of Llywelyn ab Iorwerth of Gwynedd. Coronation of Prince Dafydd at Gloucester
1249		Accession of Alexander III	
1258	Provisions of Oxford		Llywelyn ap Gruffudd, prince of Wales

	England	Scotland	Wales
1264	Battle of Lewes. First Parliament of three estates. Montfort ascendancy		
1265	Battle of Evesham		
1266		Treaty of Perth with Magnus VI of Norway	
1267	Fall of Kenilworth		Treaty of Montgomery
1272	Accession of Edward I		
1277			Defeat of Llywelyn ap Gruffudd
1282			Death of Prince Llywelyn. Annexation of principality of Wales to the Crown of England
1283			Execution of Dafydd ap Gruffudd
1286		Death of Alexander III	
1290		Death of Margaret of Norway	
1294	Outbreak of war with Philip IV of France in Aquitaine	John Balliol awarded kingdom of Scotland	
1296		Deposition of Balliol	
1305		Execution of William Wallace	
1306		Robert I the Bruce claims Scotland	
1307	Death of Edward I		
1311	The coup of the Ordainers		

	England	Scotland	Wales
1312	Assassination of Gaveston		
1314		Battle of Bannockburn	
1316			Rising of Llywelyn Bren in South Wales
1320		Declaration of Arbroath	
1322	Battle of Boroughbridge. Execution of Thomas of Lancaster		
1325	Queen Isabella abandons Edward		
1326		Treaty of Corbeil with France	
1327	Deposition of Edward II		
1329		Treaty of Edinburgh with England. Death of Robert I	
1330	Fall of Mortimer regime		
1333		Edward Balliol claims Scotland	
1337	Edward III claims France	David II takes refuge with Philip IV of France	
1341		Return of David II	
1346	Battle of Crécy	Battle of Neville's Cross. Captivity of David II	
1348	Black Death in England		
1349		Black Death reaches Scotland	
1356	Battle of Poitiers. Captivity of John II of France		
1357		Release of David II	

	England	Scotland	Wales
1360	Peace of Brétigny		
1371		Stewart succession to David II. Robert II becomes king	
1372			Owain ap Thomas of Gwynedd formally claims Wales
1376	The 'Good' Parliament		
1377	Death of Edward III and his son the Black Prince		
1378			Assassination of Owain ap Thomas by English agent in Poitou
1387	Coup of Appellants against Richard II		
1388		Battle of Otterburn. Death of James Douglas. Lieutenancy begins in Scotland	
1390		Robert III becomes king	
1397	Arrest and execution of Appellants		
1399	Bolingbroke seizes crown as Henry IV		
1400	Richard II murdered		Owain Glyndŵr's rising begins
1403	Battle of Shrewsbury		
1404			Welsh parliament at Machynlleth

	England	Scotland	Wales
1409			Fall of Harlech and collapse of Glyndŵr's regime
1411		James I captured at sea and English captivity begins	
1413	Accession of Henry V		
1415	Southampton Plot. Battle of Agincourt		
1420		Death of Albany	
1422	Minority of Henry VI begins		
1424		Release of James I	
1429		Battle of Badenoch	
1431	Coronation of Henry VI at Paris		
1435	Death of Bedford		
1437	Henry VI assumes rule of England	Assassination of James I	
1448		James II assumes rule of Scotland	
1453	Fall of Bordeaux and end of Plantagenet France		
1455		Overthrow of the Black Douglas affinity	
1460	Death of Richard of York	James II killed at Roxburgh	
1461	Henry VI deposed by Edward IV	Henry VI in exile in Scotland under Stewart protection	

	England	Scotland	Wales
1469		Cession of Orkney and Shetland by Denmark	
1470	Restoration of Henry VI		
1471	Battle of Tewkesbury. Edward IV returns. Murder of Henry VI		
1483	Death of Edward IV. Murder of Edward V. Usurpation of Richard III		
1485	Battle of Bosworth. Henry Tudor seizes throne		Henry Tudor lands in Pembrokeshire. Welsh revolt in his favour
1487	Battle of East Stoke		
1488		Battle of Saucieburn. Murder of James III	
1498		Treaty of Ayton with England	

11 Redefining Britain, 1217–1327

OVERVIEW

The century or so after Magna Carta is one of the most transformative in British history, though not necessarily in a good way. Politics was transformed by the 'Great Charter'. What before 1215 had been an informal relationship between royal power in England and the consent of the governed, characterised by compromise, became an abrasive ideological relationship revolving around the interpretation of a text, which as usual in such circumstances bred zealotry and suspicion bordering on paranoia. The old understanding of Britain was also now in a hostile environment. In part this was due to developments in the study of law, which fed into the understanding of the extent of royal power. The new breed of professional lawyers, and eventually the king they served, wanted to know what were the grounds on which privileges were claimed, so as to justify them. It fostered an aggressive attitude by royal justices towards customary and unwritten rights, which under Edward I became an invasive national inquisition. The same mind-set was applied to the relationship of England to the lesser polities of Britain, with catastrophic results.

The long reign of Henry III of England (1216–1272) is not easy to make into a narrative, as several historians have found. In part this was because of the king himself: a vacillating man, by turns kindly, waspish and peevish; overblown in his political ambitions, and consistent in very little. He was a good husband and father, and a man serious about both his kingship and his religion. There is much to recommend the view that he suffered from trying to match in royal state and reputation his charismatic cousin, brother-in-law and contemporary, Louis IX of France (1226–1270). But Henry had little ability to enthuse, organise and attach his magnates, and was much too generous with lands and revenues to his relatives at a time when Englishmen were increasingly xenophobic and the Crown increasingly cash-starved. His years as king were littered with discarded favourites and petty feuds, of which the most disruptive by far was that with his brother-in-law, Simon de Montfort the younger, earl of Leicester (died 1265), which festered into one of the most damaging civil conflicts England experienced in the middle ages, with major long-term consequences for civil peace and government. For the purpose of this book it is possible to pick out two of the many strands which make Henry's reign significant, at least in retrospect. The first is the way the principles of Magna Carta became embedded in English political life sufficiently to motivate the self-conscious political community of England into action. On several occasions it made a stand against the king on the interpretation of the clauses of Magna Carta, notably and unsurprisingly those relating to noble privilege. The second strand is the silent shift in the position of England within Britain. King John had operated with some success in Ireland and Wales, enforcing respect from the lesser rulers of the British Isles in much the same way as his predecessors had since the eleventh century. Henry III, but much more so his son Edward I (1272–1307), saw Britain differently, which was hardly surprising as it had become their principal political theatre and focus. Dynastic recovery in France north of the Loire became an increasingly unrealistic ambition. In contrast, Scotland and Wales were often at the forefront of the later Angevin kings' attention; they were within easy reach and weak enough to dominate. The English kings and their advisers developed a more proprietorial attitude to the British realms outside England which went beyond the vague, imperial overlordship of earlier centuries, and so they transformed the histories of both Wales and Scotland.

Henry III and the English Political Community

The first decade of the boy-king's reign was dominated by his aristocracy: by the regent, William Marshal until 1219 and thereafter the definitive Angevin warrior-bureaucrat, Hubert de Burgh (died 1243). It was the adherence of the aristocracy which made these men's rule effective. As usual, the aristocracy acquitted itself reasonably during its period of dominance. If so, it was because its members monitored jealously the ambitions of the others and reined each other in. Nonetheless its leaders did pretty well out of their time in power, not least the marshal himself and his eldest son and namesake. Justice and government were slowly re-established, though on a new basis. Society after 1217 was not the same as it had been in the twelfth century. One legacy of John's reign was a more powerful and militant aristocracy, inherently suspicious of the king (see pp. 121–3) and apt to combine against him when it felt its interests threatened. Their touchstone for the future was Magna Carta and its core principles, reissued with the consent of the papacy in an edited form by the regency on the defeat of Louis of France in 1217, a defeat which was itself a corporate triumph for the English aristocracy.

While government was apparently being carried on within Magna Carta's principles after 1217, the emerging political community remained quiet. So when King Henry graduated into adulthood it was into a new atmosphere in terms of Angevin monarchy. After his father's many defeats, dynastic prestige was depleted and the oxygen of royal power was thin. It is significant that Henry's first major independent act in 1225 was to issue under his seal his own definitive text of Magna Carta, under no constraint whatsoever and of his own free will, as he said. He was trying to avoid the appearance of being beholden to the community that had imposed it on both his father and himself. Not only was the aristocracy more powerful after 1216 and able to exert itself both morally and politically in a body in Henry's time, but also the post of justiciar of England as occupied by De Burgh became a formidable rival powerbase, for he was head of both the judiciary and executive. In the days of Henry's grandfather the justiciar was a necessary alter-ego for the king. Now he was an intervening power between the king and the process of government, which was what eventually doomed the office to extinction.

For all his efforts, Henry III found himself in constant and often unwelcome dialogue with the magnates of his realm (ecclesiastical and lay) about the exercise of his power. Already in 1227 the new generation of great earls was willing to mobilise against him under the leadership of his own younger brother, Richard of Cornwall. They held a rally at Stamford to protest at what they claimed was De Burgh's and the king's determination to rule in defiance of the principles of Magna Carta by reclaiming forest rights conceded a decade previously. A similar attempt to rally the political community against the king and his new mentor, Bishop Peter des Roches, by Earl Richard Marshal in 1233 degenerated into a damaging marcher conflict which sucked in the military power of Prince Llywelyn of Gwynedd against the king, and led to the earl's tragic death in Ireland the next year. In the meantime, the constant resort to Magna Carta as a rallying cry against supposed royal misgovernment fed a national debate that went much deeper into society than just the court nobility and bench of bishops. Monasteries and even county knights were motivated to obtain copies of the Charter for reference, in its 1217 and 1225 versions.

A national political community emerges unmistakably at work for the first time in the events of 1235. In pursuit of elusive international eminence and an alliance to help him against France, King Henry III negotiated a marriage for his sister Isabel to the Hohenstaufen emperor, Frederick II. It was an expensive undertaking and a cash dowry of £20,000 was agreed, which has to have been a large fraction of all the available currency in circulation in England at the time. To meet this demand, the king had to summon a council of barons and prelates to secure consent for taxation. He also had to argue against the principles of Magna Carta, which allowed him to ask help from his realm to marry off a daughter, but not a sister. Taxation to raise the sum by levies on knights' fees and clergy incomes was eventually agreed in England and – when that fell short – in Ireland also. But in the meantime there was a debate both in council and in the wider nation, reports of which still survive from a contemporary schoolbook from Oxford, where the arguments before the king were a matter of clear fascination to the author.

Here for the first time in the historical record we find the ominous question posed by the community of his people to their king: 'Why do you resort to us, when you have rents and farms with which you might enrich your treasury?'[1] The debate assumed that the king should finance his own policies and campaigns and that the real problem that lay behind the king's difficulties with money was incompetent administration. The king got his tax in 1235, and the emperor got his wife, but the money was the devil to collect and Henry had to promise his barons and bishops that his request created no precedent. The ultimate price the king had to pay was an almost paranoid conviction at all levels of political society that the king was set against the Magna Carta agenda, an impression that his own waywardness and his peevishness under pressure did nothing to lessen. Public protestations by the king that he only wanted to rule in accordance with the law and custom of England had as little weight as the same words in the mouth of his tyrannical father.

The Incompetence of Henry III

Henry III's erratic government stumbled on to no one's satisfaction after the Marshal war of 1234, with the king veering from one ill-conceived policy initiative to another. A major source of difficulty was his innate generosity to family, which sometimes was lavished on undeserving or even dangerous recipients. So in 1240 in a grand ceremony at Gloucester Abbey he recognised his nephew, Dafydd ap Llywelyn, as prince of all the Welsh, placing a coronet on the young man's head and putting him at the head of the magnates of Wales, as they were obliged to do homage to him as prince. Henry seemed unaware of how his grandiose act would upset the balance of power in native Wales and help consolidate the national aspirations of Gwynedd, an outcome which could not be to the king's own advantage. Even more perilous was Henry's determination to promote in England his wife's Savoyard relations and, later on, his half-brothers, sons of his mother Queen Isabel of Angoulême by her second marriage to the count of La Marche. The king's obnoxious foreign friends and officers were already a rallying point for opposition in John's reign, and when Henry III briefly took up with the worst (because most capable and greedy) of his father's Angevin favourites, Peter des Roches, in 1232, the consequences were all but civil war.

Henry married Eleanor of Provence in 1236. She was then twelve years of age, the daughter of Ramon Berenguer, count of Provence. Her elder sister was already married to Louis IX of France. The marriage was a successful one, and Henry's affection for his wife extended to her uncles, one of whom, Boniface, was made archbishop of Canterbury in 1241. The patronage was not necessarily wasted in this case, for the queen's most cosmopolitan and influential relative, Count Peter of Savoy, became a useful international intermediary for Henry with the Empire and France; Peter was endowed with the lands of the confiscated earldom of Richmond. The problem was with the next wave of foreigners, the king's young half-brothers: fiery and often violent men who colonised his court and monopolised his patronage in the later 1240s. The term 'Poitevins' was soon being used by the native aristocracy to stigmatise these foreigners, who were perceived not to share the English national agenda and to be behind much of the king's misgovernment. Ironically, the most resentful of Henry's 'native' earls, Simon de Montfort of Leicester, had come to England himself from Capetian France only in 1231 to claim his family's English inheritance and been received with just as generous a reception, granted an earldom and the king's sister Eleanor as wife. But Simon, like the other earls and barons, subscribed to what had been won from King John at Runnymede. His foreignness was therefore ignored, for he was a keeper of the flame. In contrast, William de Valence's notoriously oppressive and corrupt seneschal, William de Bussey, though an Englishman born, was stigmatised by his enemies as a 'Poitevin'.

The Coup of 1258

Henry III's weakness for foreign ventures was his ultimate downfall. Some were unavoidable. He inherited claims to two-thirds of France, and fitfully pursued them. He had no choice because – whatever his magnates thought of the practicality of it – his honour demanded that he should, and the fact that his aristocracy was mobilised in his support on several occasions shows that they were willing to recognise this, up to a point. His expedition to France in 1230 brought an English army as far as the western border of Normandy where it skirmished, though achieved nothing much overall, other than the subsequent death of a number of important English magnates through disease and injury. His 1242 campaign was focused on Aquitaine and was stimulated by Louis IX's inflammatory move in making his brother count of Poitou, which was one of the titles of the duke of Aquitaine, and one which Henry had already conceded to his own brother Richard. This time Henry's aggressive move into Poitou provoked a retaliatory strike from King Louis himself, and drove Henry humiliatingly back on Gascony, allowing the Capetians to consolidate their hold on southern and central France.

Things went from bad to worse in Gascony when the province was confided to Simon de Montfort as seneschal. His confrontational attitude to the local aristocracy led to civil war and opened the door for the king of Castile to revive his claims on the duchy. Henry this time managed to stabilise the situation by a personal appearance in Gascony. An astute marriage between Eleanor, the king of Castile's half-sister, and Edward, Henry III's son, added further buttresses to English rule in south-west France. In 1254 – now sixteen – Edward (called 'the Lord Edward' in his father's days) was created duke of Aquitaine which, with the lordship of Ireland and the earldom of Chester, brought him into the position which was to make him very influential in the latter years of his father's reign in both England and France. The young Edward was to take his rule of Gascony seriously, and his periods of residence there went a long way to solving for a generation many of the problems of distant Angevin rule, as well as giving him a commitment to his family's continued rule there.

It was not in the end his French claims which brought Henry III down, for his barons could sympathise to some extent, and his demands on them never came anywhere near those his father and uncle had made on them for money and support. It was diplomatic overreach that drove Henry's erratic government into its final desperate crisis. With the death in 1250 of his former brother-in-law, Emperor Frederick II, Henry saw opportunities for dynastic advancement. The papacy was eager for Henry to assist it in its Italian problems by persuading him to make a bid for the throne of Sicily over the head of Frederick's son. So Henry accepted the throne of Sicily and undertook to provide the papacy with troops and the astonishing sum of 135,000 marks to offset papal debts already incurred in the pope's fight against the Hohenstaufen empire. Not surprisingly, the increasingly insular English political community saw no advantage to itself in supporting such a faraway venture. Money was not to be had, even following the election of Richard of Cornwall to the kingship of the Romans by the German electors in 1256, which at least added to the scheme's political credibility.

In 1258, Henry III was under threat of excommunication for not fulfilling his undertakings in the treaty, and the English political community was seething about the favour shown the Poitevins by the king. Seven magnates, including the queen's uncle, Peter of Savoy, swore an oath to break the influence of the Poitevins and reform the realm, obliging the king to agree. Under their constraint, the council at Oxford in 1258 instituted measures comparable to the fateful precedent of 1215. So far as the legate was concerned, he was brusquely told that the king could not impose a debt on his subjects without their consent. The four Poitevin half-brothers of the king were rounded up and expelled from England. The magnates followed this up by presenting a list of grievances to the king relating to the way they perceived the Magna Carta agenda was being once again abused. They proceeded to co-opt a committee of fifteen from members of the king's own advisory council to monitor his decisions, and to get him to swear to uphold the 'good customs' of Magna Carta. A new measure was that this time the magnates elected their own nominee to occupy the revived office of chief justiciar. The officer's new purpose was to take control of the judicial system and displace the king from it, for Henry was by now a man whom no one trusted to do the right or sensible thing.

What happened in June 1258 was in effect a coup carried out by a group which called itself 'the whole community of England', though it was carried out with more consideration for the king's position than was shown John in 1215. Henry was warned in advance of the Oxford meeting and what would occur there. He was respectfully presented with demands for which his assent was asked, and he gave it, as if he had a choice. The king's friends as well as his critics were deliberately included among the Fifteen. The events of 1258 were, however, the reassertion by the magnates of what they had in effect possessed for a century now, a partnership in power with the king on terms their ancestors and predecessors had devised long before. It was not, therefore, the revolution that one or two historians have chosen to call it. The king might fitfully recognise, ignore or resist this dialogue, but it was a reality he could not escape, for it had title deeds of unimpeachable legitimacy. The magnates went out of their way to be seen to be even-handed in 1258 and take the whole realm along with them: the same reforming zeal they turned on the king's officers was applied to their own (equally criticised) bailiffs and seneschals. There was in fact an orgy of self-examination by the political community that created inquest after inquest and that lasted for more than a year.

 The Civil War of 1264–1267

The king himself remained marginalised in all these events until the end of 1259, when he went to Paris to visit Louis IX and re-negotiate the English position in France in person and so evade baronial control, though a group of their councillors travelled with him. Henry III returned to England without his former French titles of Normandy and Anjou, which he had given up, but buttressed by his French cousin's support and provided with French money and knights. He found the baronial regime had fallen apart in his absence, disrupted by an extremist party led by his brother-in-law, Montfort, who appointed himself guardian of the spirit of the Provisions of Oxford. For a while the king was able to isolate Montfort and escape monitoring with the aid of more moderate magnates. His advantage did not last long. By 1263 Henry's government was again in crisis, and his son Edward had been seduced into his uncle Montfort's party.

Once again Henry was subjected to the supervision of a council, but this time Montfort was in control of it. The earl's inflexibility and aggression went on to rob the baronial regime of broad appeal and caused dissent within it. By 1264 the only peaceful solution to the bitter hostility between royalist and baronial parties was to submit the quarrel to Louis IX. In view of the French king's high notions of kingship, Louis's subsequent rejection of the English tradition of consensual authority could not have been a surprise; the French monarchy had developed in an entirely different direction. Civil war inevitably followed, in which the Lord Edward abandoned his uncle and rallied to his father. Henry III, Lord Edward and King Richard of the Romans, the king's brother, were captured on the disastrous field of Lewes on 14 May 1264, when England found itself in an entirely new situation, which was this time truly revolutionary. Power had passed by military means to a small cabal of aristocrats, and the king became an impotent political catspaw.

Not surprisingly the Montfort regime was unstable and vulnerable to counter-attack. But in its vulnerability it searched around for allies, and in June 1264 Montfort deliberately sought to identify the county knights and urban elites with his regime, by summoning their representatives to a parliament. He had some success, particularly with enlisting the Londoners. His intention was to broaden his power base, and he was not the first to try this tactic (see p. 47). King John had summoned shire knights in groups or as a body to his presence with that in mind. John had not been seeking their consent to his rule, however, simply information and views independent of his distrusted magnates. But John's action helped politicise the leaders of local society. The step of inviting local representatives as well as lay magnates to councils was therefore an obvious one to take, especially when taxation was an issue. Eventually in 1254 shire knights had been summoned to a council along with the magnates, who had spoken for the lay subjects of the king since the twelfth century. The commoners had been intended to be more than just witnesses to the debate of their betters. It was not an experiment that was repeated during the 1258 Oxford meetings. It was still the barons who had considered that they embodied 'the community of England' during that sixteen-month upheaval. But in 1264 the precedent of 1254 was useful for the Montfort regime in its leader's search for a consensus to bolster his position; indeed he had attempted to do it in an earlier crisis in 1261. Pragmatic stratagem or not, it was to be the longest-lasting legacy of his fourteen months in power.

Montfort had a talent for falling out with his allies, and his attitude to Gilbert de Clare, earl of Gloucester, caused the young earl to defect to the king's son Edward when he escaped from custody in May 1265. By this time the political elite had tired of Montfort and saw nothing to gain from his continued leadership. By the time Montfort was cornered at Evesham in August 1265, it was the Lord Edward who was more the representative of the community of England than him. At this point, Montfort's support had largely declined to his own Midlands political affinity. His death in battle and the defiling of his corpse as if it were that of a convicted traitor had their significance. Though Montfort's political defeat was total, Edward's determination that his enemy must meet death on the field and that his principal supporters must go down with him injected a new strain of vengefulness into English political life which would become very evident over the next two generations in all three of the British realms. Such violence also provoked vendetta. Edward's cousin and close friend, Henry of Germany, son of Richard of the Romans, was to be knifed to death in a cathedral in Italy by Montfort's sons a few years after Evesham. Montfort for a while was regarded as a martyr capable of performing miracles, though enthusiasm for his sanctity lapsed after a generation. It was not to revive until he achieved a political cult among Victorian constitutionalists, who apotheosised him as the 'founder of Parliament'. But in fact the mandate of heaven in terms of the embodiment of national consensus passed in 1265 to Montfort's nephew, the Lord Edward, who recognised the usefulness of a parliament which could express the community of England, so long as what it expressed echoed his own will. In this way, the chaotic reign of Henry III had one coherent and positive outcome: it moulded future English political life into a formal discourse in the forum of Parliament between the national community and the executive king who ruled it.

The Destruction of Native Wales

Edward I succeeded his father in 1272, while he was returning across the Mediterranean from his crusade in Palestine. He did not in fact reach England until August 1274, having first toured Savoy, Burgundy and the Île-de-France. The stability of the realm he had left behind was remarkable considering its recent history, but the fact that the magnates had embraced the young heir to England as their true leader in 1265 smoothed away all problems. Edward was well fitted to be a king respected by his magnates rather than resisted by them. Unlike his father, he was an enthusiast for elite military culture, notably the tournament. A French writer hailed him in 1278 as the international leader of the sport in his day.[2] One of Edward's first actions when power came into his hands by default after the fall of Montfort was to lift his father's ban on the tournament in England. English writers, in their nationalistic way, loved stories in which he humiliated foreigners by his prowess. On his way home to England he attended a tournament in Châlon in which the Anglo-Aquitanian team he headed was heavily outnumbered by the rival French. His opponents took this as licence to cheat in anticipation of likely victory, and deployed infantry to round up ransoms in the grand charge. But Edward's military skills were formidable enough to defeat the count of Châlon, whom he wrenched off the back of his horse in person, and after his triumph he besieged the city and extracted a huge fine for its sheltering of the cheats. This was the sort of man contemporary barons could respect, and as a result Edward was a king who was able to develop ambitions in which he would be supported by his natural associates, his magnates. Over the first decade of his rule, these objectives developed in a British direction which would have major long-term consequences for its history, not least for Anglo-Scottish relations, which came to be entirely redefined by King Edward.

The crucible of transformation in Britain was to be the principality of Wales. An emerging Welsh state there had suffered a setback on the premature death of Prince Dafydd ap Llywelyn in 1246. In the first half of the thirteenth century, the house of Gwynedd had made a determined effort to introduce unigeniture (inheritance by a single son) as a custom of succession fitting to a princely dynasty with European ambitions. This novelty collapsed on Dafydd's death, when his dynastic lands were divided and disputed among several heirs descended from his illegitimate half-brother, Gruffudd. None of these would-be princes had Dafydd's advantage of close kinship with the Angevin royal dynasty, advertised prominently as it was in the late prince's coat of arms. However, after a decade of infighting, Gwynedd was reassembled once again by one of Gruffudd's younger sons, Llywelyn. The new prince revived Gwynedd's ambition to be the core of a principality of all the Welsh, and in 1258 Llywelyn ap Gruffudd was already going by the title 'prince of Wales' first embraced by his uncle. As with his grandfather and namesake, Llywelyn was in a good position to profit from civil discord in England. The baronial rebellion of 1264 was a golden opportunity, and allowed Llywelyn to negotiate recognition of his ambitions first from Montfort and then in 1267 at the Treaty of Montgomery from Henry III and his son. In return for a substantial indemnity, the treaty left Llywelyn in the position his uncle Dafydd had achieved in 1240, as pre-eminent among the native Welsh magnates, recognised as a semi-autonomous prince under the English Crown in the same relationship as the great dukes of Brittany and Burgundy were to the Crown of France.

The collapse of Llywelyn's achievement began on King Edward's return to his realm in 1274, though it has to be said in his defence that it was not the king's plan that it should. Llywelyn ignored the invitation to attend the coronation as the king's leading lay vassal. He added to the provocation by refusing four summonses to perform the homage he owed as prince of Wales, even though he was allowed the privilege princes enjoyed in France: performing homage to the king on the border of his own principality. Llywelyn's intention was to try to extort from Edward some advantage in his own bad relations with the English marcher lords and to demand the handover of dissident members of his family who had taken refuge in England. But it was a serious miscalculation. Edward was initially (and surprisingly) diffident about taking action against Llywelyn, but once he engaged with the problem he demonstrated what was to be his characteristic remorselessness in countering opposition to what he considered his rights. A savage and expensive campaign in North Wales broke Llywelyn's power in 1277. Though Llywelyn remained 'prince of Wales', the title was an empty one. His rule was limited to the historical provinces of Gwynedd, which he was obliged to share with his restored relatives. His overlordship of the other significant Welsh magnates was stripped from him. Unfortunately, in this crisis, Llywelyn lacked the statesmanship and patience slowly to rebuild trust and influence at the English court. By 1282 he was in a hopeless armed confrontation with Edward and the marcher barons.

A complication which emerged at this point was Edward's assumption that his rights as king of England in Britain were rather more than the vague British imperium of earlier days. The roots of this went back to his grandfather's time. King John had openly pursued a policy of imposing English law and custom on his Irish lands, and so eliminated the claims of the barons there to the same sort of marcher liberties they enjoyed in Wales. In 1207 and again in 1210 John had forcibly made his point, to the extent that a version of Magna Carta was sent to Dublin where its provisions held sway in Ireland in a way they did not in Wales and the March. As an active and aggressive lord of Ireland in the 1250s, the young Edward had direct experience of his grandfather's project there, which had created a bureaucratic lordship placing native and settler alike under the direct power of the Crown whether they liked it or not. Wales too experienced encroachments from the English state during this period. Fear of John's intervention there was the reason why in 1215 Magna Carta insisted that the Welsh and marcher lordships had their own laws, separate from those of England. This did not stop Henry III frequently and heedlessly meddling in marcher disputes and peremptorily removing legal cases within marcher lordships into his own court. So it was perhaps inevitable that judicial and bureaucratic overspill from England should disturb the balance of Wales and the March in the 1260s and 1270s. What was not inevitable was the way that this tendency gathered momentum and shattered the ancient understanding of the king of England's informal supremacy within the British Isles. That change was entirely down to the nature of Edward I's personality.

As late as 1281 Edward was still tolerant of the continued existence of a native Welsh principality, however truncated and powerless, but then his view abruptly changed. Hostilities were initiated by Llywelyn's brother Dafydd, whom Edward had until then furthered and supported. Llywelyn was dragged into the war alongside his brother regardless, and likewise attracted Edward's rage. The king became fixated on the final extirpation of the 'family of traitors', as he called the house of Gwynedd. During the last negotiations in November 1282 between the king's agents and Llywelyn, the English demand was that the prince should surrender his realm, and take up instead an earldom in England. The king's mind was clearly on the elimination of native-ruled Wales and a remodelling of the country on revolutionary lines which erased two centuries of experience and precedent. Llywelyn died in a trap laid by his marcher enemies, to be followed briefly as prince of Wales by his brother and rival, Dafydd. Llywelyn left no direct male heir, only a daughter who survived until 1337 confined to an English nunnery.

The treatment afforded to the bodies of Llywelyn and Dafydd echoes the way Edward had the corpse of his enemy Montfort defiled in 1265. Llywelyn's head was lopped off his corpse and paraded mockingly along Cheapside on a pike before being exhibited at the Tower, while Dafydd was executed in the revolting way the English had developed to dishonour traitors to the state. Edward's grim perspective was that these men, princes or not, had committed treason to his idea of the realm of England, and deserved everything they got as a result. The occupation of the former principality and the rapid construction of a ring of massive fortresses to secure it for the Crown are a statement of the same sentiment in stone and gold, for their cost has been estimated at a staggering £80,000. In what was intended as a final statement about Wales and the Welsh, the surviving lords of the house of Deheubarth and Powys Fadog were likewise subjected to the royal lordship Edward created out of Wales. This new principality of Wales was reorganised in 1284, as Ireland had been decades earlier, into administrative shires on the English model with the familiar range of royal officials, for it was now pronounced to be 'a land annexed and united to the Crown of England'. The lesser princely house of Powys Wenwynwyn survived, but on English terms. Powys was converted to a marcher lordship, its lord taking a French surname and a seat in Parliament.

The Alienation of Scotland

Scotland and England were at peace for all but the first year of Henry III's long reign. Relations between the English and Scottish royal houses were in fact remarkably close for much of the thirteenth century, as circumstances encouraged mutual friendship. The consequence of this was highly beneficial for Scotland. The reign of Alexander II (1214–1249) might have begun in warfare with the formidable adversary of King John, from which the Scots gained very little, even when John was entangled in civil war and his boy successor was clinging to a tottering throne, but what followed was different. Henry III's sister Joan was married to Alexander in 1221 as a consequence of a peace settlement, and the two kings struck up a family relationship. Continuing peace with England allowed Alexander by 1228 to finally destroy the mac Williams, his longtime northern rivals for the crown of Scotland, and consolidate his kingdom north of Inverness. Alexander's principal need was for time for consolidation in the face of Norwegian aggression around the edges of his kingdom and persistent internal aristocratic rivalries. In 1237 he settled many outstanding claims against England in a major treaty reached at York. Though he failed to recover the earldom of Huntingdon at the extinction of his family's English cadet branch after 1237, he had perhaps some useful compensation in more convenient estates across Northern England. Just as importantly, the English wrote off debt claims against Scotland and accepted in future a diplomatic equality of Scottish to English kingship. So Henry III played a supportive role during the minority of Alexander III (1249–1286), to whom he had married a daughter in 1251, a second marital alliance between the two dynasties. In return, Alexander despatched troops to support Henry and his son during the Montfortian ascendancy. This identity of interest had much to do with the fact that throughout the century several of the greatest barons of Scotland were also English barons, and such men naturally looked to London in any crisis.

A relationship based on homage was perhaps no more comfortable for the Scottish king than that the king of England owed for Aquitaine to his cousin of France. Edward could hardly object to Alexander III's declaration in 1278 on doing homage for his English lands that 'nobody but God himself has the right to the homage for my realm of Scotland', since Edward might well have said exactly the same about England to Philip III of France. Indeed the kings of England and Scotland seem to have enjoyed a genuine and sympathetic personal friendship at this time, which was hardly surprising since Alexander had been married to Edward's sister until her premature death in 1275. Edward maintained his good relations with Alexander until the Scottish king's unfortunate accidental death in a fall from his horse on a dark night in 1286, an event which was to trigger a fatal dynastic crisis. In what followed, it is tempting to see the brutal thoroughness and implacability Edward I displayed in subjugating and assimilating Wales as a precursor to his subsequent treatment of Scotland. The idea indeed occurred to at least one contemporary commentator, a Cistercian monk in Surrey, who pictured the king informing his magnates in 1291 that it was his intention 'to subdue the king and kingdom of Scotland to his authority, in the same way he had recently subdued Wales'.[3] But there is no other evidence that his Welsh success spurred any ambition in Edward to assimilate the other kingdom in the British Isles into his own. However, the traits Edward had revealed in Wales were to be exhibited later in Scotland, not least his remorseless reductionism when it came to the extent of his authority in Britain, which was just waiting its chance to come into play.

Crises such as happened between England and Scotland in the 1290s do not come entirely out of the blue. The developing nature of the Scottish state had been drawing an increasingly clear line between it and England for the past several decades, for all the tokens of friendship between the two royal houses and the cross-border dealings of their aristocracies. Alexander III was a masterful king who pursued a distinctly expansionist policy for Scotland on the outer fringes of his kingdom where there was space to exploit and claims to contest. Secure in the support of his own earls and with material help from England, Alexander waged constant war in the 1260s against Norwegian ascendancy in the Isles and against the independence of the Norse colony of Man. After several years' hard resistance from the king of Norway, Alexander bought out the claims of King Magnus VI Haakonsson in the treaty of Perth in 1266, leaving Norway with control only of Orkney and Shetland. The kingdom of Man was occupied, and both it and the Hebrides were subjected – as it was significantly stated in the treaty – to the 'laws and customs of Scotland'.

This idea of a Scottish law developed in the south and east of the realm, where there were royal sheriffs and co-ordinating justiciars. Thirteenth-century Scots even gave this law a founding figure in King David I (1124–1153) so as to endow their law with the sort of antiquity that argued respectability, just as the English looked back to the good laws of Edward the Confessor and the Welsh to Hywel Dda. In fact, elsewhere, in the great earldoms of the north and in the province of Galloway, there cannot have been any common agreement as to what those laws and customs were, for Scotland continued to be a land of diverse lordships with only a limited degree of the centralisation and bureaucratic specialism so familiar in England. The Scottish king remained a peripatetic ruler of a colourfully diverse realm, and there was no parallel in Scotland to the settled place Westminster enjoyed in the expression and enforcement of English kingship and government (see pp. 111–12). Nonetheless, the very assertion in 1266 that there was a 'law of Scotland' which was imposed and upheld by its king was an unarguable and indeed aggressive claim to Scottish statehood which would sooner or later conflict with any claim England asserted against the Scots. The ideological grounds for Anglo-Scottish conflict were already forming before Alexander III died.

King Edward did not in fact rush to exploit the dynastic crisis that followed the king's death, nor was he consulted by the Scots in setting up a regency council, which their magnates managed to do with an admirable degree of consensus and concern for civil peace. Scotland at this point had an heir, Alexander's granddaughter, the child Margaret, daughter of King Eric II Magnusson of Norway, a child who was also King Edward of England's great-niece. Edward might therefore have been brought into the process of succession through family concerns as much as because he was Scotland's suzerain. But it would be more than two years before he made his wishes clear and facilitated Margaret's move from Norway to Scotland. The Scottish magnates, embodied as the 'community of Scotland', agreed with Edward in 1289 that the child was to be their queen and that he had some right to be consulted in whom she married.

However, by July 1290 the scheme under discussion had significantly changed focus; now Margaret was to be married to Edward's eldest son. This agreement would have in due course led to a union of crowns in Britain, and it is significant that Edward was required by the Scots to acknowledge when making the deal that a future Plantagenet Scotland would retain its identity and be governed according to its own customs. It was a necessary precaution because it is clear that during that summer Edward at last began to wake up to the possibilities for future intervention in Scotland. The possibilities multiplied when the child Margaret died on Orkney as she was being transported from Norway to Scotland, throwing the question of who was to rule Scotland into a very competitive and well-populated arena where the king of England was allowed by all sides to be a self-interested referee. As of 1290 there were numerous rival claimants to the Scottish throne, descendants of the daughters of Earl David II of Huntingdon (died 1219), the younger brother of King William the Lion (1165–1214), or their sister Ada, who had married the count of Holland. It was at this point that Edward's remorseless and reductionist intellect came once more into deadly play.

The Scottish Succession Crisis, 1290–1296

Factions were already forming around the magnates who had a claim on the throne, and English adjudication was one obvious and desirable way to avoid civil war. But Edward wanted it understood he was allotting the throne as Scotland's overlord, not just as a concerned neighbour. He intended that his rights were to be acknowledged, both by the Scots and by the testimony of history. He ordered that a dossier should be compiled from the royal archives and the various annals and chronicles of England to justify his claim to imperial authority over Scotland. The result was a summit held at the bishop of Durham's border castle of Norham in May 1291, where the Scots envoys attempted to deflect the English claim to legal overlordship but, in handing Edward the kingdom for him to allot to one claimant or other, they did in effect acknowledge it. He consolidated his claim by requiring each of the claimants to agree to his suzerainty before his decision would be made. The decision was eventually made by an elaborate, time-consuming and expensive hearing which did not conclude until November 1292. It awarded the throne to the man who did in fact have the best claim in customary law: John Balliol, the eldest surviving male descendant of Earl David's eldest daughter, who had the additional advantage in 1290 of succeeding to the lordship of Galloway, which made him one of the greatest lords of Scotland. Significantly, a proposal to divide the kingdom between the rival candidates was rejected. It was in no one's interest to treat the by now ancient unitary kingdom of Scotland as if it were a partible aristocratic estate. Scotland was duly handed over to its new king, but with the troublesome caveat that he was subject to the king of England's overlordship, a condition that Edward did not intend to let rest, as it turned out.

As acknowledged overlord of Scotland, Edward immediately asserted a right to hear appeals to his court from Scotland, as the king of France did from Aquitaine. Since Edward was now, in his mind, in the same relation to Scotland as he was to the king of France, such a superior jurisdiction would have seemed to him a logical consequence and, if Edward's mind had any intellectual focus, it was on his position as king in law. Perhaps he should have reflected more on history. It seems to have escaped him that, when Philip II of France moved to exert such a right over the Angevin lands in 1202, the consequence was political armageddon for the Angevin dynasty in France. Edward himself was liable to summons before the Parlement of France in Paris as duke of Aquitaine if his vassals appealed against his rule in Gascony. It does not seem to have occurred to Edward that others might resent such treatment. He was not tactful as to how he went about his intervention in Scotland, bullying the new king Balliol into waiving the caveats about exercising such power that Edward had himself conceded several years earlier. Balliol's former status as a lesser baron of the North of England did not put him in a good place to defy his king and overlord.

Edward was relentless in his interventions, ruthlessly undercutting Balliol's stand-ing as king, going so far in 1294 as to treat him as little more than a superior English vassal in Scotland, who could be summoned for service in English wars in France. Balliol's refusal to be provoked to defiance led to a coup against him in 1295 by his mag-nates, who promptly negotiated in his name a treaty with Edward's enemy, Philip IV of France. By the spring of 1296 England and Scotland were at war, something unknown in eight decades. As a result, cross-border Anglo-Scottish landowners had to make the same uncomfortable choice as Anglo-Normans had in 1204: to support the king of England or the king of Scotland. This forced choice marked the fracture point between the old British world and the new, because the subsequent ferocious decade of warfare allowed no reconciliation or repair in the broken Anglo-Scottish political world. Each national community was to go its own way in the end.

The Breaking of Britain

The defeat and capture of Balliol, and his forced surrender of the Scottish throne in July 1296, prompted Edward to take the next logical step, which was to do to Scotland what he had done to Wales: absorb it as a territory (*terra*) under his crown. This may be seen symbolically in the way that the Scottish government records and the regalia of Scotland, including the portable altar table called 'the stone of Scone', were taken to Westminster, just as had been the crown, sword and insignia of Gwynedd in 1282. But at a critical point in 1297 Edward's attention was fatally subverted by his ambi-tious, expensive and ultimately disastrous war with France. He confided Scotland to his old friend and cousin, Earl John of Warenne, a reluctant viceroy who found the northern climate bad for his health. Rebellion broke out in 1297 and provided the cause with a hero in the Ayrshire landowner, William Wallace, one among several local leaders of resistance to the intruding English regime. The spirit in which these men fought was, in Wallace's words, 'to avenge ourselves and to free our country'. Wallace's defeat of the earl of Warenne's army at Stirling Bridge in September 1297 was seen as divine sanction for the national uprising. As far as Wallace and his men were concerned, John Balliol was still their king, and it was in his name that Wallace assumed the guardianship of Scotland. The summer of 1298 brought King Edward back to Scotland and, although the Scots were decisively defeated in the field at Falkirk, the rebellion continued to ferment, while Edward found himself at odds with his own earls as to how the conquered realm should be divided. Inconclusive campaigns in 1299, 1300 and 1301 took the king and his eldest son into Galloway, Ayr and as far north as Elgin. But at this point Edward was unable even to recapture the key castle of Stirling. Scottish national feeling was allowed to embed itself and identify with broad hostility to the English, forcing the gulf between the peoples ever wider.

Despite the capture and execution of Wallace in 1305, the rebellion continued, as it was by now a movement considerably bigger than one man. A somewhat unlikely new leader appeared in Robert Bruce (earl of Carrick from 1304), grandson of John Balliol's principal rival for the Scottish throne in 1290. Bruce had in fact enlisted with the English in 1302, when the negotiated return of Balliol to Scotland was a strong possibility. In 1305 he was still deeply implicated with the maintenance of English rule, and had done well out of it. But this changed in February 1306 when Bruce assassinated John Comyn, his rival on the council for the favour of the king of England and another claimant to the Scottish throne. Going for broke, Bruce declared his intention to take the throne of Scotland, and succeeded in obtaining coronation at Scone in something resembling appropriate royal state. Despite a disastrous first year on his rickety throne, the Scottish political community rallied to him and he had the support of the major northern earls. So when Edward I died in 1307, the new King Robert had accumulated sufficient credit and victories to discourage the renewal of English campaigns. This allowed him time to destroy his rivals within his new kingdom. In 1309, a parliament at St Andrews voiced the support of the community of Scotland for their king, received French envoys recognising Robert's claims and asserted the entire independence of Scotland from England.

By 1314 only Berwick, Roxburgh, Edinburgh and Stirling were still in English hands, and the catastrophic defeat that year of Edward II at Bannockburn at Bruce's hands brought to an end the Plantagenet attempt to absorb Scotland, along with Ireland and Wales, into their British realm. It was so shattered, in fact, that Robert Bruce had sufficient credibility to seize Ulster in 1314 and have his brother Edward (killed 1318) declared king of Ireland, an ambition inconceivable under the old understanding of the place of England in Britain. With English prestige undermined in the British Isles, anything was now apparently possible. It was in this mood that the Scottish community of the realm in 1320 addressed letters to Pope John XXII (1316–1334) in response to his excommunication of King Robert and his placing of Scotland under an interdict. In these letters is found the sentiment that the Scots were a people historically distinct and independent from any other in Britain. One of these documents, called the Declaration of Arbroath, makes some celebrated remarks about the Scottish desire for freedom, and its view of Scotland itself is clear: the king of England 'ought to be satisfied with what belongs to him, since England used once to be enough for seven kings or more; he ought to leave us Scots in peace, who live in this poor little Scotland, beyond which there is no dwelling-place at all, and who covet nothing but our own' (see Fig. 11.1). The two nations were mutually hostile kingdoms and peoples, and the ancient idea of Britain as an informal empire of peoples under the English king's presidency was entirely dead.

Fig. 11.1 Declaration of Arbroath. A letter dated 6 April 1320 to Pope John XXII sent by the commune of Scotland, sealed by eight earls and thirty-eight barons, seeking to vindicate Robert Bruce in the face of papal excommunication. It famously justifies the national struggle against the English and states: 'as long as a hundred of us remain alive, never will we on any condition be subjected to the lordship of the English. It is in truth not for glory, nor riches, nor honours that we are fighting, but for freedom alone, which no honest man gives up but with life itself.'

The Rise of Parliament in England

The story of much of Edward I's reign in England is of extension of governmental scope and of the remorseless pursuit of legal and financial efficiency. Like that of Henry I, Edward's government had an insatiable thirst for information, and one of his first acts on returning to England was to set up the most thorough survey of landholding, rights and liberties England ever experienced in the middle ages, the enquiry that resulted in the Hundred Rolls. The inquisition was followed up by a requirement that landholders justify by what authority (*quo warranto*) they claimed particular privileges. Angevin government had been doing this fitfully for decades, but now the requirement was applied across the board. A series of national statements of law or assizes addressed issues of corruption that the inquests revealed. The 1270s also saw currency reform, a more organised approach to loans to the government and new duties on the wool trade which enhanced the stability of government revenue. Reform of the administration of royal estates was also attempted, though with less success. The king was still nowhere near able to 'live of his own'. But Edward was able to negotiate a reasonable level of taxation from the political community over these decades, to the extent that his credit was high on the international loan market. He entered into a long and mutually profitable relationship with Luccanese financiers that raised the phenomenal total sum of £392,000 in the first two decades of his reign. Such resources were the reason Edward could conquer Wales the way he did and pose as a convincing equal of his Capetian neighbour in France.

However, when Edward's government came under pressure in the 1290s, as the king simultaneously pursued warfare in Scotland and France, the underlying fragility of its finances became all too obvious. Edward's success until then had relied on credit and good management; now he had reached their limits. It was at this point that the perennial problem posed by the political community re-emerged: the fact that the magnates as a body might demand an account from the king of his governance in return for their agreement to his requests, and might even seek to impose their ideas on him. Despite this, Edward remained firmly committed to the idea of Parliament as a focus for the political community, an idea which might seem paradoxical in his current situation. But Edward routinely included representatives of the towns and shires in his summonses, and two or three parliaments were held in most of the years of his reign. He retained the youthful enthusiasm for the institution he had exhibited in the Montfort years. He was in the 1290s a man still possessed by the spirit of 1258. The king genuinely valued the enactment of his kingship with representatives of the entire political community, secular and ecclesiastical. He wished for dialogue, actively soliciting petitions from Parliament in 1278, thus inaugurating a new element in the way the king of England exercised his rule and communicated with his people. His measures also assisted the transformation of Parliament into a superior court of law, as petitions were heard and determined there just as they were in the Parlement of Capetian Paris. The political return in this for the king was substantial, because England experienced two decades of uninterrupted political stability, even though the king was resident in Gascony from 1286 to 1289.

The mid 1290s nonetheless brought disruption to the balance between king and community, and finance was as ever the catalyst for confrontation, as it had been in 1235 and 1258. The conquest of Wales had been managed through existing resources and a ready loan market, but the defence of Gascony against the overmastering power of King Philip IV of France was an entirely different order of conflict. The problem itself had come out of maritime differences between the sailors of Normandy and the semi-piratical galley masters of Plantagenet Bayonne and the English Cinque Ports, which degenerated into unlicensed naval warfare in 1293. High-level diplomacy between Westminster and Paris failed to prevent the two realms blundering into general warfare, largely because it turned out that Philip IV was wilfully determined to use the tension to impose a more definitive overlordship on Edward as duke of Aquitaine. The French demand for the surrender of Gascony and Edward's appearance for judgement at Paris was met, as it had to be, with formal defiance and military resistance in the summer of 1294. Distracted by Scotland and Wales, and unable to put together an overwhelming coalition against the Capetian king, Edward was thoroughly outmanoeuvred over the next three years. His commanders in the field proved ineffective, and indeed the campaign saw the death of his beloved brother and greatest support, Edmund of Lancaster. Most of the effective resistance to the Capetians was generated within Gascony itself, not by Plantagenet viceroys. The cost of subsidies to Gascon nobles and Edward's Rhenish and Low Countries allies was phenomenal, let alone the wages of English troops sent to Flanders and the south.

The huge financial demands of war were impossible to meet, not least because of the failure of Edward's Luccanese agents, the Riccardi, in 1294. Other Italian firms were unenthusiastic about filling the financial gap. Edward began to revisit methods his predecessors had used, not least forced loans. The Church was in the front line of his demands, and was his first resort for taxation, but by November 1294 an approach was at last made to Parliament, and money duly appeared, in quite large amounts, despite open muttering. But it was never enough. By January 1296 English finances were in a desperate state. Edward was by then contemplating extraordinary measures to raise troops, including revival of the antiquated summons of individuals to actually perform the knight service with which their estates were burdened. Food was requisitioned across England through the hated mechanism of the **prise** to a degree unknown previously. Though the magnates and Commons continued to grant taxation, the relentless pressure was causing even the Church to mobilise in resistance. In November 1296 the prelates summoned to Parliament refused to pay up. This was the catalyst for the explosion of resistance to the king which shook his government to its foundations in 1297 and brought the magnates once more to the position their fathers had taken in 1258: spokesmen for the community against the king.

With the king's political allies heading his armies outside the country, and his most powerful subject and faithful brother, the earl of Lancaster, now dead, the disgruntled and disaffected earls and barons sided with the bishops. The spring of 1297 saw the king willing to go as far as his obnoxious grandfather and intimidate the clergy with arbitrary fines and confiscations, and, just as in John's day, the magnates retaliated by refusing to serve in his army. The magnates rallied against the king in the March in ways not seen since the Marshal rebellion of 1233 and refused his summons to muster for service at London. Just as his father had in 1258, Edward found himself in receipt of a written statement of grievances, the Remonstrances. The rallying cry of the king's abuse of Magna Carta was once again raised, forcing the king to issue yet another confirmation of the great charter and its companion, the Charter of the Forest. Edward was also obliged to try to present his case reasonably, which he failed to do convincingly.

In August 1297 the earls of Hereford and Norfolk appeared at the Exchequer with a large party of knights and prevented the collection of the taxes and prises the king had tried to impose. They declared that they spoke for the community of England which the king was attempting to reduce to servitude. So one of the most adroit and effective executive kings England ever had in the middle ages was defeated by the innate weakness of his monarchy, and the alienation of the political community. The king at this point became elusive, something he had never been before; income was forthcoming only with immense efforts, and his parliaments returned again and again to the same complaints. The obstructiveness and ill-feeling did not dissipate until 1302, by which time the leading opposition earls had died and the French wars had come to a bloody and disastrous end as the Capetian nobility died in irreplaceable numbers on Flemish pikes on the catastrophic field of Courtrai, thus discrediting the rule of Philip IV without any assistance from Edward of England.

 ## Faction and Vendetta

Edward II inherited in 1307 the same bad financial position, combined with military failure in Scotland and a fitfully rebellious Wales. He did not inherit his father's formidable reputation for unforgiving remorselessness to his enemies. As a result, his chances of effectively managing the hostile political community depended a lot on his own character and abilities. But Edward II proved to be entirely lacking in managerial abilities or sympathy with his aristocracy. He was an emotionally needy man, even more apt than his grandfather to over-invest in relationships. Henry III had favoured and lavishly patronised men whom he hoped could give him political direction and security. His grandson fixated on men who offered him the exclusive friendship and affection he lusted after, to the point where people assumed, probably correctly, that he took them as male lovers. Edward II's judgement in his choice of favourites was invariably appalling. The first of them set the pattern. Peter de Gabaston (the Piers Gaveston of English history books) was in fact a noble man enough, descended through his mother from a particularly important Gascon dynasty, the family of Marsan, barons of the Landais who had been closely attached to the Plantagenet interest since the reign of Henry II. It was not Peter's birth which was the problem, but his greed, stupidity and arrogance. He first appeared in England as a refugee from the Capetian invasion of his homeland as an attractive adolescent around 1296 and by 1300 was a member of the household of the young Prince Edward. The two young men were intimate friends within a few years, Gaveston being the prince's inseparable body squire. Their relationship was sufficiently objectionable for the troubled father to exile Gaveston from England and his son's company in the year before his death.

Gaveston's destabilising effect on the new king's court was just as troubling to the opposition barons in 1308 as to the old king the previous year. They too wanted him banished from England. Newly made earl of Cornwall (a dignity held since 1140 by cadets of the royal family), Gaveston also managed to spark an international crisis. Both Edward and he seemed unable to understand that the French would be offended that the tapestries displayed in Westminster Hall on the day of the coronation should not display those of allied England and France, but the arms of the king and of Gaveston. At least one English earl is said to have contemplated assassinating Gaveston on that ill-omened day. It was a gesture revealing blind and besotted homosexual passion, not misplaced homosociality and masculine brotherhood as heterosexual historians of the pragmatic English tradition are inclined to argue. The counter-argument they bring that both men had relationships with women and indeed that both were fathers does not mean that they could not be passionately attracted to each other too. Human sexuality is not and never has been so simple an equation, and same-sex attraction was not characterised as an exclusive category of human sexual behaviour until the nineteenth century.

The relationship between Edward II and Gaveston followed its inevitably catastrophic course. The crisis of 1308 was in part defused by temporarily bundling Gaveston off to be the king's lieutenant in Ireland, but the political community and the king were set on a course of confrontation, in which Gaveston was to become the first of several casualties. The earls of England continued to be the leaders of the opposition, and their personal distaste for Gaveston and his behaviour towards them was the issue, rather than his political ambitions, which seem to have been more or less non-existent; he was simply not that bright. The king's cousin, Earl Thomas of Lancaster, developed a particular distaste for the favourite and took the lead in pushing for reform. Issues of debt, maladministration and the Gaveston irritant led in March 1311 to the king's forced acceptance of commissioners to supervise his executive function, under threat of deposition according to one well-informed source, on the ominous grounds that he had broken his coronation oath (see pp. 94–6). The twenty-one men, including eight of the greatest earls, were called the 'Ordainers' from the ordinances or grievances drawn up in Parliament.

The Ordainers broke no new ground in the way they addressed the constant friction between king and community, but one of their priorities was the expulsion of Gaveston once more from England, clearing away his objectionable influence so the process of financial reform could proceed in ways under discussion since the 1290s. In November

1311 Gaveston left for the continent. He was not gone long. He reappeared in Yorkshire in the new year, to be rapidly joined by Edward, who may well have solicited his return. The king attempted to make a coup of it, repudiating the Ordinances and so directly challenging the earls. The Ordainers' retaliation was in line with the vengeful and bloody style of politics which the king's father had begun promoting in the 1260s. As with earlier crises, troops were assembled in the guise of tournaments, and the council took executive charge under the chief earls, who by one account swore an oath against Gaveston. In May 1312, the man himself was run to earth in Yorkshire and surrendered to the earls of Pembroke and Warenne. Within a month, he was seized from his custodians by the earl of Warwick and, with the connivance of Lancaster, he was condemned as a traitor. Taken from Warwick to the nearest patch of land within the liberties of the earl of Lancaster, Gaveston was butchered by two Welsh soldiers, and his head severed, as was by now customary for convicted traitors.

The king was utterly defeated and never forgot the humiliation and emotional trauma his cousin Lancaster had imposed on him. But at this point Edward II displayed for the first time an ability to bide his time. He waited two years before he was able to get the embalmed body of his beloved Gaveston moved from its temporary home in Oxford to be fittingly and lavishly buried in the house of the Dominicans next the royal palace of Langley. The settling of the debt with Lancaster took much longer, and was not assisted by the king's attempt to renew the war in Scotland in 1314, which came to a catastrophic end on the field of Bannockburn. The Ordinances now governed England, by means of the magnate-dominated Parliament. The magnates themselves had in 1311 significantly dropped their old claim to represent in themselves 'the community of England'; it was now Parliament which was the explicit means to express the corporate will of all the estates of the realm: Church, magnates and Commons. Within the political world, it was Lancaster who was supreme from 1315 when his ally Warwick died. Earl Thomas's eminence was assisted by the fact that he could use in his own support the great wealth and estates his father had amassed to retain influential local bannerets, knights and justices throughout England. It was the first of several Lancastrian affinities which would trouble the kingdom over the next century. The king recognised the danger, and by 1316 was actively recruiting his own retainers as a counterbalance, including a new crop of favourites: ambitious and greedy courtiers, whom contemporaries reckoned to be worse than Gaveston.

Edward II was assisted in his fight-back by the fact that Lancaster had his predecessor Montfort's ability to antagonise his fellow earls, not least the young earl of Warenne, grandson of Edward I's friend and confidant, who in 1317–1318 was in a state of open hostility with Lancaster in Yorkshire. Aristocratic divisions, and the king's obstructionism and vengefulness, crippled the government and debilitated the Ordinances. By 1321 Lancaster was being seen by some as the problem, as much as Gaveston had been, while the king's dominant and greedy new favourites, the Midlands banneret

Hugh Despenser and his son and namesake, were pushing affairs to a crisis. This came with the Parliament of July 1321 which met at a Westminster packed with armed and uniformed magnate retainers. It duly exiled the Despensers. The king retaliated with force, and for once proved able to take the field with decision throughout the autumn and winter of 1321–1322. At the conclusion of the campaign, Lancaster was cornered by royal forces at Boroughbridge in Yorkshire and was forced to surrender himself. His fate was inevitable: he was tried and executed at his own castle of Pontefract, beheaded as Gaveston had been, and a vicious purge of his followers followed, all subjected to death by quartering. The confiscated Lancastrian estates enriched both the Crown and the king's supporters, and for a while put royal finances in a reasonably healthy state.

 ## The Fall and Deposition of Edward II

The ascendancy of the Despenser faction that followed Lancaster's death set a new low in English governance, however. Likely opponents of the king were forced into crippling and artificial debt by sealing 'recognisances', deeds committing themselves to pay sums quite of the scale that King John had demanded to keep his aristocracy cowed, had they ever been called in. But unlike King John, no assets were ever offered in exchange for the money that was extorted. The situation was grotesquely tyrannical, and fostered a mood of growing crisis under what was an oppression unknown in England for more than a century. It also exposed a growing rift between the king and the queen, who appears to have displayed a resentment towards the Despensers in ways she had not previously done to her husband's favourites. She was later to write of her personal fear of the elder Despenser and the 'dishonour' he did her through his outrageous behaviour at court. War in Gascony proved to be the tipping point. Sent to France to negotiate on her husband's behalf in a time-honoured diplomatic strategy, Queen Isabella chose in 1325 to defy her husband and refuse to return to England on the grounds of Edward II's infidelity, of which she doubtless had abundant right to complain. Her defection was all the more dangerous as she had her son with her, the young Edward, duke of Aquitaine. Unfortunately for her footing on the moral high ground, she immediately embarked on a very public affair with the exiled Roger Mortimer, a marcher baron of the former Lancastrian party who had ended up in Paris. The queen's subsequent resolute invasion of England in September 1326 on her son's behalf with a party of exiles, including the king's own brother, the earl of Kent, and a company of mercenaries led to the abrupt and deserved collapse of the hated Despenser regime. The problem then was what to do with the captured king.

Attempts had been made to depose English kings before 1327, and from Stephen's and John's reigns we have evidence that people had at those times got round to discussing how it could be both done and justified. As Edward II settled into the custody of his cousin, Henry of Lancaster, at Kenilworth in December 1326 the political community of England began to debate how such a remarkable thing – unknown until that date in England, France or Scotland – was to be accomplished. It was done in a series of steps and in the public arena of Parliament, so the whole realm could be seen to have acted as one in the face of the intolerable problem represented by Edward II. The idea of 'defiance' was already an ancient mechanism by which vassals repudiated an intolerable lord. The magnates gathered in Parliament duly did so, but renounced their allegiance to Edward as a body, not as individuals, in this way enacting England's rejection of its unrighteous king. This defiance was transmitted to the king from Westminster to Kenilworth by a representative delegation. It then insisted – with threats – that he resign his crown to his eldest son, to which he consented, robed in black and in a highly emotional state. On 21 January 1327 the reign of Edward II formally came to an end, and his household broke their staves of office, as they would otherwise have done at the king's graveside. Edward's death, of course, did follow, but not for another eight months. His period of captivity was troubled by a border war with the Scots and plots by his former friends to secure his release, which underlined the source of political instability Edward still represented. One does not need to be a Tudor dramatist to suspect that the former king's death was too fortuitous to the new regime for it to have been a natural one.

POSTSCRIPT

Britain in 1327 was as transformed as were its component realms. A new pattern of politics was set which pitted the two kingdoms against each other in a way which was remarkably corrosive, in part because the restored Scottish kingdom defined itself and its legitimacy through the mortal enmity with Edwardian England in which it had emerged. A renewed period of antagonism between the suspicious community of England and its king brought its political culture to a new low, despite the innovation of Parliament as a theatre of consensus and kingship. The extinction of Wales as a polity was all but total, for all the resentments that smouldered amongst the native gentry. Its national history for a time becomes local history.

KEY TEXTS

Carpenter, D. A. *The Struggle for Mastery: Britain, 1066–1284* (Penguin, 2003), the most authoritative chronological study of the British, as opposed to English, thirteenth century. • Davies, R. R. *The Age of Conquest: Wales 1063–1415* (Oxford University Press, 1991), comprehensive and unsurpassed study of late medieval Wales, its politics and culture. • Davies, R. R. *The First English Empire: Power and Identities in the British Isles*

1093–1343 (Oxford University Press, 2002), in many ways the key revisionist history of the British middle ages. • Prestwich, M. C. *Edward I* (Methuen, 1988), the classic study of the watershed reign in British history.

FURTHER READING

Alexander II, ed. R. Oram (Brill, 2005). • Burt, C. *Edward I and the Governance of England, 1272–1307* (Cambridge University Press, 2013). • Carpenter, D. A. *The Minority of Henry III* (Methuen, 1990). • Carpenter, D. A. *The Reign of Henry III* (Continuum, 1996). • Clanchy, M. T. *England and Its Rulers, 1066–1307* (3rd edn, Oxford University Press, 2006). • Fryde, N. *The Tyranny and Fall of Edward II, 1321–1326* (Cambridge University Press, 1979). • Maddicott, J. *Simon de Montfort* (Cambridge University Press, 1994). • Oram, R. *Alexander II, King of Scots* (John Donald, 2012). • Penman, M. *Robert the Bruce* (Yale University Press, 2014). • Phillips, S. *Edward II* (Yale University Press, 2010). • Pollock, M. A. *Scotland, England and France After the Loss of Normandy, 1204–1296* (Boydell, 2015). • Powicke, M. *The Thirteenth Century, 1216–1307* (2nd edn, Oxford University Press, 1962). • Prestwich, M. C. *English Politics in the Thirteenth Century* (Ashgate, 1990). • Prestwich, M. C. *Plantagenet England, 1225–1360* (Oxford University Press, 2005). • Prestwich, M. C. *The Three Edwards: War and State in England, 1272–1377* (Routledge, 1980). • *Scotland in the Reign of Alexander III, 1249–1286*, ed. N. H. Reid (John Donald, 1990). • Smith, J. Beverley. *Llywelyn ap Gruffudd, Prince of Wales* (University of Wales Press, 1998). • Spencer, A. *Nobility and Kingship in Medieval England: The Earls and Edward I, 1272–1307* (Cambridge University Press, 2013). • Stacey, R. *Politics, Policy and Finance Under Henry III, 1216–1245* (Oxford University Press, 1987)

NOTES

1. British Library, Additional MS 8167, fo 105r–v. Compare Edward IV's promise to Parliament in 1467 under equal financial stress that he would 'live upon my own and not charge my subjects but in great and urgent causes': *Rotuli Parliamentorum ut et Petitiones et Placita in Parliamento* (London, 1767–1832), V: 572.
2. *Le Roman de Ham*, in *Histoire des ducs de Normandie et des rois d'Angleterre*, ed. F. Michel (Paris, 1840), 225–6.
3. *Annales de Waverleia*, in *Annales Monastici*, ed. H. R. Luard (5 vols., Rolls Series, 1864–69), II: 409.

12 Scotland, 1306–1513

OVERVIEW

The reign of Robert I was a watershed in the history of Britain,
not just in that of Scotland. Robert himself represents the
change. He began his career as very much a magnate of the
old Scotland: with cross-border links and an impeccable Anglo-
French background. His surname derived from Brix in the
Norman Cotentin. Before 1306 he had pursued accommodation
with Edward of England, as his family background and landed
interests dictated. But once king he brutally cut those old links.
His reign produced the definitive statement of a new Scottish
identity, the Declaration of Arbroath, which repudiated English
pretensions to absorb Scotland and direct its future. The
consequence of this – and indeed persistent English refusal to
accept Scottish autonomy – was centuries of armed confrontation
between two mutually hostile states within Britain.

The new Britain created by the acrimonious divorce between the English and Scottish political communities makes any integrated study of both kingdoms after the accession of Robert Bruce difficult, though they interacted often enough, if as unhappily as any other separated partners. Both in fact entered a state of intermittent warfare and prolonged hostility which was not to find any resolution within the period of this volume. One irritant was a factor that had already acted on relations between the English and the other insular peoples since the wars of 1173–1174 when the dominant Welsh prince, Owain ap Gruffudd of Gwynedd, had opened a diplomatic relationship with Louis VII of France against England, and King William the Lion of Scotland had invaded England as a second front against Henry II. When the king of England was at war with his French enemies and his back was towards Britain, there was always the opportunity for the French to ally with the king's British rivals. When King John Balliol of Scotland came into conflict with Edward I it was an inescapable strategy for him to negotiate an alliance with Philip IV of France in which he arranged a marriage with Philip's niece. When after 1337 the king of England embarked on a long-term war of succession with his French cousins this factor would continually involve the Scots in warfare as a way of gaining an advantage in their dysfunctional relationship with their southern neighbour. The occasionally disastrous consequences of this long-term alliance allowed no chance to restore the amicable links which had once existed between England and Scotland, even had both communities wanted to go back to those pre-Edwardian days.

Reconstructing Scotland

The death of Edward I in 1307 did not by any means end the war in the north, but it did allow a period of grace for the new king of Scotland to establish himself. He did this in part by reviving the old links between Scotland and Ulster, which had been a feature of King John's campaigns in Ireland a century earlier and which had much older roots in the Gaelic world out of which the kingdom of Alba had crystallised in the tenth century. The preoccupation of Edward II with his hostile aristocracy meant that by 1309 King Robert had not just established control in the west and centre of his realm, but had also secured Fife and successfully held a parliament at St Andrews. At this time several Scottish earls still maintained their allegiance to Edward, and there were still English garrisons in Perth, Dundee, Stirling and Edinburgh. Edward eventually renewed the war and entered Scotland in response to calls for support from these Scottish allies, and arrived north of the Tweed with a sizeable army in July 1309. He found no enemy army willing to confront him, and another campaign in 1310 had the same result, accomplishing little more than the reinforcement of existing English garrisons. It did, however, lead in October to a diplomatic approach from King Robert to the English court in a conciliatory mood, seeking to open negotiations towards a settlement. It led to a meeting with English envoys but no further progress. Edward remained in the field in the north until the summer of 1311 but was unable to force any confrontation with his elusive enemy, decisive or otherwise. On the king's departure, however, Bruce immediately marched south and raided the northern counties of England to such devastating effect that they had to negotiate truces in return for large sums of money for the next couple of years.

The crisis came in the summer of 1314 when the Scots resumed raiding and made determined and successful attempts to take back the remaining English fortresses in Scotland. It was the siege of Stirling and increasingly desperate pleas of the English adherents in the Lowlands which motivated Edward II to renew his campaigning. In May 1314 an army of between 15,000 and 20,000 infantry and cavalry was assembled at Berwick ready to relieve Stirling, which had negotiated a surrender if no English army had appeared in its support by 24 June. The king reached Stirling the day before the deadline and encountered a numerically inferior Scottish army blocking the road to the castle in a strong position above a tidal creek called Bannock Burn which emptied into the Firth of Forth. Trying to force a constricted causeway and hindered by boggy terrain, the English army was unable to make much headway in a day of unsuccessful skirmishing which inflicted high-profile casualties on the English forces. The second day of fighting found the English trying to advance on Stirling but blundering into a poor position which allowed a Scottish assault that Edward had not expected. The English cavalry was trapped on the spears of the Scottish infantry, and the English archers who might have saved them were deployed to the rear, out of range. Edward barely escaped the massacre on the field, swearing as he fled that if he survived he would establish a house of Carmelite friars in Oxford. He owed his escape back to England to one last gesture from the past. The earl of Dunbar, heir to an Anglo-Scottish dynasty which had flourished for centuries between the two kingdoms, chose not to capture him, but to shelter the king as he rode to escape the pursuing Scots. He was put on a boat by the earl and shipped in safety to Berwick.

The battle of Bannockburn may not have ended the Anglo-Scottish war but it made continued adherence to England by Scots magnates a pointless exercise. Stirling fell, and with it so did central Scotland and much of Lothian (Berwick was eventually regained by the Scots in 1318). It was at this point that King Robert could begin the reconstruction of his realm, while the discredited and impotent Edward II fell into the hands of his cousin, the earl of Lancaster. Robert Bruce did not rest on his laurels, but being well aware of the weakness of English rule in Ireland sent in 1315 his brother Edward with an army to Ulster by means of a fleet provided by the Gaelic magnates of the Isles. Edward Bruce seized the province and began a long-term war against the English barons in Ireland, with the fitful assistance of Irish allies. He claimed the kingship of the island, and even invited the native Welsh to join his alliance, but never came near attaining any sort of victory before his death in battle in 1318. The significance of his campaign was that, like the devastation of England's northern counties, it put pressure on Edward II to recognise Robert as rightful king of Scotland. There was little immediate chance of this and Robert's intransigence in the face of peace-making efforts by the church brought him a papal excommunication in 1320. He was vulnerable enough that year to become subject to an aristocratic conspiracy to assassinate and remove him, which was bloodily avenged on the plotters, itself a sign that King Robert was not sitting comfortably on his throne. The renewal of border warfare in 1322 by the Scots was an opportunistic attempt to take advantage of political instability south of the border, and was as unsuccessful as Edward II's retaliatory campaign. Subsequent talks did not gain Robert recognition, but they did agree a truce of thirteen years from 1323 and restore some peace to the borders.

The last years of the reign of the first King Robert set the agenda for the coming century. Most significant was the formal alliance he entered into with the king of France at Corbeil in 1326. It was a mutual defence pact though, since it obliged the Scots to attack England whenever France went to war with their southern neighbour, it amounted to more than that. The following year brought the deposition of Edward II and the seizure of power by Queen Isabella and Roger Mortimer. Just as in the earlier instability in 1322 it brought an opportunistic Scottish strike south of the border in 1327, ignoring the truce because Bruce argued it was invalidated by Edward II's loss of the throne. Mortimer's attempt to resist the Scots incursion in Northumberland nearly led to tragedy at Stanhope in the Wear valley, when the fourteen-year-old Edward III, taken on campaign by his guardian, was caught up in a night raid on the English camp led by James Douglas. The complications of the situation and the inability of Mortimer to evict the Scots from the north finally brought about the situation King Robert had wanted. The treaty of Edinburgh (ratified in Scotland in March 1328 and at Northampton by the English the following May) recognised Robert to be rightful king of Scotland and his kingdom as wholly independent of English lordship. The terms of the Franco-Scottish alliance of 1326 were not voided by the new bond of amity with England, and the child-heir of Scotland, David, was to marry Joan, Edward III's younger sister. This was a good bargain, for the Scots were obliged to pay £20,000 in return for the match, which might be seen as the restoration of some of what they had extorted from the north by force over several years. But the young Edward was furious at what his contemporaries called a 'shameful peace' and refused to sanction a marriage portion for his sister.

David II (1329–1371) Between France and England

The subsequent death of Robert I in June 1329 at the age of fifty-four did not by any means deprive his reign of its gloss. Though he left a child as heir, he also left a Scotland successfully re-established and re-oriented towards a new and very different century, one which would be dominated by protracted warfare between England and France, not between England and its insular neighbours. The legacy of the Edwardian wars was not yet entirely played out, not least because the young Edward III took personal offence at the way his grandfather's schemes had finally been thwarted. As with the brief minority of Margaret of Norway, the rule of Scotland in 1329 was resigned once more to its magnates on the accession of young David, in a council of guardianship headed by the distinguished warrior and diplomat, Thomas Randolph, earl of Moray, who continued the late king's work in rebuilding the Scottish state. Initially, good relations were continued with the Mortimer regime in England, no better demonstrated than in 1329 when Sir James Douglas was handsomely entertained in London as he carried the embalmed heart of Robert Bruce south in its silver casket on its way to a crusade its original owner had never made. But the fall of Mortimer allowed the teenage Edward III to look for an excuse to renew the wars. Three days after Mortimer's fall, the young king called over from Picardy Edward Balliol, son and heir of the dispossessed king of Scotland, who had died in France in 1314. The English king's sponsorship of Balliol was enough to destabilise a Scotland whose child-king still awaited inauguration at Scone, and several of whose great earls had never fully committed to a Bruce monarchy.

The consecration of the child-king and his queen, as a direct response to the threat posed by Balliol, finally occurred in 1331, employing the new privileges of anointing and coronation conceded to the Scots by the pope. It was while Randolph was taking measures to secure the southern border in July 1332 that he died as a consequence of a long-term illness, probably cancer. The next month Edward Balliol landed in Fife with English support and on 11 August defeated and killed the new guardian, the earl of Mar, at Dupplin Moor, near Perth. The council of guardians nonetheless rallied and was able to expel Balliol and his force from Scotland after their defeat at Annan in December. But by then Edward III had fully revealed his aims, and in a parliament at York had renounced the treaty of 1328, reasserting his grandfather's claim to be overlord of Scotland. In May 1333 the English king himself arrived outside Berwick to assist Balliol's siege of the town. On 19 July the English besiegers were offered battle by a Scottish relief force at Halidon Hill, where it became the first victim of Edward III's new military machine, which inflicted disastrous losses on the Scottish leadership.

A new English occupation of the south and east followed, legitimated by the restoration of a Balliol as king. But the international situation had changed since the days of the Edwardian conquest. The terms of the treaty of Corbeil were activated, and King Philip VI of France declared his support for the boy-king David II. In May 1334, David, now around ten, and his little queen with their tutors and a retinue of noble Scots children took ship for France and successfully made the perilous voyage to Normandy. The exiled Scottish court was established at Richard the Lionheart's great fortress at Château Gaillard on its rock above the Seine, a relic of an earlier Plantagenet empire. Here King David was to grow to manhood while his enemy, the present king of England, shifted his dynastic ambitions from the renewal of his dynasty's British hegemony to the acquisition of the throne of France, which he formally claimed in 1337. Young King David was to ride under the banner of Scotland with the French army that confronted his brother-in-law, Edward III, on the border of Flanders in 1339. At the age of seventeen, in 1341 David II embarked for Scotland on a couple of ships with his retinue and a small number of French knights, to land on the coast of Angus on 2 June ready to take up the rule of his kingdom, which, as far as his French sponsors were concerned, should include fulfilling the terms of the treaty of Corbeil, and attacking the common enemy.

In 1341, despite two major campaigns by Edward III in person, Scotland had evaded the lordship of Edward Balliol, largely due to the doggedness of Bruce loyalists amongst the aristocracy. Balliol himself in 1338 had lost much of his interest in the fight and retired to Northern England, which by 1340 was experiencing once again unrestrained raiding by the Scots. Scottish leadership had passed to the king's nephew, Robert, the steward of Scotland, son of King David's half-sister, Marjorie Bruce. Though he was the king's nephew, Robert was in fact a vigorous young knight of twenty-five when David, still in his teens, returned from France. The interplay between royal uncle and nephew would shape the course of Scottish history for much of the rest of the century.

It was not an easy relationship from the beginning. Robert Stewart had not refrained from using his position to enrich himself and his friends out of royal revenues, as aristocratic lieutenants tended to do, and this was bound to cause tensions with a returning king who had his own priorities. Robert's designs on the earldom of Fife did not ease the tensions. Nonetheless, with Edinburgh recently reclaimed for the king and Stirling under close siege, the steward had a lot to show for his period of rule when the king returned, so it is hardly suprising that the two young men fell into rivalry. Scotland was in fact in a good position to pressurise Edward III to abandon Balliol and his revived claim to the overlordship his father had abandoned, and heavy raids were launched on an England now fully committed to an expensive and prolonged war of succession with the Valois king, a danger that the English themselves recognised. When King David marched south in October 1346 in the biggest raid of all, it was in the aftermath of the great English victory of Crécy, which the young king may have calculated would soon reverse his chances of success if he did not move fast. He may also have calculated that a successful southern campaign would help assert his dominance over the fractious nobility of his kingdom.

The king came south looking for a decisive battle with the defenders of the North of England. He came in force also, deploying the combined military retinues of the nobility of the south and west of Scotland. The Scots marched through Cumberland across the Pennine spine to the city of Durham, where David encamped and demanded a large sum in protection money. Here on 17 October at a place called Neville's Cross the king was surprised by a sizeable English force that he had probably not counted on meeting. The English archers proved as decisive there as they had been at Crécy some weeks earlier, and indeed at their hands King David experienced a face wound through his visor similar to the one King Philip VI had suffered at Crécy. Robert Stewart's division began to retreat as the king's attack faltered, and in the subsequent massacre six Scottish earls died, while King David was captured as his household was cut down around him and he was wrestled to the ground by a Northumbrian squire, whose teeth he punched out with his armoured gauntlet. The king entered into his long captivity in the Tower

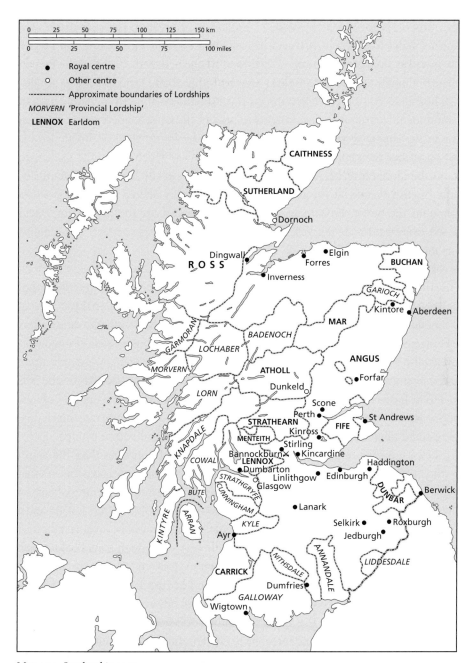

Map 12.1 Scotland in 1340

of London, and Robert Stewart regained the power his uncle refused to share with him, validating his own acts as guardian with the imprisoned king's great seal.

There was no hurry to pay the inevitable ransom that Edward III would demand for David's release, which was not to occur until 1357. It was a long negotiation, including at times proposals for the acceptance of English overlordship, the succession of a Plantagenet cadet to Scotland if David proved childless, and the retention of border castles, as well as a payment of money. David was not helped by the fact that the French were happy enough to deal with Robert Stewart rather than David as long as Anglo-Scottish hostilities continued. When in 1351–1352 David was allowed on parole back to Scotland under a guard of English knights to present the latest English terms, his own nobility in Parliament were supposed by one (English) source to have threatened his deposition, rather than compromise their independence, which (since the same idea occurs in the Declaration of Arbroath) is likely to have really happened. Eventually, after the English victory at Poitiers in 1356 had radically altered Edward's position in France for the better, Edward was willing to settle just for the money for David (£66,666) to be paid over ten years, not even insisting on his overlordship. English support for Edward Balliol was finally abandoned.

The ebbing of warfare in France had a tidal effect on Anglo-Scottish relations, not least since the treaty of Berwick committed Scotland to a 27-year truce. With King John II of France now incarcerated in London, where he and David II were occasionally to meet at social functions and (presumably) commiserate with each other, the aggravating effect of the Franco-Scottish alliance was lessened. Edward III's government even seemed willing to establish something like normalised relations: Scottish students were once more permitted to study at English universities, trade resumed and the Scottish pound was restored to its former parity with English sterling. It was, after all, in the English interest for the Scottish economy to prosper, as it would help fund King David's ransom.

The restored king was still only thirty-four, and he returned with a grudge against Robert Stewart, but he had also returned a more practised politician than the angry youth who had been captured at Neville's Cross, and his first priority was the same as that of his own people, some sort of normalisation of governance and a lessening of faction in politics. The balance between the king and Stewart was now in the king's favour, and a brief rebellion by Robert in 1363 was decisively met, to be followed by an abject Stewart submission to the king. War with England was not renewed, though David held out an offer to the French that he might do so if they paid off his ransom. The ransom itself was the chief problem of the second reign of David II, and in 1360 he simply stopped payments. This led to renewed negotiations, which David and Edward conducted face to face in 1363, involving a promise of the succession of one of Edward's sons to Scotland after David, but guaranteeing its full independence. Edward did rather cannily add the two-edged inducement of the restoration of the king of Scotland's former estates in England, which would have made the king his subject by another route. The Scottish Parliament rejected the offer decisively. Eventually Edward settled for annual payments of £4,000, about half the Scottish king's annual normal revenue, and reduced it further to 4,000 marks (£2,667) in 1369, in return for a continuing truce as the war with France flared up again. Even after David's death in 1371, the payments continued until 1377.

The Stewart Succession

King David's failure to produce offspring of any sex, legitimate or illegitimate, was already a major factor in Anglo-Scottish relations in the 1350s. Queen Joan had left him in 1358 to spend the rest of her life in retirement in England, as a guest of her brother. David's open infidelity in his English captivity is assumed to be the reason for their alienation. His second marriage in 1363 to Margaret Drummond, who had already produced a son for her first husband, was clearly as much for dynastic calculation as for love. This union too proved childless and David divorced her in 1369, despite her energetic resistance to being cast off. The obvious heir now was Robert Stewart, and before the end of his reign David II appears to have accepted this weary fact, despite contemplating a third marriage with a member of the Dunbar family. David's sudden death early in 1371 was followed by an uneasy hiatus marked by hostility between the Stewart and Douglas factions in his nobility, until Robert bought off Earl William Douglas with offices, a pension and a marriage which assured his ascendancy in Lothian. Robert II was crowned first Stewart king of Scotland at Scone on 26 March 1371. A major carve-up of the kingdom promptly followed between the new king and the Douglases, with the many Stewart legitimate and illegitimate offspring and cousins being awarded any available title and estate that came to his hand, a process which has been called the 'Stewartisation' of the Scottish aristocracy.

The reigns of Robert II (1371–1390) and his son Robert III (1390–1406) can be seen as something of a watershed in Scottish history. The actions of Robert II to ensure his succession dictated Scottish politics of the rest of the medieval period, while the historical propaganda he sponsored so as to legitimise his rule constructed Scottish national identity on the foundation of its antagonism to all things English. The new king gave his eldest son John (the future King Robert III) the Bruce domain of Carrick, and another son Robert (the future duke of Albany) gained a broad swathe of the centre of Scotland, including Fife, Menteith and the south-west Highlands, while another, Alexander of Badenoch, had Buchan and dominance in the north-east and central Highlands. This carve-up might well have given a powerful underpinning to the rule of the first Stewart king but, just like Edward III's lavish endowment of his several sons, it carried the seeds of instability in the next generation. Robert II's measures appear nonetheless to have unified Scotland to a more marked degree than the previous reign had. The Stewart heartland in the south-west was brought into closer contact with the monarchy than it had been before. The new reign also promoted a vernacular history of Scotland, which took as its title deeds the heroic resistance of the Bruce, Robert II's namesake and grandfather, to the Edwardian invasion, along with his faithful friends Walter Stewart and James Douglas (see pp. 299–300). It was a national unifying myth that served the Stewarts well, but could only consolidate the Anglophobia of the Scottish political community.

It was a myth designed to cement the legitimacy of Stewart kingship, going so far as to trace King Robert II's lineage back to the age of Brutus of Troy.

For all the bellicose propaganda associated with the new dynasty, Robert II had little intention of renewing the war with England, and the treaty he reached with the French after his succession excluded any action until the current truce ended in 1384 while he refused an opportunistic French offer to intercede with the pope to void its terms. He kept up payments of his predecessor's ransom until Edward III died. The Scots got away with border raiding at this time of English political weakness, and reclaimed much of what little of Lowland Scotland the English still held on to. It was the expiration of the truce that ended what had been until then a stable and prosperous reign. It coincided with the death of the earl of Douglas, and allowed a new generation of magnates, headed by the ageing king's son John, earl of Carrick, to bid for power; the new earl of Douglas was particularly eager to press his own agenda. Robert II also came under French pressure to renew the border war, which led to a French expeditionary force arriving in Lothian in 1385, and combining in a joint Franco-Scottish campaign which penetrated the North of England, though the French and Scots fell out over strategy and it accomplished little other than forcing a new truce. Political turmoil in England in 1387–1388 invited a renewal of war, however, and it inspired a coup against Robert II by his own son John, in alliance with Earl James Douglas. Though the subsequent campaign led to the Scots victory at Otterburn in August 1388, the death of James Douglas led to a counter-coup, when the king's second son Robert now seized power as guardian, a position of real power he was able to maintain even after the death of Robert II in 1390 and the succession of his elder brother John as King Robert III.

The Lieutenancy and Governorship of Robert Stewart of Albany, 1388–1420

The guardianship of Scotland under Robert Stewart, earl of Fife and from 1398 duke of Albany, is an instructive example of the difference between the dynastic politics of the Scottish and English royal houses. King Robert III was, for whatever reason, incapable of commanding the support of the political community. The mental and physical consequences of a bad fall from a horse at the end of 1388 are cited as the major factor in his incapacity as king. Yet there was never a serious move to pass him over for the succession in 1390. The new reign was not perhaps an unrelieved failure, but an ailing and ineffective king was a medieval literary commonplace for a very good reason. Such kings compromised their realm's prosperity and fortunes, and Scotland for a while had its own Fisher King. Yet in some respects the reign had its successes. In 1389 a stable truce was negotiated with England which was to last for over a decade, and there was for some time in Richard II's reign a degree of friendly interaction between the

Scottish and English courts to an extent unknown since the death of Alexander III. This rapprochement coincided with the period between 1393 and 1399 when King Robert ruled without the official constraint of an appointed guardian, so the king himself may take some credit for it, as much as improved political and economic circumstances. Guardianship for that matter did not necessarily weaken Scottish kingship. It might be taken as demonstrating a high idea in Scotland of the place of the community of the realm in promoting national unity in co-operation with an infirm king.

After 1399 King Robert's worsening health led to his retirement to his dynasty's ancestral estates on the Isle of Bute, while direction of affairs as lieutenant fell between his eldest son David, duke of Rothesay, and his uncle Albany. There followed a violent period, with Henry IV marching into Scotland in 1400 as far as Edinburgh, the last English king to lead an army north of the Tweed in person. Duke David's ineffective rule led to the inevitable coup against him by his uncle in 1402, and the young prince of Scotland subsequently died in prison at Falkland, most likely through dysentry, though some assumed otherwise. Albany replaced his late nephew as lieutenant of Scotland with the support of Parliament and was still in that office when Robert III died in 1406.

An unfortunate series of events occurred before the king's death. In his last violent years, with war going on between England and Scotland, there was factional conflict in Lothian between the Black Douglases and David Fleming, the tutor of the boy James of Carrick, Robert III's heir. So Prince James was placed on a Hanseatic vessel anchored off Leith rather than fall into Douglas hands. Then, with perhaps some memory of the exile of the young David II, James's tutor took sail with his young charge for France. Unfortunately, the ship was taken by pirates off Flamborough head, and the heir to Scotland was traded with Henry IV of England into captivity. Henry sardonically observed that he could teach young James French quite as well as Charles VI. Robert III died not long after the news of his son's capture reached him in Rothesay Castle.

The new King James was proclaimed in due form, but would spend the first eighteen years of his reign in captivity in England. Scotland remained under the rule of his uncle Albany, acting with the consent of the Scottish estates. The duke chose to rule in his own name and to issue acts under his own seal. This was not, however, because of his arrogance and personal designs on the crown; it simply was a consequence of the fact that the captive boy-king whose regent he was had never been crowned or anointed and had no great seal. Albany's English policy was dictated by the consequences of the war he had picked with Henry IV in 1400, which culminated in the disaster of the battle of Homildon Hill (1402) when a raiding Scottish army was intercepted by the earl of Northumberland and the rebel Scottish earl of March and massacred by expert English bowmen; eighty-two Scottish nobles were killed or captured (including Albany's own son, Murdoch). It marked the end of large-scale Scottish military enterprises against England, but more fortunately it also disenchanted the new Lancastrian monarchy with the prospects of any decisive campaign in Scotland. Henry IV hung on to the captives, which with the custody of the boy-king James gave him a decisive diplomatic hold over Albany, whose son also remained in English captivity until 1416. Both young men were held together in uncomfortable quarters in the Tower of London from 1413 to 1415. The situation meant that Albany's title to govern Scotland could always be contested by the king's English captors.

Anglo-Scottish relations in the early Lancastrian period revolved around the perpetual negotiation for James's (and Murdoch's) release, and the king proved a useful counter for the English at times. James was hauled off to France with the English army by Henry V in 1420, and his presence there was the pretext for the execution of Scottish soldiers serving with the French at Melun. Henry also used his control of James as a way of destabilising the relationship of the papacy with the Scottish Church. Within Scotland, Albany was left attempting to keep a precarious balance between the powerful aristocratic affinities which dominated the kingdom. In this he deployed forfeitures, marriage alliances and promises to some good effect, though there were times when only military action was left, as in the conflict with Donald MacDonald, lord of the Isles, over his claim on the earldoms of Buchan and Ross, which led to a bloody reverse at Harlaw (1411) at the hands of the governor's nephew, Alexander Stewart, earl of Mar, and Donald's forced submission to Albany's authority the next year. Perhaps the best testimony to Albany's effectiveness is the way the political community fell apart on his death in 1420.

James I to James IV: Late Medieval Scotland, 1424–1513

King James I re-entered Scotland at the beginning of April 1424, after prolonged negotiations which eventually agreed to his release in return for an 'expenses' payment of £40,000 and a marriage to Joan Beaufort, a granddaughter of John of Gaunt. There had been no urgency on the part of Duke Murdoch of Albany, his cousin and former fellow inmate at the Tower, to secure his release. The urgency was all on the part of Henry VI of England's regency, which wanted to negotiate a long-term settlement with the Scots and which found an ally in the earl of Douglas, Albany's rival for power. Once returned and secure on the throne, James in March 1425 had Duke Murdoch and several of his close relatives arrested. The duke was tried and beheaded after a state trial before Parliament, something not seen in Scotland since the days of Robert I, though familiar enough in England, where James learned something of the dark side of statecraft. Duke Murdoch and his allies had in fact been increasingly marginalised from the summer of 1424. He was possibly arrested initially in order to be shipped to England as a hostage for the king's ransom, but his son's immediate and unsuccessful rebellion on his father's arrest doomed the family. The king had enough reasons – between the corruption of the two Albany governors and suspicions about their complicity in his elder brother's death – to want Murdoch dead. More surprising is the willingness of the rest of the nobility to go along with such a drastic measure, but the monopoly of power the two Albany dukes had enjoyed for more than two decades was perhaps reason enough: plenitude of power was the property only of kings.

James's subsequent rule may have given his aristocracy reason to regret its willing-ness to go along with him in 1425. Everywhere royal ambition to control encroached on the magnates, even on the earls of Douglas and March who had been James's early allies. March was arrested and dispossessed by legal chicanery in 1435, thus bringing to an end a lineage that had exercised power on the Borders for nearly five centuries. James's successes reached their peak in 1429. The previous year he had rounded up the most troublesome Gaelic kindreds and their leaders as they came to a council at Inverness. This was a challenge to Alexander MacDonald, lord of the Isles, who was the overlord of many of these 'reivers' and who was agitating for the consolidation of his mainland power by the recognition of his right to the earldom of Ross. MacDonald was taken prisoner along with his men and like most of them released after making submission to royal authority. But, under increasing pressure and forced into a corner, MacDonald chose to take a stand or lose all credibility. His rebellion in 1429 was met by the rapid assembly of an overwhelming royal force and, at Badenoch on 23 June, the army of the Isles was dispersed and Alexander MacDonald captured. The power of the lord of the Isles had suffered a reverse and it took until the 1440s to recover. Five decades of royal weakness in Scotland was thus erased by a masterly act of royal devi-ousness, courage and determination. The new masculine energy of the Stewarts was underlined by a deliberate campaign of spending and building, with the construction of a new unfortified palace at Linlithgow, west of Edinburgh, to echo in a smaller way the show-place of monarchy built at Sheen on the Thames upriver from London by James's royal mentor, Henry V of England.

Subsequent Scottish history was dictated by this resurgence in Stewart royal power in the 1420s, of which James I was the architect. For all that the four Jameses of the fifteenth century came to rather unfortunate and premature ends, their monarchy was never compromised and disputed as was that of contemporary England, and it is per-haps not surprising as a result that it was in Scotland rather than England that the idea of imperial kingship was first publicly mooted in Britain as the justification for royal ascendancy over the political community, rather than as a partner in dialogue with it. Increased Stewart power did not trigger any serious Anglo-Scottish warfare. Though James I renewed the alliance with France in 1428, it was a ruse to allow him to suspend payments of his ransom to England. He did not carry out his undertakings to despatch a Scottish army to the assistance of Charles VII, who found it elsewhere, in Joan of Arc, a woman who made some cutting comments on the subject of the reliability of the Scots. James preferred quiet on the frontier and in the North Sea, as he depended on customs revenue from the wool trade with England's ally, Burgundy.

It was only when the Anglo-Burgundian alliance that sustained Lancastrian claims on France collapsed that James commenced hostilities. It had been better had he not tried to be quite so clever. An all-out Scottish bid to recover Roxburgh in August 1436 led to a humiliating rout in which James lost his artillery train, whose expense and possession was by those times an expression of royal prestige. By this date, general Scottish opinion was that their king in his undependability, suspicion and greed was 'nothing other than a tyrannous prince'.[1] The spectacular assassination that followed within eight months was a consequence of his failure before Roxburgh. He had sufficiently offended and alarmed enough of his nobility, and particularly his uncle Walter Stewart, earl of Atholl, that the king's weakened position made him vulnerable. James's failure before Roxburgh had already led to a refusal by Parliament to grant taxes to pursue the war against England and an abortive attempt by one of the chamber to arrest him (by his eventual assassin) for breaking the terms of his coronation oath, the traditional way to attack a king's legitimacy. In 1437 the earl of Atholl decided to go further and conspire to regicide. A band of assassins broke into the king's crowded chamber at the Blackfriars at Perth just after midnight on 20–21 February, cornered him and stabbed him to death in full sight of the queen and their household.

James II's minority was a different order to that of his father. James I had come to adulthood outside his own realm as an English prisoner, while his son endured a minority at the mercy of his own subjects, to whom he was inevitably a pawn. James II was a younger twin, his elder brother Alexander having failed to survive infancy. He was seven years of age when his father was murdered, and he was crowned within days of the assassination, while his father's murderers were still being hunted down. A powerful lieutenancy led by Earl Archibald Douglas was soon agreed amongst the parliamentary peers, while the king was confided to his mother's care. Unfortunately this promising arrangement collapsed at Douglas's death in 1439, leading to a prolonged period of insecurity as the queen, her second husband and household officers competed to control the boy-king, and the Douglas family itself fell into internecine conflict. The great territorial earldoms that had once dominated the Scottish aristocracy had for the most part fallen, and with Earl Archibald's death there was no other such figure available to offer ersatz kingship in the person of a lieutenant or governor of Scotland; Archibald's heir was only a teenager. Until the king's majority, the chief influence on Scotland's government was thereafter the Livingstone family, who had control of the kingdom's bureaucracy, which was by now sufficiently developed to be an effective power base. It was the king's marriage in 1448 and the subsequent fall of the Livingstones in a governmental coup that heralded James II's assumption of full power.

The ascendancy of the earls of Douglas had slowly reasserted itself during the minority, and the queen's death in 1445 removed its only impediment. As the king emerged into adulthood he had little choice but to rely on the earl's power, to the extent that he felt obliged to attempt a coup against Earl William Douglas's castles and affinity in the earl's absence on a pilgrimage to Rome in 1450. The difficulty was smoothed over, but the king's suspicions of the earl gathered, especially as there was evidence of his treasonable alliance with the lord of the Isles and others. In February 1452, the 22-year-old king stabbed Earl William in Stirling Castle in the course of a heated personal encounter, the earl falling to the floor to be finished off by the king's associates. The new earl of Douglas and his affinity had little choice in their response, and a formal letter of defiance was nailed to the door of the Parliament at Edinburgh in June 1452. Though himself exonerated by Parliament of any evil intent in the deed, the king had in the end to get the new Earl James to submit and forgive the participants, which was done in August. But no real peace was secured. The settlement had to be rearranged the next year in the face of further tensions and, eventually, in March 1455 full-scale warfare broke out between Earl James and the king in the Lowlands, during which the Douglas castles were seized and the earl fled to England. There he lived on for decades thereafter as a dispossessed English pawn and pensioner.

James II's personal war on the Black Douglases was an extraordinary episode in European kingship, and not comparable with the contemporary problems of Henry VI of England with his own aristocracy. James was dramatically raising the stakes in the exercise of strong and aggressive kingship, while Henry VI was weakly floundering in a morass of incompetence. It was the king of Scotland's extra-legal use of force which was so striking, even though he used Parliament to retrospectively validate his high-handed and brutal actions. The theory of kingship up to that time had hinged on the fulfilment of the king's contract of his coronation oath and his rule in accord with the will of the community. James II was raising his will above law in a way that King John of England had done centuries before. But, unlike John, he did so despite the existence of a body which represented the will of his realm, and yet still did not suffer the penalty of its censure. In part that might be because the territorial power of the Douglases in fifteenth-century Scotland was perceived generally to be a dangerous relic of the past, just as the Albanys had been before the fall of Duke Murdoch. It was the tyranny of the earl rather than the king that the Parliament may have feared in the 1450s. Once eliminated, there was no noble connection left to rival the capacity the earl of Douglas once had to destabilise the kingdom.

The defeat of the Black Douglas affinity allowed the king to restructure the Scottish aristocracy in a sustained series of acts of patronage, which created new earldoms for his close followers from amongst Scotland's upper gentry and for his youngest son John. His second son Alexander was given the revived dukedom of Albany. The other branch of the Douglas family (headed by the rather less powerful 'Red Douglas' earl of Angus) was favoured so as to block any revival of their cousin's dangerous affinity. A further source of stability in the reign was the way the king's numerous sisters could be deployed in strategic marriages across Europe in France, Brittany, Germany and Austria, liaisons which both exalted and strengthened Stewart kingship. James exerted himself on a wider theatre than the British Isles, negotiating with Denmark about the future of Orkney and with France about the succession to Brittany. Within Britain, it was the continued English occupation of Berwick and Roxburgh that engaged him. The collapse of England into civil war in 1460 was a golden opportunity for James II to wipe out his father's humiliation of 1437. Siding with the Yorkist faction, he moved his army and artillery train to the siege of Roxburgh in August 1460, and it was when one of the pieces was primed to salute the arrival of the queen at the siege on 3 August that the gun barrel exploded and its shrapnel ripped into the body of James, who was standing close by, wounding him mortally.

The new king James III was only eight at his father's unexpected death, so for a third time in the fifteenth century Scotland had to endure a long period when others had to shoulder the rule of the kingdom while the king was unable to exert his rule in person. James III's reign began with the more traditional regency of his mother, Queen Mary of Gueldres, whose regency, though brief (she died at the end of 1463), was singularly accomplished. She was luckily able to exploit the weakness of the new Yorkist regime, and indeed supported a Lancastrian insurgency in Northumberland, where the dethroned Henry VI was more or less her puppet at Bamburgh Castle. Queen Mary was thus able to manipulate the factions in the ongoing English dynastic civil war to recover Berwick bloodlessly.

The boy-king James III passed after his mother's death into the control of successive aristocratic factions, the Kennedys and the Boyds, though without bloodshed being involved. The support of Parliament was ranged behind his successive guardians. The guardianship of Robert Boyd achieved the remarkable feat that had eluded the Scottish kings for centuries: the acquisition of Orkney and Shetlands from Denmark, as the dowry of the young James's marriage with Margaret, daughter of King Christian I in 1469. By that time Boyd was in exile, having deeply offended the young king by an act of temerity in marrying his eldest son to James's sister. In some ways, therefore, the transition between the reigns of James II and James III was seamless, despite the king's minority. As the new reign developed, James III also continued his predecessors' policy of avoiding any sustained conflict with England. Since all the ancient kingdom of Scotland south to the Tweed was now in his hands, he had little cause for war in any case. In 1474 he abandoned the alliance with France and arranged a marriage treaty between his son and heir and a daughter of Edward IV of England. This did, however, have the consequence of losing James the leverage in Europe that alliance with France had given Scotland. So the French alliance was renewed in 1484 after an outbreak of Anglo-Scottish hostilities had demonstrated the dangers of James's international isolation to his position in Britain.

James III was the least successful of the fifteenth-century Stewart kings, and for the usual reason: a personality incompatible with the even-handed exercise of power. He was a king like John of England, who found security in amassing treasure, with a lack of scruple in how he did it. He harried Parliament for extraordinary taxation, which won him no friends, and took the unwise option of deliberately debasing the currency (to produce the well-named 'black money'), which badly affected Scottish trade, even if it secured the king large profits in silver. His selling of pardons for serious crimes was a flagrant breach of contemporary expectations of what a just king was, and it was condemned in his own Parliament. His greed made him diffident about rewarding even his professed supporters and offended contemporary ideas about good lordship. James had a controlling personality, which came out in his statements about the 'imperial' (that is, untrammelled) nature of his royal authority, and in his moves to centralise power and justice for the first time in Scottish history on the rising town of Edinburgh, the largest city in Scotland, with approaching 12,000 inhabitants. To complete the parade of classic kingly faults, James trusted low-born counsellors over his own nobles.

James's personality was resentful and suspicious, and with a new crop of close Stewart siblings, uncles and cousins, he had a lot of relatives to suspect. Internal conflict focused on his two younger brothers, Alexander Stewart, duke of Albany, and John earl of Mar. He fell out with the duke over alleged differences concerning the king's pro-English policy, and the king's dramatic and ill-judged response was an attack on Albany's headquarters in the Border March at Dunbar. Albany fled to France, and his flight was followed by the arrest and subsequent suspicious death of Mar, of which common opinion convicted the king. Opposition grew to James, and Parliament significantly refused to forfeit Albany's estates at his request. In 1482, the king summoned an army to resist an imminent invasion by Albany, in alliance with the English; his brother by then certainly exploring the idea of taking the crown from James as 'King Alexander IV'. The king was arrested by his own men and imprisoned at Edinburgh while Albany was left to make what he could of the situation by his English allies, who benefited by the re-taking of Berwick.

The remainder of the reign was an unsatisfactory standoff, with sufficient northern nobles willing to sponsor the return of James III to power, and Albany unable to find enough support to assume the role of governor of Scotland which the first duke of his name had occupied in the reigns of Robert II and Robert III. Eventually, after the death of his ally Edward IV of England in 1483 removed his protection, Albany was driven abroad and after a fruitless bid to invade Scotland in alliance with the dispossessed earl of Douglas, died an exile in France in 1485. Despite that, the king did not succeed in fully re-establishing his authority, and indeed a personal and deadly rift opened up between himself, and his influential wife and their son. A rebellion against his authority by the Hume affinity in the March became ever more dangerous as the king alienated even his own supporters by refusing negotiation and resorting to force. Significantly perhaps, the trigger was James's characteristic declaration that resistance to his expressed royal will was in itself an act of treason. Carried to its conclusion, such a position would have denied the political community any voice in the conduct of the realm's affairs. It was as much as to invite regicide. In the early summer of 1488 James campaigned west of Edinburgh and deliberately sought battle with the rebels near the field of Bannockburn, carrying with him Robert Bruce's sword, to make the point. But his army collapsed and, at a place called Sauchieburn, the king was cornered and killed by magnates in alliance with his own son, now King James IV.

Stewarts and Tudors

The teenage King James IV came to the throne in the shadow of his father's assassination, an act in which many believed him complicit, probably correctly. That his subsequent reign transcended its gloomy start is a testimony to the young king's intellectual energy and abilities, which were quite possibly the most brilliant of any medieval king who ruled in the British Isles, exceeding that of his grandfather, himself a man of no mean talents. James's many gifts, artistic and musical, and his intellectual curiosity made him fit to compare with other great princes of his day, not least his brother-in-law, Henry VIII of England. In many ways it was his relationship with the parvenu Tudor dynasty to the south that has defined him in the eyes of posterity, but there was more to him than that. James wanted to act on a European stage and took measures that would give him more weight amongst his fellow princes, as was demonstrated by his military intervention in a civil war in his mother's homeland of Denmark in 1501–1502 (see Fig. 12.1).

The construction of a large Scottish navy was James's most striking move. It gave him the ability to project Scottish royal power beyond the Atlantic rim where the dark galleys of the Islesmen had previously operated mostly on their own account. The English time and again raided along the coast of Lothian whenever the two nations were in conflict, which presented another reason to invest in large ships as a counter-measure. But, like the royal artillery train, the financing and building of great warships had become in the later fifteenth century an expression of the monarchical state, as Henry VIII would demonstrate for England in his day. At the very least it made possible the suppression of the piracy that had plagued the North Sea for over a century, and indeed had been responsible for King James I's English captivity. James was to deploy his fleet against England in the North Sea in 1513 in a new variation on the way that Scots had supported their French allies. James's ambitious gunships, the *Margaret* and the *Michael*, were comparable in their day with the *Mary Rose*, and indeed Henry VIII's programme of naval construction followed in the wake of James's. It was in fact James IV who was the British king in 1500 whose rule and personal conduct had passed beyond medieval ideas of rulership and majesty, not Henry VII of England.

James took until 1492 to master the instability caused by his father's assassination. It was the same year that the French and English concluded the latest outburst of warfare, which had been going on since Louis XI's meddling in the Lancastrian and Yorkist

Fig. 12.1 Portrait of James IV. Like any great Renaissance prince, King James IV was the subject of state portraiture; this late fifteenth-century image now in the National Gallery of Scotland was painted in Scotland by an unknown artist.

confrontation of 1470–1471. The consequence was an Anglo-Scottish truce reached in 1493, though the truce was fragile. James was happy to exploit the last tremors of the War of the Roses in England, and notoriously accepted as legitimate the pretender Perkin Warbeck in his masquerade as the murdered Richard, younger son of Edward IV. This was followed by active raiding into the North of England in which James acquired military stature, though little in the way of concrete results. His wider ambitions resulted in Scottish intervention in 1501 in the conflict that had challenged his uncle, King Hans of Denmark, in his control of Sweden. The Scottish force did not cover itself with glory, but the very ambition in sending it signalled Scotland's rise to a new level of European importance, beyond its earlier place as a fitfully reliable French auxiliary. In 1502 this was consummated by Henry VII's willingness to include marriage with his thirteen-year-old daughter Margaret in the negotiations for peace between the two kingdoms, a union celebrated with unheard-of magnificence at Edinburgh the next year. The marriage was highly successful on a personal level, though it did not secure the 'perpetual peace' which was the name the diplomats had settled on for it. The fact that Margaret Tudor's Stewart great-grandson was to succeed to England and so unite Britain into a new realm was not even dreamed of in 1502, but that was nonetheless the result of the treaty, one of the last of the attempts to deal with the wholly medieval rivalry between nations so unwisely entered on by Edward I, the English king who attempted to make real the idea of Britain as a greater England.

POSTSCRIPT

James IV of Scotland is the fit and proper person to ring down the curtain on medieval Britain, rather than his Tudor counterpart, Henry VII. He was a charismatic man with a remarkable world view, whose appreciation of his great office owed more to the Roman tradition of imperial monarchy than to the ancient consensual tradition of British kingship. His mind was cultivated in the scholarship of humanism which – amongst other things – found congenial new expressions of projecting military and naval power and expressing dynastic prestige. It was the irony of James IV's career that he was to die in Northumberland in 1513, the last British king to fall on a battlefield, on the sort of invasion in support of his French ally pioneered by his medieval predecessors.

KEY TEXTS

Grant, A. *Independence and Nationhood: Scotland, 1306–1469* (Edinburgh University Press, 1984), a level-headed and comprehensive assessment of Scottish politics in the Bruce and early Stewart era. • *Scottish Kingship, 1306–1542: Essays in Honour of Norman Macdougall*, ed. M. Brown and R. Tanner (John Donald, 2008), the most comprehensive treatment of Scottish monarchy during the period, organised on a reign-by-reign basis.

FURTHER READING

Boardman, S. I. *The Early Stewart Kings: Robert II and Robert III, 1371–1406* (John Donald, 1996). • Brown, M. *The Black Douglases: War and Lordship in Late Medieval Scotland, 1300–1455* (Tuckwell, 1998). • Brown, M. *James I* (John Donald, 1994). • *England and Scotland in the Fourteenth Century: New Perspectives*, ed. A. King and M. Penman (Boydell, 2007). • Macdougall, N. *James III* (John Donald, 2009). • Macdougall, N. *James IV* (3rd edn, John Donald, 2006). • McGladdery, C. *James II* (John Donald, 1990). • Penman, M. *David II, 1329–1371* (John Donald, 2004). • Penman, M. *Robert the Bruce* (Yale University Press, 2014).

NOTE

1. John Shirley, *The Life and Death of King James the First of Scotland* (Maitland Club, Glasgow, 1837), 49.

13 Dynastic Struggles, 1327–1485

OVERVIEW

The history of England in the fourteenth and fifteenth centuries is dominated by the demands and burdens of the dynastic war for the crown of France between Plantagenets and Valois. During the course of it, and because of it, the Plantagenet dynasty itself collapsed into internecine warfare amongst the grandchildren of Edward III. The result was a debilitated political system which only a king of the capacities of Henry V could transcend, and which destroyed several of its possessors.

The Mortimer Regime, 1327–1330

The period between the coup which established Edward III on the throne and the young king's own coup which brought Mortimer down is a curious one, with no parallels in English history before this date, though it was to have several parallels in fifteenth-century Scottish history. Roger Mortimer was not a regent governing with the consent of the magnate interest, as had been William Marshal and Hubert de Burgh between 1216 and 1227. Nor was he much like Simon de Montfort, who saw himself as the leader of a reform movement which again depended on the community for its authority. Roger Mortimer had been associated with the Ordainers and a follower of Earl Thomas of Lancaster, and in the winter of 1325–6 as an exiled dissident from England he had gravitated to the court of the refugee Queen Isabel. What gave him authority was not ideology but his sexual liaison with the queen and control of her son, the young Edward. When Mortimer escorted the queen back to England and rode the wave of popular hatred of the Despensers to engineer the downfall of Edward II, he did so as Isabel's captain. Following the deposition of Edward II, it was still his personal closeness to the queen and her son, the new king, which gave him authority. For the queen saw no reason why she should not, like the great Blanche of Castile, her ancestor in mid thirteenth-century France, govern her son and the realm until Edward was of full age. Mortimer was given no office of state, but it was soon clear that he was always at her elbow and that his was the voice she listened to: the queen ruled, but Mortimer reigned, as a contemporary chronicler put it. The young king was a closely supervised and increasingly resentful cipher. The wonder is how Mortimer thought he could get away with his coup in the long term.

The new regime sought a prompt and realistic (but unpopular) peace with France over the status of the Plantagenet duchy of Aquitaine. It accepted losses of land and major reparations payable to the French. This had a lot to do with the continuing fall-out from the failed Edwardian conquest of Scotland. Edward III was taken north by Mortimer to campaign unsuccessfully against James Douglas's army, which nearly led to the boy's capture in a raid on the English camp. The lack of military success there worsened the regime's unpopularity. The news of the death of the former king Edward II in 1327 did not help; Mortimer and the queen were generally thought to blame for an assassination. The marriage of the boy-king to Philippa of Hainaut at the beginning of 1328 was in itself a challenge to Queen Isabel, who (like Blanche of Castile) did her best to diminish the standing of the new queen consort in her son's bed, a sign perhaps of her growing realisation of her insecurity as regent. When the queen's regime embraced the bitter necessity of accepting the legitimacy of Robert Bruce as independent king of Scotland and the marriage of her daughter Joan to the young heir David, the alienation from her son was complete. He steadfastly refused to offer any dower to his sister.

In the meantime he had to endure the increasingly offensive posturing of Mortimer at court, and his self-aggrandisement in the March of Wales. In 1328 Mortimer invented for himself an earldom with that very title. As the political community began to take more offence at him, Mortimer's precarious dependency on Isabel became as clear as the queen's own weakness. Rising discontent caused the great earls, Norfolk, Kent and Lancaster, to do at the end of 1328 what dissident English earls usually did: take a stand on Magna Carta and allege that Mortimer was leading the young king astray from the path of righteousness in the conduct of the realm.

Mortimer had nerve if little else and, having identified Henry of Lancaster (younger brother of the executed Thomas) as his principal opponent, he faced him down in arms with the king beside him at Bedford in January 1329. But by imposing the costs he had incurred in the military parade on Edward, he further humiliated the already resentful adolescent king. It became more and more apparent that Edward had little control over his own government and that Mortimer had secured full power, peopling the king's household with his own trusted agents. A reaction was inevitable, and Edward began plotting, perhaps even in fear that Mortimer might take things to their unpleasant conclusion in his lust for power, and murder the king.

In November 1329, Edward was seventeen years of age and about to become a father. His mother nonetheless showed no desire to relinquish her control, even though her daughter-in-law, Philippa of Hainaut, was now crowned queen. This uncertainty may explain Mortimer's sudden strike against the king's uncle, the earl of Kent, who was arrested for the treasonous fostering of the belief that the king's father was alive and still the rightful king. The earl was tried and summarily executed at Mortimer's own initiative, a sign of increasing desperation on his part. By this time people were willing to countenance any rumour, such as the particularly poisonous one that Mortimer had got Queen Isabel pregnant, and was plotting to put his own child by her on the throne. In October 1330 at Nottingham Castle, a gang of friends assembled by the king were smuggled through the fortifications; they arrested Mortimer in the queen's chamber. With a little more consideration for due process than Mortimer had afforded the earl of Kent, he was taken to London and tried before Parliament in November, then summarily hanged as a felon at Tyburn.

The Claim to France

Warfare is the theme of the long reign of Edward III (1327–1377), for as it was to his mind the chief business of kings it was a condition he was entirely comfortable with. His eagerness for military action was evident before the fall of Mortimer, for he was already then keen to resurrect his grandfather's policy for Plantagenet domination of Britain and expunge the disgrace of Robert Bruce's victories. Like his grandfather,

Edward proved to be from the first a king who very much lived up to his nobility's expectations of martial leadership. But he was further blessed with an unassailable self-belief, personal attractiveness and a cheerful and courtly demeanour that rapidly brought his associates to venerate him. His choice of capable and loyal military lieu-tenants was rarely at fault, and luck favoured him with a broad field of talent to select from in his day. Like Edward I, he valued Parliament as a stage for the enactment of his kingship, and was genuinely accessible to its concerns. In most respects, therefore, Edward was the pattern of a courtly king, and his conjunction of talents arguably made him the most formidable English king of the middle ages.

Edward's determination to pursue his dynastic claims also made him the most dangerous king his neighbours ever had to face, and not just the Scots. During the Mortimer years his uncle, Charles IV of France, had died, and for the first time in well over three hundred years a Capetian king had no male heir in the person of a son or brother. Charles's wife was pregnant at his death, but the child delivered was short-lived, and so the regent of France, the king's first cousin, the count of Valois, took the throne as King Philip VI, overriding any claim Edward of England had to France as the eldest of the surviving grandsons of King Philip IV (died 1314). The French nobility cer-tainly would not have supported an English candidacy at the time, but nonetheless in May 1328 an embassy was sent to register Edward's claim and protest Philip VI's seizure of the throne. In this way France took the first step in the direction of that protracted dynastic succession conflict known as the Hundred Years War.

Once he had freed himself from the tyranny of Mortimer and politely set aside his mother's tutelage, Edward's developing strategy closely resembled that pursued by his grandfather. He regarded Scotland as unfinished business, and the first item on his agenda. The death of Robert Bruce in 1329 and the succession of a minor made Scotland a tempting enough target, even if Edward had not already acquired a per-sonal reason to resent the Scots when James Douglas's troops had threatened to cut short his reign in 1328 and in what he regarded as the demeaning marriage of his sister to the boy-king David Bruce. Within days of Mortimer's arrest, Edward was already plotting the destruction of the Bruce monarchy with his sponsorship of the claims of Edward Balliol, son of the late King John of Scotland. War began between the Scottish guardians of King David and Balliol in 1331 and, by 1333, repudiating the treaty of 1328, Edward III himself invaded Scotland, achieving his first major military victory at Halidon Hill outside Berwick. The fact that Philip VI offered refuge to David II in 1334 in Normandy, according to the terms of the treaty of Corbeil, brought the two areas of conflict together, especially as the erratic record of Balliol and the determination of the Bruce loyalists denied Edward III any hope of quick and decisive success north of the Tweed.

As far as France was concerned, Edward had in September 1331 put the problem of Aquitaine on temporary hold by crossing to France and – in a low-key and secretive meeting with Philip VI – acknowledged that the duchy was in fact dependent on the French Crown. He did not apparently do homage for it in person, or at least he never admitted he had. Edward was in 1334 debating the extent of the historical claims of the king of England in France, while Philip VI's obligation to support the Scots brought the three kingdoms into a state of mutual hostility. By 1336 a military and naval build-up in France left Edward in little doubt that war was imminent, a war to which he was not himself averse. In November 1336 the demand from Philip VI that Edward surrender to him a political refugee, his enemy and cousin Count Robert of Artois, was the trigger for war, as there was never a chance that Edward would do so. A parliament in March 1337 was the stage for Edward's asking for consent for war from the community. In fact coastal raiding had already begun by then, while Edward had commenced the diplomatic search for allies the previous year. In September 1337 Edward 'defied' Philip as his overlord and envoys were sent to Paris to repudiate his obligations, though the mission was delayed and the necessary letters were not in fact delivered. But, slowly and indeed hesitantly, England and France passed into a state of warfare, which would be the natural state of their relations for well over a century to come.

The French Wars, 1338–1347

Edward's first strategy was to open up a distracting front in the north-east to draw Philip VI away from the Plantagenet lands in Gascony. Edward invested far more than his available resources allowed in constructing an alliance with the Emperor, the Flemings, his wife's homeland of Hainaut and the Rhineland magnates. He arrived in Antwerp ready to pursue this alliance in August 1338, to be greeted with the title of vicar-general of the Empire at Cologne, which gave him all the rights and prerogatives of the Emperor himself. Mobilising his new allies and financing their subsidies were a different matter, however. The French in the meantime were not idle. In October a great French raid devastated the port of Southampton, and the coast from Plymouth to Sussex was ravaged, while the Channel Islands were occupied. There seemed every reason to expect that Philip VI intended an invasion of England, and indeed captured documents were later to confirm that was the initial French plan. In the meantime, the plan to base an attack on France from Flanders grounded on lack of money and allied enthusiasm. A move south in 1339 did a lot of damage to Picardy but got little further than Cambrai, which resisted a siege, and a face-to-face confrontation between the armies of England and France at Buironfosse resulted in no battle. Indeed at that point Edward's brother-in-law, the count of Hainaut, defected to Philip after re-assessing the English chances.

The year 1340 brought no further luck to Edward, other than the great sea battle off Sluys where the French fleet was utterly destroyed, which at least relieved Edward of any fear of an invasion of England. But the most telling event of that year was symbolic. In January, Edward had a high throne set up in the largest of the market places of Ghent and was proclaimed there as king of France. His quartered banner of the lilies of France and lions of England was displayed for the first time, with France given the dominant position in the top left and bottom right quarters of banner and shield. The heraldry and style of France would be incorporated in the royal arms and title of the Crown of England from now until the style was finally set aside on 1 January 1801. The significance of this act was that the war was no longer about the status of the English king as duke of Aquitaine; rather it was – in the English mind – purely a fight over the Crown of France.

The campaigns that followed in the Low Countries were disappointing, gaining little ground and failing to lead to any decisive encounter, while money drained away and burdened the king with massive debt. A second front was opened in Brittany, a semi-independent duchy within the kingdom of France. Duke John III died in 1341 leaving his inheritance to be disputed between his half-brother, John de Montfort, and his niece, married to King Philip's nephew. The English supported Montfort and established a useful military bridgehead in the duchy which forced the French to divide their resources. Furthermore, Montfort was willing to do homage to Edward for Brittany as king of France, which provided more than symbolism for his title. The French may have hoped to parallel Edward's strategy by returning David II to Scotland in 1341 with subsidies to assist him in carrying warfare into the North of England. David did not disappoint the French, and forced the English to a truce in 1343. The collapse of his imperial alliance did not deter Edward from his aims, and at least his former allies no longer had any claim on his finances. By 1345 Edward had abandoned his grandfather's failed strategy and formulated a new plan to pursue the war, with the express determination of bringing King Philip to the battlefield. Money and men were assembled by extraordinary efforts in 1345–1346 for an ambitious campaign on several fronts. For all the difficulties that he had to deal with in Brittany and Flanders, Edward was encouraged by the news from Gascony where his cousin, Henry of Grosmont, earl of Derby, scored spectacular successes in reclaiming lost ground from the French.

In July 1346 Edward himself was at last able to embark for France, landing in western Normandy and conducting a devastating chevauchée eastward through the duchy, making a nonsense of Valois lordship, sacking the city of Caen which his ancestor the Conqueror had founded, and capturing its commander. The English army devastated the Seine valley as far upriver as Poissy, some twenty kilometres from the gates of Paris, then turned north towards Picardy, looting as they went. Philip VI did his best to counter Edward's progress, but Edward successfully reached his own domain of Ponthieu, a county his grandmother had brought to the Plantagenet dynasty in 1279. Here, near the village of Crécy, Philip finally caught up with the English on 25 August.

Edward deployed his army along a ridge and offered battle the next day. King Philip had little choice but to take the field and indeed had the advantage of greater numbers on his side. Philip trusted his formidable Genoese crossbowmen to offset the longbowmen the English deployed, along with the field guns Edward was the first medieval commander to employ on a battlefield. The poor command structure and indiscipline of the French cavalry were their undoing, as well as King Philip's ignorance of the devastating use English armies had been making of massed bowmen for the past two generations. The French chivalry, launching an assault when the efforts of their infantry had little apparent effect, was slaughtered on the field. The display of the French war-banner of the oriflamme had proclaimed that no quarter was to be offered, as a result of which the subsequent rout of the French army led to a massacre that lasted from late afternoon until nightfall. It was only with the morning that the English realised they had destroyed the greater part of the higher French nobility. Philip himself was lucky to escape, his oriflamme abandoned and trampled into the mud. Barely three hundred English casualties were recorded. The victory staggered Europe, and the fact that only a few days later David II of Scotland was captured near Durham entirely transformed the war, which became now one of Valois survival, rather than Plantagenet pretension.

Bad Times

The war had cost well over a quarter of a million pounds by the time the first phase ended with the fall of Calais to the English in July 1347. Circumstances also combined to frustrate its full prosecution. This was not least the arrival in Western Europe of the Black Death, whose severity was enough to suspend campaigning in 1348 and 1349 (see pp. 252–3). Setting aside the despair and horror that the pandemic inflicted on the populations of Britain, it had other marked consequences. In terms of population, maybe as many as half of the country perished during its visitation, which could only impact heavily on the economy, as labour became scarce and more expensive. There was little that could be done about that, despite the Ordinance of the Labourers (1349), which attempted to fix wages at the pre-plague level and compel shirkers to work. Food prices fell, making agriculture less profitable, and manufactured goods grew more expensive. But these were long-term changes which would take two generations to become fully manifest. The pandemic had an aggravating effect on existing social anxieties, which had been troubling the community since the disorder of the reign of Edward II. Since most people, including the king, assumed that the plague had been visited on their world as a result of its sinfulness and pride, then prayer and penance were obviously required, and to be effective penance must be followed by amendment of the sinners' ways.

The 1350s saw a determined effort to answer complaints about law enforcement and public corruption which had been periodically raised and addressed in the 'trailbaston' inquiries occasionally mounted between 1305 and 1328. Protracted lawlessness and abuse of power had been the long-term consequence of civil disorder in England after the civil wars of Stephen's reign, the Barons' Wars, the Montfort rebellion and the civil disorders of Edward II's reign. The difference in the fourteenth century is that, for whatever reason, corruption and lawlessness failed to be adequately addressed and became endemic. The political community through Parliament expressed a view that it had much to do with the contamination of the legal system and local society through unrestrained bribery and conspiracy. Historians have seen it as a consequence of the extension of magnate influence into society through the practice of building up local affinities of gentry and others so as to intimidate rivals and support their own people.

From the very beginning of his reign, Edward III made periodic efforts to get to grips with the problem. Well before the Black Death there were moves to mobilise local communities to indict corrupt officials and expose criminal conspiracies through commissions of the peace and special justices. In 1346 it was forbidden for those involved in the process of justice to take robes and fees from parties involved in a case, a common and much-resented abuse. The aftermath of the plague saw a new and more decisive intervention. From 1351 the King's Bench was sent out from Westminster on a national circuit to energise the process of prosecution in local courts and step up the rate of criminal prosecutions, the process of 'gaol delivery'. By 1352 Parliament was nervous at quite how deep into society such inquiries were going. The king gave it short shrift, assuring the petitioners that he would send his courts where he saw fit. The petty corruption represented by breach of weights and measures legislation and the rigging of markets against consumers (or forestalling) was a local irritant that the king also addressed, promoting local courts and justices to curb abuses. The results were positive, at least for Edward's reputation as a just king who lived up to his coronation oath.

The War State

England had already had in Edward I an experience of a king with ambitions to mobilise the entire nation to support his wars. The extent to which he was able to accomplish his aims was remarkable, though in the end England was unable to support the degree of warfare that was needed to subjugate the entire British archipelago and simultaneously defend distant Gascony. Edward III had rather more success after he abandoned his grandfather's French strategy and his own renewed attempt to reconquer Scotland. The success of the Crécy campaign was in part because it aggressively took the war to France and diverted French retaliation on English soil. It also revealed a fortuitous wealth of military talent available to the king amongst his aristocracy, notably the several friends and early adherents he promoted to earldoms in 1350. The remarkable military successes of Henry of Grosmont, then earl of Derby, as the English commander in Gascony in 1346–1347, were almost as important as the king's great chevauchée in tipping the balance against Philip VI. The king's own eldest son, Edward of Woodstock, was already a charismatic war leader even in his teenage years. Lower down the social scale there were talented men of the rank of knight and squire whom the king selected and employed in key commands, men such as the Hainauter Walter Mauny and the famous Robert Knollys. The quality of the troops available to the king was the product of two generations of constant warfare in the north. His infantry was rather more organised and effective than Edward I's had been, especially the highly mobile companies of archers and men-at-arms developed as a response to Scots raiding, who were customarily mounted but fought on foot. They were perfectly suited for the fast-moving chevauchées Edward began to employ as his new French strategy. Such men found attractive terms of service in magnate military retinues, as much as in contracted companies for the king's service, and were both highly skilled and disciplined. Their effectiveness lay in that rather than in the numbers brought to the king's campaigns.

To support the wars there was something of a revolution in military supply. The Tower of London became the location of the department of state which provisioned and equipped the armies in France, the Privy Wardrobe. It operated at a level of efficency one does not normally associate with medieval warfare. Mobilisation was usually by contract with individual commanders, not by conscription or military summons. Once in France, the English armies extorted food and money from the countryside, itself a form of economic warfare. The armies took pay, but the chances of enrichment through looting and ransoms added to the attractiveness of campaigning for all levels of the army. England in the reign of Edward III developed a form of aggressive warfare which transferred the costs to the enemy at minimal expense to the king and which deflected danger from the home country. It also flattered the military values of the ruling class and raised the prestige of the monarchy as long, that is, as the war delivered military success. It was in the flush of that success that Edward celebrated his military ascendancy in his formation of the noble order of chivalry which was named the Garter and dedicated to the soldier saint, St George, but most inspired by the pseudo-historical Round Table of Arthur of Britain.

Success continued to come, largely because French commanders persisted in trying to win a decisive victory in the open field, relying on the force of their cavalry when they did. The climactic confrontation came in 1356, though not before peace-making had been tried. Several schemes of peace were entertained, and in 1354, in bargaining to obtain control of the full extent of former Plantagenet lands south of the Loire, Edward was even willing to put his claim to the throne of France on the table. Negotiations continued before the pope at Avignon into 1355, and although an elaborate and expensive embassy was sent the competing claims were too complex for the parties to agree, particularly the question of when and how Edward would surrender his claim to France. The French in any case had decided to pursue a military solution by 1354, while the new French king, John II, was eager to overmatch Edward in the field and reclaim the chivalric eminence that had for over a century been reckoned as the natural property of France.

In the summer of 1355 the war was renewed, when Edward III sailed for Calais to once again pillage Picardy, while the Black Prince was despatched to take over the defence of Gascony. From there he merrily plundered and intimidated the lords of the Midi who had failed to acknowledge his father's claims. The prince's activity obliged King John of France to retaliate in force, harrassed as he was by another successful English chevauchée through Normandy, this time led by the duke of Lancaster, Henry of Grosmont. His success encouraged leading Norman nobles to abandon King John for King Edward and cede real control of the duchy to England. There was, therefore, a certain desperation in King John's march against the Black Prince, whom he intended to prevent uniting his Anglo-Gascon forces with Lancaster. The armies met on 18 September 1356 outside the city of Poitiers, where the Black Prince found himself heavily outnumbered and trapped. The catastrophic defeat of the French that followed was entirely down to squabbling and wilful insubordination by the French battalion commanders. King John himself led his forces on foot into battle, but the routing of his cavalry left him unsupported and trapped by English knights. The French king and around 2,000 knights and squires were captured, a bonanza for the ransom market. There was, besides this, a devastating number of French noble casualties on the field which decapitated the nation's remaining leadership.

With the Valois king in the Tower of London, Edward was now in a position to fashion a settlement to suit himself and impose it on King John. In 1359 the French negotiators were confronted with a demand for a ransom amounting to nearly £700,000, and the cession to Edward's lordship of France from Calais, through Normandy, down to the Pyrenees – most indeed of the land Edward's dynasty had ruled before 1204 and some areas besides, which they had never held. For this he would give up his claim to the throne. The French refused, despite the near-anarchy and devastation to which war had reduced the north and centre of the country. In 1359, therefore, Edward marched a huge army to Reims, with the intention of intimidating into acceptance the dauphin, now ruling France in his father's forced absence. But the expedition was a failure and the French evaded a battle which might have been decisive against them. In 1360 at the Peace of Brétigny, Edward settled for a ransom of around half a million pounds, and much less French land, though what he acquired was to be held in full sovereignty without homage to the king of France. Edward would no longer use the title of king of France, but the lilies stayed on his royal arms and he did not formally renounce his claim. The French had to be content with that, and at least there was a peace until 1369 in which they could recover their strength.

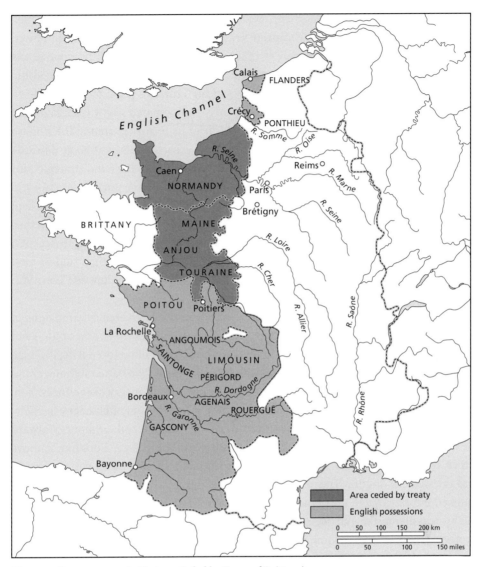

Map 13.1 France, c. 1340 (with Area Ceded by Peace of Brétigny)

❦ Inglorious Years

The remainder of Edward III's reign tends to be regarded as something of an anticlimax. Certainly there were no further great victories for English arms in France, which were exercised elsewhere, in Castile, where a war of succession drew in the Black Prince, called now prince of Wales and Aquitaine, which was fought as a proxy war, with the English backing Pedro the Cruel and the French his half-brother, Henry of Trastamara.

Though Prince Edward scored a great victory over Henry at Nájera (1367) he badly mishandled the aftermath, and the campaign left him with a long-term disabling illness. His incapacity did not assist his rule over Gascony, where he was not popular in any case. In 1369 Charles V of France was emboldened to resume his claim to overlordship over Gascony, which was a breach of the treaty of Brétigny, as a result of which Edward III once again assumed the title of king of France, and prepared a new campaign. But successive naval and land reverses robbed the war of its former glamour. The English forces in Gascony were unable to prevent French encroachments, and King Edward's younger son, John of Gaunt, duke of Lancaster, proved not to have the strategic gifts of his father when he was placed in command of the expeditionary armies in 1369 and 1373, even though he was able to roam freely across France. The French simply kept to their fortresses and avoided battle, deploying the same strategy that had proved so frustrating for the English in Scotland. In 1375 the English were willing to accept a truce rather than continue an expensive and inconclusive war, which is said to have cost £650,000 for very little return indeed. So the first phase of the Hundred Years War sputtered in this way to an unhappy conclusion.

How much the disorganisation and incoherence of the later French campaigns of Edward III were due to the ageing king's increasing debility of mind and body is not easy to say. He was active enough until 1369 and the death of his beloved wife, Philippa of Hainaut. He was certainly able to articulate in the early 1360s an ambitious grand diplomatic strategy in the Low Countries by which he would marry his youngest son, Edmund earl of Cambridge, to Margaret, daughter of Louis count of Flanders, the heiress not just of her father but also of Burgundy, Artois, Brabant and Limbourg. Edward III creatively promised to settle Calais, Ponthieu and Guines on Edmund, a move which would have created a new super-principality dominating north-eastern France and the western Empire. The new king of France, Charles V (1364–1380), readily recognised the danger and the opportunity. He deployed his own considerable diplomatic talents to frustrate the marriage, which he successfully did, securing the girl for his own brother, Philip, who would unite all those areas into a powerful new state, which would in due course be a major player in the war and politics of fifteenth-century Western Europe, and beyond.

The war, once so glorious, became an expensive embarrassment in Edward's last years. The king's mental faculties declined, and a mind once decisive, subtle and astute faded into dependency on his private household and a squalid relationship with a corrupt mistress. His eldest son was himself chronically ill and was to die before his father. Leadership increasingly fell therefore to Edward's fourth son, John of Gaunt duke of Lancaster (1340–1399) who from 1369 was the principal English commander in France. It was he who headed the English response to the attempt of Pope Gregory XI in 1375 to get the warring parties to conclude a peace, or in default of that an extended truce. In the end the warfare was suspended only until 1377. An increasing instability in the English political community was a consequence of the physical incapacity of the king and the Black Prince, manifested by rumours that Duke John intended to take the throne over the head of his nephew, Richard of Bordeaux, as an earlier royal John had done over Arthur of Brittany. The duke had to deal with an aggressive Parliament out of royal control and dissatisfied at military failure as much as the corruption at court and in the country. It went so far as to presume to 'impeach' (that is, 'accuse of wrongdoing') several royal councillors, a procedure the 'Good Parliament' of 1376 invented, and a development of the way that local communities had for two generations been 'presenting' suspected corrupt local officials, who were then prosecuted in the king's name. It was a process that would have many long-term consequences for English history, for through Parliament the English nation was in effect prosecuting offences committed against itself independently of the king. John of Gaunt won no friends when he chose, as the king's designated representative, to pardon the impeached officials and retaliate against those who had procured the charges. As a result he was not chosen as regent when the old king died on 21 June 1377, to be succeeded by his eleven-year-old grandson.

Richard II and the Retreat from War

Perhaps the grandeur of the Edwardian period looks all the more glorious because of what succeeded it. There were to be decades of military failure in a state locked into what was an unwinnable war. There was also domestic civil and religious strife culminating in an act of dynastic dispossession. As ever, the character of a king was an aggravating factor in this period of political and social instability. But Richard of Bordeaux was a minor on his succession, and so can hardly be blamed for the disorders of his early reign or the problems with which his realm was beset; those were entirely the fault of the preceding regime. The financial pressures of unrelenting warfare and the consequences of plague were at the root of the problems. Nonetheless, when Richard II assumed direction of the kingdom at the end of 1383 at the age of seventeen, his lack of talent for governance and his inept handling of the political community, as well as his personal diffidence and unapproachability, made a bad situation much worse.

Unlike his father and grandfather Richard II did not wholeheartedly embrace the military culture of the male elite of his day (though he shared his grandfather's expensive tastes in lavish pageantry, objets d'art, relic-collecting and rich fabrics). His idea of expressing his kingship was to match or even exceed the extravagances of foreign courts, especially that of the rival Valois king of France. Richard enforced the sort of formal court protocol the Valois had embraced, and in so doing distanced himself from the political community to whose moods his grandfather had been so alert and attentive. It is perhaps significant that a flatterer described him as a noble king 'who governs in sublime fashion not so much by force of arms as by philosophy and the two laws'.[1] But

Fig. 13.1 Portrait of Richard II. The Wilton Diptych, painted in the last years of the reign, is a dramatic statement of the king's concept of his own glory. He is presented to the Virgin and Child by a group including the two English royal saints, Edward the Martyr and Edward the Confessor (whose heraldry Richard appropriated). Richard is here asserting the sacrality of his kingship against his Valois rivals, who flaunted their own royal saint, Louis IX. The angels who form the court of Heaven are partisan. They carry the banner of England and wear the English royal livery badge, the white hart.

though he may have compared himself to the wise King Solomon, his critics compared him to Solomon's son, the ill-advised and tyrannical Rehoboam, criticising his partiality for flatterers rather than his working with his magnates, his natural counsellors. These he alienated by personal slights and by wilfully destabilising their local power bases, deliberately constructing a rival royal affinity of retainers to challenge their own local retinues. His self-absorption as a person meant he could work only with people who made him the centre of attention. He was therefore a born tyrant, as the middle ages looked at it, and not above the personal vindictiveness of tyrants (see Fig. 13.1).

Richard earned most criticism through his quite realistic assessment of the dim prospects of war with France. His strategy was to get out of its consequences as soon as he could. To take that view openly was, however, to forswear the brilliance of English arms under his father and grandfather and the war state that they had set up, which had been so much to the advantage of the magnates and the stability of his own realm. This led to the first political crisis of his reign, when Richard resisted the pressure of his uncle, Duke John, to renew the war in France. He was expected himself to lead an expedition into Flanders in 1382 to mark his coming of age, which was the traditional time for a warrior 'tyro' to show his physical mettle. His refusal to join the expedition earned the suspicion of his father's generation of nobles, who had defined themselves in war. His personal insecurity demanded he create a coterie of like-minded young magnates around him, and he favoured them past the point of offence, not least Robert de Vere, earl of Oxford, whom he promoted successively to the rank of marquess and then duke of Ireland in 1385 and 1386.

It was Richard's exclusive concentration of lavish patronage on such men that alienated the political nation, particularly the older, established magnates. They turned inevitably to John of Gaunt as their leader against the king, and so the duke was forced unwillingly into the unenviable role of his predecessor at Lancaster in the days of Edward II, Earl Thomas, as spokesman for the outraged magnates against an objectionable king. Confrontation at a parliament in Salisbury in April 1384 between the seventeen-year-old king and his uncle on the subject of his loyalty led to high words and an open rift. Relations had deteriorated by February 1385 to the point where a party among Richard's courtiers plotted to assassinate the duke at a tournament. Differences between the pair on military matters caused Richard's first military campaign against a French expeditionary army in Scotland in the summer to end in disarray, even though the French themselves got little return for their military efforts. The first crisis of Richard's adult reign duly followed, after Gaunt quit the realm on his own expedition to seek to secure the crown of Castile.

Gaunt's disappearance did not much help Richard, for he himself could not provide the direction and expertise in policy his uncle had. In October 1386 a parliament was confronted with demands for taxation to finance a response to continuing threats from France. Its abrupt refusal, due to the mismanagement of the session by the chancellor, Michael de la Pole, affronted the king, who made things worse by leaving the capital in what looks very like a huff. The Commons in response impeached and removed Pole for failure to reform finances and for mismanagement. In doing this, Parliament cited not Magna Carta (as in past conflicts with the executive) but its supposed right to supervise the administration of the realm, and, when the king protested, it alluded to a fictious 'statute' that allowed a king who reneged on his coronation oaths to be removed by his people. The threat was obvious and indeed crude. Richard felt obliged to consent to a commission to take charge of reform, which was granted access even to his household accounts.

The Appellant Regime

In its year of office the commission had the luck which never favoured Richard, and an English squadron under the earl of Arundel sank a much larger French invasion fleet in the Channel, decisively removing that threat for the rest of the century. Perhaps

Arundel's triumph merely fuelled the king's frustration and resentment. In the summer of 1387 he privately took legal advice about Parliament's recent impositions. Finding it favourable to his view of the royal prerogative, he decided to fight, but he was outflanked, for word got out of what he had done, thus confirming everyone's suspicions about him. At the end of 1387 the five leaders of the aristocratic opposition 'appealed' (or challenged) his household intimates as traitors. These 'Lords Appellant', who had long had differences with Richard over the French war, went for the kill, helped by confusion amongst the royalists. The Appellants moved an army against Robert de Vere, by now duke of Ireland, the king's most capable and resented courtier. De Vere's retinue was dispersed in Gloucestershire and he and his confederates were arrested or driven abroad, leaving Richard powerless and indeed at one point apparently temporarily deprived of his kingship by his Appellant uncle, Thomas, duke of Gloucester, who was clearly determined on deposing Richard if he could get away with it. The tension was satisfied in the Parliament that met in February 1388 by the death sentence (in absentia) on De Vere, and the executions of others of the king's intimates and the virtual disbanding of his household, the only real charge against them being that they had opposed the policy of Gloucester and his gang, which was defined as treasonous in a new way: it interfered in the natural rights of Parliament to counsel the king.

Kingship in England had in 1388 reached a very low point, and for the same reason as it had earlier found itself in troughs: a king unable to communicate with his magnates and secure their confidence. The difference this time was that there were now legal mechanisms by which the king could be constrained and his rule curbed, for Parliament, originally set up to amplify royal authority and assist communication with the political community, could now be turned against the monarch as being the truer representative of the interests of the realm. The remainder of Richard II's reign featured his vain attempts to escape the consequences of his unenviable position, beginning with the theatre of March 1388 at Westminster when he solemnly repeated his coronation oath in the presence of his magnates.

It did not take long for the Appellants to discredit themselves, being as unable as the king to re-establish any English edge over the French. In the end they too looked to make peace with Paris. Meanwhile at the end of 1389, John of Gaunt returned to England in a mood to reinstall harmony in the body politic and Richard had to be content for a while with being more of an ornamental than an executive king, though admittedly he did do ceremony and festivities rather well. The kingdom in the meantime, under the direction of Gaunt, coasted in 1393 into the harbour of peace with France with the conclusion of a new truce, for which Richard himself could not be blamed by his critics, as it was his uncles who negotiated it. For many months following the death of his beloved queen, Anne of Bohemia, in June 1394, Richard was even out of England, travelling in Wales and crossing to Ireland deliberately to avoid, as he said, places where he and his wife had been together. He even had the palace of Sheen where she died demolished.

Descent into Tyranny, 1397–1399

It was the king's delight in his expensive schemes and entertainments that was eventually to disturb the equanimity of his reign. The 1397 Parliament was energised on the subject of his extravagance which led to a brief confrontation and challenge. It seems that, in the course of that year, Richard came to believe he was in a stronger position than he had been since the beginning of his reign, strong enough to deal with his old enemies. In July he had three of the Appellant lords arrested and, in an act of malicious theatre, had the Appellants themselves appealed of treason by a group of younger lords acting on the king's instructions. Gloucester was murdered at the king's instigation at Calais before he could come to trial, but not until he had signed a confession of his treason. The subsequent Parliament, held in a Westminster teeming with the king's soldiers, voided what its predecessor of 1388 had dared to do. There the surviving Appellants were tried and, with Gaunt's acquiescence, all but one were sentenced to death or banishment, the noble earl of Arundel inconveniencing the king by making a rather dignified end to the open distress of the watching and supportive Londoners as he was led through their city to his beheading on Tower Hill. What followed was a period of royal tyranny, supported initially by a clique of younger magnates, including Gaunt's son and heir, Henry of Bolingbroke, earl of Derby, promoted by the king his cousin to be duke of Hereford in (temporary) gratitude. The attitude of the general populace may be guessed from the fact that Arundel (like Simon de Montfort and Thomas of Lancaster in their days) was said to work miraculous cures at his tomb in the church of the Austin Friars in London.

Richard's last years were not spent in any ease, despite the decisiveness of his coup against the Appellants and his critics in 1397. Plagued by nightmares, the insomniac king formed a guard company of Cheshire gentry and archers whose loyalty was secured by lavish pay and privileges. His subjects and magnates found them threatening. Richard himself brooded on the ominous fate of his great-grandfather, Edward II, whom he promoted as a candidate for canonisation. He spent months after the so-called Great Parliament in pursuing enemies, real and invented. His nemesis was of his own creation, however. Initially, Henry Bolingbroke had been happy with the events of 1397 and ready to believe that the king meant his protestations of future good lordship. When another of his fellow dukes, Thomas Mowbray of Norfolk, fell into conversation on the road from Windsor to London, and Duke Thomas gave it as his opinion that the king was only biding his time before turning on the Lancaster family, Duke Henry was genuinely shocked. When invited to join a conspiracy against the king, he went promptly to Richard and reported it.

The matter was put to trial at a parliament held in Shrewsbury in January 1398, to which Mowbray failed to turn up, though he later surrendered to Richard. The king was able to intimidate the Commons into giving him the right to deal with the resulting case between the two dukes. In April 1398 the pair were awarded a day to decide the issue by battle between them. The two finally met at Coventry before the king on 16 September, the event being by then a matter of European celebrity: the duke of Milan sent Bolingbroke a fine suit of steel armour, and several great German, Bohemian and French nobles sent their heralds as observers and bearers of gifts to one or other duke. The king of arms of Brittany was to be the arbiter of the lists. In the event, the king peremptorily intervened from his throne and exiled both men from England so as to avoid the 'dishonour' that the affair might impute to them. Bolingbroke was to leave England for six years and went with a parting gift of 1,000 marks from the king. But the tyrannical nature of Richard's act was nonetheless clear to everyone, for Bolingbroke had been punished for an act of loyalty and as a way of getting him out of the realm. Ominously, the king made a point of securing Bolingbroke's son and heir, the boy Henry of Monmouth, and kept him in his household, a strategy for which an earlier tyrant, John, was noted.

 Usurpation

Duke John of Gaunt died in February 1399. Though Richard II had breezily allowed that Henry of Bolingbroke could succeed his father, when the duke's death actually happened it was too tempting to him to withhold succession. He had better have resisted the impulse, for the magnates now saw that even the greatest magnate house in England could not hold its lands in any security under such a tyrant. Bolingbroke was at the time living in Paris in style, and so in a good position to exploit differences within the council of Charles VI on relations with England. Allying with the rising faction of the duke of Orléans, Bolingbroke was able to gather shipping and support, embarking at Boulogne for England in June 1399. He landed on the Humber estuary at the end of the month and by 14 July was at his castle of Pontefract, surrounded by a loyal Lancastrian army. King Richard in the meantime had made things easier for the coup by taking himself off to Ireland. By the time the king was able to return, the duke of York, whom he had left in charge, had been entirely outmanoeuvred and had capitulated to Bolingbroke, and so England was lost to Richard in a matter of a fortnight. Even Cheshire abandoned the king, who finally surrendered on 15 August, in a fearful state of depression, to the earl of Northumberland, just outside Conwy in North Wales.

Henry of Bolingbroke had concluded already by then that the only future security he had was in displacing King Richard, though he was willing to pretend to the king that he had every intention of respecting his dignity. Initially he posed as the defender of justice in the realm, justifying his rule by a novel interpretation of what had been until then the largely ceremonial office of steward of England, which had been linked with his earldom of Leicester since 1153. In fact Henry formed a committee of academics and lawyers to research the subject of the deposition of a ruling king, and ordered clerks to stop dating letters by the year of Richard's reign long before the issue came to trial. Henry found the process not an easy one, as the only obvious precedent, which had ended Edward II's reign, was an abdication, not a deposition. In the end, Henry and his advisers had to use the papal deposition of the Emperor Frederick II (1245) on the basis of his tyranny and perjury as the only workable precedent. For Henry this provided other problems, as he was by no means the nearest male heir to the childless king once he was ousted from his throne. Bolingbroke even went so far as to research whether it was possible to claim that Edward I had not been the eldest son of Henry III, but that it had been his own forebear and Edward's brother, Edmund of Lancaster (a fond fantasy John of Gaunt had apparently entertained). In the end, all Bolingbroke could offer was his descent from Henry III as his justification for taking the throne, an ominous and unsatisfactory claim, for numerous others could say as much.

Richard was eventually intimidated into resigning the throne, though only under protest and not in Henry's favour. The day afterwards, 30 September 1399, a parliament was summoned in the name of Henry Bolingbroke as his successor, Henry IV. The ex-king Richard of Bordeaux was not put on trial for the crimes with which he was charged but was eventually confined to the Lancastrian fortress of Pontefract. By the end of the year, he was already the focus of plots by members of his displaced household. In mid February 1400, after an abortive rising had occurred in his favour, the former king was dead. The new king's canon law consultant, Dr Adam Usk, chose to believe Richard had starved himself to death in a fit of depression. Few other people were so wilfully naïve. His body was taken south to London, the face of the embalmed corpse displayed at each stop so he might be recognised. Henry IV himself attended the funeral mass at St Paul's, but Richard was buried out of common sight at the royal manor of Langley, not being moved to Westminster to the lavish tomb he had ordered for himself and his beloved first wife until after the usurper's own death in 1413.

 Lancastrian Kingship

The vulnerability of the new king was evident from the moment the crown descended on his head. New ways of exalting English kingship were devised for the occasion, to try to repair the damage Henry had himself done it. An 'imperial' crown was ordered for the new king, that is, a crown with cross bars enclosing its top, rather than the open circlet previously employed. Also, the anointing was carried out with a phial of holy oil produced for the occasion, supposedly one that the Virgin Mary had conferred on Archbishop Thomas Becket but which had somehow ended up in the treasury of Poitiers Cathedral, where it was found and liberated by Henry IV's grandfather and first duke of Lancaster, Henry of Grosmont, in one of his triumphant chevauchées across France. The allusions in these symbols were to the crown of the Emperor and the coronation of the king of France (whose phial was said to have been given by the Holy Spirit to Archbishop Rémi of Reims for the coronation of Clovis as first king of the Franks). The insecurity of the new king's title to his crown was implicit in the hollowness of these symbolic supports to its legitimacy. The nature of the reign that followed showed that few were fooled by the façade of royal power and legitimacy. Henry IV's coronation was followed by an unrelenting decade of conspiracy and rebellion, the aftershocks of which continued into his son's reign. The king proved to be not up to the challenge. After only five years on the throne his mental health gave way and he collapsed into a state of what we would regard as clinical depression. He was unable to engage fully with public affairs, and indeed in 1406 his abdication was under discussion. This was compounded by what seems to have been cardiac illness which culminated in a series of strokes in 1408 and 1409.

The first serious rebellion against Henry IV occurred in Wales. It may have been the result of the sudden power vacuum caused by Richard's removal, for he was the dominant landowner in Wales and the Marches, especially after he had taken over the Lancastrian lands there. There was no authority in Wales to offset the sudden native rising in favour of Owain Glyndŵr, who in September 1400 proclaimed himself prince by hereditary right after seizing most of the principality and its fortresses. His military successes gave a reality to Owain's realm until at least 1406, and they debilitated Lancastrian rule elsewhere in Britain as the war sucked in money and troops. Systematic raiding by Welsh soldiery took the warfare into the English border counties and added to the disruption. Glyndŵr also proved adept at exploiting the fissures in Henry's rule in England, allying with his enemies to bring Henry IV to bay on the battlefield of Shrewsbury in 1403, when the future of his dynasty depended on the chances of combat. Glyndŵr was able to negotiate support from Charles VI of France, who in 1405 landed troops in South Wales in support of the Welsh. Glyndŵr's own problem was the mirror image of King Henry's. He too had to assert his legitimacy, and in the end his military success was not lasting enough to enable him to consolidate Wales as a parliamentary state. There was never a chance the Welsh and marcher English would unite under his rule.

Even so slight a danger to the English state as the Lollard heresy seemed to challenge Lancastrian legitimacy, and ultimately provoked a harsh orthodox reaction. The reason the Lancastrian regime survived its first king was in part because – within it – kingship was more or less resigned to the sort of conciliar regime we find in the twelfth and thirteenth centuries, where the powers of the Crown were delegated to loyal magnates and officials while the king was absent or a minor. In this case the arrangement worked because his young heir, Henry of Monmouth, was loyal to more than his own personal interests, and the Lancastrian council worked hard and with some talent at managing the political community through a sometimes fractious Parliament. Luckily, perhaps, the political community did not have much of an alternative to Henry IV, such was the poisonous legacy of Richard II's rule to any future opposition faction to the Lancastrians. In this way the regime rode out the challenges of insurrection, not least the existence of a powerful and hostile magnate interest in the North, represented by the Percy earls of Northumberland. The regime was also cautious about getting involved with hostilities in France, though that became more difficult as Charles VI's increasingly feeble rule led to competing factions within France which drew the English into what became a situation of civil war.

This was the situation when Henry IV died in March 1413. Such was the continuing insecurity of his throne that it is not surprising that his son had to deal with a major insurrection within a year. The rising was provoked by the harsh measures that archbishop of Canterbury, Thomas Arundel, had been pursuing against Lollard heretics since 1409, and it was focused on the charismatic knight and MP John Oldcastle, an enthusiastic Lollard but also one of the new king's former associates as prince of Wales. But Henry V could not get Oldcastle to repent his heresy and so had to allow action against him. Oldcastle's escape into hiding in London led to openly rebellious rallies, and their contingents converged on the capital. The king had to seal the City gates and disperse thousands of rebels to the north of London in an armed confrontation in January 1414. Scores of captives were subsequently executed as traitors, though Oldcastle escaped once more. He remained at liberty until arrested in North Wales at the end of 1417 seeking to ally with Gruffudd, son of the by now deceased Owain Glyndŵr. He was promptly executed. The defeat of the Lollards did not end the dangers to the new king. As he was preparing to embark on his chevauchée in France in July 1415, a startling noble conspiracy to assassinate Henry V as he embarked at Southampton was uncovered. The conspirators intended replacing Henry with the earl of March, a descendant of John of Gaunt's elder brother, Lionel duke of Clarence. The leaders included the younger brother of the duke of York, the first tremor of the dynastic rivalry that would destabilise the realm in the second half of the fifteenth century. All were rounded up and promptly executed by beheading.

The Great Gamble: Renewal of Warfare in France

Success in battle in France solved many of Henry V's problems, for after the triumph of Agincourt he could pose convincingly as the true heir of Edward III, his great-grandfather, the victor of Crécy. Henry had proved himself a brave and accomplished knight since his teenage years fighting his father's enemies in Wales, being wounded in the face at the battle of Shrewsbury in 1403, weeks before his sixteenth birthday. War with France was threatening before his father's death, as factions battled for control of the council of the demented Charles VI, particularly the Burgundian faction, which had murdered the duke of Orléans, Henry IV's former patron in exile. The other faction, the Armagnacs, alienated the English by their professed hostility to English rule in Gascony. Henry IV himself planned to lead an expedition to France in 1412, by which time the Armagnacs had won him over, but his health prevented him from carrying out his promise if, that is, he had ever been sincere. Henry V was left with the problem, and his solution was to favour the Burgundians while pressing English claims on France dating back to the unpaid remainder of King John II's ransom, in the hope of gaining some diplomatic advantage. The French king's heir, the dauphin Charles, added to the pressure by stonewalling negotiations and recklessly provoking Henry by personal slights.

So Henry V led his army to Normandy in the autumn of 1415 and besieged Harfleur, a port at the mouth of the Seine, which he took after a five-week siege, perhaps contemplating using it as another Calais, a bridgehead for future English domination of Normandy. He did not, however, stay there long after taking the port. In the second week of October he mounted a great chevauchée across the Seine and northwards towards Calais itself. Crossing the Somme in Picardy, Henry was confronted by a French army drawn principally from the region and from Flanders, perhaps half as large again as his own, and on 25 October he fought it at the village of Agincourt. His army was stronger than the French had perhaps believed and their commanders were poorly co-ordinated. The French were also attacking across waterlogged ground. The English bowmen inflicted terrible slaughter on the French cavalry and heavy infantry as they were trapped in mud within a horseshoe of fire. Several of the dukes of France were either killed or taken prisoner, and the leadership of the king of France's council was decimated.

Agincourt transformed Henry V's strategy to one of open conquest, and it restored the English liking for war in France as a solution to domestic problems. The Lancastrian regime experienced a boost to its legitimacy, for it was garlanded with victory in the same manner as the Edwardian war state had been. It was up to the king to make the most of the windfall victory. He focused on Normandy, rather than distant Gascony, and achieved what Edward III had not, a complete conquest of the duchy. Some measure of the European significance of what Henry had achieved was the crossing of the Emperor Sigismund to England in August 1416 to attempt to make political capital of the humiliation of France. Henry found a dazzled Parliament patriotically ready to grant taxation in the pursuit of conquest. In 1417 English forces were able to seize Caen, the city founded by William the Conqueror, and siege by siege Henry V reduced Normandy to his authority while the faction-ridden French leadership sat paralysed in Paris. His success was assisted by his heavy investment in what was becoming a new royal attribute in Western Europe, a mobile siege artillery train, first deployed effectively in warfare in his reign. The capital of Rouen and almost all the duchy was in Henry's hands by the summer of 1419.

The final collapse of the French came in the September of that year, with the assassination of the duke of Burgundy by members of the household of the dauphin (the future Charles VII). The new duke promptly allied with Henry V, and the result was the treaty of Troyes (May 1420) by which Henry married Katherine, sister of the dauphin, whom Charles VI disinherited in favour of Henry, who thus became regent of France. For two years he ruled from Paris and fought the dauphin's supporters, producing a son with Katherine, but Henry was to die on the last day of August 1422 from dysentry, resigning the guardianship of his infant son and of English France to his younger brother, Duke John of Bedford. He died just seven weeks before Charles VI and so was cheated of the coronation as king of France that had been promised him at Troyes.

The Minority and Incompetence of Henry VI

Despite the great military talents of the duke of Bedford, the future direction of English warfare in France did not go well. Bedford underlined the legitimacy of Lancastrian rule in France by having the child Henry VI crowned king of France at Paris at the age of ten. It had been better had it been done at Reims, but the dauphin beat the English to it in 1429 and now ruled from the Loire valley as Charles VII. By the time Henry VI came to full age in 1437 Bedford was dead, the Burgundian alliance defunct and the fortunes of Charles VII on the rise. Henry VI came to the English throne at the age of only nine months. Initially the kingdom was confided to the dukes of Bedford and Gloucester, his uncles, and to Henry Beaufort, bishop of Winchester, his great-uncle, half-brother of Henry IV, who together were the leaders of the royal council which became the repository of the infant king's powers. As had already been the case several times in English and Scottish history, aristocratic regencies might be times of relative political tranquillity.

Henry VI's regency council had its internal rivalries (particularly those tensions caused by Gloucester's jealousy of his colleagues), but under the ascendancy of Bedford until 1435 it did in fact keep the realm quiet, and under his direction it assisted him in mounting a stubborn defence of English gains in France. Henry, however, proved unable to live up to expectations of him when he finally came into his own in 1437. He was a king of no political acumen, heedless and vacillating. In due course it became evident that France was not the only inheritance he had from his grandfather, Charles VI, for he developed some form of congenital mental illness. Even before his insanity became undeniable in 1455, observers found him odd and unpredictable; he had irrational hatreds and, like Richard II, was widely criticised for his childish and petulant nature. As a character he was unfixed and strange, held together perhaps only by his deep piety, which gave some sort of structure to his mental life.

In the circumstances, England could only suffer when such a king sat on the throne, as more ambitious and competent characters made their bid to control him and his realm. There were handsome rewards for those who controlled the king's household, as Henry's generosity to those about him knew little restraint. But such favour destabilised the political community and the impression the nation gained of its king after he took power at the age of sixteen was that he was not strong in council. The first beneficiary of the new situation was William de la Pole, earl and later duke of Suffolk. By 1440 he had quietly built up a position of dominance within the king's household and council, while the duke of Gloucester and Cardinal Beaufort publicly squabbled and English control in northern France crumbled. By 1444 Suffolk had used his closeness to the king and his common interest with Beaufort's faction to sideline the council and was actively pursuing a peace in France and a royal marriage, which took place the next year when Henry VI married Margaret, daughter of René of Anjou, king of Jerusalem, a cadet descendant of King John II of France.

The position of the likes of Suffolk, depending on precarious royal favour, was never a safe one. He himself was a problem, using the king's supposed will as his only authority without the back-up of the political community who were more and more distanced from power by his monopoly of the king. As the military position in France decayed, a new leader emerged to fill the part of a Simon de Montfort and Thomas of Lancaster in earlier crises in personal monarchy. This was Richard duke of York, the king's cousin, who had heavily invested in the French wars and got little thanks for his efforts. As a French invasion began to oust the English from Normandy in 1449, Suffolk's regime began to be the useful focus of blame for discontented magnates, and London in particular became restive. In February 1450, as Normandy fell to Charles VII, Suffolk was impeached by an angry Parliament, to be banished at the king's insistence rather than executed. Unfortunately for Suffolk, the restive country disagreed. His ship was intercepted off Dover by local sailors and he was beheaded, his head lopped off over the side of his vessel. The angry and turbulent Commons were not pacified, and the summer of 1450 was notable for the rising known as Cade's Rebellion, named for John Cade, a colourful Irish mercenary who was employed by his Kentish gentry backers to give military direction to their rising. The rebels' complaints show that the country had been deeply disturbed at the polarisation and ineptitude of the court, the profiteering amongst the king's household, local corruption and the isolation of the king from his natural advisers, his magnates, especially York. It showed that the community of the realm had a pretty clear idea of what was going wrong in England. The rebellion petered out ignominiously for all concerned. Briefly Cade's men occupied London and attempted a witch-hunt against the household faction. The king and his allies proved ineffectual in attempts to defuse the situation, and in the end the rebels were dispersed only by wholesale issuing of pardons.

The War of the Roses

Another violent usurpation of the throne was not inevitable in 1450, but in retrospect the circumstances that made it so began to appear in the aftermath of Cade's Rebellion. Duke Richard of York had been prominent in representing the interests of the opposition magnates, and he was happy to remain the focus of discontent. Around him grew a party of 'Yorkists' within the fractious and directionless nobility of England, which was not in general that keen to submit to Duke Richard's self-assumed moral authority. The Beaufort faction around the duke of Somerset had its own independent policy agenda and saw no reason to defer to York. This rivalry was the seed of what has come to be known to historians as the War of the Roses, though in fact there was only episodic military activity in the decades it spanned, and that only affecting the nobility and its retinues. The red and white roses which were supposedly the party badges of each side in the conflict were in fact not the favoured livery devices of either Lancastrians or Yorkists at the time. It is better viewed as what it was, the collapse of confidence in the insecure dynasty that the usurper Henry IV had established within the political community. As the king himself proved unable to rule, aristocratic cliques bid to fill the political vacuum with the additional civil peril that the Lancastrians had, by unseating Richard II, provided a precedent to other similarly qualified Plantagenets to resolve any dynastic crisis the same way Henry IV had. So England entered three or four decades of structural failure in the political class, whose tensions could be resolved only by periodic factional confrontations which on several occasions led to blood-letting amongst the nobility.

Richard of York was not by any means the most successful statesman in England when the 1450 crisis hit England. He had an undistinguished record in defending Normandy in the 1440s (his son Edward was born in Rouen), and he had not enjoyed much success in his period as lieutenant of Ireland. He failed to have much impact on the council, where the Beauforts maintained power. His response in 1452 was ominous, and not unlike that of the frustrated Kentish gentry in Cade's Rebellion. York raised a force to march on and confront his rival, the duke of Somerset, but was forced into a humiliating climbdown when the council mobilised against him. The king's collapse into a schizophrenic illness the next year opened the final gaping crack in the fabric of the state, as nothing now could be hoped for from his direction. Since the king was evidently insane, the council had to appoint a protector. It did so in the same way as had Scotland, where the senior male member of the royal family, the duke of Albany, had stood in for King Robert III on his descent into mental incompetence and then maintained power while James I was a captive at the Lancastrian court. In 1454 the senior member of the English royal dynasty was Richard of York, who now assumed power and immediately proved his inadequacy by settling his personal score with Beaufort, whom he placed in the Tower. Things got worse with the king's temporary recovery and Beaufort's subsequent release the next year, when York lost power and chose to regain it by marching against Beaufort, who was cut down during a skirmish at St Albans. Whatever the state of the king's health, he was now a pawn in the hands of murderous rival factions, for Beaufort's son, the new duke of Somerset, entered into a blood feud with York, finding an ally in Queen Margaret, who now had a young son with interests to defend.

By 1459 the queen was ready to move against York as the only solution to the perpetual crisis at court, setting herself against the duke and his allies in the Neville family, the earls of Salisbury and Warwick. There may have been an assassination attempt on Warwick at court, or so he believed, for he fled to Calais. York and his supporters tried the option of rebellion with the excuse of removing the king's evil councillors, the sort of justification that brought Richard II down in 1387. York lost his nerve when confronted by a large royal army at Ludlow and fled to Dublin. In his absence, Parliament passed a bill depriving him and his heirs of their lands, a bill called an 'attainder' (a tactic first used against Edward II's favourites). So York had little choice left but to risk all in an invasion in 1460, a gamble that he initially won at Northampton, where his allies led by the earl of Warwick destroyed a royal army and slew the Beaufort duke of Somerset, capturing the king, who had been brought along. York made no secret on his return to England that he intended to solve the problem of Henry VI by taking his throne over the head of the seven-year-old prince of Wales, a fatal decision. He could not persuade the subsequent Parliament to depose the king and, when the queen struck back at him in Yorkshire, Duke Richard and one of his sons, as well as his ally Salisbury, were killed. Her victory, however, merely reinforced the feud mentality that had gripped the English aristocracy. Edward of Rouen, the new duke of York, was now locked into a struggle to survive against Queen Margaret, and he did so with a vigour and intelligence his late father had not possessed. A series of battles in February 1461 gained him London and proclamation as king, and eventually on 29 March Edward risked the chances of battle at Towton. He decisively defeated the queen, who fled with her husband and son to exile in Scotland.

The Yorkist Kings

A second usurpation had now worsened the already unstable nature of English monarchy and political culture, the violent option always being the easier one in any difficulty. Succession customs had long been a problem, as a comparison with the relatively stable nature of Stewart kingship in Scotland demonstrates. English successions between 1154 and 1377 had at least respected the link between father and son, even when Edward III had succeeded his deposed father in 1327. But Henry IV's seizure of the crown from the head of his cousin Richard II had further destabilised the institution. Henry V had been able by luck, talent and the chances of war to unite the nation around his kingship, and the situation might have stabilised even on the succession of his child-heir in 1422, for his family and nobility rallied around the boy and real hopes of further victory in France were built upon him and his uncles. But when incompetence and mental illness wrecked any faith in the adult Henry VI, the violent precedent of 1399 reduced political options to usurpation, while it also encouraged the practice of murder as a way of clearing the political gaming board, for those of an impatient nature.

Edward IV, like Henry IV, tried to find ways in his coronation ritual to shore up the rickety structure the English throne had become. The tactic he and his council devised was the curious one of promoting the legal nature of his investiture over the sacral. The political community assembled in Westminster Hall before the consecration was offered a lecture about his right to the crown. Setting symbolism at nothing, Edward already had the sceptre of kingship in his hand when he did it. The message to the assembly was that his kingship was possessed by him before even he was crowned, and so he deliberately demoted the consecration liturgy to be the second act of his inauguration theatre. Edward even went so far as to offer an additional lecture on his rights to the abbey congregation after he was crowned. There may have been many who witnessed the occasion who found his protestations rather too much. In fact the Neville affinity which had been principally responsible for lifting him to the throne might well have been among them, for he ruled as much by their grace as by God's. It was the Nevilles who were to colonise the Yorkist nobility, offices of state and council during the first half of his reign. Their leader, Richard Neville earl of Warwick was not known as the 'kingmaker' for nothing. He was a talented and dynamic man with boundless ambition and considerable talent as a strategist, not easily daunted by political or military danger. He was still only twenty-one when he became earl in 1449 and found himself straightaway caught up in the turbulence of that year, as Normandy was falling to the French and the council was in disarray. His choice was to tie his fortunes to the duke of York, all the easier for him as the Neville family had long been great in the North of England.

Edward IV, still not twenty when he became king, proved an inevitable disappointment to his new subjects. He was unable to provide any instant resolution to his kingdom's problems, as Henry V apparently had. The expectations on him were that he should reclaim English control in France, restore an effective council, balance the finances and root out corruption. A man a lot older and with more experience would have been equally helpless in the face of such a task. His initial mistakes were a young man's. Instead of offsetting English weakness by following Warwick's plan for a foreign marriage, he married Elizabeth Woodville, the daughter of a courtier. This added further instability to the realm, as her family inevitably competed with the Nevilles for favour. The Lancastrians were also still able to cause Edward trouble. Queen Margaret found sympathy and support for an invasion of the North in late 1462, and she and her husband were left unassailed in Northumberland with Scottish support until the summer of 1464. When the government finally evicted the Lancastrian troops the old king lived on abandoned in the North for a year on the run with the help of local sympathisers, until finally cornered by Yorkist agents in Lancashire in July 1465. He was placed in the Tower for safekeeping.

The inevitable crisis between Edward and Warwick finally came in 1469. Warwick allied with the duke of Clarence, the king's younger brother, in taking up arms to force on Edward what they regarded as necessary reform of his household and court. The king was duly challenged in what amounted to a coup in the summer of 1469, when the Woodville faction was rounded up, many of them executed and the king himself seized and put under house arrest, while Warwick assumed power. He found, however, that the nobility would not answer to him as protector, and in the end he had to release Edward or murder him in favour of Clarence. He took the first option, expecting that he had made his point, but found that, whatever else Edward was, he was not easily daunted. The two men edged around each other, but no reconciliation was possible, and within five months Warwick's position was so undermined that in April 1470 he boarded a small fleet of his own warships and sailed into exile. Thwarted in an attempt to take Calais as a base, he set up for a while as a pirate preying on the Channel trade, his fleet sheltering in Norman ports. Without much other option, Warwick abandoned his alliance with York and was persuaded by Louis XI of France into an uncomfortable reconciliation with Queen Margaret at Angers in June 1470, with the intention of mounting an invasion of England and a restoration of Henry VI. The expedition, backed by several exiled Lancastrian earls and the French, arrived in Devon in September, despite what preparations King Edward could make in alliance with Louis's enemy, the duke of Burgundy, whose not inconsiderable naval power was based on the Flemish ports. Edward's support melted away with the reappearance of Warwick in England, and on 2 October he rode in haste to King's Lynn and a boat that would take him to exile in the Low Countries. He had very little to hope for, had he been taken captive by Warwick and his accomplices.

The brief restoration of Henry VI (or 'Readeption', as it is called) lasted a little over six months. The Lancastrian regime had little ability to reward its adherents, and counted for survival on a certain respect for the unworldly and harmless old king and an edgy caution towards the charismatic earl of Warwick in the political community. In the end it was not enough. When Edward took refuge at the Burgundian court, he found it on the verge of war with France. When hostilities broke out (especially when Warwick opportunistically joined the French against Burgundy) Edward found Duke Charles amenable to financing a Yorkist attempt to reclaim England. Edward proved for the first time to possess the determined intellectual resources in terms of diplomacy and calculation to rouse foreign and domestic support. He landed on the Humber estuary at the same location as Bolingbroke had, more than seven decades before, giving out that he had only come back to claim the duchy of York. The support of the earl of Northumberland was of great use to Edward, since he did not meet with much popular sympathy. His estranged brother, Clarence, finally joined him as he marched south, and the reunited brothers mounted a risky strike at London, which dithered but surrendered to him; with the fall of the City, King Henry was taken captive once again. When Warwick pursued Edward, their armies met at Barnet on Easter Sunday (14 April) 1471. It was a battle in which for the first time in England batteries of field artillery played a major part in the action. It was by mistakenly opening fire on his own allies that Warwick lost the battle, which left him dead and his corpse defiled on the field by Yorkist troops. Edward then turned on Queen Margaret and her son Edward, prince of Wales. Three weeks after Barnet, the Yorkist army met the queen's forces at Tewkesbury, where the Lancastrian army was broken and Prince Edward, his dynasty's last hope, cut down in the retreat. The Beaufort dukes also perished there, leaving as heir to the dynastic cause the marginal figure of Henry Tudor, earl of Richmond, the offspring of an illegitimate son of Katherine of France, the widow of Henry V, and Margaret Beaufort, a great-granddaughter of John of Gaunt.

The day before Edward IV's re-coronation Henry VI was murdered, a victim, in truth, of the original sin of his own dynasty. Edward's 'second reign' had little new to offer the realm. He was obliged to go to war with Louis XI after Louis's backing of the Lancastrian invasion, which naturally also involved war with Scotland. This was not by any means an unpopular decision in England, and Edward seemed initially enthusiastic in adopting the old claims that had energised Anglo-French warfare since 1337. He was indeed urged by the Burgundians to claim France and displace the hated Louis. But it took until 1475 for Edward actually to finalise preparations to his satisfaction and to neutralise Scotland by marrying his sister to James IV. He landed at Calais with an impressive artillery train and a sizeable force in the summer of 1475. The campaign that followed was marred by lack of Burgundian support and the failure of a promised Breton force to materialise. Within a month, Edward was disillusioned enough to conclude a truce with Louis despite Burgundian anger, and he walked off with promises of subsidies and a royal marriage for his daughter Elizabeth. The truce of Picquigny gained Edward no popularity or prestige, as Louis defaulted in the end on the subsidies and the marriage. It might have been a pragmatic decision in the circumstances, but the truce proved that the Yorkists were unable to sanctify their kingship in blood by feats of arms. Nor could they deliver stability and good governance. Edward and his council could not find resources to balance the books and generate a surplus, and could barely afford to pay the key garrison of Berwick on the Scottish Marches.

The death of Warwick did not end political instability, which now focused on the mercurial and insecure figure of Edward's brother, the duke of Clarence, who had conspired with the Lancastrians to unseat him in 1470. By 1477 Clarence was suspected of plotting with the Burgundians to take the throne, a suspicion Louis XI was happy to foster. Clarence made things worse by his extravagant and petulant interventions in the council and indiscreet plotting. He was arrested for treason, tried in front of Parliament and in February 1478 done to death privately within the Tower, the king fraternally unhappy to have him exposed at a public execution. Edward's surviving brother, Duke Richard of Gloucester, played a much cannier hand. Edward increasingly relied on him to defend England from the inconveniently dynamic Stewart kingdom in the north, and deliberately constructed to that end a quasi-principality for him in Cumbria and Yorkshire. The concentration of patronage this involved – which was paralleled by other noble power blocs in the Midlands, the Welsh March and the south-west – may have given stability to the realm, but it proved fatal to Edward's sons.

On Edward IV's death, his government lacked the money even to pay off the legacies in his will, and England had been successfully neutralised as a credible threat to Valois France. Though Edward left two sons, neither survived the calculating ambition of their uncle, Richard of Gloucester, who succeeded to the position of protector, an office which his own namesake and father had not filled with any distinction. The new reign brought the nadir of English kingship, as murderous kin strife had now become endemic within the royal house in a way unknown in centuries, apart from amongst the predatory dynasties of princely Wales. The new king seems to have had little sensibility of the house of York as a corporate enterprise, as the Lancastrian family had demonstrated when it rallied to its king in the reign of Henry V and the subsequent minority of Henry VI. The debasement of English political culture and the instability in the upper reaches of the political community were what gave credibility to the marginal claims to a succession bid by the exiled Henry Tudor, earl of Richmond, whose paternal descent was from the upper gentry of the principality of Wales, and whose English royal blood came by way of his Beaufort mother. King Richard III's reign (1483–1485) deserves perhaps its notoriety, but in terms of the history of English kingship and the state its only significance was that it was the point where the nation touched bottom in terms of political culture and corruption. Richard, like the tyrant John before him, was a king who secured his magnates' children as guarantees for their compliance, but unlike John he was actually capable of killing them.

 ## Tudor Postscript

Henry VII (1485–1509) cannot have been a king in whom the decimated nobility and wearied political community would have initially seen much hope. The fact is, however, that his reign proved more significant than that of Henry V in reconstructing England, though his methods were not those of his predecessor and namesake, who rallied the nation in war. It cannot have been until he had been on the throne for a decade that the impact of Henry's governance on England became apparent. It has long stopped being the practice to date the end of the (English) middle ages to his accession in the aftermath of the battle of Bosworth. The kingship of Henry VII was not initially distinct from that of his predecessors, and indeed in 1487 and again ten years later he had to take to the battlefield to defend his throne. His decision to marry Elizabeth of York was, however, the first indication of a king determined to re-establish the royal family as a central institution within the realm, a focus of unity rather than dissension, as symbolised famously in the 'Tudor rose' badge, a device which folded a white rose of York within the red of Lancaster.

Like Edward IV, Henry Tudor was capable of threatening the renewal of war in France so as to gain diplomatic advantage, though unlike him Henry was never personally enthused by the prospect. This was not because he lacked the medieval passion for noble military culture. He expended a huge amount of money on chivalric feasts and tournaments, at which he was an avid spectator. He was as much an enthusiast for hunting and hawking as Harold Godwineson, who wrote a book on the subject. Henry was as devoted to his mother and source of his dynastic claims, Margaret Beaufort, as had been Henry II to his mother, the Empress Matilda, who had brought him the royal blood of Wessex. His grasp of governmental detail and finance was that of the young Edward I, the true creator of parliamentary kingship. Like the better medieval kings, he was friendly and accessible to his court, and inspired personal devotion. When he came to name his eldest son, in whom was united the claims of rival branches of the Plantagenet royal house, not to mention the blood of the even more ancient royal house of Gwynedd, he chose to name him after the avatar of British medieval kingship, Arthur of Britain. It might therefore be said of the first Tudor king that he united in himself the better traits of established medieval kingship, and it is to that he owed his ultimate success.

POSTSCRIPT

So as Scotland under James IV emerged into a new humanistic era under an innovative and charismatic monarch, England under Henry VII slowly recovered its stability largely by an intelligent use of tried and tested medieval expedients. However, one thing that was characteristically medieval did change in England. The balance of power that had tipped away from the king towards the magnates in the twelfth century, and which had been behind all the many instances of political confrontation within the political community since, began to reverse itself in Henry's reign. His rule was characterised by the many risings and Yorkist conspiracies against him, and the battle of East Stoke in 1487 could easily have seen the abrupt end of Tudor rule. Yet, exposed and precarious though Henry VII's rule was, accomplished diplomacy found him acceptance abroad, and he was able to convince Parliament to levy the taxation he needed to survive. After surviving the disorder of 1497 and achieving the dynastic glory of the marriage of his son Arthur with Katherine of Aragon, Tudor monarchy began to assume a prestige of its own and become a focus for unity. Henry VII controlled his nobility – like Henry I had – by imposing debt upon them, but not calling it in as long as they behaved themselves. Like his greater medieval predecessors, he avoided reliance on noble factions and looked for talent rather than flattery in his officers, though he was happy enough to employ in government magnates whom he found reliable. Though he did not challenge noble liberties and franchises in theory, the former great palatinates (apart from Durham) were now in his hands and were no longer a challenge to royal authority. But his principal move was to curb the military dimension and social disruptiveness of the affinity, which had corrupted local society for generations. From 1504 recruitment of retainers had to be licensed and, though Henry still relied on such retinues for military support in crises, it was no longer an unchallenged noble right to go around attended by armed retainers. New royal councils in the North and West of England and the March of Wales were formed to monitor more closely noble activity in local society. So here, certainly, one of the great weaknesses of medieval monarchy was being addressed. The question for the future was how the weakening of the magnates would affect the dialogue between executive king and community of the realm.

KEY TEXTS

Carpenter, C. *The Wars of the Roses: Politics and the Constitution in England* (Cambridge University Press, 1996), a clear assessment of the turbulent fifteenth century with an emphasis on the 'constitution', meaning the dialogue between king and political community as expressed through central institutions. • Harriss, G. *Shaping the Nation: England 1360–1461* (Oxford University Press, 2005), a detailed and very authoritative study of the process of Plantagenet government and its politics. • Prestwich, M. C. *The Three Edwards: War and State in England, 1272–1377* (Routledge, 1980), a study spanning the first three Plantagenet reigns with a concise breakdown of the part that war played in defining their monarchy. • Sumption, J. *The Hundred Years War* (4 vols., Faber & Faber, 1999–2015), a detailed and colourful extended study of the central struggle which formed later medieval England and its relations with its neighbours.

FURTHER READING

Allmand, C. *Henry V* (Methuen, 1992). • Bennett, M. *Richard II and the Revolution of 1399* (Sutton, 1999). • Castor, H. *The King, the Crown and the Duchy of Lancaster* (Oxford University Press, 2000). • Cunningham, S. *Henry VII* (Routledge, 2007). • Curry, A. *Agincourt: A New History* (Sutton, 2005). • Davies, R. R. *The Revolt of Owain Glyn Dŵr* (Oxford University Press, 1995). • Dockray, K. *Henry V* (Sutton, 2004). • Fletcher, C. *Richard II: Manhood, Youth and Politics, 1377–1399* (Oxford University Press, 2008). • Given-Wilson, C. *Henry IV* (Yale University Press, 2016). • Goodman, A. *John of Gaunt* (Longman, 1992). • Green, D. *Edward the Black Prince: Power in Medieval Europe* (Longman, 2007). • Griffiths, R. A. *Conquerors and Conquered in Medieval Wales* (Sutton, 1994). • Harriss, G. L. *Henry V: The Practice of Kingship* (Oxford University Press, 1985). • *Henry V: New Interpretations*, ed. G. Dodd (Boydell, 2013). • Hicks, M. *Edward IV* (Bloomsbury, 2004). • Horrox, R. *Richard III: A Study in Service* (Cambridge University Press, 1989). • Johnson, P. A. *Duke Richard of York, 1411–1460* (Oxford University Press, 1988). • *Kings and Nobles in the Later Middle Ages*, ed. R. A. Griffiths and J. Sherborne (St Martin's Press, 1986). • Luckett, D. A. 'Crown Office and Licensed Retinues in the Reign of

Henry VII', in *Rulers and Ruled in Late Medieval England: Essays Presented to Gerald Harriss*, ed. R. E. Archer and S. Walker (Continuum, 1995), 223–38. • McFarlane, K. B. *England in the Fifteenth Century: Collected Essays* (Oxford University Press, 1981). • Maurer, H. E. *Margaret of Anjou: Queenship and Power in Late Medieval England* (Boydell, 2003). • Ormrod, W. M. *Edward III* (Yale University Press, 2011). • Pollard, A. J. *Richard III and the Princes in the Tower* (Sutton, 1991). • Pollard, A. J. *Warwick the Kingmaker: Politics, Power and Fame* (Continuum, 2007). • *The Reign of Henry IV: Rebellion and Survival, 1403–1413*, ed. G. Dodd and D. Biggs (Boydell, 2008). • Rogers, C. J. *War Cruel and Sharp: English Strategy Under Edward III* (Boydell, 2000). • Ross, C. *Edward IV* (2nd edn, Methuen, 1997). • Saul, N. *Richard II* (Yale University Press, 1997). • Smith, J. Beverly. 'Crown and Community in the Principality of North Wales in the Reign of Henry Tudor', *Welsh History Review*, 3 (1966–7), 145–71. • Strohm, P. *England's Empty Throne: Usurpation and the Language of Legitimation, 1399–1422* (Yale University Press, 1998). • Tuck, A. *Richard II and the English Nobility* (Edward Arnold, 1973). • Walker, S. 'Rumour, Sedition and Popular Protest in the Reign of Henry IV', *Past & Present*, 166 (2000), 31–65. • Watts, J. L. *Henry VI and the Politics of Kingship* (Cambridge University Press, 1996). • Waugh, S. L. *England in the Reign of Edward III* (Cambridge University Press, 1991). • Wolffe, B. *Henry VI* (Methuen, 1981).

NOTE

1. N. Saul, *Richard II* (Yale University Press, 1997), 358, translating the dedication of a book of philosophical tracts compiled for the king (Oxford, Bodleian Library, ms Bodley 581).

Conclusion

A half-millennium of the history of three separate nations occupying the same island was not an easy book to be asked to write. But the result does illustrate some major disruptions in the history of Britain which affected all three of those peoples. The first is that the thirteenth century discarded the earlier medieval idea of England's tributary empire across the British Isles it had inherited from the distant past. Henry III and Edward I both wanted to convert that relationship to something more legalistic and formal: to actually pull the emerging lesser British states within that of the English. In part this might have been an ambition inspired by what the Capetian monarchy had imposed on the Plantagenet family (as dukes of Normandy and Aquitaine) in France. In part it may also reflect a change in society, where legally trained minds (as the minds of kings and aristocrats often were after 1180) were no longer content with their political world being informally understood, and not formalised overmuch. They wanted the dependency defined and nailed down tight. Edward I got his way with Wales, the least developed polity in Britain. The failure of all three Edwards in their ambitions to execute a new level of control over Scotland was, however, catastrophic to that earlier and productive way of understanding Britain. It destroyed the vision of Britain as a loose confederation of peoples under English presidency and replaced it with two hostile nation-states, the northern one forging its identity in the anger and visceral hatred Edward I wilfully generated amongst the Scots. The old way had made possible a shared aristocracy and a remarkably open cultural, economic and social border between England and Scotland in the thirteenth century. The new state of affairs made warfare endemic between the two countries and brought about a sharp separation between peoples: a pressing problem which the English and Scots had to find ways to accommodate in the subsequent centuries.

A second major change also affected all three peoples, though the Welsh less than the others. This was the absorption of eleventh-century Britain into the dominant European Francophone culture. Earlier Britain had not been by any means immune to the international Latin culture which also overlaid the peoples and institutions of Europe and united its intellectuals and clergy in the same thought world. But 1066 deserves its headline status as a key date. The Norman Conquest did not immediately change much about the English government and economy; indeed, the 1070 decision of the Conqueror to use Latin as the language of his government reinforced England's place within Latin Europe. It would not be until 1752 that a British government rescinded the privileged place Latin had in its government's records. What 1066 did was to reorient England and eventually Scotland towards the south and the emerging culture of France, the reach of whose literature, aristocratic culture, schools and military technology already in 1066 spread much wider than the small realm the Capetian king of France actually controlled. As the Capetians rose to political dominance, French culture became even more pervasive, colonising the Germanic culture of the Empire to the east as much as Britain to the north. England was not, however, a colony of this Francophone world, but a vibrant part of it. Until 1200 its kings were more often the cultural leaders of the zone than the Capetians were. French literature, culture and education developed in parallel within the two kingdoms, and this remained the case until perhaps as late as the 1250s. But the headwind of xenophobia against which Henry III in his day had to contend changed this. Court culture remained French-dominated for the rest of the period, but increasingly England (like Scotland, Aragon, Castile and the Empire) moderated French influence through its own vernacular and insular culture.

Any narrative of progress in social and cultural history during this period would then be misplaced. If one was in search of golden ages, then Britain in Europe experienced a unique period of profitable cultural interaction between 1180 and 1260, which was coincidentally a period of major expansion in its wealth and populations. Edward I was by this view the harbinger of a troubled, harsher and more insular Britain in the last two medieval centuries. The irony was that his family's history and claims pulled his successors into a continuing but very different relationship with the French, as their would-be conquerors. There were, however, changes and developments in the sophistication of medieval technology, social organisation and particularly in cultural presentation, which were evidently on a developmental arc. Some may not have been that welcome. The mind-set of precedent and narrow definition which emerged out of the professionalisation of law was a mixed blessing to society and had some unpleasant consequences, not least for the agricultural poor. It may also have been one of the triggers for the increasing bureaucratisation of government, which again was a mixed development. Literacy may or may not have increased in the period of this book, but Britain's rulers certainly found new uses for it.

There were other new things in Britain between 1000 and 1300. Technology did make some slow advances. From the 1180s Britain became a land of windmills, as a new source of power was harnessed. The technology of building in stone made a major advance on the old forms inherited from Rome at much the same time. Domestic brick architecture appeared in the fourteenth century and would begin to change the quality of domestic housing, as well as the appearance of cities and villages alike, well before the end of this period. The fifteenth-century technology of the printing press would soon transform communication. Perhaps the most obvious changes in British society in this period were in matters of presentation. The medieval mind was very fertile in the sophistication of the ways it presented central features of its society, principally its faith and its ideas of social eminence. The appearance of churches and palaces was radically different between 1100 and 1400. Though the furniture might not have changed much, by 1300 the noble hall was figured with murals, tapestries and rich fabrics, well lit by tall windows bearing heraldic stained glass and warmed by hearths under carved chimney pieces. By 1400 Britain's many great churches were not just marvels of vaulting and carving, but hosted an elaborate and aesthetic worship, which answered to the direction of the chimes of painted and gilded mechanical clocks. There were great wind organs to accompany chant all through this period, but the polyphonic voices of the trained and disciplined choirs that sang the office and mass were something new, and a sound that remains inspiring.

Ceremony too became a new art, not that the earlier society had been unable to stage great events and festivals: the shape and processional ritual of the medieval coronation were already set by 1142 in England and probably had been since at least 1099. But the emergence of the art of the herald is perhaps the most illustrative way that society can be seen to have changed between 1000 and 1500. It encapsulates what was the later medieval genius for linking aesthetic, social power and symbolism into a new form of cultural currency. From being a hanger-on at tourney events and the fringes of noble households, the herald (MFr. *hiraut*: 'military attendant') found a new role by 1200 as consultant in ceremony and specialist in the art of representing and recording noble devices and coats of arms. Already in 1180 the Angevin royal household included a 'king of arms' to marshal events, act as state messenger and offer young heralds training, in much the same way as common law justices were then offering lectures to aspirants to the bar. By 1300 heralds had a career structure and a technical vocabulary, and had generated a copious and colourful literature about their art, in both England and Scotland. Eventually in 1483 in England, just before the end of this period, kings of arms, heralds and their apprentices (pursuivants) were incorporated into a college with premises in London and given a royal charter to regulate their profession. And there, in Queen Victoria Street, they still ply their trade, as eloquent a testimony as might be needed that we are not quite as distant in thought from our medieval ancestors as some might believe.

Glossary

acolyte   One of the junior orders of clergy, of which there were seven.

affinity   A retinue of local followers, clerics and legal advisers recruited and rewarded by a magnate to bolster his local and national influence.

anchorite   Someone pursuing a life of religious contemplation in isolation from the world, though not necessarily having taken religious vows (as a hermit would).

Angevin   Name applied to the French noble dynasty which ruled the county of Anjou (MFr. *Angeus*) from the ninth century. Used of the kings of that family who ruled England between 1154 and 1272, by which time the kings of England had given up their claim on Anjou. Thereafter customary to call the family by the name Plantagenet.

Anglian   English language and culture in North Britain which was both outside and within the lands ruled by the king of England.

annals   Year-by-year accounts of events.

appanage   An estate reserved for a junior member of a royal dynasty.

archbishop   A senior bishop in control of a province, which was made up of a number of dioceses ruled over by other bishops.

atheling   A noble rank developed in England, and later found in Wales. It was held by men of royal descent who formed a pool of princes from which a new king might be selected, and in Wales (as *edling*) applied to a king's designated heir.

Augustinians   An order of regular canons which became popular in Italy and France at the end of the eleventh century, taking as its patron St Augustine of Hippo, the great theologian. It was very popular in the England of Henry I. Also known as the Black Canons.

bailiff   All-purpose French word for any officer having his lord's authority.

banneret   A rank of superior knighthood which appeared in the 1180s. A knight banneret led a company of his own knights and carried a square banner as the sign of his rank.

baron   Leading follower of a medieval king, though also applied to a follower of a great magnate or to a citizen of London.

Bede   A Northumbrian monk and scholar of European reputation whose *Ecclesiastical History of the English People* (completed 731) was a fundamental historical text for the medieval understanding of Britain and its peoples.

bench   Bishops and justices customarily shared a long bench when presiding over assemblies, so the word came to be a group noun for judges and bishops.

burh   Old English term to describe a fortified and garrisoned town, found in tenth-century England and later applied as a burgh or borough to any medieval walled and privileged urban area.

canon   A secular canon was a clergyman holding an endowed prebend (source of income) in a large church, governed by a chapter under a dean or other head. A regular canon was a priest living most of the time like a monk in a celibate community to a rule of life, but still going out into the world to offer teaching and the rites of the church (see also **Augustinians**, **Premonstratensians**).

Capetians   A dynasty which provided kings for the Western Frankish kingdom (i.e. France) from 860, and continuously from 987. Although the direct line ended with Philip IV in 1337, various junior branches of the family provided kings of France until the French Revolution and afterwards, up to 1848.

Carolingians   A powerful noble dynasty of the Franks who seized the throne in 751 and under Charles the Great (**Charlemagne**) ruled modern France, Germany and Italy as Western Emperor.

Carthusians   An offshoot of the Cistercian order, which strictly enforced contemplation, its monks living in individual hermit cells around a cloister, and only gathering for the office hours.

castellanry   A lordship or territory dependent on a castle.

cathedral   A chief church where a bishop set up his throne, in Latin *cathedra* (see also **see**). Some dioceses, such as York, Dublin and Chester, had several cathedrals, but most only one.

Charlemagne   Charles 'the Great' (died 814), king of the Franks in 768, crowned Western Emperor in 800. His reign was immensely significant for the future shape of Europe and the revival of its Latin culture.

chevauchée   A mounted expedition whose intention is to waste and pillage a region rather than conquer it.

Cistercian   A monastic order of austere principles which appeared in Burgundy in the late eleventh century, developed a unique form of governance and spread across Europe in great numbers. Also called White Monks.

Cluniacs   A major tenth-century offshoot of the Benedictine order which emphasised liturgy and music in its worship, and looked to its chief monastery of Cluny in Burgundy for direction.

copyhold   A property which had once been liable to unfree peasant service but which had come into its owner's full control. Got its name because records of changes of ownership were copied into the manorial rolls. Copyhold had some vestigial small annual charges owed to the manor, notably 'chevage' (head money) which became a form of rent rather than being a badge of servile status.

count   Originally a regional official of the Roman Empire, adopted by the Frankish and other successor kingdoms, universal across Western Europe in 1000.

crusade A territorial war for religious ends declared by the pope, the participants generally marked by a cross stitched to their clothing.

cult From the Latin *cultus*, meaning an expression of devotion, as to a particular saint or to one of the attributes of Jesus Christ or His mother.

curia Usually the word applied to the pope's household and court, which is what the Latin word means.

diocese The area of authority of a bishop, a name borrowed from the Late Roman Empire, where it signified a province. In England (just as in the Roman Empire), dioceses respected secular administrative boundaries. Outside England, dioceses were formed on the template offered by Celtic and Gaelic sub-kingdoms.

Dominicans The second of the major orders of friars, taking their name from their founder, the Spanish intellectual and theologian St Dominic (died 1221). The order was founded in 1216 to combat heresy in the south of France (see also **Franciscans**).

dysentery A deadly form of enteric (bowel) infection caused by the bacterium *shigillosis*. Killed far more medieval soldiers than did violence.

ealdorman An ancient high office granted by English kings to favoured supporters giving them control over one or more **shires**. It was equivalent to the continental duke, though was held only at the king's will, and was not hereditary. The term was discarded for the Anglo-Scandinavian title **earl** in Cnut's reign.

earl An Anglo-Scandinavian title which replaced that of **ealdorman** in England in the 1020s. Originally equivalent to a duke, but demoted by the Normans to the equivalency of a continental **count**. The rank penetrated Scotland by the end of the twelfth century, replacing the native title **mormaer**.

epic Early form of literature defined as a heroic poem concerning the deeds of a people or family where the male predominates.

escheator An officer whose responsibility it was to inquire into rights or heirs who ought to come into the king's hands.

estates The three principal groups of people within the leadership of a realm. The first estate was the clergy, the second the **peers** and the third the Commons.

Exchequer In England and Normandy, and later in Scotland, an auditing and accounting meeting which collected debts to the ruler and registered payments. Took its name from the checker-board cloth on which calculations were made (Latin *scaccarium*: 'chessboard').

farmer Not necessarily an agriculturalist. Anyone who took an office, mill or land in return for paying a set rent in cash (*firma*) was a 'farmer' (*firmarius*).

fealty An oath of loyalty or good faith.

Franciscans An order within a new form of organised preachers called *friars* (Lat. *fratres*: 'brothers'). This particular group was named after the originator of the concept, Francis of Assisi (died 1226). Also called Grey Friars, Friars Minor or Minorites (see also **Dominicans**).

Frankish   The Franks ruled a kingdom that once covered most of France, Germany and Italy in the eighth century. By the end of the tenth century they had permanently separated into East and West kingdoms, and the 'West Franks' were becoming recognisably French.

freehold   Property which is generally free of any obligations other than to the king, and which is at the disposal of its owner, the freeholder.

genitive   One of the several 'cases' of nouns (a 'case' is a way a noun changes its form depending on where it is in a sentence) found in many languages. The genitive (or possessive) case changes a noun to express possession, in modern English by adding apostrophes and the letter 's' (as dog does in 'a dog's breakfast').

gentry   A term applied to local landed elites in Britain, families operating usually at the level of a single manor or township, though there were some greater families who operated at the shire level, the county gentry.

Gilbertines   An English order of canons founded in the twelfth century by St Gilbert of Sempringham (died 1190).

imperium   Latin word meaning not just 'empire' but any realm whose ruler acknowledges no superior.

interdict   A ban on clergy offering the sacraments of the Church, imposed by a bishop on an individual or his diocese, or by the pope on an entire realm.

justiciar   An office which evolved in twelfth-century England as the king's alter-ego in matters of justice and administration. It lapsed in the early thirteenth century when the king was no longer routinely on the continent. Its importance was as a step towards centralising executive government and making it a process independent of the king.

Justinian   Eastern Roman Emperor (527–565) whose legacy was the *Corpus Juris Civilis*, a collected edition of the laws of the Roman Empire, which remains the foundation for civil law in many European states.

knight   A professional horseback warrior who appears as a type of soldier in the late tenth century in France and western Germany. By the end of the twelfth century it became increasingly seen as a noble rank.

Lateran   The principal palace of the Pope in Rome until 1589, when he moved to the Vatican.

magnates   Literally the 'great men' of a realm: the leading barons and bishops with whom a medieval king had to consult.

March   A border area, of which there were two principal ones in Britain: the *Welsh March* (the English-ruled lands west of **Offa's Dyke**) and the *Merse* (the borderland between Lothian and Northern England). 'Marcher' lords were those whose principal possession was a privileged lordship in Wales.

mass   The central Christian rite, ceremonially re-enacting the Last Supper of Christ before his arrest with sacramental bread and wine. Sometimes also called (from the Greek) a eucharist.

mormaer   High provincial official of the kingdom of Alba. Later equated to the French **count** and English **earl**.

Offa's Dyke   A demarcation of the boundary between English and Welsh lands undertaken in the reign of King Offa of Mercia (757–796), and still the eastern border of Wales.

Ottonians   An East Frankish noble dynasty which replaced the Carolingians as kings of the East Franks (i.e. Germany) in 919.

origin myth   Most national or ethnic groups developed a legendary account of their origins explaining their distinctive national character. The Gaels, Welsh and French copied the Romans in claiming to have been descended from refugees from ancient Troy.

Pale   The district around Dublin under direct royal control.

papal legate   A cleric, usually a bishop or cardinal, granted a commission to act in the pope's name in a named realm, and with all papal prerogatives while he exercises them, including the right to dress in papal robes.

peasant   General term for any worker on the land, whether a bonded serf or a freeholder.

peers   From the Latin *pares* ('equals') meaning, from the later thirteenth century, the privileged great magnates of the realm: dukes, earls, barons and bannerets, who had the right to be summoned to the king's great council or Parliament.

pietism   A form of religious observance where individuals seek personal sanctity without much acknowledgement of the Church's right to direct them.

pipe rolls   The annual accounts of the English Exchequer, which dated back to at least 1118. So called because they are parchment rolls the size and shape of a drain pipe.

polity   Like state (see Chapter 5), a vague but useful word indicating an area under a distinct political system.

Premonstratensians   An order of regular canons founded in eastern France by St Norbert of Prémontré, inspired by the austere ideals of the **Cistercians**. Also called White Canons.

prerogative   The rights of jurisdiction that go along with an office.

prise   The royal right in England to requisition provisions for the court at a fixed rate.

romance   Any language and culture deriving from Late Latin, such as the French, Occitan, Italian and Spanish tongues.

scutage   Cash payment made to a lord in place of fulfilling military service in the field. Also a form of property tax introduced by King Stephen and King Henry II.

see   Another name for a diocese, the seat of a bishop. The Holy See was Rome.

seigneurial   Something attached to a lordship (Fr. *seigneurie*).

sergeant   A term used in medieval armies for trained infantry ('foot sergeants') or medium cavalry ('mounted sergeants'). It was also a term for the enforcement officers who worked for sheriffs. Just to make it more complex, sergeant was also a term which by 1260 signified a senior lawyer working the central courts of Westminster.

sheriff   An officer who was appointed to manage the king's interests and estates in a **shire** in England, Wales, Ireland and Scotland.

shire   Originally an administrative subdivision of the kingdom of Wessex, but later extended to other areas of England. Under French influence it became equated with the continental county. All England was shired by 1200, and shires were extended across Britain in the thirteenth century, including most of Wales and Ireland as well as Scotland.

sinecure   Office with a salary but making little demands (Latin: *sine cura*, 'without responsibility').

tally   A hazelwood stick issued as a receipt for a payment, cut with notches and with the sum written on it; it was split in two, one kept by the payer and the other by the payee.

Talmud   Ancient writings supplementary to the Jewish scriptures, summarising the verdicts of scholarly rabbis on the interpretation of the Books of Law in contexts from an era centuries before Christ up until after the fall of the Roman Empire. It was much studied and commented on in European Jewish communities after 1050.

thurifer   In an ecclesiastical procession, thuribles (incense-burners) carried and swung by attendants wafted scented smoke representing prayer. Angels were often depicted as thurifers in medieval art.

tournament   Definitive medieval aristocratic sport whose origins lie before 1100; a mock combat on horseback. Superseded by jousting events (one-on-one tilting contests) during the thirteenth century.

township   The basic unit of civil administration in Britain from the twelfth century until 1866, focused on its larger villages, which were expected to elect representatives to answer to the bailiffs of hundreds and sheriffs for any offences against public order within their boundaries.

Vikings   A mixed Scandinavian movement of peoples that raided and eventually colonised the British Isles and North Sea world from the end of the eighth century. Norwegians principally colonised Ireland and the North of Britain. Danes were dominant in England and along the French coasts. The 'Northmen' who colonised northern France and created Normandy were a mixed group of Norwegians and Danes, some of whom had previously colonised Britain.

Vulgate Bible   The Latin text of the Bible, the work of St Jerome in the fourth century, though not an 'official' translation recognised by the papacy until after the end of the middle ages.

writ   A sealed order from the king written in English before 1070 and in Latin afterwards. In Scotland called a brieve.

yeoman   A later medieval word for the owner of a substantial acreage within a township or townships, whether **copyhold** or **freehold**, whose life style and home were superior to those of his neighbours and who often occupied local office. The ancestor of the farmer of later centuries.

Chronology of Rulers

RULERS OF ENGLAND

West Saxon Dynasty
Æthelred II (978–1016)
Edmund Ironside (1016)

Danish Dynasty
Swein Forkbeard (1014)
Cnut (1016–1035)
Harold I (1035–1040)
Harthacnut (1040–1042)

West Saxon Dynasty
Edward the Confessor (1042–1066)

Godwine Dynasty
Harold II (1066)

Norman Dynasty
William I the Conqueror (1066–1087)
William II Rufus (1087–1100)
Henry I (1100–1135)

Blois Dynasty
Stephen (1135–1154)

Angevin–Plantagenet Dynasty
Henry II (1154–1189)
Henry the Young King (1170–1183) *Associate King*
Richard I Lionheart (1189–1199)
John (1199–1216)
Henry III (1216–1272)
Edward I (1272–1307)
Edward II (1307–1327)
Edward III (1327–1377)

Richard II (1377–1399)
Henry IV (1399–1413)
Henry V (1413–1422)
Henry VI (1422–1461, 1470–1471)
Edward IV (1461–1470, 1471–1483)
Edward V (1483)
Richard III (1483–1485)

DOMINANT RULERS OF GWYNEDD

Kings of Gwynedd
Cynan ap Hywel (999–1005)
Aeddan ap Blegywryd (1005–1018)
Llywelyn ap Seisyll (1018–1023)
Iago ab Idwal ap Meurig (1023–1039)
Gruffudd ap Llywelyn (1039–1063)
Bleddyn ap Cynfyn (1063–1075)
Trahaearn ap Caradog (1075–1081)
Gruffudd ap Cynan (1081–1137)
Owain ap Gruffudd, alias Owain Gwynedd (1137–1170)

Princes of Gwynedd
Dafydd ab Owain (1170–1195)
Llywelyn ab Iorwerth (Llywelyn the Great) (1195–1240)

Princes of Wales
Dafydd ap Llywelyn (1240–1246)
Llywelyn ap Gruffudd (1246–1282)
Dafydd ap Gruffudd (1282–1283)

DOMINANT KINGS OF ALBA

Coinneach III (997–1005)
Máel Coluim II (1005–1034)
Donncadh I (1034–1040)
Macbethad (1040–1057)
Lulach (1057–1058)
Máel Coluim III (1058–1093)
Domnall (1093–1094, 1094–1097)
Donncadh II (1094)
Edgar (1097–1107)
Alexander I (1107–1124)

RULERS OF SCOTLAND

David I (1124–1153)
Máel Coluim IV (1153–1165)
William (1165–1214)
Alexander II (1214–1249)
Alexander III (1249–1286)
Margaret (1286–1290)
John Balliol (1292–1296)
Robert I Bruce (1306–1329)
David II (1329–1371)
Robert II Stewart (1371–1390)
Robert III (1390–1406)
James I (1406–1437)
James II (1437–1460)
James III (1460–1488)
James IV (1488–1513)

Index

Search terms have been selected with essay and project research in mind.